The Nature of the Beasts

ASIA: LOCAL STUDIES/GLOBAL THEMES

Jeffrey N. Wasserstrom, Kären Wigen, and Hue-Tam Ho Tai, Editors

STUDIES OF THE WEATHERHEAD EAST ASIAN INSTITUTE, COLUMBIA UNIVERSITY

The Weatherhead East Asian Institute is Columbia University's center for research, publication, and teaching on modern and contemporary East Asia regions. The Studies of the Weatherhead East Asian Institute were inaugurated in 1962 to bring to a wider public the results of significant new research on modern and contemporary East Asia.

The Nature of the Beasts

Empire and Exhibition at the Tokyo Imperial Zoo

Ian Jared Miller

Foreword by Harriet Ritvo

UNIVERSITY OF CALIFORNIA PRESS
Berkeley · Los Angeles · London

University of California Press, one of the most distinguished university presses in the United States, enriches lives around the world by advancing scholarship in the humanities, social sciences, and natural sciences. Its activities are supported by the UC Press Foundation and by philanthropic contributions from individuals and institutions. For more information, visit www.ucpress.edu.

University of California Press
Berkeley and Los Angeles, California

University of California Press, Ltd.
London, England

Library of Congress Cataloging-in-Publication Data

Miller, Ian Jared, 1970–
    The nature of the beasts : empire and exhibition at the Tokyo Imperial Zoo / Ian Jared Miller ; foreword by Harriet Ritvo.
        pages cm — (Asia—local studies/global themes)
    Includes bibliographical references and index.
    ISBN 978-0-520-27186-9 (cloth : alk. paper)   1. Ueno Dobutsuen (Tokyo, Japan)—History.   2. Zoos—Social aspects—Japan—History.   3. Philosophy of nature—Japan—History.   4. Nature and civilization—Japan—History.   I. Title.
    QL76.5.J32M55 2013
    590.52'135—dc23
                                                    2013002001

Manufactured in the United States of America

22 21 20 19 18 17 16 15 14 13
10 9 8 7 6 5 4 3 2 1

In keeping with a commitment to support environmentally responsible and sustainable printing practices, UC Press has printed this book on Rolland Enviro100, a 100% post-consumer fiber paper that is FSC certified, deinked, processed chlorine-free, and manufactured with renewable biogas energy. It is acid-free and EcoLogo certified.

For Crate

Contents

Figures

Foreword

HARRIET RITVO

In a way, there is nothing new about animals as the focus of learned investigation. The ancient genre of the bestiary, a massive compendium of known and unknown animals, continued to flourish in Europe through the medieval period. Since at least the late seventeenth century, which is when the *Oxford English Dictionary* identifies the first occurrence of the word "zoology," animals have occupied their own scientific discipline. (Animals continue to occupy the attention of these scientists, of course, even though recent developments have made them increasingly uneasy with that characterization of their research; thus in 1996, after a century as the American Society of Zoologists, their disciplinary organization rechristened itself as the Society for Integrative and Comparative Biology.) Animals have traditionally figured in analyses of literary and religious symbolism. Their physical remains have provided important evidence for paleontologists and paleoanthropologists. And accounts of them, both numerical and verbal, have provided fodder for historians of science and of agriculture and economics.

But in another way, there is something very new. Scholarly attention to animals has expanded exponentially over the last few decades, spreading to nearly every discipline and subdiscipline within the humanities and social sciences. During the same period, "animal studies" has emerged as a multidisciplinary research area, now institutionalized in scholarly societies, conferences, and journals. As is often the case with such enterprises, the extent of this success has tended to undermine its multidisciplinarity. That is, the more numerous the scholars interested in animals become, the less need they have to engage with colleagues outside their own methodological comfort zone. Nevertheless, most scholars whose work is subsumed under the animal studies rubric share a novel understanding about how to approach their nonhuman subjects: one way or another, they attempt to take the interests or the perspectives of animals into account, along with those of people.

Despite this convergence and consolidation, or perhaps because of it, some fundamental questions remain unresolved. The most important is the simplest: What is an animal? According to zoological taxonomy, Kingdom Animalia includes sponges, jellyfish, and worms as well as fish, birds, and mammals; some animal studies scholarship repackages this under the expansive rubric of "the animal." At least for historians, however, that definition may be overly generous. Humans (at least those who are not invertebrate zoologists) tend to interact most frequently with and think most fruitfully about the animals that they resemble most strongly. In consequence, most historical scholarship that falls under the rubric of animal studies concerns our fellow vertebrates. And there are other reasons to acknowledge that people tend to distinguish between their relationships to mollusks and arthropods, and their relationships to horses, eagles, and snakes. Some of these reasons reflect politics, either of academia or of the wider world. For example, *Black Beauty* would probably have inspired a very different reception if its protagonist had been a lobster, even though the fate of Victorian lobsters was not necessarily preferable to the fate of Victorian draft horses. Underlying these definitional or boundary issues is yet another question: Is the most significant way to characterize the human relation to other animals as a binary (the human vs. the animal) or as a continuum on which humans take their place among many other species?

Even if the term "animal" is taken in its most restrictive sense—of vertebrate, or even of mammal—its referents engage with humans in numerous ways. The foci of scholarly attention have been correspondingly varied. Zoos have figured frequently in this emerging literature, for several reasons: they are conspicuous and discrete institutions, they have often been sufficiently self-conscious to preserve their records, they command large popular audiences, and they have practical and symbolic connections to politics and diplomacy. They have ancient antecedents but are distinctively modern. And they are obsessed with classification but are inherently liminal. They present wild animals in close confinement, juxtaposing security and peril. In addition, zoos are frequently landscaped to suggest that they preserve or encapsulate bits of nature within an urban or suburban setting, and problematic as this suggestion may be, the questions it implicitly poses are reinscribed on the bodies of captive animals and on the contexts in which they are displayed. To what extent do they remain natural, when separated from their native environment and way of life by thousands of miles, tens of thousands of dollars, or multiple generations?

Most scholarship about the history of zoos, like most scholarship about the history of human–animal relations more generally, has focused on Europe and North America (with occasional acknowledgment of ancestral menageries maintained by the potentates of ancient Egypt, Persia, or India). But, as Ian Miller shows in *The Nature of the Beasts: Empire and Exhibition at the Tokyo Imperial Zoo*, by the latter part of the nineteenth century those were not the only places to host large collections of exotic wild animals. The modern zoo may have been born in London, Paris, and Vienna, but it was an idea—or an institution—whose time had obviously come. It was widely imitated by states and municipalities wishing to stake their claim to various forms of modernity—imperial and scientific, among others. To imitate, however, is not necessarily to replicate, and the significations of even a close copy may shift when it is embedded in a different cultural context. The design and purpose of zoos inevitably reflect the attitudes and values of the society that produces them, and their history inevitably reflects the larger history of which they are a part. If such differences emerge when the zoos of cultural neighbors are compared (Britain and Germany, for example, or Britain and the United States), they become much more apparent as cultures diverge. Thus as Miller unravels the fascinating history of the Ueno Zoo in Tokyo, the flagship zoo of Japan, the implicit comparison to Western practices provides a fresh perspective on living animal collections more generally, and therefore on modern understandings of nature and environment.

Beginning with a pair of chapters that link the birth of the Japanese zoo and changing attitudes toward the natural world, this richly detailed account also allows the Ueno Zoo to stand as a synecdoche for the complex relationship between Japanese culture and the culture or cultures of Europe and North America over the last two centuries. They share many similarities, of which some result from parallelism or convergence, and some from borrowing or exchange. For example, Japanese practices with regard to the display of captive exotic animals strikingly paralleled those in the West, not only as embodied in the distinctively modern institution of the zoological garden, but also with regard to the popular sideshows and private menageries that were its predecessors, whether acknowledged or not.

Although such parallelism, whether the result of influence or ancient shared descent or of an inherent logic that guides human treatment of captive wild animals, is significant, it is far from the whole story. One of the most paradoxical or ironic features of the modern zoo is its vulnerability. Because they are both expensive and technically difficult to maintain, zoos are always at risk of institutional failure, and for this reason alone the survival of animals wrenched from very different habitats is inevitably precarious. Their symbolic triumphalism, whether with regard to colonial territories or nature more generally, makes them tempting political targets; like the looting of national museums, the slaughter of iconic zoo animals is a frequent concomitant of conquest. That is, if they last that long. In times of extreme hardship, their caloric value may come to outweigh their charisma as exhibits, as was famously the case in the siege of Paris during the Franco-Prussian war. After the introduction of aerial bombardment in the twentieth century, the possible release of dangerous zoo animals to roam city streets became a civil defense concern, leading wartime officials in Europe to require the slaughter large carnivores if local zoos lacked remote facilities to which they could be rusticated.

Part 2 of *The Nature of the Beasts*, entitled "The Culture of Total War," concerns the period of Japanese militarization in the mid-twentieth century. Its two chapters illustrate both the extent to which Japanese practices and understandings paralleled those of the West, and the extent to which they were starkly idiosyncratic. "Military Animals" explains how the inhabitants of the Ueno zoo, and animals more generally, were incorporated into wars on the Asian mainland in the 1930s, and subsequently into the broader global war in the Pacific. Although the details of their service naturally diverge somewhat, in general these creatures accomplished rhetorical and practical missions similar to those accomplished by their analogues in London or New York. But "The Great Zoo Massacre," the most arresting chapter in this compelling book, makes a very different point.

Japanese leaders were not unique in their decision to slaughter beloved zoo animals for military or political purposes, and they also followed the pattern of their international colleagues in imposing a veil of secrecy around the actual killings—to spare the feelings of a sentimental public and also to forestall the possibility of protest. But the formal and elaborate "Memorial Service for Martyred Animals" does not have many parallels, even though its impact depended on the widespread human tendency to see other animals as furry (or feathered or scaly) people. Eliding the role of the officials who ordered the massacre and the often excruciating manner of the animals' deaths, it transformed the dead victims, and especially the popular elephants, into fellow sufferers with the Japanese citizenry, willing to lay down their lives for the greater national good, and (as Miller suggests, this was more important though less explicit) preparing themselves to share in the traumatic national experience of defeat. Equally notable was the vigorous postwar life of this dreadful episode. The slaughtered elephants were enshrined in children's literature, and ultimately in national mythology, as representatives of the Japanese people, who were thus equally defined simply as victims of war, not as parties to it.

Like its nineteenth-century origins, the more recent history of the Ueno Zoo—addressed in the final two chapters of the book—again converges with that of similar institutions elsewhere. Changes in global political realities and in the sensibilities of local audiences inspired alterations in the figurative valence of collections of live exotic animals. (Or at least they led to attempts to make such alterations; at some level the message conveyed by large animals in confinement remains intractable, one reason that the very existence of zoos has become the focus of criticism.) The regions that had been the sources of most star zoo pets were no longer so readily exploitable, and it became impossible to ignore the effect of decades of hunting and habitat destruction on animal populations. Zoos increasingly had to breed their own exhibits (or buy or trade with other zoos), and to rebrand themselves, however implausibly, as genetic reservoirs from which the wild might be restocked at an imagined future time when vanished habitats would reappear. As zoo animals became rarer, they also became more precious in every sense: more expensive to acquire and maintain, as well as more desirable in the eyes of zoogoers. Concession stands had been part of the zoo experience since the nineteenth century, but twenty-first-century fans could purchase an unprecedented array of physical and virtual replicas of their favorites, adopt them (again virtually), watch them on webcams, and correspond with them by email.

The Nature of the Beasts concludes with the species whose zoo experience epitomizes all these distinctively Anthropocene pressures. Giant pandas, whose appealing looks made them the poster children of the WWF (originally the World Wildlife Fund), are easily the cutest of carnivores. Although they are big enough to do damage, they live on bamboo and so do not kill for food. They are objects of intense desire on the part of zoo directors anxious to maintain attendance figures. Never common, pandas are now confined to a single habitat in central China, and their international travel, along with their germplasm, is tightly controlled by the Chinese government, which deploys them as part of its diplomatic outreach. Over the last four decades, the Ueno Zoo has played host to almost a dozen pandas, more than all but a couple of zoos elsewhere in the world. For the most part, these animals have done their jobs—they have engaged the affection of the admission-paying and souvenir-buying public, and they have submitted to high- and low-tech interventions in their sex lives. But, as Miller suggests, it is difficult to consider their residence at the Ueno Zoo an unqualified success. The recent death of an expensively produced and breathlessly awaited panda cub (which would in any case have been eventually repatriated to China if it had lived) exemplifies the special historical ironies that surround the Ueno Zoo. And the long story of which it is the current culmination trenchantly evokes the larger ironies—characteristics captured in what Miller calls "ecological modernity"—that have come to entangle zoos, wild animals, and people at the present time.

Acknowledgments

Books, like zoological gardens, are shaped by conventions, hierarchies of things and ideas that often remain hidden in plain sight but which nonetheless carry considerable meaning. I am grateful for those conventions now, since the format of the book requires that I place the acknowledgments where they belong: at the beginning. *The Nature of the Beasts* could not have been written without the care, support, and inspiration of dozens of people and institutions, and I am proud to recognize them here, since their generosity and influence is evident on every page that follows. All flaws and oversights are my own.

This project began in an archive. I did not set out to write about a zoo, but when I stepped into the archives of the Tokyo Zoological Park Society (TZPS), tucked away at the edge of the Ueno Zoo, I knew that I had to do something with those materials. The institution has been collecting documents since its founding in the 1880s, and its holdings, while small, include everything from diplomatic agreements and conservation statements to the ephemera—tickets, maps, architectural blueprints, and letters to the zoo director—that give archival form to the everyday politics of the past. The wartime collection—materials of the sort destroyed at many state-run institutions in 1945—is especially rich. It is also especially controversial, and I am grateful to the Tokyo Zoological Park Society for their support. Though this book is at times critical of the zoo, it is important to emphasize that the target of analysis is the problem of modernity and its troubled relationship with the natural world, not necessarily the institution itself. The point is that the zoo offers a uniquely evocative picture of that problem, and it deserves our attention as such. It is an argument that has been made in different ways by many of the staff at the Ueno Zoo, TZPS, and the Japanese Association of Zoos and Aquariums, and this book could not have been written without their work. I am especially grateful to Doi Toshimitsu, Ishida Osamu, Komiya Teruyuki, the late Komori Atsushi, Mochimaru Yoriko, Nakagawa Shigeo, Nippashi Kazuaki, Ohira Hiroshi, Shōda Yōichi, and Sugaya Hiroshi. Ken Kawata, formerly of the Staten Island Zoo, also offered helpful comments.

I walked away from that first visit to the archive puzzled by what I had found. Like many scholars of Japan, and most Japanese my age, I had heard rumors of the events described in chapter 4, "The Great Zoo Massacre," wherein the zoo's most valuable animals were slaughtered in the service of a wartime cult of sacrifice and martyrdom, but I had always assumed that it was the stuff of fiction. "This actually happened?" I asked myself as I called my graduate mentors, Gregory Pflugfelder and Carol Gluck. Those conversations—like so many with Carol and Greg—were transformative. It is impossible to convey in a single paragraph my gratitude to them for the vibrant community that they nurtured at Columbia University, together with Henry D. Smith II, William Leach, Charles Armstrong, and others; I can only say that I strive to share their wisdom and passion with my own students. That community included Joy Kim, Fabio Lanza, Lee Pennington, and Tak Watanabe, who all read multiple drafts of the project. Jessamyn Abel, Victoria Cain, Adam Cluow, Dennis Frost, Federico Marcon, Laura Neitzel, Suzanne O'Brien, Scott O'Bryan, Aaron Skabelund, Sarah Thal, and Lori Watt all contributed readings or ideas. Kathleen Kete contributed generously to my dissertation committee. A grant from the U.S. Department of Education, Fulbright-Hays, allowed me to work with Obinata Sumio at Waseda University.

My thinking on history in general and environmental history in particular came together in several scholarly communities. Louise Young and Harry Harootunian at New York University, Donald Roden at Rutgers University, and David L. Howell, formerly of Princeton University and now happily a colleague at Harvard, each pushed me to think more deeply about the methodologies and philosophies that define what Japanese historians call "problem consciousness." Kevin M. Doak, the late David Goodman, and Ronald P. Toby at the University of Illinois galvanized my passion for Japanese history. The late Jackson H.

Bailey and Chuck Yates demonstrated the ethical dimensions of historical praxis. My appointment in the Department of History at Arizona
State University, while brief, was an important driver in my shift toward environmental history. Roger Adelson, Anthony Chambers, James
Foard, Brian Gratton, Monica Green, Paul Hirt, Peter Iverson, Rachel
Koopmans, Stephen MacKinnon, Catherine O'Donnell, James Rush,
and Hoyt Tillman offered friendship and collegiality. I benefited from
comments received when presenting my work at many conferences and
at the University of Arizona, Brandeis University, Claremont McKenna
College, Cornell University, Earlham College, Indiana University, the
University of Michigan, the Needham Research Institute at Cambridge
University, the University of North Carolina, Oxford University, Penn
State University, Sophia University, the University of Tokyo—Komaba,
Waseda University, and Yale University.

I wrote most of *The Nature of the Beasts* while an assistant professor
in the Department of History at Harvard University. I gratefully acknowledge my students and colleagues in Cambridge; their curious,
intelligent company enabled me to think more creatively about the
project. Andrew Gordon is a truly inspiring friend and mentor. I learn
something new each time we talk. Emmanuel K. Akyeampong, Henrietta
Harrison, Erez Manela, Afsaneh Najmabadi, and Hue-Tam Ho Tai
all read portions of the manuscript, as did members of my writing
group, Robin Bernstein, Elizabeth Lyman, Sindhumathi Revuluri,
Adelheid Voskuhl, and Joanne van der Woude. Jennifer van der Grinten
and Michael Thornton provided invaluable research assistance, Claire
Cooper shared her research on the Iwakura Mission, and members of
my seminars on "Japanese Imperialism" and "History's Environmental
Turn" suffered through drafts of their professor's chapters with grace
and insight. I had the good fortune to join the faculty together with
Maya Jasanoff, Andrew Jewett, and Kelly O'Neill. I have also found
intellectual community and financial support thanks to Ted Bestor,
Ted Gilman, and Susan Pharr at the Reischauer Institute of Japanese
Studies and Emma Rothschild at the Joint Center for History and Economics. Shigehisa Kuriyama is a constant inspiration. Kuniko McVey
and the staff at the Harvard-Yenching Library are treasures. Grants
have also come from the Harvard Asia Center, the Faculty of Arts and
Sciences Tenure-Track Publication Fund, and the Weatherhead Center
for International Affairs. Sheila Jasanoff and the Harvard STS Circle
and the Harvard Humanities Center both kindly hosted workshops on
chapters. I also gratefully acknowledge research leave supported by the

National Endowment for the Humanities and the Harvard Faculty of Arts and Sciences.

Three scholars from outside of my various institutional homes deserve special thanks. Brett L. Walker, Harriet Ritvo, and T. Walter Herbert, Jr. have each read and commented on the full manuscript in its penultimate stage. Harriet's seminal work defined the field within which I now work. Brett has pushed me to think more critically about the relationships between representation and the natural world, reminding me that animals can bite and images can kill. Walt's wit and eloquence have helped to harness my unruly prose to a larger argument. David Ambaras, Barbara Ambros, Andrew Bernstein, Todd Henry, Trent Maxey, Jordan Sand, and Julia Adeney Thomas kindly commented on chapters, as did Sabine Frustuck and Tak Fujitani.

Working with Reed Malcolm and Stacy Eisenstark at University of California Press has been a pleasure. I am grateful for their enthusiasm for the project and for Reed's insightful framing of the book. Daniel Rivero of the Weatherhead East Asian Institute helped to usher the book into publication, and Elizabeth Lee offered her editorial skills to an early draft. Parts of the introduction and chapter 1 appeared previously in *JAPANimals: History and Culture in Japan's Animal Life* (Michigan Monograph Series in Japanese Studies), edited by Brett L. Walker and Gregory Pflugfelder, Ann Arbor: University of Michigan Press, 2005.

My parents, Nann and Bill Miller, set me on this course when they allowed their sixteen-year-old son to board an airplane for China and Japan alone. They are a brave and caring pair, who responded with curiosity rather than panic when I called, lost in Tokyo. Their faith in basic human decency and hopes for social justice have shaped my thinking in ways that I continually rediscover. My grandparents were the source of my earliest "travel grants," allowing me to encounter the wider world while still young. My in-laws, Walter and Marjorie Herbert, contributed intellectually and materially to the project through childcare and long discussions.

It is fitting that my son, Liam Herbert-Miller, was born with the dissertation that preceded this book. I write about environmental issues in the hope that it may, in whatever small way, help to sustain a verdant, robust natural world able to nourish his sense of wonder at life. My thanks to Liam's mother, my wife, Crate Herbert, are boundless and fundamental. Thank you, Crate. Your dedication to our shared lives is the foundation for all other things. Your ability to bring laughter and quiet into lives filled with complex travel schedules, daycare pickups, and conflicting deadlines is nearly as breathtaking as your capacity to see through to the heart of things, intellectual and emotional. You and the rest of our family are the axis around which my universe spins. This book is for you.

Note on Transliteration

East Asian names are given in the customary order, with family name preceding personal name. Names of authors with works in English, however, follow the order given in the publication and the author's preference for the use of macrons.

Japanese words are transcribed in the modified Hepburn system used by *Kenkyūsha's New Japanese-English Dictionary*. Korean words are rendered using the McCune-Reischauer system.

Macrons are omitted from common place names such as Tokyo.

Introduction

Japan's Ecological Modernity

Observe that each and every zoo constitutes both a playground and a prison. For each and every zoo is founded on
certain acres which have been captured by civilization, from
civilization, on behalf of civilization and which acres are
themselves the homes, and captors, of certain essentially
non-civilized entities, commonly referred to as "animals."
From one point of view, the typical zoo means a virtual
chaos, whereby human beings are enabled temporarily to
forget the routine of city life; while, from another point of
view, it means a real cosmos, possessed of its own consciousness, its own quarrels and even its own social register—
which, as we shall soon see, is indirectly our own social
register. These two aspects, "human" and "animal," interact;
with the result that the zoo, in comprising a mechanism for
the exhibition of beasts, birds and reptiles, becomes a
compound instrument for the investigation of mysterious
humanity.

—e.e. cummings, "The Secret of the Zoo Exposed"

Over the course of the nineteenth century, Japanese redefined and reshaped their place in the natural world. A new understanding of the
animal—and thus the human—was central to that transformation. When
United States Commodore Matthew C. Perry steamed into the bay of
Edo (present-day Tokyo Bay) at the head of a naval squadron that included four coal-burning "black ships"—intimidating machines that
belched black smoke into the skies above the vulnerable capital city—
his arrival announced more than a change in Japan's international

position. It foreshadowed the onset of Japan's industrial age and the reconfiguration of dealings with the natural world to suit the demands of "civilization." That transformation was both intellectual and material. As Japanese scholars and officials quickly recognized in the wake of Perry's carefully staged military and technological pageant, whoever holds the power to project a vision of civilization and humanity, and to make that vision prevail, holds a truly decisive power. All the more so in an age when the line between civilization and savagery was often synonymous with that between colonizer and colonized.[1]

The pursuit of such power in modern Japan took one of its most spectacular forms in the institution of the zoological garden, which redefined the relation between human beings and animals in keeping with the requirements of the dawning global age. The institution was a new kind of didactic medium that symbolically marshaled the animal world in the service of Japanese claims to Western-style "civilization," as modernity was called at the time, in the era of industry and empire. This book is about the creation of the first modern zoo in Japan, Tokyo's Ueno Park Imperial Zoological Garden, popularly known as the "Ueno Zoo," and the industrial and imperial culture that it helped to bring into being. It is a culture that I have chosen to call "ecological modernity" because it was so persistently concerned with Japan's place in the modern world and the place of flora, fauna, and other natural products within that modernity.[2] The defining irony of this culture was that even as it intensified the human exploitation of the natural world through the mechanics of industrialization and the expansion of the market, it imagined real nature to be elsewhere. It is a culture, I argue, that remains in force to this day.[3]

Nowhere was the paradoxical character of ecological modernity more evident than in the taxonomic perfection of the Ueno Zoo, a manufactured ecology that brought humans and other animals together—often across vast distances and at considerable expense—for the purpose of setting them apart. The zoo's agents imported living exotic animals into the heart of the modernizing Japanese capital and made them into icons of the "wild," exiles from a natural world somewhere "out there"— always elsewhere—beyond the manufactured world of the gardens, the human bustle of the capital city, and the increasingly industrialized landscapes of the Japanese islands. My principal argument holds that when the Ueno Zoo made caged animals into representatives of pristine "nature" it instituted a separation between people and the natural world, introducing a break between humanity and animality that recast

Japanese—together with Westerners—as the rational masters of a new natural history based on Linnaean nomenclature and the tenets of evolutionary theory. The primary consumers of this culture were the Japanese people themselves.

I use the term "ecological modernity" to designate this doubled process of intellectual separation and social transformation. At the zoo, it was a culture that took form in the juxtaposition of living animals and people. Binary frames of this sort belonged to a panoply of nineteenth-century dualisms, categorical distinctions used to debate the character of Japan as the country modernized: East and West, science and society, rationality and superstition. Even today, intellectual and popular cultures remain trapped by the Manichean logic of such over-powered dualisms.[4] It has long been commonplace for scholars to portray modernization—and thus modernity—as a process of denaturing and disenchantment, a slow disentangling of humans from animals and society from nature.[5] At one level, the reasons for this are obvious: urbanization, population growth, industrialization, and technological development have fundamentally altered our relationships with natural forces. But the history of the zoo—and that of ecological modernity more broadly—tells us that the modern story did not always play out along such neatly bifurcated lines.

Ecological dynamics do not stop at the edge of the city or at the doors of the factory, but the zoological garden thrives on the idea that such must be the case, that cities such as Tokyo are intrinsically unnatural. The Ueno Zoo, one of its directors was fond of saying, was appealing mainly because it was a refreshing "oasis of nature" in the middle of an industrial city.[6] Such assertions are premised on the idea that industrialization and modernization are the opposite of natural. This book begins from a very different point. It is an attempt to think beyond the simple juxtaposition of nature and society given form by the zoo and other institutions of ecological modernity. It assumes that people are always embedded in the natural world and that modernization meant, not the physical separation of nature from society, but their increasingly rapid interpenetration. Nineteenth-century factories burned coal—fossilized sunshine, as one scholar has called it—and cities, as public health officials in Tokyo concerned with cholera bacilli and other opportunistic organisms knew all too well, can be fecund ecologies. Cities, factories, parklands, and markets—the centers of human culture and industry—are understood here as what urban ecologists call "hybrid ecologies," sites where natural and manmade elements blur into one another in a manner that does not respect any absolute divide between material and cultural realms.[7]

The Ueno Zoo was an especially public form of hybrid ecology. It was a manufactured environment, to be sure, but an environment nonetheless, and many of the cultural dynamics that concern us here played out in physical interactions between people and animals within that built environment. When the zoo projected images of "nature" and the "wild" outward onto the forested edges of the Japanese archipelago or inward onto captive animals framed as fragments of exotic nature it also invited patrons into one of the most biologically diverse landscapes in the country. It did so in an effort—state-led by the 1870s—to alter how people saw themselves by changing how people saw the animal world. This was the nature of the beasts at the zoo: the effort to substitute a single "modern" or "civilized" vision of animals and nature for diverse early-modern cosmologies, and to give that new vision convincing form in the nation's largest and most diverse collection of exotic animals.[8]

Like many other aspects of nineteenth-century modern culture, ecological modernity announced itself as new and foreign in the Meiji period (1868–1912) despite the fact that Japanese had long drawn distinctions between people and other animals.[9] It marked itself off through the creation of a new lexicon, new social roles, new forms of specialized knowledge, and a host of new institutions. Its advocates struggled to align Japanese public practice with Western—self-consciously "modern" or "civilized"—norms. Indeed, although Japanese had been looking at captive animals in sideshows and the like for centuries, the zoo was introduced as something entirely novel when Japanese discovered it in their mid-nineteenth-century European travels. The modern Japanese term for "zoological garden" was coined by Fukuzawa Yukichi (1835–1901) in his widely read compendium of Western culture, *Conditions in the West* (*Seiyō jijō*), published serially in the 1860s. There, together with notes on steam engines and gaslights, republicanism and corsets, Fukuzawa included an entry on the "dōbutsuen," or "animal garden," a popular institution that "holds rare and marvelous creatures from all over the world."[10]

At a time when only a handful of Japanese were able to travel internationally, it was through such books—and later through the zoo and related institutions such as the schoolhouse and the museum—that many people first discovered the ideas and institutions of Western-style "civilization and enlightenment" (*bunmei kaika*), the cultural program through which elite nineteenth-century Japanese sought to reform the nation and its subjects in the face of foreign imperialism and domestic instability. It was in this fraught political context that the zoo appealed to Fukuzawa and his contemporaries, including many of the architects of Japan's industrialization such as Ōkubo Toshimichi (1830–1878). An important advocate for official exhibitions and museums, Ōkubo seized on the idea that it was the government's duty to teach people to control natural forces in the service of national development. The result was a state-led effort to alter how people saw the natural world. The proper exhibition of caged animals before curious crowds, Meiji-era exhibitionary policy suggests, had weighty implications at a time when notions of biological race and the "struggle for survival" (*seizon kyōsō*) were beginning to politicize, in an explicitly global context, the distinction between people and other animals.[11]

Despite origins in the exotic West, the zoo and its associated culture quickly took root in Japan, where natural history exhibits and acts of pilgrimage had long been commonplace, unfolding to become an accepted feature of the country's social landscape by the close of the nineteenth century. The drivers of this change were diverse. Over the course of the Meiji decades the efforts of bureaucrats, scientists, educators, tour guides, and publishers combined with the popular appeal of animal spectacle to transform the world of the zoo into a "natural" foil for everyday life in the city. The institution offered patrons a convenient, entertaining, and educational escape from the routines of daily life into a world that celebrated exotic animals and human ingenuity. For managers, it offered a way to address a self-selecting clientele who chose (in most cases) to open themselves up to suasion in the name of education and entertainment.

This book focuses on that transformation and its ramifications. It shows how managers and marketers created a vision of animals and nature and then put that vision to work, eventually themselves coming to believe that the new vision was, in actuality, a simple picture of "nature as it is" (*shizen sono mono*) rather than a highly mediated and carefully crafted depiction of the natural world. It was a vision that strove to be comprehensive, to claim for itself the symbolic power of a "real" nature—assumed to live outside the zoo—through the exhibition of living creatures. It was meant to celebrate—and reinforce—the modern, "civilized" order of things in the guise of staging an escape from that order.[12]

One of the central assumptions of this book is that the categories of "animal" (*dōbutsu*) and "nature" (most often *shizen* or *tennen*) are human fabrications that overlay and define living creatures and living environments, and that whoever lays definitive claim to these categories also lays claim to a subtle and powerful social influence.* The Ueno Zoo is a large organization with an annual budget to match, and thanks to the survival of abundant archival materials, there is much that can and will be said about its financial and bureaucratic dynamics. But those institutional particulars serve the telling of a cultural story, about changes in the way that Japanese understood themselves in the world, and the particular consequences of those changes. I try, whenever possible, to give voice to the patrons who were the subjects of this culture, but the interior world of the viewer is beyond the reach of even the most in-depth archival work, and such materials are scarce, especially during the early decades of the zoo's functioning covered in the first part of the book. By definition, the cultural story that I tell was neither purely interior nor fully individual; it was played out in public, in the whole range of activities by which the zoo declared its role in Japanese life and in the purposes it sought to pursue. My focus is on those public acts of fabrication.[13]

People are quite accustomed to recognizing the importance of animals in so-called primitive societies—a bias enabled by the progressive sense of time that became fixed in Japan in the nineteenth century—but animals are also woven into the fabric of the modern political economy in myriad ways, whether as labor, livestock, specimens, or companions.[14] Animal imagery was ubiquitous in modern Japan. Just as twentieth-century American children could not learn the English alphabet without discovering that "'Z' is for 'zebra,'" Japanese children could not learn the hiragana syllabary without learning that "'A' is for 'ahiru,'" or duck, or that "'TO' is for 'tora,'" or tiger. Such plain facts, addressed to children and by extension their parents, were given political color in a variety of ways. "Tigers are ferocious like [our] soldiers in China," added one 1940s flashcard, bringing masculinity and empire into the simple act of learning syllables. Through such means the cultural politics of ecological modernity arrived in youngsters' lives before they ever visited the zoo.

---

*I assume that human beings are animals, but I have chosen to maintain the distinction between "animals" and "humans" because it more clearly reflects the worldview of my subjects.

Much as Disney and other corporations work to saturate the private lives of today's children with dissatisfaction and desire, creating a wish to visit Disney World to see the "real" thing, girls and boys often arrived at the Ueno Zoo, stuffed animals in hand, hoping to *re*discover something that they had already learned in school textbooks, children's magazines, or through word of mouth. "Since I was little the lions, tigers, and elephants of picture books and magazines have called out to me," wrote one boy to the zoo director in 1943. "And then one day, my mother took me to the zoo, and there right in front of my eyes, weren't those the very same lions, tigers, and elephants from the books moving around right in front of me?" Mass culture and mass literacy helped to knit the zoo into the broader social fabric of modern Japan.

Zoos developed out of the eighteenth- and nineteenth-century traffic between European nations and their colonies to become something truly global. First in the West and then in Japan, they were created as metropolitan natural historians and collectors struggled to come to terms with the stunning biodiversity of newly colonized ecosystems. In their sheer will to collect, catalog, exhibit, and write about exotic fauna in increasing volume and with a seemingly insatiable hunger for new and unusual specimens, the managers of those institutions helped to forge connections between their patrons, the international world, and the natural environment. In the process they helped to craft a new set of habits and assumptions about the relationship between people and animals, ideas that were often framed as "scientific" but that moved most vigorously in the social, cultural, and political realms. Those habits and assumptions were not simply mimicked in Japan; they were translated, localized, made useful, and at times returned to international circulation as concepts and objects (animal and otherwise) moved through the institutional network of the zoo.[15]

The institution of the zoological garden ceased to be novel as millions of patrons stared into its cages and thumbed through its guidebooks. Managers continued to feature recent acquisitions, celebrate the births of baby animals, and promote new or renovated attractions, but like the broader culture of ecological modernity, the zoo itself eventually became an accepted part of daily life in metropolitan Japan. One result of that transformation was a commonsense understanding of the world that remains vibrant to this day, a vision in which nature appears as a different order of creation, a world apart from the engines of culture and industry that are typically taken as the locus of modernity and modernization. This book concerns itself with the history of that distinctly modern form of "common sense"—captured in the split between animals and people—as well as its ramifications in and beyond the miniaturized world of the gardens.[16]

ANIMALS IN THE ANTHROPOCENE

The Ueno Zoo was the first modern zoo in East Asia and the first zoo the world not built under the sway of a Western imperial regime.[17] The earliest modern zoos were opened in Paris in 1793 and London in 1828. Fueled by the competitive cosmopolitanism of the nineteenth century and the sheer volume of fauna moving through expanding global networks, similar institutions soon began to open in capitals and cities across Europe. By the 1870s, when zoos opened in Australia, India, and North America, the trend was global. There were more than one thousand elite accredited zoological gardens worldwide by the close of the twentieth century, visited by some 675 million people each year, or approximately 10 percent of the world's population. That number swells when we take into account nonaccredited animal theme parks, sideshows, and the like. Conservative estimates place the total number of such attractions worldwide at roughly ten thousand. By the late twentieth century Japan itself was home to more zoological gardens and aquariums than any other nation on earth, save the United States, where more people visited zoos each year than attended all professional football, baseball, and basketball games combined. Nearly two-thirds of the Japanese population (some fifty million people) visited a zoo or aquarium each year in the 1980s.[18]

In its global development and myriad localizations the zoological garden gave exhibitionary form to one of the defining events of modern times: the transformation of the world's human population into ecological actors of global significance. Human beings have always shaped our physical environments, but the scale of those changes expanded together with material and economic modernization. We live today, Nobel Prize–winning chemist Paul J. Crutzen argues, in an age when human influence has become so pervasive that it has overtaken geophysical factors as the dominant driver of the earth's climate and ecology. Crutzen's research suggests that in the past three centuries human beings have bought, built, planted, and bred our way out of the Holocene—the epoch, some ten to twelve millennia in the making, whose relative stability was crucial to the development of human civilization—into a turbulent global ecology fashioned in our own image. Crutzen, working in the chronological idiom of geologic time, has dubbed the new epoch the "age of man," or the "Anthropocene."[19]

The Anthropocene provides the global environmental context for Japan's ecological modernity. Although global warming has come to define the environmental crisis in the popular imagination, it is only one dimension of the problem. Crutzen and his colleagues have identified three major areas of anthropogenic ecological change in addition to rising average temperatures: biogeochemical cycles of elements such as nitrogen, phosphorous, and sulfur that are crucial to life on earth, altered through the use of chemical fertilizers and other means; modified terrestrial water cycles achieved through civil engineering and intensive agriculture; and the mass extinction of nonhuman animal species on a global scale, the so-called Sixth Great Extinction Event, the result of habitat destruction and intensive exploitation.[20] Unlike each of the previous five mass extinctions (the most recent was approximately sixty-five million years ago), this one appears to be driven mainly by human actions, concentrated in the modern age. Each of these three dynamics deserves close historical treatment, but the zoo's function has been most obvious in the last area, mass extinction.[21]

The Ueno Zoo became a theater of Anthropocene culture in Japan. Over the course of its short history the institution has gone from a place where captive wild animals were framed as exotic reflections of nature's ferociousness or fecund abundance to one where the animals themselves appear as figures of loss, disappearance, and extinction.[22] This representational shift echoes changes in international and domestic biodiversity even as it suggests that our notions of "modernity" must be far more attendant to ecological factors if they hope to capture the complexity of a global transformation that is at once social and environmental.

Globalization and industrialization were ecological events that ensnared millions of nonhuman animals. As of 2011, the International Union for Conservation of Nature and Natural Resources estimated that 19,265 species out of the 59,507 assessed worldwide—roughly 32 percent—were threatened with extinction. The number was slightly more encouraging for mammals, the core of most zoological garden collections, because they are the creatures with which human beings share the most in both emotional and morphological terms. Mammals look and behave more like us than other fauna, and so we tend to find them most engaging. Of the world's 5,494 known mammal species, 78 were extinct or extinct in the wild (a designation made meaningful by the existence of zoos and related organizations). Another 191 were

Mass extinction [handwritten margin note]

critically endangered, 447 more endangered, and 496 vulnerable.[23] This means that slightly more than 20 percent of the world's known mammal species were threatened with extinction or already extinct. Globally, the rate of extinction has accelerated to more than one hundred extinctions per million species per year, between one hundred and one thousand times the rate that scholars estimate took place in preindustrial times.[24]

Domestically in Japan, the extinction *rate* slowed dramatically in the late twentieth century. It was pushed downward by the simple reality of species depletion, as well as the radical simplification of environments through industrial forestry and agriculture undertaken in the service of commodity standardization (builders prefer certain kinds of trees, consumers prefer particular strains of rice, and so on). More optimistically, increased vigilance through improved conservation legislation, especially from the 1970s to today, has also had an effect. Positive developments notwithstanding, as of 2002, according to the Organization for Economic Co-operation and Development (OECD), slightly more than 20 percent of known mammal, amphibian, fish, reptile, and vascular plant species in Japan were threatened by extinction, an aggregate figure on par with global numbers.[25] This number does not register earlier extinctions, which have tended to take place over the course of only a few human generations.[26] Human beings have altered the ecologies of the Japanese islands for as long as people have lived there, but those processes have been amplified dramatically by the same social and technological dynamics that drove Japan's rapid material development. Ecological modernity was a handmaiden of industrialization.

These environmental developments pose historical problems, and scholars have begun to recognize that the scale of the Anthropocene threatens to overwhelm traditional frameworks and methodologies of history writing. As Dipesh Chakrabarty and Julia Adeney Thomas have both argued persuasively, the very notion of the "Anthropocene," framed in timescales typically reckoned in millions of years, envisions action by the human population as a singular, biologically defined global force rather than by classes or even nations of individuals. This baseline fact calls into question the meaningfulness of the individual human agent who occupies center stage in most histories, as well as the assumption (and significance) of a continuity of individual human experience between past, present, and future. How can questions of individual agency and experience matter when the human *species* has become an ecological force on par with the movement of continents?[27]

At first glance it is an odd question, but a sense of radical environmental change is now tangled into social consciousness at both global and local levels, whether as anxiety, denial, or studied apathy. If we wish to make our histories speak to present-day politics and hopes for the future, our own "problem consciousness" as historians must shift to address these new global realities. In this sense, the Anthropocene asks us to do more than simply recognize the importance of natural resources or biodiversity loss in the master narratives of human history. It suggests that information coming out of the environmental sciences and into public discussion has begun to unsettle the epistemological and social grounds that prefigure the act of writing history.[28]

The problem is one of scale and agency. The truly global dimensions of the Anthropocene require historians to ask what role the individual agent—and therefore histories that work at the level of the individual actor—might play when living things as such are endangered, living now at human sufferance. In this context, Chakrabarty argues, "Species may indeed be the name of the placeholder for an emergent, new universal history of humans that flashes up in the moment of danger that is climate change." We have moved from being merely biological agents—a theoretical innovation at the center of environmental history—to becoming geological agents at the level of the species, instigating an extinction event that appears to be on par with the one that wiped out dinosaurs. In such a situation the distinctions between the natural and the social at work in so much history—distinctions at the core of the ecological modernity given form in the zoo—appear to be simply out of synch. The human species has made itself into something more than an assemblage of biological actors. We have become a natural force, arguably *the* natural force of the epoch.[29]

Where are the connections between everyday human experience and these global changes? Framed in this way, the problem becomes one appropriate to the work of a cultural history such as this one. Politicians and pundits may argue otherwise, but the biological, chemical, and earth sciences in Japan, the United States, and elsewhere are in basic agreement on the facts: climate change is taking place, biodiversity loss is accelerating, and these changes are in no small measure driven by human actions.[30] The basic problem is not—and has not been for some time—one of science. It is one of politics and culture. Or, put another way, it is a problem of science in society. The technical processes that produced scientific consensus around climate change are at odds with the emotional and social needs of the local communities and individuals who must make them meaningful and, importantly, socially actionable.[31]

The problem, Sheila Jasanoff argues, emerges in the gap between the *is* and the *ought* of sense making. Representations of the natural world attain persuasive power not through the objectivity of scientific facts but rather when such concepts are found to be socially and culturally useful. Seen in this way, the trouble with the Anthropocene is not ontological (we *know* that the climate *is* changing) but social and normative: the behavior that this abstract knowledge recommends is at odds with ingrained power structures and assumptions about the natural world. It displaces the familiar (if not always comfortable) categories of nature, nation, and society—even person—in favor of the impersonal scientific knowledge of global transformation, nitrogen cycles, terrestrial water cycles, extinction events, and so on. It is unsettling. "To know climate change as science wishes it to be known," Jasanoff observes, "societies must let go of their familiar, comfortable modes of living with nature." I would add that climate change is just the tip of the Anthropocene iceberg, perhaps the clearest aspect of the problem because it appears so dramatically.[32]

ECOLOGICAL MODERNITY IN JAPAN

This book shows how one mode of living with and thinking about nature—Japan's ecological modernity—took form within a single institution across the late nineteenth and twentieth centuries. In situating my study within the discrete space of the Ueno Zoo, I seek to give a sense of human scale and historicity to the Anthropocene, to suggest that it is coeval—if not conterminous—with modernity itself. The close focus on a single institution allows us to see how ecological dynamics, social practice, and political intention became intertwined as Japan modernized. In a mass-culture, mass-consumption society such as Japan's, the problem of the Anthropocene is at least as much a question of culture, affect, choice, and "common sense" as it is one of industrial or scientific policy. Given this situation, where do we find the political and imaginative resources to reconfigure the ingrained practices of everyday life that have, in the aggregate, yielded up the "age of man"? A meaningful step forward might be to begin to analyze the cultural and political mechanisms that drove such environmental choices, to incorporate environmental issues into those corners of the historical discipline that seem, at first glance, to be distinct from the "environment" rather than dividing them out into separate studies in environmental history or the history of science. As Lynn K. Nyhart has shown in the German case, zoos and exhibitions played important roles in the development of what she has called the "biological perspective." Likewise, ecological dynamics—most often in the histories of captive animals—occupy a significant place alongside more traditional questions of capitalism, imperialism, and power in the present study. They are *a* central concern rather than *the* central concern of my inquiry.[33]

No environment in Japan was more consciously oriented to making the natural world meaningful than the Ueno Zoo.[34] The institution sought to "offer [patrons] a living picture of true nature," in the words of former zoo director Koga Tadamichi, and this very mission makes it a valuable case study for the cultural dimensions of modern Japanese attitudes toward the natural world.[35] But Koga's evocative summary of the zoo's function did not go far enough. The Ueno Zoo was built as a microcosm, yes, but not as a true reflection of nature. It offered instead a contrastive representation of the natural and social worlds as managers believed they *ought* to be experienced, a relationship defined, we might say, echoing Weber, by the bars of an iron cage. The zoo was a didactic institution whose main purpose was the inculcation of norms rather than the depiction of how things really were, an act of interpellation whose ultimate goal was not the faithful representation of the natural world but rather the use of those representations—the contrastive and mutually defining figures of the "animal" and the "human"—as social and political tools. This pull between the *is* of patrons and animals and *ought* of managerial intention is a driving spring in the narrative mechanism of my story.

Setting this history in a single site also facilitates the creation of a narrative of change over time. Few subjects are so compelling as animals. Animal characters can conjure human emotion without eliciting the ambivalence and categorical judgment often inspired by human characters. They are at once like us and unlike us, and in the oscillation between like and unlike they provide sympathetic figures that draw readers into the fabricated world of the story. The centrality of animals in children's literature is perhaps the most obvious example. From Aesop to *Where the Wild Things Are* or *The Poor Elephants* (*Kawaisō na zō*) featured in chapter 4, animals have brokered the socialization of children across cultures. I have paid close attention to such animal stories (aimed at children and adults alike) in the zoo and presented the most salient here: the highly politicized protest for elephants in the postwar, postimperial, occupation-era zoo discussed in chapter 5, for example. Through such stories this study narrates the intersections between natural and cultural politics within the Ueno Zoo in order to show that the exhibition of animals—icons of "nature"—is itself a political act.

At times animals figure as historical actors—as distinct from agents—in the stories recounted here, especially in later chapters, as dictated by available archival materials. Agency in its standard usage implies conscious, deliberative action. As R.G. Collingwood put it, "man is regarded as the only animal that thinks, or thinks clearly enough, to render his actions expressions of his thoughts."[36] The study of animal cognition has developed considerably since Collingwood penned that sentence in 1946—we now know that crows, chimpanzees, and other species work with forethought and "mental maps"—but I do not follow the recent trend in some scholarship to ascribe thoughtful *agency* to animals. This is not an act of disdain; it is a methodological choice. Such questions are beyond the scope of the archive, and so there will be no attempt to "give voice to the animal other" here. Such ventriloquism would, in fact, be a disservice since it would invariably be an act of dominance, no matter how well intentioned, in significant ways akin to the imperial historian who wishes to speak for the subaltern.[37] Indeed, as I show in chapter 3, when zoo officials did attempt to speak for the animals, it was most often as a means of disciplining human subjects.

To argue that animals were not agents is not to relegate them to the status of voiceless passivity. The term "actor" implies physical presence and emotional influence, and such influence was clearly registered in the gardens. Children's stories and adult fantasies notwithstanding, the Ueno Zoo was not an abstract "imagined landscape" populated by fictional creatures. It was a manufactured ecology full of living, feeling animals who inspired thoughts and emotions in those who interacted with them. When the sources allow, this book is attendant to the embodied aspects of the stories it tells. It asks us to rethink who, or rather what, counts in our histories and *how* they should count. Even within the tightly controlled world of the zoo, animals managed to influence the world around them; they were not inert objects. People may have become ecological actors of global significance in modern times, but they shared the stage with a host of other creatures—from prions and pests to predators and pets. In situating my analysis within the specific spaces of the zoo, I aim to show how cultural and environmental dynamics were intertwined at the scale of everyday life within the broader frame of the Anthropocene.[38]

Narratives—stories—are the most powerful tools available to historians, and scholars have only just begun to narrate the vexed relationship between modernization and environmental change in Japan. The majority of that work has focused on pollution cases and other environmental disasters, devastating events that have shaped the course of Japanese history. Much of the work, in both Japanese and English, has been excellent, and this book could not have been written without it. At the same time, seeing the whole of Japan's environmental history through the lens of "environmental problems" (*kankyō mondai*), the standard approach in many Japanese works, is itself part of the problem. It simplifies the story, falling too easily into what William Cronon has described as the "declensionist mode" of history writing, stories of terminal decline and callous disregard for human and nonhuman life. As Brett L. Walker has argued so eloquently, the reasons for this approach are well founded. Japanese have fundamentally transformed their physical environment—and thus their physical selves—through the work of nation building and industrialization in the modern period, and in large measure those changes have been negative.[39]

But the history of the Ueno Zoo refuses to fall into a neat story of decline. The institution was, to be sure, home to episodes of cruelty and neglect. As we will see most clearly in chapter 4, "The Great Zoo Massacre," such events were all the more chilling because they occurred at the zoo. Cruelty is perversity in an environment where animals are so completely under human control, "the abrogation of civilization's promise," as the animal-protection advocate Hiraiwa Yonekichi once put it. But such cases were exceptional rather than normal at Ueno. Indeed, the norm at the zoo was most often expressed in the ill-defined and changeable notion of "civilization" (*bunmei*), a term born in Japan's collision with the imperialist West but which continued to find life in the zoo long after Perry's black ships faded from memory. The institution was purpose-built as an emblem of civilized behavior, "a mechanism for the manufacture of civilized people and animals," as Director Koga put it nearly a century after Perry's departure. Zoos such as Ueno marked a country's international place according to an increasingly homogenized set of criteria and channeled heterogeneous cultural practices into landscapes that were in the process of being replicated, in various configurations, in capitals and cities around the globe.[40]

The gardens were also home to acts of remarkable, at times poetic, human effort on behalf of animals and the natural environment. Within the same horrific episode of the "zoo massacre," for example, keepers risked censure or worse as they advocated for the animals in their care. Similarly, Ueno Zoo staff played important parts in the effort to make Japan a signatory of the Convention on International Trade in Endangered Species of Wild Fauna and Flora (CITES) in 1980. CITES is, without question, the most important policy instrument currently available to those who would stop the trade in endangered and threatened species. Its implementation in Japan made work at the zoo more difficult rather than easier, but administrators pursued the application because they believed it was the right thing to do. The institution has also made marked contributions to causes ranging from animal cruelty legislation to the conservation of endangered domestic species such as the Japanese Crane (*Grus japonensis*) and the Japanese Crested Ibis (*Nipponia nippon*). Director Koga led the expansion of international conservation efforts through the World Wildlife Fund and numerous other organizations.[41]

My purpose here is not to counter narratives of decline with naïve assertions of progress. To do so would be to fall prey to the Ueno Zoo's own folklore, a mythology in which the zoo becomes ever more indispensable as the broader environment degrades. The zoological garden, some in Japan have suggested, must become an "ark of biodiversity" (*shu no hakobune*) against the flood of habitat destruction.[42] Drawing on a national faith in technology that rivals even that of the United States, these arguments overestimate the capacity of the gardens to answer such global questions. They also fail to recognize the zoological garden's historical role in producing and strengthening the very dynamics that they seek to stymie. The Ueno Zoo has thrived in the culture of industrial modernity that made it seem indispensable, a tense dynamic that is at the heart of ecological modernity.

My desire, rather, is to suggest that Japan's ecological modernity found its rhythm in the point and counterpoint of contradiction. Tracing those rhythms will help us to understand the cultural dynamics that tie everyday behavior into the Anthropocene. As David Blackbourn argues in his analysis of related dynamics in Germany, the modern conquest of the natural world was a Faustian bargain. It brought gains and losses both. The broader transformation of the natural environment in modern times delivered benefits to many Japanese: a more secure food supply, potable drinking water, and new sources of energy that brought heat, cooling, and the material comforts of modernity. Postwar Japanese took reasonable pride in the fact that they were the longest-lived people on the planet. But plentitude in the midst of increasingly insistent environmental losses—and now the crisis of March 11, 2011—has led many Japanese, like Germans and others, to begin asking whether the culture of mass production and mass consumption can be maintained, and if so at what cost?[43]

The staccato rhythm of contradiction is most audible today in the questioning and tension between *ought* and *is*. The new, urgent, scientifically sophisticated understanding of the emerging global ecological crisis is at odds with the familiar, timeworn, and symbolically rich vision of animals and nature that is woven into the fabric of everyday life in modern Japan. The stories, myths, and beliefs of ecological modernity came together over the course of more than a century, and they drew on an even older universe of practices and symbols. They will not change overnight or without dissent.[44] But the weight of the Anthropocene problem bears down on the accepted binary that encompasses nature and society. As we struggle to come to terms with the realities of climate change, diminishing natural resources, and the rapid eradication of other species, it is increasingly clear that the crisis emerges most forcefully along the frontiers where people seek to make sharp distinctions between these two realms. Nowhere in modern Japan was the border between the natural and social worlds more spectacularly rendered than in the Ueno Zoo.

THE NATURAL WORLD AS EXHIBITION

The Ueno Zoo used animals to set the natural world up as a picture of itself. In the process it introduced the idea that nature was being represented—rather than reshaped—within the zoological garden. Across most of the institution's history, keepers and curators have not seen anything natural in the cages and enclosures of the Ueno Zoo beyond the bodies of the animals themselves. This sense of displacement is partially produced by the structure of the zoological garden. The unquestioned authenticity of the animals on display—the fact that they are, unlike museum artifacts, *alive*, and thus possessed of instincts and motives that push up against the barriers that constrain them—has served to highlight the perceived artificiality of the institution that confines them and, by extension, the manufactured character of the modern culture that created the gardens in the first place.[45]

This dynamic, at the very heart of ecological modernity, drew part of its energy from a quiet revolution in Tokugawa-era taxonomy.

Beginning in the early nineteenth century, as I show in chapter 1, practitioners of natural history (honzōgaku) sought to bring the diverse creatures of the living world together under a single new master metaphor, that of the "animal," or dōbutsu. It was a move inspired by post-Linnaean Western taxonomy and driven by the pursuit of professional distinction within Japan. Practitioners of honzōgaku late in the Tokugawa era wished to set themselves apart from hobbyists in order to secure income and position. In the process, they worked to define nature as a world apart, a realm best understood through the application of specialized knowledge garnered through close examination and the application of the new Western theory.[46] This book begins with that effort. Where early-modern cosmologies celebrated the creative multiplicity of the natural world or spiritual connections between people and other creatures—in Buddhist cycles of rebirth, the animism of Shintoism, or the moral mirror of Confucian nature, for example—advocates of ecological modernity sought to draw clear distinctions between humans and animals based on the capacity for reason (chinō), perceived to be the sole domain of Homo sapiens.[47] Emotional connections between people and animals were ancillary, always framed as incidental, and the idea of spiritual or karmic affinity eventually came to be seen as irrelevant "superstition."

Commodore Perry's arrival breathed political urgency into this esoteric discussion, amplifying the question of the "dōbutsu"—together with its supplement, the "savage" (yaban)—into a matter of national concern, thus elevating the status of the nascent biological sciences.[48] The Ueno Zoo was born of this moment, and it drew much of its dynamism from a contradiction that lay at the root of the new natural history. Human beings, the tenets of evolutionary theory said, were always still dōbutsu (animals) at the dōbutsuen (zoological garden), and so the work of separation—what the historian of science Bruno Latour calls "purification"—could never be complete.[49]

Even those who proudly celebrated a special Japanese (as opposed to Western) attitude toward nature or animals, or who claim that no such divisions existed in Japan, made those arguments on grounds laid in the Meiji era, the same moment that gave rise to the institutions that concern us here—the zoo, the botanical garden, the expo, and the museum. Records and letters from visitors tell us that the picture of nature on exhibit at Ueno was familiar—in its formatting and framing—to men, women, and children from Berlin to the Bronx. Exhibits were formatted by such comfortably exciting ideas as the "wild" and "wilderness," "safari" and "specimen," and even "animal" and "human" that structured zoos everywhere.[50] And while Ueno's managers aggressively pursued new containment designs, the material culture of the zoo's cages and enclosures was also decidedly transnational. Ideas, plans, planners, and animals all moved back and forth in a manner that renders claims of essentially Japanese attitudes toward nature (familiar to anyone who has lived in or studied Japan) suspect, at least to the extent that the vision at work in the zoo can be taken as indicative, a vision that was ubiquitous in popular culture and directly experienced by more than three hundred million people at Ueno alone over its first 120 years in operation. Particularities were there, and they are fascinating in their distinctiveness, but they were expressed on a stage built of transnational materials.

Such binaries endured because they were useful. Reformers from inside and outside of the zoo used the juxtaposition of authenticity and artifice, for example, to argue for improved funding, greater legal oversight, or expanded breeding programs. "Progress in the techniques of animal care [shiiku gijutsu] at zoological gardens" becomes increasingly important as extinction accelerates in the wild, the Director of Kyoto's Imperial Zoo, Kawamura Tamiji (1883–1964) argued in 1940. Zoological gardens, the former professor of zoology at Kyoto Imperial University went on to say, must be made into a more faithful mirror of nature in order to reproduce nature itself.[51] Kawamura's comments were balanced between the critical and the celebratory, and they drew on a longer tradition that elevated the artificiality of the zoo as a marker of civilization itself. Zoo and museum administrators often praised what Timothy Mitchell has called the "realism of the artificial" in displays.[52] In a context where the proper techniques of exhibition were themselves definitive of civilization, as they were under ecological modernity, administrators took not just the accuracy of the displays themselves but also the capacity to produce such mimicry as an index of progress.

The experience of the natural-world-as-exhibition was at once global and local. Whether in Toronto or Tokyo, zoogoing is a rationalized, sanitized event more akin to a stroll through the mall or along a shop-lined street than it is to the safaris, hunts, and expeditions that the word "zoo" evokes in the minds of children—and for many adults. We look past bars, across moats, and through layered polycarbonate-glass composites when we look at most animals in the gardens. The aesthetics of that experience are shaped by the careful use of light, color, glass, sound, and smell. Zoological gardens (including Ueno) now regularly pipe in edited "nature sounds." Animal odors are washed away as quickly as possible because they are visceral reminders of the physicality we share with the creatures on the other side of the bars or perhaps instinctual cues to the fact that we are, in purely biological terms, potential prey for the beast that we are looking at, or who is looking at us. We stand apart from the animals behind the glass, which sit isolated, enclosed by manmade architecture.

Ecological modernity entailed, not the natural world's disappearance, but a reorganization of the ways in which most people engaged with animals and the natural world. As Akira Mizuta Lippet has argued, animals and nature, as abstract categories, can never simply disappear. Rather, the social and economic changes concomitant with modernity in Japan and around the world have seen many species driven to extinction—the Japanese wolf, for example—and others sequestered behind the walls of institutions or, to the extent such things are possible, confined to wildlife preserves and national parks. As Andrew Gordon has shown, Japanese social experience was increasingly aggregated under large-scale bureaucratic and commercial organizations as the country modernized, and so too were Japanese dealings with animals. Institutions ranging from the zoo to the laboratory to the puppy mill to the factory farm dominate the landscape (often overseas in the Japanese case). Mediating increasingly impersonal and attenuated interactions between humans and animals, they feed a growing sense of alienation from the natural world even as they have amplified humanity's impact on living nature.[53]

This is part of the darker side of the zoo's story, the unintended consequence of the Meiji era's bright pursuit of "civilization and enlightenment." The zoological garden thrives in a culture of alienation that it helps to produce. Together with the sense of separation from nature that was definitive of the natural-world-as-exhibition—what Heidegger called the world-as-exhibition—came the sense that nature itself was the wellspring of authentic humanity, something that had to be *rediscovered* in order to recover one's true self in a landscape that felt increasingly barren and artificial.[54] Social bureaucrats, writing in the same interwar moment as Heidegger and his Japanese colleague Watsuji Tetsurō (1889–1960), realized that the zoological gardens could play an especially important role in this context, which was, for them, pregnant with the threat of mass disaffection. Alive, their authenticity only augmented by the architecture that enclosed them, zoo animals became ever more enchanting as industrial capitalism consolidated in Japan after the First World War. The charisma of unusual animals brought unprecedented numbers of people to the gardens, where the mechanics of spectacle induced a state of wonder that opened visitors up to influence "without thought and without consciousness" (*fuchi fushiki*), in the words of zoo director Kurokawa Gitarō. Zoogoers, Kurokawa and his colleagues believed, experienced encounters with strange and unusual animals on a pre-ideological level. The zoo was a "comfort institution" (*ian shisetsu*) that helped people to see the social order as a natural one.[55]

This combination of popularity and political utility led to a boom in zoo construction. The Japanese empire was home to more than thirty zoos by 1942, and total attendance at those institutions approached fifteen million people annually. By 1965 the total number of accredited zoological gardens topped fifty, and by 2010 it climbed to ninety, down from a peak of over one hundred during the economic "bubble years" of the 1980s. The Ueno Zoo—already the "world's most popular zoo" by 1942, according to zoo administrators—became so overburdened by crowds that a subsidiary garden, modeled on German nature parks and specializing in species indigenous to Japan, was opened in suburban Inokashira Park in 1934. Another much larger garden was opened in the distant suburbs of Tama Township in 1958.

Public fascination with the zoological garden amplified as wildlife and animals other than pests and pets—the bane and the boon of bourgeois domesticity—were progressively removed from the day-to-day experience of most Japanese.[56] In the century or so encompassed by this text, the portion of the Japanese population engaged in agricultural labor as its primary source of livelihood went from roughly 75 percent in the 1880s to less than 5 percent in 1990. Across the same period the population of Tokyo increased from slightly more than one million to nearly twelve million (the metropolitan area now holds nearly thirty million), and the proportion of Japanese who lived in cities climbed above 75 percent, up from 38 percent in 1950. Zoo attendance rose steadily but not evenly over the same decades, spiking in counterpoint to political events and new animal acquisitions as it illustrated a deeper groundswell of interest in and desire for the zoo and the vision of nature on display.

This was the institution's greatest achievement. Whether they found what they wanted there or not, people visited the zoo voluntarily and with pleasure. Tokyoites did not go to the zoo to "develop technical skill through the education of the eye" or to "situate themselves on the empowered side of the animal-human dualism." They went to have fun and to escape from the increasingly alienating landscape of the modern city. Visitors went to pull their children away from the television, to look at Ueno's famous cherry blossoms, to discover for themselves exactly what an okapi might be, or perhaps to satisfy a craving for a "panda bun," "panda ice cream," or "panda yakisoba." A popular cliché holds that all Tokyoites visit the Ueno Zoo at least four times during their lifetimes: first when they are children, then as teenagers on a date with their sweethearts, next when they have children of their own, and finally as grandparents escorting their grandchildren.[57] Once a beacon of Japanese aspirations to Western-style civilization, the Ueno Zoo is now seamlessly woven into the fabric of the nation's capital and consciousness. Our concern is how that transformation happened and what it meant.

PART ONE

The Nature of Civilization

CHAPTER I

Japan's Animal Kingdom

The Origins of Ecological Modernity and the Birth of the Zoo

There is no document of civilization which is not at the same time a document of barbarism.

—Walter Benjamin, *On the Concept of History*

BRINGING POLITICS TO LIFE

Ecological modernity began to quicken in Japan when Udagawa Yōan completed his *Botany Sutra* (*Botanika kyō*) in 1822, an act of translation that claimed revolutionary social and scientific consequences. It was in that short essay that Udagawa (1798–1846), already a noted translator of Western medical and scientific texts at the age of twenty-four, proposed the Japanese word for "animal" that is still used today. The characters that he chose for the word—*dōbutsu*—signify a moving or animated thing, a description that he linked with breath, air, and life force: ideas that share important elements with both the Latin term *anima* and the Buddhist recognition of affinity between people and animals.[1] It was a choice that signaled the young scholar's careful engagement with botanical and zoological texts, foreign and domestic. It also indicated the scope of his ambitions. Beginning with *Botanika kyō* and continuing in a series of original and translated works, this practitioner of *honzōgaku*—a discipline rooted in *materia medica* but best translated as "natural history"—sought to transform the study, classification, and cultural meaning of the natural world in Japan.[2] The Chinese-style nomenclature used by Japanese specialists from the early Tokugawa era was, he claimed, lacking in precision. It had been superseded by the work of such Western scholars as Conrad Gesner, John

Ray, and Carl Linnaeus. "People, lions, dogs, pheasants" and all manner of other "ambulatory things," he wrote, listing sixteen different creatures in the style of older encyclopedias, shall henceforth all be "dōbutsu." The confused abundance of traditional nomenclature, Udagawa argued, must be consolidated into two Linnaean kingdoms: Animalia (*dōbutsu*) and Plantae (*shokubutsu*).[3]

Udagawa brought a religious sensibility to his task. The *Botanika kyō* was written in the form of a Buddhist sutra. Many graphs begin with the phrase "Thus I have heard that" (*nyoze gamon*), a pattern typical of the sutras referenced in Yōan's title. In nineteenth-century Japan the phrase would have been recognized as a nod to the recitations of Ānanda, the longtime attendant to the historical Buddha who was said to have perfect recall. In local temples and domainal schools, children in the Tokugawa era (1600–1868) were taught that after the Buddha's death it was Ānanda who recited his master's sermons verbatim from memory so that they could be transmitted within the monastic community.[4] Only in the case of the *Botany Sutra*, it was not the Buddha from whom readers were to receive teachings, but a pantheon of foreign botanists and zoologists. The sutra begins with a litany of Western scholars labeled as *taisei*, or "great sages," and Udagawa plays the role of Ānanda, a faithful reporter of correct teachings.[5]

The *Botanika kyō* has been something of a riddle for historians of science in Japan. Why phrase a treatise on nomenclature—even one so full of ambition and new ideas—in the language of a religious text? Was Udagawa the only one to write in this manner? Historian Nishimura Saburō argues that Yōan was not alone. Another translator and scholar of Dutch Studies (*rangaku*, or the study of Western science and medicine), Yoshio Nankō (1787–1843), also presented an essay—a seminal piece on Western astronomy—as a "sutra" at around the same time. Focused mainly on economic and professional motives, Nishimura speculates that Udagawa and Yoshio may have hoped to see the principles of Western taxonomy spread like those of Confucianism or Buddhism, transmitted by disciples who would gain prestige through association with the "sages."[6] To me, the *Botanika kyō* says that and something more. The *Sutra's* format suggests a purpose at once sociological and cosmological.

Like all religious texts, the "sutra" was concerned with the relationship between one world and another, and the short treatise argued for a new kind of separation between its readers and the natural world. The work gave lexical form (what Nishimura calls a "new systematics") to a broader shift in attitudes when it posited the existence Linnaean "kingdoms" (*kai*) as objective categories independent of human history and culture. It was not the natural world's creativity, therapeutic qualities, or moral content that Yōan celebrated, as Buddhist theorists and others had earlier in the Tokugawa era, but rather the rational order that he came to discern beneath its profusion of forms. This was a decisive shift. When Yōan argued that knowledge of nature was valuable in and of itself, he also suggested the possibility of a nature apart from (and prior to) human concerns. In doing so, the young theoretician accelerated a shift that gathered force across the Tokugawa era away from traditional ways of seeing life and being in the world.[7] He drove an intellectual wedge—the idea of the animal—into the nascent gap between people and nature. Understood in this way, the sutra marks a moment of basic continuity as well as one of epistemological rupture. It suggests, in microcosm, the complexity of a transformation in attitudes toward animals—and by extension people—that began long before the 1853 arrival of U.S. Commodore Matthew Perry and which emerged only through engagement with existing philosophies and practices (including older iterations of European theory).

Even as it placed humans (*hito*) at the head of the list of *dōbutsu*, the *Sutra* suggested a distinction between people and other animals premised on the capacity for intelligent thought (*chinō*). The very qualities that helped to ease distinctions between human beings and other creatures in other modes of classification—animation and sensation, for example—here became "characteristics" (*sei*) to be described in the rational pursuit of a better model.[8] Yōan drew on Buddhism's recognition of similarity (not sameness) across species and an early-modern neo-Confucian ethic that made it a moral duty to exploit natural resources to outline a more remote relationship between humans and other living things. People certainly share physical traits with animals, later work in the field argued, but only human beings render those qualities into objects of rational contemplation.[9]

The human capacity for reason, then, became a pivot in the double movement of ecological modernity. On the one hand, Yōan's theory facilitated the categorical separation of people from animals. This externalization—enabled by the homogenization of a hugely diverse set of living creatures as "animals"—took on unanticipated political importance after 1853, when Japan was more fully opened to international capitalism and imperialism. "Savagery" was the inverse of "civilization" in the bipolar worldview of the nineteenth century. On the other hand, Yōan's *Sutra* internalized that same dualism *within* the human. This was a defining contradiction. People and other *dōbutsu* shared breath, air, and life force—the fact of living—but that contiguity had to be disavowed in the nation's pursuit of civilization and autonomy. Differentiation was politically critical but biologically impossible, and so it was always incomplete, a circuit that remained open rather than a process that could reach a conclusion. This tension—along with the sheer spectacle of extraordinary creatures held in captivity—gave the zoo its dynamism.[10]

As in Europe, no single discovery led to this new way of knowing nature in Japan. Udagawa was innovative, but as Federico Marcon has argued, practitioners of Dutch Studies and natural history were involved in a process of professionalization across the Tokugawa period, defining disciplines and setting themselves apart from amateurs. Together with later works from Itō Keisuke (1803–1901), Tanaka Yoshio (1838–1916), and a small group of scholars focused on the study and translation of Western books—a subdiscipline that took form in the Institute for the Study of Barbarian Books (Bansho Shirabesho) in 1856—Yōan's sutra gave new force and coherence to these changes, primarily in the form of language. As Barbara Ambros has shown, before the *Botany Sutra* the creatures classed as "dōbutsu" were either named individually (using what scholars of classification today call "common names") or allocated into a diverse range of midlevel taxa associated with (to choose the most common examples) moral concepts of beastliness (*chikushō*) rooted in Buddhism, religious philosophies of being and sentience (*ikimono, kigyō*), and spiritual notions of divinity or monstrosity (*misaki, mono no ke, bakemono*).[11] Yōan's "dōbutsu" named a unifying idea that percolated through the scholarly community across the nineteenth century. It also enabled the imagination of a categorical distinction between humans and other animals akin to that at work in other modern societies.

"Dōbutsu" became part of the national vernacular after the Meiji Restoration of 1868. Propelled by state policy, conditioned by the flood of Western texts and ideas into the country, and fueled by broad social utility, the term was in wide usage by the 1880s. It was a classic "sticky idea": novel, concrete, easy to use, at once simple and profound. Readers encountered it in journals and newspapers, students learned it in school textbooks, and technicians put it to work on behalf of agricultural and industrial development (*shokusan kōgyō*), which targeted animal resources as well as human and mechanical work. By the late

1880s, the "animal" was commonly understood within an encompassing notion of "nature" (most often *shizen* or *tennen*) whose nomenclatorial and ideological consolidation tracked many of the same pathways and dynamics.[12] In the most basic terms, animals and nature remain locked in this relationship today. By the end of the Meiji period in 1912, the vision of the world outlined in the *Botany Sutra* was widely accepted as common sense. In this way, Udagawa's short, hybrid tract—at once sutra and science—was an important document in the development in Japan of the basic distinction between nature and culture (or the nonhuman and the human) that historians of science such as Bruno Latour use to mark the threshold of modernity.[13]

Tokyo's Ueno Zoological Garden was built on that threshold. It was a consciously constructed mechanism for the separation of people from other animals, an anthropological machine whose primary purpose was to help create a certain kind of person—curious, docile, productive, and "civilized"—through the didactic exhibition of live animals. Opened as part of the country's new National Museum complex in Ueno Park in 1882, the Ueno Zoo rendered Udagawa's animal kingdom into an object of spectacle and difference. In doing so, the zoo helped to popularize the idea that the Japanese people stood apart from the animals on the other side of the bars, separate from the nature that those creatures were made to represent.[14]

The carefully ordered displays of the *dōbutsuen*—or "animal park," as the new institution was called—harnessed the taxonomic abstraction of Yōan's *dōbutsu* to something real, observable, and undeniably *present*: living, breathing, moving animals. In the process, the zoological garden helped give rise to the broader sense of a natural order that existed apart from (and prior to) the representational work of the zoo itself, and thus apart from the everyday realities of politics, culture, and historical (as opposed to evolutionary or geological) time. It then put that vision of the natural world—rendered into an exhibition meant to educate and fascinate—to work in the service of a host of political and social goals. This chapter is about that transformation, its implications, and the creation of the Ueno Zoo. It takes us from Japan's first state-run museum and menagerie, through the Ueno Imperial Zoo and the European and American zoos that inspired it, and into the politicized world of social evolution in modernizing Japan, where the figure of the animal became an inescapable reminder of Japan's impossible struggle to detach "civilization" from the natural world. It shows, in sum, how ecological modernity altered attitudes and how, in turn, that transformation changed what it meant to be human in the age of "civilization and enlightenment."

SORTING ANIMALS OUT IN MEIJI JAPAN

According to one visitor, the most popular exhibit at Japan's first museum was neither a graceful Buddhist statue nor a piece of fine porcelain. Rather, it was a dancing Ezo Bear and his two Ainu keepers. The men—bearded indigenes from the northern island of Hokkaido—traveled to Tokyo together with their animal charge as part of the country's first state-run survey of natural and cultural treasures, carried out just three years after the Meiji Restoration. The trio performed (and may have lived) in a small building at the end of the visitor path that guided patrons through the grounds of the Yamashita Museum, a collection of exhibition halls, warehouses, offices, animal pens, gardens, and greenhouses located just inside of the Yamashita Gate at the edge of the Imperial Palace. The museum was home to the nation's first state-run menagerie, the Yamashita Animal Hall, or *Dōbutsukan*, a large wooden hall whose seventy-plus inhabitants ranged from badgers and bears to dogs and dormice. The land that held the museum was previously home to a residence owned by the Satsuma Clan, one of the main drivers of the Restoration, and after the museum closed in 1881 it became the site of the Rokumeikan, or "Deer-Cry Pavilion," a government-run guesthouse and ballroom where Japanese leaders famously danced to the tune of Western-style cultural diplomacy.[15]

The Yamashita Museum was the first institution in Japan to be called a "museum," or *hakubutsukan*. The appellation underlines the strong connections between Meiji-era scientific and exhibitionary culture—the institutions at the center of Japan's ecological modernity—and natural history of the sort practiced by Udagawa. Scholars have often placed Dutch Studies (*rangaku*) at the start of Japan's scientific modernization because of its explicit connections with the West (the Dutch were the only Western country permitted to trade with Japan during most of the Tokugawa era), but Dutch Studies developed out of the broader discipline of *honzōgaku*, which in turn took its name from the Chinese study of materia medica (*bencaoxue*) in the early years of the Tokugawa era. China preceded the West in the Tokugawa imaginary, and so too did *honzōgaku* precede (and prefigure) aspects of *rangaku*. By the mid-nineteenth century "honzōgaku" had become a terminological victim of its own disciplinary openness, however. As the medical aspects of natural history were first folded into Dutch Studies and then, after the Restoration, further bifurcated into Western-style (*igaku*) and Chinese-style (*kanpō*) medicine, "natural history" came to be known as "hakubutsugaku," or the "study of myriad things." *Hakubutsugaku* connoted a general interest in the material world rather than the close study of *materia medica*. The *hakubutsukan* ("hall of myriad things") derived its name from this *hakubutsugaku*.[16]

The museum was more than a showcase. It was an epistemological workshop, a place where categories were tested and created through the separation of artifacts and animals. The staff at Yamashita was consciously engaged in a process of taxonomic innovation in the service of the state. Items arrived in Tokyo (itself recently renamed from Edo) two-by-two from each of the nation's new prefectures (*ken*). One of each kind was slated for the Vienna World Exposition (held from May to November of 1873), the other destined for domestic display. When they arrived they were sorted, labeled, and prepared for exhibition by technicians who were themselves only recently reclassified, transformed by government fiat from members of Tokugawa Japan's status system (*mibunsei*)—which separated the ruling samurai from peasants, artisans, merchants, and outcastes based on birth and occupation—into imperial subjects. Each subject was now theoretically equal before the emperor, but "liberation" came at a cost. Individuals were laid bare to imperial law with the eradication of status-based institutions, and hierarchy was reinscribed in the past tense: samurai became "former samurai," outcastes became "former outcastes," and so on.[17] With people and animals alike, the modern taxonomic revolution was as much an exercise of power—of opening people and things up to change (*kaika*)—as it was the realization of any ideal of "civilization" (*bunmei*).

The Vienna Expo marked the Meiji state's official debut in the competitive world of national expositions and fairs, and Tanaka Yoshio oversaw the natural-history portions of the exhibit. Tanaka, who credited Udagawa for inspiring his taxonomic zeal, was the first person to use the modern term for "zoology" (*dōbutsugaku*, or "the study of *dōbutsu*") in the title of a published work. Based on close readings of Dutch and German texts, *Zoology* (authored just as the museum was opening) is larded with other neologisms, most notably *hachūrui*, which is still the accepted term for "reptilia." "There are few words in our language for these [things]," Tanaka wrote in the preface, "so I have had to coin new words [for them]." It was not that Japanese had never known of turtles or crocodiles or most of the other creatures described in

Dōbutsugaku before, he suggested in a Linnaean spin on the neo-Confucian practice of "rectifying names," but they had never named them accurately. Proper names would bring proper knowledge, Tanaka later argued in a set of articles aimed at educators, and proper knowledge of the natural world would help to secure Japan's place as a "civilized country" (*bunmeikoku*).[18]

The museum at Yamashita was a liminal institution. It was suspended between the modern state's nascent program of official exposition and the profit-oriented sideshows (*misemono*) and natural-history exhibits (*bussankai*) that were common in Tokugawa times. Like the National Museum and zoo that followed it, the museum attempted to draw on these cultural antecedents, recalibrating and regulating them according to the emerging logic of modernity, a logic that was itself the stuff of spectacle in the 1870s.[19] Curious about the changes sweeping their country and eager for distraction in the wake of the Boshin Civil War (1868–1869), people were happy to put the habits of Edo-era *flanerie* to new use.[20] They poured into the grounds when the museum opened for a temporary, two-month stint in April 1873. When they entered the exhibition, patrons encountered a carefully organized collection of several hundred items, each categorized through the work of Tanaka and his colleagues. Officials extended public hours as crowds continued to push through the gardens, into the display halls, and on to the pen where the Ainu and their bear performed. By the end of the year Yamashita was open on days ending in "1" and "6" (marked, it is worth noting, according to a newly instituted Gregorian calendar that was itself the subject of a small display inside the museum).

At once museum and menagerie, Yamashita was a hybrid institution, a middle ground between the human and the natural worlds where the relationship between those two realms—essentialized into opposition and mutually defining—was worked out and put on display. Animals and nature were weeded out from people and civilization as Tanaka and his colleagues went about their work. Classification at Yamashita was as much a material process as it was a theoretical exercise, and as technicians dealt with specific objects—animal and otherwise—they refined a working distinction between products of human manufacture (*jinkō*) and things that were "made by nature" (*tenzō*). The grounds embodied this basic division between the human and the nonhuman. Over time, the division, which drew authority from Western texts and early-modern natural-historical theory, developed into a normative split—a master metaphor—that shaped the entire Japanese exhibitionary complex. In the short term, the separation was most clearly evident in the creation of a separate Division of Natural Products (Tensanbu) administered by Tanaka. In the midterm, it influenced the configuration of the Ueno Park exhibitionary complex, where the human world of the museum was severed from the imported nature of the zoological garden. Nature served culture in this institutional configuration; Tanaka's colleague Machida Hisanari (1838–1897) supervised the handling of historical, artistic, and cultural artifacts at Yamashita. He became the first director of the National Museum (and Tanaka's boss) when it opened in 1882.[21]

The vision of nature on display at Yamashita was far from "made by nature." It was the result of human labor and, oftentimes, confusion. "Things do not sort themselves," Machida wrote in frustration in 1878, "and many items are difficult to classify in actual fact." This was especially true of natural products (*tensan*), he continued, which seemed to slip between categories "depending on use." His annoyance is understandable. After all, how does one separate nature from culture when dealing with silkworms or thoroughbred horses? As Tanaka and Machida recognized, domesticates such as the horse are bred by human beings over generations. Silkworms—indispensible to Meiji industrialization—were entirely dependent on human beings for breeding and food. Were these things *jinkō* or *tenzō*? In both cases the answer at Yamashita was "made by nature," but placement was debated and questioned. It was, in part, through such debates that the idea of nature itself became naturalized at the museum. While the classification and naming of individual species and artifacts continued to elicit consternation and debate, fewer and fewer people stopped to question the fact of division itself. The assumption that human beings were separate from nature was normalized at Yamashita in the 1870s and, as Stefan Tanaka has shown, elsewhere in the archipelago across the nineteenth century.[22]

Difference implied hierarchy, and as patrons walked through the museum they enacted a descent through the official order of things. The largest building in the grounds was the Hall of Antiquities (Kobutsu-kan), a rambling wooden structure of twenty-odd exhibition areas, each dedicated to some aspect of human history or culture (*jinkō*). The original guide for the building listed five departments in English: "Art, History, Education, Religion, and Arms [military paraphernalia]."[23] With nearly one thousand square meters of exhibition space, the Kobutsukan was bigger than all other interior spaces at Yamashita combined. The garden leading up to the hall's graceful entrance was divided into eleven separate plant beds, each filled with a selection of floral specimens

defined by use: "edibles" (*shokuyō*), "medicinals" (*yakuyō*), and "orna-
mentals" (*kinshō*). Even the lawns at Yamashita performed taxonomic
work.

When visitors exited the Hall of Antiquities they walked out of a
monument to Japanese cultural accomplishment and into an architectural rendering of the new natural history. Where Udagawa, in his focus
on life and living creatures, posited a bifurcation between Animalia and
Plantae in the *Botany Sutra*, the layout at Yamashita echoed the tripar-
tite model of Linnaeus's canonical 1735 *Systema Naturae*, a model that
influenced a host of Western and Japanese taxonomists, including
Udagawa himself in his later work. Tanaka divided the products of
the natural world (*tensanbutsu*) at Yamashita into three kingdoms: animals, plants, and minerals. The plant kingdom was further subdivided
according to utility, and animals were split between the living and the
dead, the popular and the scientific. In each display, the labor of classification was actively celebrated. Rather than trying to hide the human
origins of taxonomy (the norm in later institutions where the categories
of modern life were more fully naturalized), Yamashita rendered the act
of classification itself into an object of exhibitionary attention emblematic of the new age.[24]

The museum's Second Hall used the exhibition of lifeless fauna (*dō-
butsurui*) to underline the diversity of the animal world and to demonstrate the efficacy of the new nomenclature. In a profusion of objects
reminiscent of European cabinets of curiosity or popular Tokugawa-era
exhibitions, the hall included dozens of taxidermy specimens ranging
from peacocks to porcupines, skeletons and skulls, jars of preserved marine life, the skin of a tiger, an assortment of tusks and teeth, and a collection of butterflies and insects assembled by Tanaka. Each of Tanaka's
specimens were pinned in series under glass next to a label that included
the appropriate Latin binomial, common name, and a note on distribution. It was, in the estimation of the historian Ueno Masuzō, Japan's first
"truly modern" natural-history exhibit. The butterflies were eventually
sent on to Vienna, where they garnered considerable attention.[25]

Fauna was followed by flora (*shokubutsurui*). The visitor path took
patrons through the exhibit on animal species and on to two buildings
dedicated to Plantae. The first was full of medicinal and ornamental
specimens, many of them new imports brought to the country in the
course of expanded foreign trade. Botany texts were displayed along
with selections from the country's rich tradition of natural-historical
prints. The next hall was dedicated to agriculture and forestry. Here

was botany of a different sort, a representational world that drew on Tokugawa-era survey practices—notably those used by Tanaka's teacher, Itō Keisuke, who sought to apply *honzōgaku* in struggling domainal economies during the late-Tokugawa era—that presaged the modern discourse of "natural resources."[26] Exhibits on rice cultivation, silviculture, and foreign farming methods were arrayed alongside notations on fertilizers and seed stock. This focus on material wealth and the place of natural products in industrial development carried over into the last of the halls located in the front half of the grounds, the Hall of Minerals, where copper, gold, coal, and silver were arranged behind glass along with descriptions of their various qualities and uses. Though records from these displays are fragmentary, it bears mention that the dominant theme in the Hall of Agriculture and Forestry and the Hall of Minerals was one of plentitude and promise. The specter of resource scarcity that troubled twentieth-century Japan seems to have found little purchase in Yamashita's prolific universe.

Living nature was walled off from the formal front gardens by a barrier that bisected the museum grounds. When patrons exited the Hall of Minerals and walked into the rear gardens, they stepped into a world that must have looked—and smelled—quite different. The Animal Hall dominated the back portion of the museum. Rather than taking them directly to the menagerie, however, the visitor path first directed patrons through a series of three narrow halls dedicated to domestic and foreign technology. These exhibits were a logical extension of the displays on iron, copper, and coal in the Hall of Minerals, of course, but they also highlight important connections between animal husbandry and the nineteenth-century political economy. Animals were living machines in Japan's early-modern and early-industrial economies, technologies for the conversion of the solar calories stored in plants into labor or food calories useful to humans. Tanaka clarified this connection in a series of influential works on "useful animals" (*yūyō dōbutsu*) published in the 1870s and 1880s. The logic of those essays was reflected in the gardens themselves. The very back of the grounds was given over to breeding pens used for experiments with acclimatization inspired by Tanaka's 1867 visit to the Jardin des Plantes in Paris.

The precise contents of the menagerie at Yamashita are hazy and they changed over time, but the historian Sasaki Toshio estimates that by 1875 as many as thirty-three different species of live animals were on display in different parts of the gardens. These ranged from a small herd of water buffalo imported from China to a lively five-foot-long

Japanese giant salamander (*ōsanshōuo*). Highly sought after by European collectors at the time, the salamander shared space in the hall with a rabbit imported from France by Sano Tsunetami (1823–1902). Sano was a close colleague of the revolutionary leader Ōkubo Toshimichi (1830–1878) and a leading voice in early exhibitionary policy. Trained in Dutch Studies by Ogata Kōan (1810–1863), Sano began to advocate for the creation of a national zoological garden, botanical garden, and museum following his visit to the Paris Exposition Universelle in 1867. Much like Tanaka and Machida, who also visited the expo, Sano returned home convinced that proper exhibitionary representation could distract Western imperial attention and ease domestic unification. The rabbit that he donated (part of an odd early-Meiji craze for pet rabbits) was displayed alongside a crate full of dormice, a friendly Newfoundland dog, and Japan's first live imperial trophy: a small leopard cat (*Prionailurus bengalensis*) acquired by the Imperial Army during the 1874 Taiwan Expedition.[27]

Even in the midst of such exhibitionary wonders, the Ainu and the bear stood out. Playful and overweight, the bear "danced" for treats. The Ainu appear to have been the subject of considerable attention as well. Located next to a small pond that may have held a performing seal—also collected in Hokkaido—the Bear House was a special favorite of visiting children. It was less appealing to Machida and his subordinates in the cultural affairs section of the Exhibition Bureau, however. Tasked with the creation of a national artistic tradition, Machida's team denigrated such performances as "mere *misemono*," sideshows evocative of the outdated Tokugawa past. Class and aesthetics swirled together in such judgments, offered for the most part by former samurai whose identity was built through distinction from urban commoners, rural peasants, and especially "outcastes" (*eta*), who suffered discrimination based, in part, on their work with dead animals (seen as sources of pollution) as butchers and tanners. Aimed at the plebian crowd and evocative of the Western circuses that started to tour Japan at midcentury, live animal displays became the antithesis of "civilization" in the eyes of Machida and his staff. This bias—drawn in class colors along the border between the human and the animal, civilization and savagery—informed the design of the institutions that followed Yamashita, institutions that one can still visit in Ueno today. Indeed, the Yamashita Museum was always seen as a step in the direction of more permanent and imposing structures.

ANIMALS IN THE EXHIBITIONARY COMPLEX

Animals and art were definitively separated when the National Museum complex opened in Ueno Park on March 20, 1882. The zoo—formally the museum's Second Exhibition Hall—occupied a wooded valley at the edge of the park overlooking Shinobazu Pond, chosen for its easy access to fresh water. The museum, in contrast, presided over the grounds. It occupied the terminus of the longest sightlines available within the park. The construction itself was a political event; the Meiji regime appropriated a precinct sacred to the Tokugawa house for its new exhibitionary complex. One of the Shogunate's three funerary temples, Kan'eiji, was located on Ueno Hill together with the graves of six of the fifteen Tokugawa Shoguns and a shrine, Tōshōgu, dedicated to Tokugawa Ieyasu, the founder of the dynasty. Ueno Hill was also the site of a bloody revolutionary battle between Tokugawa loyalists (the storied Shōgitai) and imperial insurgents in 1868. Imperial enlightenment—in the form of a museum and the new "zoological garden"—was mapped over the top of a landscape of early-modern religiosity and feudal fealty when this politically charged acreage was opened to the public as a "park" (kōen, or "public garden," another neologism) five years after the battle.[28]

Ueno Park—as a new kind of space designed to call forth a national public in the service of the state—was a stage for the enactment of a new relationship between the people and the government, Japan and the world. As Thomas R.H. Havens has shown, Ueno Park became one of the premier sites for spectacles celebrating the Meiji regime after its opening in 1873. As crowds filled the park's central promenade, strolled through its temples, and enjoyed its cultural institutions they were encouraged to associate the pleasures of *flanerie* and the satisfaction of curiosity with the largess of the new government. State-sanctioned parades and official events filled the area's formal schedule, and a police station was added in an effort to ensure proper behavior. Officials urged people to visit the area not only to witness the fruits of state-sponsored "civilization," but also to take in the spectacle of the crowd itself, orderly multitudes drawn from the capital's various classes engaged in government-approved activities in an area once claimed as sacrosanct by the old regime. It was in part through the awareness of such shared experiences that urban crowds were slowly converted into a self-conscious national "public."[29]

Both the zoo and the museum were built with an eye to shaping the minds and behavior of the populace. The two institutions differed in some key ways, however. The museum, like the Yamashita Hall of Antiquities that preceded it, sought to secure the nation's cultural provenance by rendering the diversity of the archipelago's human past into a national narrative. The zoological garden, by contrast, drafted animals and nature into the service of the Japanese nation-state and its claims to civilization. In performing these functions, both institutions addressed domestic and international audiences. Internally, they worked as didactic spectacles, communicating information and speaking to the redistribution of social and cultural power as the country's fractured political landscape was knit into a single nation-state. Externally, they served as venues for the exhibition of Japanese claims to cultural parity with the West.[30]

The Ueno Park complex was planned as part of Japan's answer to Western institutional modernity. When Sano, Tanaka, and other travelers such as the prominent enlightenment advocate Fukuzawa Yukichi visited Europe and North America in the 1860s and 1870s, they were taken on tours of the zoos, museums, botanical gardens, and expositions that proliferated in nineteenth-century Western capitals. It quickly became evident to Japanese observers that the European culture of didactic spectacle might be one of the keys to Western commercial productivity and national strength. These institutions—the core of what Tony Bennett has called the modern "exhibitionary complex"—were perceived as a set from the start. Fukuzawa, for example, placed the museum, the zoological garden, and the botanical garden alongside such related institutions as the exposition, the zoological museum, and the medical museum in his widely read series of books, *Conditions in the West (Seiyō jijō)*.[31]

Fukuzawa coined the term *dōbutsuen*, or "zoological garden," in *Seiyō jijō*. He introduced it as follows:

> There are places called zoological gardens (*dōbutsuen*) [in the West]. Live animals, fish, and insects are kept in zoological gardens. Lions, rhinoceroses, elephants, tigers, leopards, black bears, brown bears, foxes, badgers, monkeys, rabbits, ostriches, eagles, hawks, cranes, geese, swallows, sparrows, snakes, toads, all of the world's rare and wonderful creatures are kept there. Food is given to them according to their character (*sei*) and temperature is adjusted to keep them alive. Fish are kept behind glass and fresh water is provided as needed.[32]

Fukuzawa was one of the first Japanese to travel abroad at midcentury. *Conditions in the West* was based on his travels to the United States in

Western
/ modernity desire

1860 and Europe in 1862 as part of the first Tokugawa diplomatic missions after Perry. The ten-volume series became a best seller when it entered publication in the late 1860s. The books—perhaps best described as travelogues-cum-encyclopedias—offered a compendium of things Western and "civilized." From hospitals to poor houses, schools to mental asylums, Fukuzawa defined many of the key institutions of Western modernity, and the terms he coined for those institutions often held. In the case of the zoo, rather than following other early travelers in selecting more familiar terms for animals such as *kinjū*, which we might translate as "creatures" or "beasts" today, Fukuzawa chose to set the institution off through the use of Udagawa's exotic "dōbutsu." The term was *honzōgaku* jargon before the publication of *Seiyō jijō*. It was known to specialists such as Fukuzawa, who trained in Dutch Studies before leaving for the United States, but unfamiliar to the broader reading public. Like the institution that it named, then, the term "dōbutsuen" communicated a sense of novelty and specialized knowledge.[33]

As Fukuzawa noted, the idea of putting unusual animals or objects on display was hardly new to nineteenth-century Japanese, but Japanese travelers quickly realized that the exhibitionary complex differed from the sorts of visual practices that were familiar at home. For one thing, Europe's governments and upper classes poured capital into public institutions dedicated to focusing the wandering eyes of their subjects. The scale and detail of those exhibits outpaced anything that one could have encountered in Edo or Kyoto. The period saw the transfer of tremendous quantities of cultural and scientific property from the realm of private ownership—typified by cabinets of curiosities but inclusive of sideshows and the like—into public institutions administered by the state on behalf of the extended general public. There, they were subjected to new techniques of organization and display meant to convey, not a complete microcosm, but the sense of a greater reality beyond the exhibition. They became, in the eyes of Fukuzawa and other Japanese visitors, indexes of an abstract and universal "civilization." The Ueno Park complex was built in an attempt to appropriate that civilization.[34]

The zoological garden occupied a strange place in the exhibitionary complex. As Bennett notes, the institutions involved were generally characterized by the movement of bodies and objects into progressively more public arenas where, through the representations to which they were subjected, they formed vehicles for broadcasting messages of power throughout society. The special dynamics of the zoo inverted this: it imprisoned in the act of exhibition, and this aligned it with yet

prison-like

another modern institution: the penitentiary. In Japan and the West, the zoo and the penitentiary developed at much the same time, with similar controls on display. Rather than shifting objects into public view, these institutions—the one like the other—enclosed them. As Michel Foucault famously noted, the disciplinary gaze at work inside Jeremy Bentham's (1748–1832) Panopticon was increasingly hidden, concealing discipline behind the solid walls of the penitentiary. Inside its gates, inmates were subject to constant scrutiny; like zoo animals, they were always available for observation.[35]

Like all modern zoological gardens, the Ueno Zoo shares elements of both the exhibitionary complex and the carceral archipelago. It sits uneasily between the two, a circumstance that may help to explain the peculiar feelings of sadness that frequently accompany visits to the zoo. The nineteenth-century zoological garden was a theater of disciplinary techniques—built around the simple distinction between people and animals—in which discipline was often represented as play or pedagogy. As Watanabe Morio points out, modern penitentiaries and zoos owe a debt to the technologies developed in the menageries of Europe's royal houses.[36] In these gardens, typified by Schoenbrunn and Versailles, the seat of the sovereign was located at the hub of a representation of the natural world, encircled by animal enclosures that appeared to radiate outward from the royal center. In theory, at least, the captive animals held in the enclosures were to be visible to the sovereign at all times. While royalty dined or entertained, their centrality to the natural order was symbolically confirmed by the landscape in which they took their leisure. Foucault notes the same dynamic: "The Panopticon is a royal menagerie; the animal is replaced by man, individual distribution by specific grouping, and the king by the machinery of a furtive power."[37]

The zoological garden, one can argue, is a penitentiary in which the inmate is replaced by the animal. Criminal classifications become biological nomenclature. And the furtive power of the disciplinary gaze becomes that of the eager eyes of spectators. The zoo is a modern menagerie in which the gaze of the spectator mimics the gaze of the sovereign, and these masquerading monarchs or child emperors can be every bit as demanding as the absolutist rulers they impersonate. Zoo administrators in Japan and around the world are accustomed to complaints that certain animals—perhaps instinctually given to remaining concealed—are not fully visible at all times. The cost of admission, many zoogoers assume, buys one the right to see each animal at one's own leisure.

Two very different kinds of power were exercised along the axis defined by animals and civilization within the nineteenth-century zoo. On one side of the bars the institution exemplified the premodern regime of punishment in which the king (or Shogun or feudal lord) exercised power negatively, through the right to kill—or, as Takashi Fujitani puts it, by allowing subjects to live. Foucault called this "sovereign power." In the zoological garden, however, it was animals, rather than human subjects, who were laid bare to sovereign power, and that power was exercised only rarely. As with human subjects under absolutism, the public application of lethal force marked exceptional circumstances in zoos in Japan and in the West. Euthanizing surplus animals behind the scenes is a regular part of animal husbandry, but in the decades before the Second World War killing became public only in emergencies such as escapes or attacks on keepers. Zoological gardens have always been associated with the protection of life, and care itself is an elaborate performance at most zoos (public feedings and so on), but it is implicit that such care comes as a gift or an obligation, both of which can be revoked *in extremis*.[38] The institution was (and still is) an object lesson in power.

Life was even more carefully nurtured on the "civilized" side of the bars. When nineteenth-century zoos laid the animal world at the feet of their patrons, they exercised a different form of power. The institution afforded visitors an opportunity to play, at least temporarily, at dominion. There, in the act of play, the double movement of Udagawa's *dōbutsu*—at once external and internal to the human—took on a new political significance. Through the exhibition of animals the zoo became a mechanism for the expression of what Foucault has called "biopower," a form of positive discipline rather than negative punishment. Power in biopolitical regimes is first and foremost *productive*—of behavior, of discipline, and in the case of the zoo, of mindset. It turned power into something internal to (and definitive of) the human subject. To Foucault's way of thinking, this form of politics—born in the eighteenth and nineteenth centuries—marked the "threshold of modernity" for any given society, but it is important to note (as the zoo makes clear) that sovereign power and biopower coexist and overlap in modern societies.[39]

The zoo asked patrons to look across the threshold of animality without crossing it. In the process of looking at animals, spectators were encouraged to internalize the attitude that was generated within the exhibitionary complex, in effect becoming self-knowing and self-regulating.

Much as with the museum, the institution asked them to identify with power, to see it as theirs, as a force regulated and channeled by the government and elites for the benefit of all. This is the counterintuitive work of the zoological garden: it is not just the animals that are subjected to discipline within the exhibition. We monitor ourselves and others as we pass through the spaces of the zoo, and we are asked to see the worldview on display as an expression of nature, not as an effort to order society and shape our consciousness.[40] This is what Koga Tadamichi, the director of the gardens from 1933 to 1962, meant when he called the gardens a "a mechanism for the manufacture of civilized people and animals."[41]

Nineteenth-century Japanese were hardly immune to the empowering thrill that accompanied encounters with caged beasts. Members of the elite government-sponsored Iwakura mission, who visited Western Europe and the United States from 1871 to 1873, were themselves intrigued by the elaborate animal spectacles of modern European zoos, and they apparently delighted in the feelings induced by the vision of exotic animals held captive for their viewing pleasure. The official account of the mission's travels, written by Kume Kunitake (1839–1931), who was special assistant to Iwakura Tomomi (1825–1883), the head of the mission, describes numerous visits to zoological gardens and other components of the exhibitionary complex.[42] The company's visit to London's Regent's Park Zoo, opened to the public in 1847 and destined to become one of the models for Ueno Zoo, is particularly telling:

> In the gardens, paths meandered among hills and woods and lakes. The greenness of the trees and shrubs was offset by the brightness of the gravel paths. The wooded hills were charming in appearance. At every step one paused; at every turn one raised one's head. There was not enough time to gaze at everything. In the midst of this landscape, enclosures had been created with various different structures, and in them were kept birds and animals which had been sought and trapped all over the world. There were placid beasts such as the elephant and the camel, and ferocious creatures such as bears, wolves, and jackals. The woods quaked at the roaring of the lions, tigers, and leopards; the air shivered at the screeching of eagles, hawks, and falcons.[43]

Kume's paean to the zoo continues with a lengthy listing of the exotic animals that the group encountered. The text reveals his excitement and his desire to provide a comprehensive inventory of the creatures observed during the visit, perhaps inspired by the claims to encyclopedic representation made by the zoo itself. In a pitch-perfect evocation of one of the slogans of the modern tourist industry, Kume gushed, "There were so many things to see that we were oblivious to the fact that night was falling."[44] They were captivated by spectacle.

The vision of Regent's Park conveyed in Kume's account is edenic. After describing bounding kangaroos and frolicking peacocks at peace in their enclosures, Kume notes: "Inside the tropical house, where the humidity of spring was maintained by steam heat, parrots squawked and monkeys played. The air was fragrant with the scent of flowers. Small, brightly colored birds twittered as they flitted about their cages." Kume's zoo is a place where humans express technical command over the entirety of nature, even over the seasons. When Kume recounts the vast numbers of tropical birds stored in the garden, he is struck not only by the beauty of the specimens but by the marvel of the technologies devoted to keeping them. "If they are not kept in conditions appropriate to their natures, then even if they do not die they will waste away and will not be worth seeing. By that alone can be seen the degree to which the care of animals has progressed as a science in this country."[45]

Clearly, the experience was more than one of simple innocent wonder—although wonder is certainly a crucial aspect of the subjectivity that the zoo seeks to elicit. Kume tied the pleasures of the zoo to concrete concerns. In the nineteenth century, zoological gardens were a recognized gauge of national strength. Zoos could express a nation's technological progress, its control over natural resources, and its ability to shape populations into productive, self-supporting citizens. They were measures of progress and prestige. Kume, like his Western counterparts, seems to see this relationship as self-evident. He heaps praise on Regent's Park and England—"We saw nothing in Europe to compare with the richness of this zoo,"—and he ranks Holland a close second. In the end, however, the Dutch zoo was judged to be slightly "inferior" because its landscape was lacking and the number of species represented did not match London's broad collection. The index of nature provided by the Dutch zoo was less authoritative. Less impressive zoos reflected poorly on the nations that house them, and Kume repeatedly passed judgment on a country's ability to manage its natural resources based on the state of its zoological gardens.[46]

That these modern gardens shared something with Japan's sideshows and natural-history exhibitions was evident to Kume and his companions. Nevertheless, the zoological gardens surpassed Japan's existing animal displays in terms of both scale and efficacy. One of the first discussions of a zoological garden, written about the mission's arrival in San Francisco, their first stop, highlights the novel function of zoos' didactic displays, as well as the perceived benefits that accrued to the nation through such focused visual encounters:

> In the West there are botanical gardens and zoological gardens in every city. In Japan, too, there are gardens and parks where people can look at animals and birds, but the scale is not the same. These gardens may look somewhat similar to those in the West, but the original aim in setting them up is very different. In the West, they are intended to attract people's eyes and ears so they can actually see things for themselves and discriminate, in order to promote industry and to promulgate knowledge and learning. Such projects are expensive, but the cost is not a worry because eventually there is a great profit.[47]

Zoos, it was recognized, productively focused the gaze of their spectators, sharpening their powers of perception and thus their ability as workers. Botanical and zoological gardens "promote the material sciences and encourage the discovery of advances in agriculture, industry, and commerce" and "serve, therefore, as a means to promote national wealth."[48] The pursuit of productivity was not decadent or luxurious, as certain moralists might have seen it during the Tokugawa era; it was the motor of national growth and the guarantor of national independence in an imperial age.

Kume and other officials saw exhibition as a tool of governance. Museums and expos, he argued, had led to the "utter transformation" of Europe over a relatively short period of time, an interpretation that boded well for their use in Japan. "It is since 1800 that Europe has attained its present wealth," he wrote, "and it is only in the last forty years that it has achieved the truly remarkable level of prosperity that we now see." British industry had developed especially rapidly, Kume argued, and much of that was thanks to the "efforts of the queen's consort, Prince Albert," who sponsored the "Great Exhibition held in Hyde Park in 1851." To Kume's eye, the outcome of the Hyde Park exhibition was nothing less than a revolution in British manufacturing: "The British became aware for the first time of the reason for the poor design of their products. After much reflection, they put behind them the undesirable practice of copying the French and began to seek out instead their own country's individual style. The view taken of British goods at the next international exhibition, held in France in 1855, was very different, and from then on the number of industrial products imported from France began to decline. The change was due entirely to the effects of

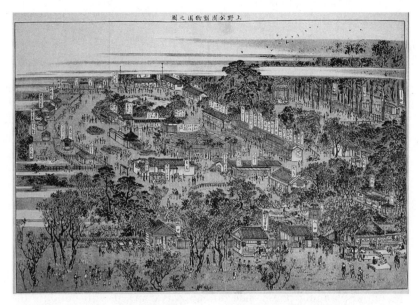

FIGURE 1. Map of zoological garden in Ueno Park, c. 1896. Space is flattened in this illustration from a special number of the journal *Fūzoku gahō* (Customs Illustrated) on Ueno Park. The Elephant House greets visitors soon after entry; a large circular flying cage dominates the central gardens; and cages for leopards, tigers, camels, monkeys, bears, and pigs can be seen in the notataions above each cage or enclosure. "Shinsen Tōkyō meisho zue, Ueno Kōen no bu," in *Fūzoku gahō*, no 131 (Tokyo: Tōyōdo, 1896). Image courtesy of Tokyo Zoological Park Society.

the exhibition."[49] The Great Exhibition's success, he continued, led to the construction of public museums and related institutions throughout Europe, and international competition via exhibitions fostered an industrial revolution. "It was thus a mere dozen years or so ago that the industrial arts attained the heights of beauty throughout Europe." It was as if exhibition—simply by focusing public attention in the service of the state—could condense time, speeding a nation along the rails of progress.[50]

THE UENO ZOO

The Ueno Zoo came into being as part of the Meiji state's efforts to institutionalize the new ways of seeing encountered in Europe. In the words of Sano Tsunetami, the first person to use the word *dōbutsuen* in Meiji government documents (in a policy paper written in 1875), the purpose of Japan's exhibitionary complex was to "develop people's knowledge and technical skill through the education of the eye" (gan-moku no oshie ni yorite hito no chikō gigei o kaishin seshimeru). For Sano and most other officials, the museum, not the exhibition or the zoo-logical garden, was the ideal medium for these efforts to increase produc-tivity (shokusan kōgyō) via what he called the "power of the gaze" (ganshi no chikara). The zoo was not far away, but it played a support-ing role. Sano envisaged a "grand, pristine, beautiful park surrounding the museum" that would contain botanical and zoological gardens. This imagined concentration of institutions influenced the form of the future Ueno Park complex. In his requests for funding, Sano argued that these institutions would not only provide healthy distraction for urban resi-dents but would also focus the eyes of patrons, helping them to see for-ward into new realms of learning and knowledge by fostering their "powers of discrimination."[51]

Construction of the zoological gardens was placed under the control of the Home Ministry's Exhibition Bureau (Hakubutsukyoku) during the initial planning phase. The bureau was charged with building the Ueno complex in addition to managing the Yamashita Museum. In 1881, the year before the museum complex in Ueno opened, adminis-tration was unexpectedly moved to the newly created Ministry of Agri-culture and Commerce, a decision that reflected a belief that exhibition-ary practices influenced the nation's commercial prowess and its ability to manage natural resources. Management of the zoo was assigned to the bureau's Natural History Section. This arrangement continued until 1886, when administration of the entire museum complex was trans-ferred to the Imperial Household Ministry as a bulwark against the com-ing uncertainty of constitutional government at the urging to Iwakura Tomomi.

When the National Museum and zoological gardens opened in 1882, the Meiji Emperor, Mutsuhito (1852–1912), became their first official patron. His debut there would not be the last appearance of an emperor on the grand stages provided by these civic institutions. The general public may have temporarily assumed the sovereign gaze on their visits to the zoo, but they were urged to believe that this play was at the plea-sure of the emperor. The royal relationship with the zoo was cinched in 1889, when the Ueno Zoo was formally renamed the Ueno Imperial Zoological Garden, the same year that the constitution authorizing the new national legislature was promulgated. The complex remained under direct imperial control until 1924, when the zoological gardens were transferred, together with Ueno Park itself, to the Parks Section of the

Tokyo municipal government. The move was said to be in celebration of the wedding of the crown prince, the future Shōwa Emperor, Hirohito (1901–1989).[52]

Finances at the zoo were a complicated affair, and records from the early years are scattered, but it is clear that the institution developed into the museum's cash cow. Animals and art may have been separated on the exhibitionary side, but the zoological garden remained under the museum administration, and animals pulled in thousands more paying visitors than did history and art. Sideshows and other private entertainments were subjected to scrutiny and control under the image-conscious Meiji regime, which prohibited certain kinds of animal shows (along with public nudity and other crimes of comportment) in its first misdemeanor code, the Ishiki kaii jōrei, enacted in 1876. The zoo may have benefitted from these changes. In any case, it is hardly surprising, given the popularity of early-modern sideshows, that the gardens drew crowds. Tickets were usually sold separately for the museum and the zoo. The cost of zoo entry was set at one *sen* (Tuesday through Saturday) and two *sen* (on Sundays) in 1882. The museum was considerably more expensive, costing three *sen* on weekdays, two *sen* on Saturdays, and five *sen* on Sundays. These institutions show us how the workweek discipline of the new solar calendar—defined, in part, through separate "leisure time"—was expressed in everyday terms.[53]

The gap between the two tickets closed slightly as managers responded to two realities. First, contrary to the fears of some officials, poorer patrons were generally not disorderly during their trips to the museum. Their behavior, it could be said, was by-and-large appropriate to the context. They acted as if they were at the nation's premier museum, not at a sideshow or circus. Second, visitors were willing to pay as much to see exotic animals as they were to view the nation's historic treasures. By 1902, twenty years after the zoo first opened, the cost of entry was four *sen* for the zoological garden and five *sen* for the museum. From an early date children paid less than adults, school groups began paying reduced admission rates in 1887, and soldiers began receiving free entry in 1905 in recognition of their service in the Russo-Japanese War.[54] Such policies seem only natural in most modern societies (certainly Japan), but they are best read as they were intended, as subtle forms of social engineering.

Gate receipts were seen as crucial to the financial stability of the museum. Administered by the conservative Imperial Household Ministry, the museum exploited the zoo's popularity while keeping capital reinvestment to a minimum. This relative lack of commitment to the zoological garden and its failure to support natural-history exhibitions in general fueled efforts in the late 1880s to sever the zoo's connection with the museum by transferring the Natural History Section to the Ministry of Education. These proposals were quashed in 1889 by Kuki Ryūichi (1852–1931) soon after he became director-general of the museum. Kuki's institutional priorities were clear. "Much of the museum's revenue comes from the zoological garden. Annual income from all components of the museum . . . stands at approximately 7,600 yen, and the zoological garden accounts for more than 4,000 of that, providing over half of the museum's revenues. The zoo is a tremendous help to our finances."[55] If the zoo was to be moved, Kuki argued, it could seriously injure the museum and, in turn, weaken a set of institutions organized under the Imperial Household Ministry. The zoo stayed where it was.

The zoo drew more paying visitors than the museum from the beginning. In the first year alone the disparity topped thirty thousand people, the museum attracting 174,444 patrons and the zoo bringing in 205,504. The gap doubled in the following year: 123,672 for the museum and 184,992 for the zoo. By 1885 the number had nearly doubled again, with the zoo boasting over one hundred thousand more spectators than its more staid sister institution (92,471 versus 195,587). In 1888 attendance broke 350,000, fueled by the display of the zoo's first elephants. Ten years later, spurred on by the zoo's new role as the display case for "live-animal war trophies" (see chapter 2) garnered during the Sino-Japanese War of 1894–1895, which included mules, large cats, horses, dogs, and camels, attendance approached one million for the first time. It was a mark that was finally topped in 1907 with the arrival of two giraffes. The pair—named Fanji and Grey—were the first of their species to be exhibited in a Japanese zoo. Lines of visitors pushed out of the gardens and into the park in the weeks and months after their arrival.[56]

As attendance surged, so did official recognition that the zoological gardens might be a useful social tool, a means of communicating with—and bringing order to—urban crowds such as those that had rioted against the government in Hibiya Park only a year or so earlier. As Andrew Gordon has argued, the Hibiya crowds were not there for leftist revolution. They were there to protest the terms of the Portsmouth Treaty that brought the Russo-Japanese War to a close. After years of individual sacrifice on behalf of the national war effort, Japan became the first non-Western country to defeat one of the European "great powers." Crowds took to the streets—in a lot adjacent to the old Yamashita Museum—not to protest the government's assertions of military superiority in Asia, but to urge greater foreign acknowledgement of Japanese power and governmental recognition of popular national sacrifice. The zoo's role as a showcase for trophies thus became especially appealing to officials.[57]

ISHIKAWA CHIYOMATSU AND THE EVOLUTION OF EXHIBITION

The politics of ecological modernity came together in a potent new configuration in the work of the man who brought Fanji and Gray to the zoo, Ishikawa Chiyomatsu (1861–1935). Ishikawa was the director of the Natural History Section at the National Museum from 1900 until 1907, when he resigned in the scandal following the untimely deaths of the two African ruminants—they were poisoned by fumes from a poorly ventilated heating system in the new Giraffe House. The most prominent scientist to follow Tanaka Yoshio into museum administration and the last zoo director trained in the protocols of *honzōgaku*, Ishikawa was an internationally recognized evolutionary biologist with a teaching position at Tokyo Imperial University by the time he left the Ueno Zoo. It was Ishikawa, more than any other person, who drafted the animals of the zoological garden into nineteenth-century debates over human social evolution, amplifying the logic of Udagawa's *Botany Sutra* into a program of social reform and popular mobilization aimed at children and adults alike. He worked at the zoo on and off for seventeen years before his resignation.

Ishikawa was a classic popular scientist who split his time between laboratory science, the zoological garden, and a wide array of popular books and articles, especially those aimed at children and teenagers. Born into a family of Shogunal retainers in Edo in 1861, he began his advanced studies at Kaisei Gakkō, the predecessor to Tokyo University, where his tutors included Katō Hiroyuki (1836–1916), the founding dean of the university faculties of law, science, and literature and a future interlocutor in the debates over social evolution. Ishikawa, who had always liked animals, focused on English and *honzōgaku* while at the Gakkō. Having fled Edo during the civil war, he returned to the city, now called Tokyo, to study at the new university (founded in 1877) with the American zoologists Edward S. Morse (1838–1925) and Charles O. Whitman (1842–1910). He also worked with Mitsukuri Kakichi (1858–1909), Tokyo University's first Japanese professor of zoology, and Itō Keisuke, Tanaka Yoshio's mentor who became a professor of botany and director of the university's Koishikawa Botanical Gardens.[58]

Ishikawa's training was not limited to Japan. He was a student of the influential evolutionary biologist August Weismann (1834–1914) from 1885 until 1889. When Weismann's precocious student (by all accounts one of the professor's favorites) matriculated in Freiburg, he was already a recognized scholar in Japan. In 1883 Ishikawa, who grew up thumbing through his father's copies of *honzōgaku* classics, published the first introduction to natural selection written in Japanese. Based on Morse's 1877 lectures at the university, *Dōbutsu shinkaron*, or *Animal Evolution*, was a watershed in the history of science in Japan. It is a small book of only nine chapters, and it skims over the major topics in the field, but as Ishikawa later argued, it shifted the course of scientific inquiry in Japan, amplifying the ideas behind Udagawa's decades-old *Sutra* and consolidating Itō's contributions into the prehistory of the new fields of "biology" (*seibutsugaku*) and "science" (*kagaku*).[59]

Until quite recently, historians of science have tended to treat the emergence of modern biology in Japan as a revolution, something akin to Thomas Kuhn's notion of a "paradigm shift," a transformation between two incommensurable systems, but the continuities within ecological modernity do not bear this out. When read closely—from Udagawa to Itō to Tanaka to Ishikawa, for example—it becomes clear that ecological modernity, while fraught and at times hotly contested, emerged through a series of adaptations and translations. Writing more than a half-century apart, scholars such as Ishikawa and Udagawa *framed* their ideas as revolutionary, but those framings themselves are best understood as part of a broader effort to secure professional distinction, to underline the separation between amateur and expert, and to set "civilization" and modern science apart from the past, much as Tanaka and Ishikawa sought to set people apart from animals within the exhibitionary complex. Such acts of professional folklore—echoed by historians—were convincing. By the time Ishikawa's students published his collected works in 1935, biologists turned to *Dōbutsu shinkaron* or Ishikawa's influential 1891 follow up, *Shinka shinron* (*New Thesis of Evolution*, revised in 1897), as foundational texts rather than delving into the suddenly arcane library of *honzōgaku*.[60]

Presented by Morse, who worked under Louis Agassiz at Harvard before moving to Japan, and shaped by Ishikawa (it is clear that this is not a direct translation, at times the voice is clearly Ishikawa's), *Dōbutsu shinkaron* offers a snapshot in the globalization of evolutionary theory. It shows how the basic ideas of modern biology arrived in Japan and took on immediate political importance. Morse spoke broadly in the lectures, sermonizing on topics ranging from the development of dog breeds to the relationship between class and order in nomenclature, but what emerges most forcefully from *Animal Evolution* is not a new understanding of animals per se but a new sense of humanity's place in the world. It was an ominous vision, and Morse (at least as translated by Ishikawa) had a knack for the dramatic. Delivered to several hundred students and faculty on October 6, 1877, the first lecture, Morse later recalled, was met with "nervous applause." It ended with a grim crescendo:

> If I were to lock tight the doors of this lecture hall, in just a few days the list of the dead would include those in the audience with weak bodies. Those of you in good health would probably die in a week or maybe two or three. Now, if the world were closed off in the same manner as the hall, the weak animals would be killed and the strong would remain because they would be able to eat when there was not enough food [for all]. If this situation were to continue over a number of years with people and animals eating each other, the people of the future would be entirely different from the people of the present. A powerful and terrible kind of human (*osorubeki jinrui*) would be born.[61]

Morse's lectures argued for a connection between the mechanics of natural selection and ceaseless human competition for resources that would, in turn, lead to ceaseless change in human nature. "All things change," he noted at the end of the second lecture. "To think that humans alone are somehow unchanging is untenable." Morse continued, taking aim at the Christian missionaries in the audience: "Humans are said to be the lords of creation. But they really just occupy the highest position on the ladder." Man, the author concluded, is "nothing more than an animal that can read books and reason."[62] In an echo of Udagawa's *Sutra*, reason—the bedrock of civilization—had become the sine qua non of biological humanity. And civilized humanity, as nothing more than "animals that can reason," was always under threat of degeneration into biological animality. This degeneration could even occur in relative terms: one nation or race could stagnate while others continued to progress.

Government and society were not overlooked in *Animal Evolution*; they were desirable "traits" selected through competition. Taking a Spencerian turn on Darwin's arguments in the *Descent of Man* (translated into Japanese in 1881), Morse moved from the study of the individual to societies in general. Here, too, conflict was the driving force. "Groups [*shuzoku*] with traits useful in war tend to survive," the author confirmed.

Examples of such traits, he argued, included shared religion or government. Technology also played a role. "It is obvious that groups capable of creating metal weapons will defeat those fighting with bows and arrows. Thus when different races (*jinshu*) met in battle in ancient times, the advanced race survived and the less advanced was destroyed. This is natural selection." War was a motor of natural selection at the level of race, and for Morse it continued to perform this function in his own day, notably among the "savage races" (*yaban jinshu*) of central Africa and the Pacific Islands. These "previously isolated" groups were being exposed to outside competition for the first time, and they were suffering in the process of social evolution. Morse was not entirely callous. He saw such encounters as unfortunate, but what is more important—and telling—is that he understood them as natural and inevitable. Social evolution took on the status of natural law in Morse's lectures.[63]

The text was thus a formative entry in the debate over race, science, and public policy—biopolitics—in Japan, and it spoke to Japanese anxieties at a time when biology seemed to predetermine the work of empire. Morse argued in the final lecture: "The primates [*enkō*] living in Africa (the 'gorilla' and the 'chimpanzee') are black and have long skulls, similar to the black people living there. The primates living in Asia ('orangs') are brown or yellow with short skulls like the 'Malay' people. This is enough to show that the African is closer to the 'gorilla' and 'chimpanzee' and the 'Malay' is closer to the 'orang.' "[64] Where does Japan fit in this worldview? Japanese were left out of Morse's zoomorphic speculation, but the American phrenologist Samuel George Morton (1799–1855), whom Morse cites favorably and at length in the previous paragraph, described "Mongolians" (which included the Japanese) thusly in his 1839 *Crania Americana*:

> This great division of the human species is characterized by a sallow or olive colored skin, which appears to be drawn tight over the bones of the face; long black straight hair, and thin beard. The nose is broad, and short; the eyes are small, black, and obliquely placed, and the eyebrows are arched and linear; the lips are turned, the cheekbones broad and flat. . . . In their intellectual character the Mongolians are ingenious, imitative, and highly susceptible of cultivation [i.e., learning]. . . . So versatile are their feelings and actions, that they have been compared to the monkey race, whose attention is perpetually changing from one object to another.[65]

Culture and science swirl together in such statements, blurring distinctions between nature and society even as they claim to speak in the objective language of science.

BIGOT'S JAPAN

The racialized logic of *Animal Evolution* helps to explain the prominence of exhibition in Meiji policy circles. Sano, Tanaka, Machida, and other leaders believed that exhibition could help Japan's lower classes learn to see through the "fog of ignorance" (Kume's words) in which they were enveloped, and that such skills, once instilled, could be carried on to future generations. It was an idea with prestigious science behind it. Morse, in a neurological spin on Lamarck's theory of inheritance of acquired characteristics (1801), suggested that "brains," like muscles, "can be improved through [intellectual] labor," and that such changes could be passed on to future generations.[66] Indeed, Morse argued that it was the development of the brain—as a physical organ—that distinguished civilized peoples from savage ones. The notion that personal development could benefit future generations through the mechanics of natural selection was especially appealing in Meiji Japan. It allowed for greater agency in the evolutionary process (what George Bernard Shaw once described as "creative evolution"), and it opened up the possibility that a nation could, through extraordinary shared effort, effectively accelerate natural selection. If one subscribed to Lamarckism or the ideas of Herbert Spencer (derivative of Lamarck on this point), education and exhibition could help to secure the national or racial future through the mechanism of social evolution.[67]

Sentiments of this sort did not remain confined to the lecture hall. They found their way onto the pages of books and into the hands of consumers. They permeated Meiji literate society outside of the zoo as well as within it. If there is one image that seems to encapsulate the cultural stakes—the feedback between science and popular culture—behind such reasoning for Japan, it is a caricature by the French satirist Georges Bigot (1860–1927). Bigot, who studied under the Orientalist painter Jean-Léon Gérôme at the École des Beaux Arts in Paris, lived in Yokohama between 1883 and 1899, where he published the popular satirical magazine *Toba-e*. The image in question, published in 1888, shows us "Monsiuer et Madame vont dans le Monde": sir and madame preparing to go out for the evening, or perhaps more accurately, "out into society." The pair is caught primping in the mirror as the Japanese characters in the upper-left corner (presumably illegible to most foreign readers) label them as "gauche" or "cheeky" (*namaiki*). The woman, long-faced and wearing a towering feather that makes her seem taller than her male companion, wears a Western-style dress with a voluminous bustle. The

Monsieur et Madame vont dans le Monde.

FIGURE 2. Aping civilization. *Monsieur et Madame vont dans le Monde*, 1888. Georges Bigot (1860–1927). Originally printed in an 1888 edition of *Toba-e*, the French painter and satirist Georges Bigot's Yokohama-based magazine, this image depicts a pair of Japanese dandies from the era of the Rokumeikan, or Deer-Cry Pavillion, a lavish foreign guesthouse and diplomatic club sponsored by the Japanese government. The men and women of the Rokumeikan, who included much of Japan's political elite, were subjected to wicked caricatures by the Japanese and foreign press alike. In this case, Bigot plays on the tensions between civilization and nature in the age of Darwin and Spencer. Image courtesy of Print Collection, Miriam and Ira D. Wallach Division of Art, Prints and Photographs, The New York Public Library, Astor, Lenox and Tilden Foundations.

man appears self-assured as he angles his elbow outward and admires himself, eyebrows raised, perhaps beginning to smile.[68]

The implications of the picture—like those of Morse's lecture—are at once blatant and complex. At first glance the mirror seems to simply reveal the "truth" of the situation. The reflected image erases the trappings of civilization—crosshatching over the umbrella, foreign-cut suit, and corseted dress—to expose the Japanese couple's innate incivility by portraying them as animals.[69] However, when we step back from the initial surprise of the reflected image and return to the couple themselves, another meaning is revealed. There is no bifurcation between savagery and civilization at work within the picture. To paraphrase Morse, man appears as merely an animal who can primp. The lines are intentionally blurred, producing a tension that drives the picture. Bigot's depiction limits the couple's alternatives to either "savagery" or "half-enlightenment" (*hankai*), to use the nomenclature of the time. His readers (Japanese or otherwise) would have understood the assumptions at work behind such depictions, and as Albert Craig has shown, many of Japan's most prominent intellectuals (not least Fukuzawa Yukichi) believed that Japan languished in the dangerous twilight of *hankai*, far from fully realized enlightenment.[70]

That a similar logic structured the satirical picture and the university lecture is obvious. Monsieur, to be certain, is possessed of simian characteristics. The waxed moustaches only emphasize his protruding teeth and maxilla, and his receding frontal bone is reminiscent of the African gorillas referenced by Morse. The species was the subject of a great deal of fascination after its 1847 introduction to Western science by the ironically named American missionary Thomas S. Savage (1804–1880). Recessed frontal bones were read as signs of criminality and a lack of creativity by nineteenth-century phrenologists such as Morton.

One assumes that neither the man nor the woman see the apes reflected in the mirror as we do, and so the joke is on them. They are, quite literally, aping civilization, engaged in the kind of imitation cited by Morton. In the act of copying they undermine their claims to genuine civilization—imagined to reside elsewhere, perhaps with the viewer, perhaps in the idealized West. Bigot's use of the mirror allowed his readers to catch the pair in the act of fooling themselves. That madame and monsieur were "taken in" by the reflection while readers of the magazine were not served not only to underline the difference between the pair's perception of themselves and their true nature; it also underlined the more crucial distinction between Bigot's readers and the ridiculous couple. Only humans, it was widely believed in the nineteenth century, could see through illusion.[71] In the act of looking, the observer was set apart, and this act of separation was, one assumes, premised on the capacity for reason.

The complexity of the caricature only increases the more carefully we look—couldn't it, in a final reading, also be seen as an act of caricatured *resistance* to scientific racism? After all, Bigot's readers, many of them Japanese, stood looking through the illusion of the mirror with the Frenchman, able to read "*namaiki*." Bigot was not a simple bigot. His attitudes toward Japan, like those of many Western residents, were notoriously ambivalent. He briefly married a Japanese woman and was a proud father to their son. He was also friendly with the progressive political theorist Nakae Chōmin (1847–1901) and other intellectuals. The target of his criticism was more often Japanese elites and officials—the "gauche" madams and monsieurs of society—than Japan as a whole. And in fact, contemporaneous Japanese satirical magazines such as the *Marumaru chinbun* used primates to lampoon politicians. As Emiko Ohnuki-Tierney points out, monkeys have been used as a cultural mirror in Japan for centuries. What changed in the Meiji era was the meaning of such satire, not the use of animals as metaphors. What emerged, in the zoo and in broader culture, was a new juxtaposition of animals and civilization in which shared biology—breath, air, and life force—threatened to imprison Japanese in the realm of savagery, subject to the sovereign power of Western imperialism.[72]

CONCLUSION

No single theorist—Darwin, Lamarck, Spencer, or otherwise—dominated social evolutionary theory in Meiji Japan. Meiji-era scientists and intellectuals such as Ishikawa and Katō Hiroyuki were voracious readers in multiple languages. As Morse recalled, they were often reading the same texts at the same time as their colleagues in Boston, London, and Berlin. Students and faculty pored over original and translated works from Ernst Haeckel (whom Ishikawa knew personally), Thomas Huxley, Charles Lyell, Herbert Spencer, Alfred Russel Wallace, and Ishikawa's teacher, Weismann, among others. In a 1902 Maruzen survey of nearly eighty academics and intellectuals, Darwin's *Origin of Species* was ranked as the single most important Western book of the nineteenth century; Goethe's *Faust* was second; Spencer's *System of Synthetic Philosophy* ranked third; Darwin's *Descent of Man* placed tenth.[73]

Morton's stereotypes notwithstanding, these ideas were neither simply mimicked nor quickly set aside. They were debated and, in the case of Ishikawa and other professional biologists such as Oka Asajirō (1868–1944), who also studied with Weismann, tested through physical experiments. Specialization brought professional differentiation. The figure of the veterinarian (*jūi*) was a manufacture of the mid-nineteenth century—the first vets were trained beginning in 1876—as was the biologist. The Tokyo Biology Society, the country's first scientific society, was founded by Morse in 1878. The society quickly became a forum for debates over Lamarckism and Darwinism, as well as Spencer's well-known formulations on the "survival of the fittest." These debates, in turn, were reflected in monographs by Katō, Ishikawa, Oka, and others, and in such venues as the *Journal of Zoology* (Dōbutsugaku zasshi), published from 1888.[74]

Ishikawa, following Weismann, was an ardent Darwinist at a time when many Japanese intellectuals—notably his old friend Katō—preferred the softer selection of Spencer or Lamarck. In his 1891 *Shinka shinron*, Ishikawa took the harder Darwinian line, arguing that selection only happened through the propagation of beneficial *inborn* traits, rather than through the inheritance of acquired characteristics, as followers of Lamarck and Spencer suggested. For social Darwinists such as Ishikawa, evolution was a matter of nothing more or less than life, death, and reproduction within a given population. Everything else, he argued, was hopeful "superstition."[75]

Katō, Ishikawa, and other intellectuals nonetheless converged around the broad implications of evolutionary theory. Ishikawa dedicated *Shinka shinron* to Katō, and his writing on cells—thought to be the smallest unit of life available to human investigation at the time—influenced the elder Katō, who put it to use in his 1912 *Shizen to rinri* (*Nature and Ethics*). For both men, and for many others policymakers, intellectuals, and scientists at the time, the nation-state was the crucial evolutionary unit of the age, not the individual. The challenge in this situation, Ishikawa wrote, was to "open people up" to proper knowledge of evolution, and thus to full recognition of their role in this "natural process." For Ishikawa, the zoo—together with schools and other components of the exhibitionary complex—was an ideal venue for these efforts at evolutionary education.[76]

It was the imperative of mass education that brought Fanji and Grey, the ill-fated giraffes, to Tokyo in the first place. As Ishikawa noted in his primer on *The History of Life* (*Seibutsu no rekishi*), "the most common example of Lamarck's theory is the long neck of the giraffe, which is said to have grown longer and longer in order to reach the leaves of the acacia tree." Despite his fervent advocacy of Darwin's position in academic discourse, however, Ishikawa did not try to draft Fanji and Grey into partisan debates over Lamarckism. He saw them instead as tools of social evolution itself. "Mass education," he wrote at the close of *Seibutsu no rekishi*, "is what will drive our national evolution. The only thing that sets us humans apart from other animals is education." It was a point that was "especially important to Japanese" because they had to accelerate social change if they hoped to stay on pace with the "more advanced" Western powers.

In a biopolitical renovation of Udagawa's *Sutra*, Ishikawa argued that human civilization was a race for survival that would be won or lost through the biological capacity for reason. In the "civilized age," however, the capacity for knowledge had to be manifested across the population of the nation-state rather than simply within the individual.[77] The defining factor was not the mass inculcation of detailed knowledge on the finer points of natural selection, then, but rather the natural assumption of the individual's "proper place" in society. "The population," Ishikawa argued, using the analogy of worker bees and soldier ants to separate specialists, scientists, and intellectuals from the laboring masses, must "realize for themselves" that they were subordinate to natural law and the state. This was where education and exhibition became essential, and where ecological modernity moved from the realm of specialized debate into public policy.[78]

The zoo's exhibits converged with Ishikawa's social Darwinism in an attempt to redefine the nature of civilization for millions of visitors. The original impulse of ecological modernity was intellectual and professional. Udagawa and other *honzōgaku* specialists wished to gain a better understanding of the natural world and to set themselves apart from amateur natural historians in the process. Perry's arrival injected power and geopolitics into that nascent separation. Japan's "opening" to Western culture—a culture defined for many through the work of exhibition—brought a sense of national urgency to the question of the "animal." It amplified debates between intellectually important but politically somewhat marginal figures such as Itō, Machida, Tanaka, and Udagawa into questions of state policy. This amplification, which yielded the institution of the zoological garden, was the crucial tipping point, not the quiet revolution of the *Botany Sutra*. Intellectuals and their manifestos did not transform the country, but they did, as Julia Adeney Thomas has shown, redefine the horizons of possible thought and action as they reworked the idea of "nature." Institution builders like Machida, Sano, and Tanaka and public intellectuals such as Fukuzawa ensured that the idea of *dōbutsu* and the encompassing notion of *shizen* became something more than jargon.

Udagawa's neologism did not remain hidden. The idea was popularized and refined, put to use in children's magazines, school curricula, newspaper articles, and a variety of public enterprises where it joined with material development to transform attitudes toward the natural world. By the time Ishikawa left zoo administration in 1907, it was no longer sideshows, *honzōgaku* manuals, or even the mountains and marshes of the Japanese hinterland that defined "nature" for many urban Japanese, but rather the "civilized" space of the zoo, an institution that had been, only four decades earlier, unnamed and unfamiliar. By the close of the Meiji era in 1912 the "externalization of nature," to use Stefan Tanaka's apt phrase, and the internal alienation demanded by social evolution had become so pervasive that animals and untamed nature were re-imagined as the locus of a lost, more authentic humanity. The exhibitionary culture of the state-run zoo, in turn, used this logic to redefine the geography of ecological modernity, projecting animal figures of wild, untamed nature outward into the nation's growing empire rather than into the Japanese countryside, as agrarian nationalists and others tended to do. As yet unconquered by civilization, the zoo suggested, authentic nature could still be found at the edges of empire.

FIGURE 3. "Animal Festival Commemorative Zoo Map," 1930. The zoo is transformed into a cartoon-like playground in this limited edition polychrome map. Automobiles bring families to new entrance gates and the grounds are shown as uncharacteristically empty. Attendance increased dramatically as new species were brought into the gardens and the zoo became a showcase of imperial culture in the early twentieth century. Courtesy of the Tokyo Zoological Society.

CHAPTER 2

The Dreamlife of Imperialism

*Commerce, Conquest, and the Naturalization
of Ecological Modernity*

In societies where modern conditions of production prevail,
all of life presents itself as an immense accumulation of
spectacles. Everything that was directly lived has moved away
into a representation.

—Guy Debord, *Society of the Spectacle*

THE DREAMLIFE OF EMPIRE

By the close of the nineteenth century, as the Japanese archipelago entered a period of sustained industrialization, the taxonomic separation
of people from animals instigated by Udagawa Yōan in 1822 had become a source of mass-culture longing and lament. When the Imperial
Household Ministry approved the construction of a popular exhibit for
living "animal war trophies" (*senrihin dōbutsu*) in 1897—the garden's
first major expansion since its opening in 1882—the exhibitionary culture of the zoo was already beginning to invert. By the end of the Meiji
era in 1912 the steel bars of the Ueno Imperial Zoological Garden no
longer marked the frontier of a state-led effort to sequester Japanese
civilization from the symbolic threat of animal savagery. For many, the
zoo's displays came to signal instead the threshold of an alienation from
the natural world so profound that it seemed to threaten the very humanity that it defined. As Japan began its fitful, violent transformation
into an industrial and imperial power, the zoological garden projected
"nature" and its wild animal figures outward onto the colonial frontier,
away from the cities that housed zoos such as Ueno and beyond the
domesticated villages of the Japanese countryside. It was there, at the

wild edges of empire, that visitors were urged to look as they sought solace from the dislocations of modern life.

The war trophy exhibit was the most obvious expression of the garden's new role as a nexus of imperial culture. Built on a wooded hillside above the central gardens, the trophy enclosures were filled with dozens of animals captured or used in the course of the Sino-Japanese War (1894–1895). Wild boar trapped by troops on "safari" (safuari) in Korea—the main battlefield in the conflict—were housed next to deer captured on the continent. Children could feed treats to purebred warhorses (gunba) ridden into battle by Japanese officers or, perhaps for the wives and children of draftees, mules and donkeys used by enlisted men to transport supplies. Funded through a public gift from the Meiji Emperor's personal coffers, the war exhibition marked the beginning of the zoo's own slow colonization of the west side of Ueno Park, often at the expense of neighboring institutions. The Ueno Zoo flourished at the intersection of imperialism and consumerism. The institution more than doubled in area between 1897 and 1937, and annual attendance quadrupled over the same years.[1]

Located at the center of a growing network of colonial zoos and collectors, Ueno's collection expanded together with the nation's reach overseas, offering visitors an increasingly elaborate figuration of Japan's imperial project. Administrators sponsored what we might call the "dreamlife of imperialism" as they drew connections between the world of the zoo and the aspirations of empire.[2] First under Ishikawa Chiyomatsu and then under his successors, Kurokawa Gitarō (1867–1935) and Koga Tadamichi (1903–1986), the Ueno Imperial Zoological Garden was remade into an imperial fantasyland, a place where fact and fiction were carefully blended in the service of political goals. "Animal war trophies" and species collected in the colonies were displayed alongside other animals that had little to do with Japan's physical empire, all arranged to elicit a sense of reassuring order and lightly educational excitement. If modern empires, in order to be successful, must generate some conception of paradise or bring to life a set of ideas, images, and symbols that elicit consent, loyalty, or devotion across diverse populations, the zoo was in the vanguard of that effort with Tokyo's kids and their families.[3] It made imperialism seem fun. As visitors strolled through the carefully manicured gardens and, from the early 1930s, looked into new barless enclosures where animals appeared to roam free, they were treated, not to a picture of empire as it really was, but to a vision of empire as administrators believed it *ought* to be: rational, benevolent, playful, and profitable.

The zoological garden depicted a world in which the exotic and the unusual were appropriated by the state and its agents—often dressed in the white lab coat of the scientist, the khakis of the safari hunter, or the evermore familiar smile of the fatherly zoo director—for metropolitan spectators. It gave the public the opportunity to witness the fruits of newly acquired colonies, urging visitors to associate the managed world of the zoo with the real work of empire building. In doing so, it underwrote the growing sense that real nature had been expunged from the everyday lives of most Japanese. Gone were the homely Newfoundland dog, the dormice, and the frisky French rabbits of the Yamashita Animal Hall. They were replaced with colonial trophies and foreign megafauna—lions, tigers, bears, and elephants. With the exception of the animals in the war trophy exhibits, domesticates and many native species were weeded out of Ueno's collection in favor of "rare" (*chinjū*), "wild" (*yasei*), and "exotic" (*gairaishu*) animals from overseas. Physically impressive big game (*mōjū*, literally "ferocious beasts") from overseas underlined the sense that the domestic landscape was all but tamed, broken by industrial power or, in the case of the nation's rural periphery, domesticated into rustic simplicity. The few remaining native megafauna—bears from northeastern Japan and Hokkaido, for example—were reframed as symbols of disappearing national nature in need of preservation. Rare exotics, in contrast, bespoke the conquest of virgin territory by Japanese explorers or exchanges of prestige between Japan and other imperial powers. As displays of power, these exhibits overwrote the histories of specific fauna—totems of conquered lands or foreign peoples—with a "natural history" generated in the metropole.[4]

This metropolitan "natural history" was singular rather than plural. It reframed diverse cultures, ecologies, and fauna as components of a unified Japanese empire or icons of Japanese national accomplishment.[5] The fiction of unity was especially important in a multiethnic, multinational empire such as Japan's, and we need to pay close attention to its appeal as well as its costs if we hope to understand how the Japanese empire generated consent in the home islands. Much as Udagawa Yōan's idea of the *dōbutsu* gathered a diverse assemblage of living creatures into the classificatory kingdom of Animalia, the imperial zoo asked visitors to envision a benevolent order that transcended the concerns of individual territories or animals, even as it gave structure and meaning to their lives. By the 1930s the Japanese empire encompassed 200 million people and some of the richest environments on the planet. It reached from the steppes of Manchuria to the atolls of Micronesia, from Sakhalin's boreal groves to Taiwan's mountain rainforests. Korea became a protectorate after Japan's victory in the Russo-Japanese War in 1905 and a formal colony in 1910. In actual fact, this compound empire was often at odds within itself, but the zoo joined with a host of political, legal, military, and cultural institutions to paper over those divisions in an attempt to provide a sense of unity where violence and dissent were often the norm.[6]

Kurokawa and then Koga played on the gap between the utopian fantasy of the gardens and the gritty realities of empire to build attendance and garner official recognition. Where Ishikawa was relentless in his advocacy of science and rationality in the service of social evolution, his successors embraced the commercial nature of the gardens. In doing so, they presided over a transformation of life at the zoo that was subtler and more enduring than the pomp and circumstance of imperial pageantry: the saturation of the gardens by the techniques and attitudes of consumer capitalism. By the 1920s the zoo at Ueno was a mass-culture mecca, a place where government ideology was able to compete for public attention with the department stores of Ginza and the amusement parks of Asakusa. It was here, in the play between explicit politics and implicit economy that ecological modernity developed most powerfully. The Japanese empire imploded in a frenzy of bloody sacrifice in the closing years of the Second World War, but to this day the Ueno Zoo—like many zoos around the world—continues to embody the tension between curiosity and exploitation that was energized through the dreamlife of imperialism.

Surging attendance brought official admiration. Tens of thousands of yen poured into the zoo budget after the institution was levered away from the Imperial Household Ministry by Tokyo City officials in 1924. Government funds helped to convert captive animals into marketable objects, commodity fetishes of the sort described by Marx. But these commodities were able to draw further force from the sensuousness of living presence, and they were deployed in the service of the state.[7] Specific prices for animals may have been recorded behind the scenes in the zoo's ledgers (animal values were noted in yen, dollars, or pounds for budgetary reasons), but the creatures were publicly displayed as priceless embodiments of pure, inexhaustible value, usually associated with rich colonial ecologies. They were incarnations of "wild nature," symbols of a natural alternative to the mechanical culture of modern city life. Alive and authentic, the zoo's animals were offered as a spiritual balm for the contradictions of the same capitalist culture that contained them.

Posed as the antithesis of enlightenment during the Meiji-era heyday of the *bunmei kaika*, the animal world—now explicitly connected to the overseas empire—was crafted into an antidote for civilization and its discontents in the early twentieth century. As the archipelago industrialized, animals seemed to come out of another time, physical reminders of an older economy that may have maintained a more balanced relationship with the natural world. That economy was said to remain in place overseas, at the edges of the Japanese empire. For some, such as the prominent ethnographer Yanagita Kunio, these changes captured the spiritual losses of the new modern order. For others, such as the social bureaucrats who took over the administration of the gardens in 1924, captive animals offered a new kind of social medium, natural symbols of life outside of modernity that could be used to address a host of "urban problems" (*toshi mondai*) that threatened to destabilize the imperial metropole.[8]

Even as bureaucrats trained in the social sciences began to assume control of the Ueno Zoo for the first time, professional biologists and zoologists retreated from public life at the gardens. The professional distinction sought by Udagawa, Itō, Tanaka, and other practitioners of early-modern natural history was social fact by the early twentieth century, and practical biology and zoology took a backseat to scientism (the promotion of a secular faith in science as a means to answer social problems) at the zoo. Ishikawa Chiyomatsu, who left public administration for university life in 1907, was the last director of the gardens who maintained an active laboratory research agenda.[9]

Municipal bureaucrats were haunted by the specter of social revolution in the early twentieth century, and they began to fear that Tokyoites had become dangerously alienated from the natural world. In opening a gateway between the "wild" edges of the empire and the "civilized" city, managers argued, the zoo provided a colonial answer to the problem of industrial estrangement, and in a form that could be almost endlessly replicated. Taiwan's forests might be logged and Manchuria's mountains might be mined, drained of value, but how does one exhaust the value of *looking*?[10] Each year millions of visitors stood in front of the same animals in the same enclosures, where they were asked to experience the same emotional responses. Crowds at the gardens became so large that they were a news story in their own right, and managers argued that the animals on display could do more than just lure people through the gates. The zoological garden, Kurokawa wrote in a 1926 policy paper, used animals to communicate at the level of emotion and affect. It addressed patrons prior to the consciousness of ideology. "When people come to see animals for entertainment," he suggested, "they will reap benefits unknowingly and unconsciously" (*fuchi fushiki*). The zoological garden could do more than teach visitors about the colonies or natural history; it could represent ideology as nature and camouflage policy as play.[11]

[handwritten annotation: ideology = capital Bon]

THE NATURE OF EMPIRE

The natural world was a very different place when Koga Tadamichi began to work at the Ueno Zoo in 1927 than it was when the institution was founded in 1882. A top graduate of the same Tokyo University zoology program founded by Edward S. Morse in the 1870s, Koga was the grandson of insurgent samurai who helped to drive the "restoration" of imperial rule in 1868. By the time the charismatic young zoologist took control of the gardens in 1933, most of the animals on display would not have been familiar to his revolutionary grandfather. Urban youngsters in shorts and shirt collars now peered across concrete moats at a diverse collection of imported fauna (over one thousand animals in all), representatives of a natural world framed as a world apart. No longer too close for evolutionary comfort, as they had been in the Meiji era, animals appeared, instead, to embody an appealingly exotic world separate from the lives of the men, women, and children who crowded onto the institution's paved pathways. Wealthy families drove up to the garden's gates in gasoline-powered automobiles. Other visitors stepped onto the crowded platforms of nearby Ueno Station from trains driven by electricity whose origins were obvious: the modern cityscape was defined by thickets of towering smokestacks. Each set of stacks marked a coal-burning power plant or factory, each pumping smoke into increasingly grey skies that had first been corrupted by the engines of Commodore Perry's "black ships."[12]

The First World War solidified the hold of industrial modernity in the Japanese archipelago. Japanese goods became competitive in overseas markets as the country became a supplier to combatant nations; Asian markets opened to Japanese producers while Western companies were distracted. New capital-intensive industries—notably petrochemicals, shipbuilding, and machine tools—began to concentrate in burgeoning urban agglomerations such as Tokyo-Kawasaki-Yokohama and Osaka-Kobe. The lure of employment in these urban-based industries combined with the push of a chronically distressed agricultural sector to fuel a population explosion in the country's cities. Tokyo's population more than doubled in the two decades after 1900, reaching 3.35 million by 1920. It continued to grow even after the beginning of Japan's second war with China, which lasted from 1937 until 1945.[13]

The zoo's animals were transfigured by the changing political economy, rendered into objects of metropolitan longing. Ecological modernity did not, in fact, spell the material disappearance of animals—or more often animal products—from the lives of most Japanese, even those who lived in cities. As Yanagita Kunio pointed out in 1930, people ate more fish and meat as production modernized, they kept pets, they sought entertainment in the natural world through hiking and sightseeing, and the country's publishing houses brought images of animals into their lives in unprecedented volume.[14]

Animals were also the subject of considerable discussion by intellectuals such as Yanagita. But even as these ideas and images arrived in classrooms and living rooms, the new symbolic economy instituted a powerful social fiction in which animals and nature were re-imagined as alien to the lives of most Japanese. "Nature has become a thing apart," the liberal social critic Hasegawa Nyozekan wrote in 1939. "This separation," he continued, "is something new for the Japanese," and it constituted a threat. "We need to reclaim our traditional connection to parklands and green space," Hasegawa warned, using distinctly modern terms for traditional nature, or risk losing track of "who we really are." This was one of the central ironies of ecological modernity. Even as the externalization of nature accelerated, the idea of nature, itself a human fabrication, was seen as a wellspring of authentic humanness, something that had to be rediscovered in order to recover one's true self in a world that seemed increasingly denatured and artificial.[15]

Zoological gardens, Koga argued, had a crucial role to play in this act of self-recovery. The Ueno Zoo was reclassified as a "comfort institution" (*ian shisetsu*) in the 1920s, a social tool designed to sooth the alienation bred by what he called the "dramatic development" (*kyūgeki hatten*) of the nation's cities. Consciously mirroring similar trends in contemporary Germany and England, Koga and his colleagues in the Tokyo Parks Department sought to remake the Ueno Zoo into a distinctly modern answer to the problem of urban modernity. It was an approach that was at odds with the cultural atavism that has absorbed so much attention from historians of the interwar era. Where Yanagita and others pursued the preservation of an idealized rural culture defined in opposition to the city, Kurokawa, Koga, and their superior in the Parks Department, Inoshita Kiyoshi (1884–1973), projected the anomie of modern urban life outward into the wilds of the nation's expanding empire. It was the unspoiled edges of empire that offered the surest satisfaction for the modern "craving" (*yokkyū*) for nature, Koga argued.[16]

At times, Koga sought to harness the pursuit of this emotional comfort to the physical pursuit of empire, but he was less concerned with the public display of imperial trophies than with the spiritual hygiene of the people who walked through the Ueno Zoo's gates. Affect was the point, not accuracy. Animals from outside of the empire—lions or elephants, for example—could still be made to serve the needs of imperial Japan. People visit the zoo for rest and relaxation, he argued, and this recreation (*rekurieshon*), taken from the English to mean "re-creation," was an important social tool. Rural and wild "scenery" (*fūkei*) of the sort protected under the 1919 Law for Preserving Scenery and Historic and Natural Monuments—Japan's first substantial conservation legislation—or found in the wild lands of the colonies could, Koga wrote, recharge the spirit of a nation enervated through the industrial separation of civilization from nature. But since it was not feasible for millions of people to visit such places on a regular basis the metropolitan zoo had a role to play.[17]

It was a romantic vision with practical policy implications. Koga sought to use the mass-culture exhibition of animals—living embodiments of disappearing nature—to inoculate the nation's children and their families against an alienation born of that same modern culture. Since untamed nature had largely been expunged from the Japanese archipelago, he suggested, metropolitan Japanese would have to draw on the uncorrupted wilderness of the empire's "uncivilized regions" if they hoped to answer the biological "need" for contact with the natural world. "Respect for nature is the very essence of our humanity [*ningen no honsei*]," he wrote, but that humanity was threatened by modernity itself. The rationality championed by Ishikawa and advocates of "civilization and enlightenment" during the nineteenth century was premised on the intellectual separation of humans from "other animals." Koga, like Kurokawa, trumpeted the fact that "people are animals," using it as a drumbeat to build curiosity and march people into the zoo, but this recognition led him to see a contradiction at the heart of each and every modern subject. Biologically, humans (*ningen*) may be animals, but they were thinking animals who risked losing touch with their natural selves.[18] The riven subjectivity of ecological modernity—torn between rationality and biology—threatened to destabilize not only individual lives but also the nation as a whole.

An answer to this contradiction lay in a colonial world that Koga framed as the natural antithesis of the civilized metropole. "The inhabitants of uncivilized regions [*bunmei no susumanai chihō*]," Koga argued, comparing colonizer and colonized, "engage with nature unconsciously or, perhaps more aptly, without care for like or dislike." The consciousness of separation, in other words, was not at work in premodern societies. "Primitive people" inhabited a world prior to alienation. "They join with the natural world. In contrast, those [of us] who are separated from nature in civilized cities come to consciously long for it. Clearly this longing should be seen as a pure expression of what it means to be human"—a biophysical need that had to be addressed. "Zoological gardens and botanical gardens," he concluded, "are essential to cities in order to satisfy this craving." They did more than answer the need for contact with nature; they soothed the social disaffection that was endemic to urban modernity, inducing a "truly peaceful comfort, a supple comfort" unavailable through other institutions in the city.[19]

The qualities cultivated by the zoo-going experience were, to Koga's way of thinking, similar to those of an effective colonial administrator. People who were estranged from nature were estranged from their own true selves, and such people made poor colonial officers because they lacked firm moral grounding. He writes, referring here to the imperial futures of Japanese children, "It goes without saying that increasingly large numbers of Japanese will have to make their way to the continent. This state of affairs demands an open and tolerant heart rather than the false heart of self-delusion. The zoological garden and similar institutions have a powerful effect on our nation's youth, teaching them to love nature and not to view it with contempt."[20] The zoological garden in this formulation opened a healthy traffic between the spiritual needs of the colonizer and the "uncivilized" nature of the colonies, which required protection rather than simple exploitation. Rendered into something external to the civilized metropole, the peoples of those regions where true nature remained intact were ascribed a status reminiscent of the zoo's animals, biological creatures in need of care but who were not

conscious of that need. Like animals, they were endowed with a precon-
scious, prerational sense of togetherness with nature. Indeed, "nature,"
as such, did not exist for them.

Koga was not arguing for a return to this prerational, premodern
state. Neither did he exhibit the fear of biological degeneration that
haunted Ishikawa and other social Darwinians. In 1939 he wrote with
a confident optimism born of imperial success. This view would change
after Japan's disastrous imperial collapse in 1943, but in the 1930s and
early 1940s Koga continued to work on the assumption that empire
was economically necessary and morally desirable so long as administrators were properly trained. It was here, in the realm of ethics and
attitude, that the linkages between the commercial world of the zoo and
the material realities of imperial administration were most evident. The
Ueno Zoo, Koga argued, was of course an important showcase for imperial acquisitions, and he did a great deal to build its colonial collection, but it was also a moral stage. The institution cultivated amiable,
respectful relationships between children and animals (*dōbutsu ni shi-
tashimu*) where less savory institutions—and less civilized nations—
merely elicited "empty amusement" from the animal world. If carefully
structured, Koga argued in his longest and most telling logical stretch,
encounters with animals in the zoological garden would help to prepare
people for the demands of imperial management. Critics may dismiss a
trip to the zoo as mere play, he reasoned, but those critics overlooked
the social significance of play in modern societies. Just as the animals on
display were echoes of a distant nature, a lighthearted trip to the metropolitan zoo could be a moral rehearsal for the dramatic realities of
empire.[21]

NATURE BEHIND GLASS

For Koga, zoological gardens were conduits between colonizer and
colonized, Panglossian "gateways" capable of drawing together the best
of both worlds. There was something like an imperial biophilia at work
in these arguments, the assumption of a biological "love of living things"
that he claimed was inborn but which was stymied by the growth of the
modern city. In his eyes, the longing for nature that drove the zoo-going
experience was a specifically modern, specifically urban symptom of the
contradiction between human biology and the modern political economy, and he began to pursue new technologies in order to make the
encounter between visitors and animals as intimate as possible. The goal

was to use the techniques of mass culture to answer the psychological needs of the "human animal." The closer the encounter between man and beast, the more effective it would be. "People must be able to see animals as if they are in nature," he said in one interview.[22] "Nature" in this formulation remained elsewhere, confined to the colonies and other "uncivilized" spaces, but animals could be used to trick people into feeling *as if* they were experiencing the real thing. It did not matter whether visitors knew that the nature of the zoo was artificial—Koga recognized that most zoo visitors saw through the artifice—so long as they felt the emotional benefits. The point, to paraphrase Roland Barthes, was a "reality effect" rather than reality itself, and this effect played on the assumed split between the rational mind and the emotional unconscious.[23]

Koga's colleagues in the Tokyo Parks Department, notably the department's director, Inoshita Kiyoshi, joined him in this conviction. An irrepressible advocate for green space and urban parks, Inoshita helped transform the relationship between the city and the natural world in the years following the Great Kantō Earthquake of 1923. The quake destroyed nearly half of the city, took more than one hundred thousand lives, and inspired a series of race riots aimed mainly at Koreans, who were rumored to have poisoned wells muddied by seismic activity, among other things. Parks served as firebreaks and evacuation sites during the crisis, and after the emergency the man in charge of rebuilding the capital, former Tokyo mayor and colonial administrator Gotō Shinpei, argued strongly for the creation of a more robust park system. In the end, approximately 3 percent of postquake redevelopment funding went into the park system. Large parcels of private land were brought under municipal control through purchase and donation. Ueno Park and the zoological gardens were the most publicized transfer of this kind. Gifted to the "people of Tokyo" from the imperial house in celebration of the crown prince's wedding in 1924, the zoological gardens were transformed by improved funding and more active management after the transfer.[24]

The quake came as a crisis and an opportunity for Inoshita and other social bureaucrats. To Inoshita's way of thinking, the riots that wracked the region after the quake were expressions of underlying "urban problems" such as poverty, unemployment, or overcrowding. If Tokyo hoped to avoid further riots and the kind of radicalization recently witnessed in St. Petersburg and elsewhere, he suggested, following Gotō and other conservative reformers, the country would need to address the unhealthy character of industrial city life. Parks and zoos were a cost-effective means of social management in the industrial age. They could, officials believed, absorb the anomie and disaffection of modernity and convert negative feelings into renewed energy.

Funding for the zoo more than quadrupled as Inoshita, Kurokawa, and Koga sought to reframe nature for a growing audience.[25] In these years the relationship between viewers and the animals on display was redefined in architectural as well as social terms. Cages had once been designed to underline separation, but now color, glass, empty space, and light were used to manipulate the viewing experience, transforming the act of looking at captive animals into something like the experience of window-shopping in the city's modern department stores. From 1924 forward, visitors' encounter with the animal world was increasingly like the encounter between consumer and commodity—both experiences were shaped by a new aesthetics of desire.

To choose perhaps the most obvious similarity, glass increasingly mediated the zoogoer's encounter with nature and the consumer's encounter with goods. Glass displays offered spectators the illusion of increased intimacy. When glass replaced bars, visitors were better able to indulge in the fantasy of entering directly into the world of the animal, a communion that Koga believed the industrialized landscape of the modern city led them to yearn for. Transparent glass seemed to allow the viewer an unmediated encounter with the animal, but it was in fact a carefully engineered experience. Much like display cases at Mitsukoshi and other modern department stores, the zoo's new displays fueled the desires and needs that they claimed to answer, but they did so in a way that capitalists and marketers could only dream of duplicating. Here, in the world of imperial biophilia, desire was natural.[26]

Window enclosures were acts of recontextualization, subtle expressions of power, and this helped to make them appealing. The Small Bird House, which opened in 1938, was emblematic of this new viewing experience. It rendered the animals on display into exquisite living exemplars. Each species was identified by a naturalists' sketch and its scientific, English, and Japanese names. Surrounded by walls that were often painted with depictions of natural scenes and lit with electric light, these windows displayed animals in an environment crafted by human beings. Selected natural artifacts—tree limbs, an artificial pond, growing plants—suggested the natural habitat of the birds in the wild. Human influence was evident (indeed celebrated) in the ersatz nature of the displays, but those same techniques also implied that the real nature

FIGURE 4. Small Bird House (*Kotori no ie*). Completed in 1938, the Small Bird House offered visitors an experience not unlike that of window-shopping in the department stores of the Ginza. Glass added a new level of abstraction to the zoo-going experience, appearing to offer unimpeded visual access while refusing other kinds of engagement. Smell and sound were reduced even as sight was aided through artificial lighting and the removal of intervening structures. Image courtesy of Tokyo Zoological Park Society.

of the birds' native ecologies remained extant elsewhere, unaltered and uncorrupted, even as human beings (often as part of Japan's imperial expansion) placed some of them in jeopardy.

Glass added another level to the process of abstraction at work in the zoo by cutting down on sound and smell. Unless the species were particularly loud or an air vent opened into the display corridor, animal sounds were muted, which disappointed bird-watcher hobbyists interested in listening to rare birdcalls. Such complaints were balanced by the relative reduction in complaints about odor. In these prewar years, as today, one of the primary complaints about the zoo concerned animal odors. Musky or soiled, many animals produce powerful scents that offended metropolitan sensibilities. In the 1880s, when such sensibilities were on the rise, administrators addressed this problem by increasing the number of janitors on hand to remove the mountains of feces produced each day at the zoo. They also increased the frequency with which the cages of particularly prolific animals were cleansed, adding the use of detergents to the menu of standard zoo practice.[27]

Just as advertisements were marketing Shiseido's newest soap—"99.5% pure"—to the human populace, the zoo was being deodorized regularly for the first time.

Likewise, touching the animals became impossible with glass displays. Although touching dangerous animals was always strictly limited at the zoo, Ueno, like most zoological gardens in the late nineteenth and early twentieth centuries, allowed visitors to physically interact with many species. One could purchase biscuits in the war trophy area, for example, to feed to a favorite mascot or animal hero.[28] Many species kept in pens rather than cages could be tempted to come close enough to pet if the treat was sufficiently enticing. Similarly, accepted behavior at Ueno during this period included tossing leftover food and unwanted treats to certain animals, even large predators. Particularly good targets for such efforts, bears quickly consumed most proffered morsels. These actions cultivated a sense of presence and interaction between spectators and the animals that appealed to zoogoers' desire to build relationships with the creatures and, more importantly, to see these fantastic specimens move. The vision of a tremendous polar bear lumbering after a tidbit discarded by a small child highlighted the animal's restricted freedom and subservience to even the smallest of human patrons. And it was far more visually engaging than watching the great creatures sleep.

For better and for worse, glass eliminated such contact. As William Leach notes in his analysis of display window aesthetics, the result of this transparent separation was a mingling of refusal and desire that almost certainly increased the feelings of frustration that often accompany a trip to the zoo.[29] Glass brought animals—particularly smaller creatures often difficult to identify in more traditional cage designs—into sharp focus and intimate proximity, but it placed them clearly out of reach. These displays offered no easy mode of interaction with the animal other than sight and the ever-alluring tap on the window. As window displays came into being, so did the ubiquitous warnings to patrons that tapping on the glass was unacceptable behavior. Even if they can see beyond the light reflected in the windows, animals quickly learn that the moving figures outside the cage (other than the keeper, who signifies food) are of little consequence—they become bored. Likewise, visitors often found themselves staring, not at the animals, but at reflections of themselves on the glass of the window, a visual metaphor for the nature of the zoo and the work of ecological modernity.[30]

BACKSTAGE AT THE ZOO

Developments in glass technology in the 1920s and 1930s, combined with increased tensile strength in the metal used in bars, allowed for the creation of new ways to produce the illusion of immediacy. Stronger steel meant thinner bars or allowed the use of high-strength wire mesh to contain large cats and other big mammals. The Large Mammal House (Mōjū shitsu) that opened in 1930 exemplified how this new technology enabled changes in architecture. The exhibit now comprised two ovoid segmented cage structures united by a rectangular concrete building that contained the animals' sleeping quarters as well as a public throughway. From the outside, the cages offered a view little different from that of older designs: barred barriers separated spectators from the animals, which were separated from one another by intervening barriers. On the inside, however, the structure ushered zoogoers into a new relationship with the animals and the institution. As patrons passed down the hallway of the Large Mammal House they experienced what may have been the Ueno Zoo's first staged views of backstage life at the zoo.

As Susan G. Davis notes in her study of Sea World, cultural institutions keep certain aspects of their functioning carefully hidden from patrons.[31] At the Ueno Zoo, as at most zoological gardens, keepers carefully sequestered sick and dying animals not only from the general zoo population but also from the view of patrons. The creation of a new Zoo Hospital, built in 1935, was proudly announced, but its occupants remained hidden. To leave sick animals on display would not only ruin the experience of the visitor and perhaps further damage the animal's health, it would also highlight unsavory aspects of institutional life and tarnish the zoological garden's carefully cultivated image as a protector of animal life. Until the late twentieth century zoos tended to be lethal places for most species. Truncated lives were the norm rather than the exception. The distinction between frontstage and backstage activities was thus necessary for the maintenance of the illusion of a healthy animal world tended by Japanese keepers and veterinarians—a metonym for the nature of empire.[32]

The Large Mammal House offered visitors an edited view of backstage life. It allowed viewers to peer into the animals' sleeping and feeding areas, giving them views that had been unavailable in older cage designs. With this new architecture, the animals, and certain parts of the infrastructure, were moved to the "front" but marked as "back." Scheduled public feedings, which Ueno implemented in the late nineteenth century, are the most obvious example of the illusion of privileged access. Popular "behind the scenes" tours restricted less savory aspects of institutional life (animal mortality, for example) to a new backstage kept invisible.[33] As the Large Mammal House shows, the Ueno Zoo's architects sought to move patrons through the zoo in particular ways, shaping the zoogoer's experience not only as they stood before each view or exhibit, but also as they moved through these carefully crafted spaces.

THE ILLUSION OF LIBERTY

The illusion of intimacy and unhindered access generated by increasingly subtle techniques of separation reached its pinnacle in the 1930s with the construction of several so-called barless cages. Prominent in zoos today, these new enclosures were first developed by the famous German animal dealer and circus owner Carl Hagenbeck for use in his Animal Park, a successful for-profit operation located outside of Hamburg. Inoshita, like other administrators of public institutions, kept abreast of the latest technological developments through such specialized magazines as *Parks and Greenswards* (*Koen ryokuchi*) and *Museum Studies* (*Hakubutsukan kenkyū*). He was aware of such displays, and first encountered them in person in New York and Berlin during a lengthy 1925 inspection tour of zoos and museums in Western nations. Determined to see them replicated in Tokyo, he incorporated these techniques into the master plan for zoo renovations drawn up upon his return in 1926.[34]

Hagenbeck's displays allowed zoogoers to indulge in the fantasy of a direct, authentic encounter with nature even as they moved animals even farther beyond patrons' reach. Rather than using the bars, fences, and roofs that were the mainstay of zoo display technology in the years before he opened his park in 1907, Hagenbeck developed systems of dry and water-filled moats that separated the wildlife from patrons without appearing to do so, leaving animals open to the elements. He accomplished his goal by carefully observing the jumping, climbing, and swimming capabilities of various animals and then building seemingly "natural" barriers that would act as effectively as cages to keep the animals contained. "Ponds" fronted by vertical walls allowed patrons to look down on swimming polar bears even as they denied the

FIGURE 5. The Polar Bear Grotto, 1927. The most expensive exhibit built at Ueno before the Second World War, the Polar Bear Grotto included a cutting-edge "refrigerated wall" along the backside of the display. Meant to keep the bears cool in Tokyo's hot summers, the machine was loud and ignored by the animals, who preferred swimming in the water-filled moat in the display's foreground. Portions of this display can still be seen at the zoo today. Image courtesy of Tokyo Zoological Park Society.

animals a pawhold upon which to lever themselves out of the enclosure; steep-walled concrete ravines only a few meters across kept elephants in place; and circular walls surrounding elevated "mountain-scapes," replicas of alpine terrain, kept monkeys or mountain goats penned up.

The appeal of such displays was manifold, and it hinged on the contradiction of animals appearing to roam free while remaining in captivity.[35] This paradoxical situation appealed to new understandings of the animal that developed as human life in Japan became increasingly urban in character and industrialization transformed urban space. Despite the fact that more Japanese lived in rural areas than in the nation's growing cities until the postwar era, mass media portrayed city life as universal and rural life as out of synch and marginal. Under these conditions, nature, increasingly defined (and symbolically confined) by park boundaries or colonial borders, came to be understood as something extrinsic to everyday life. Even as the abstract desire to seek out and experience nature intensified (and meat eating became more common), metropolitan viewers became increasingly uncomfortable with the idea that zoo animals were locked in cages. Hagenbeck's new animal enclosures, which soothed visitors' guilty consciences at the same time that they improved visual access to captive animals, addressed this contradiction of ecological modernity, celebrating the animals' freedom with invisible discipline. To hearken back to our discussion of Foucault in the pervious chapter, the displays reveal a growing discomfort with the realities of sovereign power—the power over life and death—at the zoo. Then, as now, people found it difficult to consciously recognize the importance of force in a place nominally focused on childhood education and entertainment. This discomfort, as we will see in chapter 4, offered administrators a powerful emotional lever.

Hagenbeck's designs reordered space so that the animals did not appear to require control. They were entirely self-disciplined. It was a model that thrilled Koga and Inoshita. Not only did the pits, ponds, and pinnacles constrain animals in a manner that stimulated visitors with the illusion of intimacy and even threatening proximity, they also made disciplinary use of space, working on captives and captivated alike in a manner that appeared "empty" of any ideological intent. Both people and animals seemed to roam free even as the new designs subtly defined their movements. The experience was emblematic of the "comfort" pursued by administrators in the interwar years. Patrons other than children on school trips were never required to visit the zoo. They chose to visit, and when they arrived they found themselves looking at animals that appeared to be contented and satisfied, at least in comparison to their caged brethren. Journals such as *Collecting and Keeping* (*Saishū to shiiku*), a specialized publication aimed at the nation's growing zoo movement that first entered publication in this era, noted that the incidence of idiosyncratic pacing, self-mutilation, and other disturbing behaviors was reduced in the enclosures. The animals' reactions became, in article after article, measures of technical progress, and the change was generally attributed to reduced stress and boredom—the return to a "more natural" environment. "Stress" and "boredom," then, became a policy concern for animals just as anomie seemed to threaten the people who looked at them.[36]

When the Ueno Zoo's Polar Bear Grotto, the first such display in Japan, opened to the public in 1927, it offered visitors the prospect of eye-to-eye encounters with powerful animals. Nothing but space separated fathers, mothers, and children from the two large predators—a male and a female purchased from the Hagenbecks in 1926. Though polar bears had been successfully kept in the zoo since 1902 when Ishikawa brokered a purchase from Carl Hagenbeck, Inoshita and Koga wanted simultaneously to demonstrate Ueno's achievement of technological parity with the zoos of Europe and North America and to add a new layer of technological sophistication by producing a better environment for the bears. They devoted a sizable portion of their budget for the entire zoo renovation to a cutting-edge "refrigerator wall" at the back of the enclosure. Cooled by the latest technology, the wall was intended to keep the animals refreshed as they passed in front of it, even during the heat and humidity of Tokyo's notoriously unpleasant summers. It was an expensive choice, and it indicates the paired pursuit of more suitable animal habitats and institutional prestige at the gardens. Koga and Inoshita were hardly callous about animals—Koga's writings in particular demonstrate deep emotional attachments. They simply pursued recognition through innovation. When it came down to practical use, however, the two bears dismissed the costly contraption after a cursory inspection; they spent little of the hot summer of 1928 within reach of the chilled air produced by the noisy machine, and the refrigerated wall was turned off the following year.[37]

Ueno's second Hagenbeck-style enclosure, the Seal Pool, opened the year after the polar bear exhibit. Populated by several fur seals, the Seal Pool quickly developed into one of the zoo's most popular attractions, pulling in crowds of spectators eager to see the graceful animals shoot through the water at feeding time as they pursued fish thrown by a uniformed keeper. Like the Polar Bear Grotto, the pool crafted manmade materials into iconic representations of natural scenery. The "stone" used in all such displays, which totaled four by 1931, as well as in the "natural" backdrops in buildings like the Large Mammal House and the new Hippo House (opened in 1929), was constructed of a carefully formulated mixture of concrete and wire spread over a metal and wooden armature. Inoshita brought the recipe for this mixture back with him from his world tour. He subsequently turned construction of the exhibits over to the carpenter Aikawa Motomu, who added color and texture to the mixture in order to create artificial stone that one commentator claimed appeared "more real than real rock."[38]

Aikawa's widely acclaimed masterwork was his Monkey Mountain (*Saru yama*), which opened in 1931. Aikawa, Koga, and Inoshita devoted more time and consideration to this design than others of its type in the zoo. Other than borrowing the basic idea from Hagenbeck, this

FIGURE 6. The Monkey Mountain (*Saru yama*), 1931. Modeled on the Muromachi-era paintings of Sesshū (1420–1506), the display was the progenitor of a host of similar "monkey island" exhibits. The association between Japanese macaques (*Nihonzaru*) and the displays became so prominent that it was satirized by the author Dazai Osamu in his 1936 short story, "Monkey Island" (*Saru ga shima*). Image courtesy of Tokyo Zoological Park Society.

display was largely drawn up by the team at Ueno, and its construction was plagued by difficulties. The finished product still stands on the grounds of the Ueno Zoo today, and it remains one of the zoo's most admired exhibits. Rather than denying them, the jagged "mountain" that sits at the center of Ueno's Monkey Mountain celebrated its human and national origins. Made up of complex formations of dramatically shaped artificial rock and home to a lively group of Japanese macaques (known as *Nihonzaru*, or "Japanese monkeys"), the Monkey Mountain was shaped to reflect the cultural heritage of its country of origin, constituting a three-dimensional reproduction of Japanese landscape painting in the idiosyncratic style of Sesshū (1420–1506), one of the nation's most celebrated landscape painters. The display has been reproduced throughout Japan and, on numerous occasions, overseas, especially in displays for Japanese macaques. In the decades after 1931 it was standard practice at all Japanese zoological gardens to keep Japanese macaques in Monkey Mountain and Monkey Island exhibits, which were largely modeled on Aikawa's creation. Even the Minnesota Zoological Gardens, the zoo that I visited often as a child, exhibits *Nihonzaru* in a similar "Japanese" style.[39] Imperial dreamlife first crafted in interwar Japan, then, continues to stimulate the cultural imaginationsof zoogoers in the American Upper Midwest.

IMPERIAL TROPHIES

Not all connections to empire were so subtle or attenuated as Koga's conjecture on the spiritual vacancy of industrial society. Most were intentionally blatant. As Japan's overseas holdings expanded, the dramaturgy of empire was elaborated across a broad range of concrete representations. Newly acquired colonies appeared as wildlife habitats (*seitai*), jungles (*mitsurin*), or tropical zones (*nettai*) in the zoo's literature and signage, while the metropole was cast as the governing center. Once used to assert Japan's parity with the West, the zoological gardens now celebrated the Japanese capacity to impose order on colonial possessions, territories, and animals. The "war trophy" section of the zoo, for example, brought imperial trophies and troop mascots close enough to touch. The majority of the animals on display in the area were relatively unremarkable species. Nonetheless, the area attracted large crowds that rivaled those that surrounded more overtly spectacular displays such as the Elephant House. In most cases, the animals' appeal had less to do with their foreign origins than with the manner of their acquisition. Many exhibits were accompanied by large placards explaining the occupant's species and national origin as well as a carefully edited telling of how it came to be included in the zoo's collection. The story in front of the wild boar (*inoshishi*) enclosure, for example, told of intrepid Japanese soldiers single-mindedly pursuing the animal— like the enemy—across unfamiliar foreign soil. It used the coincidence of the species' name to make a pun on the soldiers' bravery: in Japanese a "wild boar soldier" (*inoshishi musha*) is a soldier who, like the fierce boar, charges straight at the enemy with no thought of surrender or retreat.[40]

In other cases, the displays exhibited animals that represented the *means* through which empire was acquired. The most obvious example of this pattern was the display of army war horses (*gunba*), which were said to have been ridden by general-rank officers as they led Japanese troops into battle. These finely bred creatures were regularly led out of their enclosures and trotted around the area. A display of their tack was also on hand for visitors interested in military paraphernalia. Not all military displays were of such distinguished pedigree. One of the most appealing exhibits in the area was the collection of "war hero" mules and donkeys—the figurative foot soldiers to the officer's horses—which were said to have weathered great hardship in support of their infantry comrades during the war. Such displays of domesticated animals became increasingly elaborate under the military culture of the 1930s and 1940s. They gave patrons the opportunity to thank the nation's rank-and-file soldiers by offering food to their animal representatives, a form of symbolic engagement that might best be characterized as mass-mediated totemism.[41]

The area's only truly exotic—in the sense of being both rare and foreign—inhabitants were also its most popular inmates. Far from wild, the three trophy Bactrian camels were captured from Chinese troops in the bloody 1894 assault on Port Arthur and shipped back to the home islands as a gift from the commander of the victorious First Army Division to the Meiji Emperor. As with many such imperial gifts, the ruminants were transferred to the Ueno Zoo, which retained its role as the main repository of imperial animal trophies after the administrative transfer to Tokyo City. The sovereign's gift to the people was celebrated publicly, as were the camels' endurance and strength. Their arrival—all such new animals were called "new guests" (*shin kyaku*) at the zoo as if they were taking a room at an inn—was applauded in newspapers and in mass-circulation children's magazines such as *Boy's World* (*Shōnen sekai*), *Kid's Country* (*Kodomo no kuni*), and *The Student* (*Gakusei*), which shaped perceptions of the war for kids and their parents. Articles encouraged readers to visit the zoo to feed the camels. As with the mules and donkeys, the primitive display architecture—consisting of little more than wooden railings and scant decorative plantings—allowed patrons to walk up to the camel display and touch the animals.

The camels' exotic character lent itself to less generous rhetorical uses. The hapless creatures were made to speak to the bigotry of empire in the special 1902 edition of *Boy's World* devoted to the Ueno Zoo's twentieth anniversary. Just as mules, donkeys, and horses—common domesticated species all—could be fashioned into representatives of Japanese soldiers serving their country, the camels, as animal embodiments of difference, could be made to stand in for Japan's enemies or colonial subjects. The magazine offered an object lesson in such racialized animal rhetoric when it none too subtly linked the captive camels with the defeated Chinese nation. "At first glance, the camel appears to just be a clumsy, quiet, somewhat stupid animal, but its actual disposition is quite bad," the author writes. "Foreign sources say that camels are quite depraved, and this is certainly true. If camels were people they'd be just like the Chinese."[42]

Commercially speaking, "new guests" were quickly domesticated, worked into the imaginative lives of children who read magazines and storybooks to quench their thirst for depictions of unusual animals, tales of heroic soldiers, and descriptions of the world's latest technological wonders. Like different animals in the zoo, some explicitly imperial and others simply foreign or exotic, genres and items blended together in these magazines, creating exciting connections between fictional stories of adventure, cultures of nonfiction curiosity, and the facts of empire building.[43] Such stories, full of "firsthand accounts" and proper nouns, brought the empire to life, answering a desire that was partially generated by the aesthetics of ecological modernity itself. The imaginative geographies of empire and the wild were often coterminous within the boundaries of these popular subcultures, and they both elicited children's curiosity. This curiosity, in turn, was targeted for mobilization by the zoo and its administrators.

Administrators did their best to keep the institution in the spotlight. Then, as now, managers paid close attention to the media. The zoo's archives are filled with thousands of newspaper and magazine clippings from Japan's imperial heyday—faded records of popular culture, of course, but also evidence of administrative attention. Notes and marginalia in the handwriting of Kurokawa and Koga mark many of these items, exhibiting excitement and, at times, frustration over factual errors or critical comments; dates are crossed out, errors in Latin binomials are corrected, and ideas for additional articles are noted. The director of the Ueno Zoo was—and is—a public figure. Koga, Kurokawa, and Ishikawa were regular contributors to a range of magazines. Kurokawa seems to have been the first to actively pursued the avuncular title of "old man zoo" (Dōbutsuen no ojisan), posing for photos as he brushed a hippo's teeth or smiling as he cradled a newborn bear cub. By the 1920s kids were said to be as excited to meet the zoo director— a fatherly figure presiding over an orderly synopsis of colonized nature—as they were to see many of the animals.

Much like the political empire to which it gave popular form, imperial exhibition was at once a competitive and cooperative enterprise. "Old man zoo" brokered trades and did his best to maintain a steady supply of new and exciting animals. Competing nation-states offered tribute to one another through animal trophies, generating a system of mutual recognition even as they sought to best one another. The zoo's directors and their superiors understood the importance of such exchanges, which symbolically confirmed their place as brokers within the global circuits of imperial trading and gift giving, and the process was initiated early at Ueno. In 1883, less than a year after the zoo opened its gates, the Imperial Navy sent a formation of warships to Australia to execute the Japanese empire's first formal royal animal exchange. With much pomp and circumstance, a Japanese navy admiral took possession of a group of kangaroos and offered a Japanese brown bear in exchange. The gifts were presented in the names of their respective sovereigns. The emperor of the land of the rising sun and the empress of an empire on which the sun never set transacted a reciprocal exchange of recognition, power, and prestige.[44] The process acknowledged Japan as a member of the community of civilized nations—a modern nation-state that recognized the rules of exchange—rather than as an uncivilized territory better suited to safari hunting. It was a transformation that echoed Tanaka Yoshio's efforts at the Vienna Expo of 1873, described in the previous chapter. There, Europeans were asked to recognize not only Japan's unique flora and fauna but also the scientific capacities of a bright young man in samurai garb. Foreign collectors could no longer take interesting or valuable animals with the simple assumption that Japanese specialists would fail to understand their significance.

As the empire grew, so too the means by which the zoo acquired new specimens. With the move into Southeast Asia in 1941, Japan suddenly had direct access to many of the world's most prolific ecosystems. The imperial military conquered ecosystems and social systems alike, and animals flooded into the zoo. The military command expressly ordered the gathering of specimens, which often arrived as publicized gifts from general officers such as Terauchi Hisaichi (1879–1946) and wartime prime minister Tōjō Hideki (1884–1948). Terauchi sent animals to the emperor, care of the zoo, at a pace so brisk that cages and enclosures were soon filled to capacity. Hedgehogs arrived by express plane direct from the frontlines in China in 1939, various breeds of Chinese horses arrived later the same year, Korean deer were presented in 1941, and a veritable menagerie of animals arrived out of the Southern Advance in 1942, including, most spectacularly, a group of Komodo dragons taken from former Dutch colonial possessions in the East Indies. The general

FIGURE 7. Troop mascot, "Hakkō." Named after the ubiquitous wartime slogan "Hakkō ichiū," or "eight corners of the world under one roof," a metaphor for the aspirations of the Japanese empire, this young leopard was donated to the zoo by troops stationed in Manchuria. The placard displayed in front of the enclosure read: "This 'young leopard' was born in the spring of 1941. She was captured and raised by Japanese troops station in China, and her name is 'Hakkō.' She is very tame and was kept as a mascot by the troops before her donation to the zoo in 1942." Image courtesy of Tokyo Zoological Park Society.

martial flavor of institutional life during this period was highlighted in 1942 when the zoo's most spectacular wartime birth, a female giraffe, was named "Minami," or "South," in commemoration of the military's southern advance. The name was selected by popular vote on specially printed ballots distributed to children as they visited the zoo. Examination of the submitted names, still listed in the zoo archives, shows that only three children hoped for the animal to be named "Heiwa," or peace.[45]

At the same time as gifts were arriving from elite patrons, soldiers on the frontlines took it upon themselves to augment the zoo's collection, sending back a broad assortment of animals purchased, stolen, or captured as they entered new areas. The most notable of these trophies was a young spotted leopard named "Hakkō," a truncation of the wartime slogan of "Hakkō icchu," or "eight corners under one roof," a metaphorical representation of the imagined harmony of the Greater East Asian Co-Prosperity Sphere under the rule of the Japanese emperor. Hakkō was a shy animal that had been kept as a mascot by a Japanese unit stationed in Manchuria. When she became too large to keep safely, she was shipped to Tokyo with a detailed history and recommendations to the zoo staff regarding her diet and her deep affection for scratches behind the ears. A short summary of the animal's story, identifying her as a military "mascot" (*masukotto*) donated to the zoo and the people of Japan, was painted on a large placard and hung in front of the quiet cat's cage. Now a mascot for soldiers everywhere, Hakkō quickly became one of Tokyo's favorite animals.[46] In this sense, the young leopard was emblematic of the zoo's broader function. The particularity of this single animal and its story was now made to speak to the larger realities of the war. A leopard could stand in for troops, a camel could signify a conquered country, and the zoo itself could mark the space between civilization and nature, knitting the home front and the frontlines together through material exchange and public display.

IMPERIAL NATURE

As empire and economy grew, so did access to the vision of the world given form at the zoo. By 1939, when the Japan Zoological Garden and Aquarium Association was founded, there were sixteen major zoological gardens in Japan and the colonies along with dozens of research stations, collection outposts, and natural history museums that displayed live animals or taxidermy specimens. Inspired in part by British efforts to create imperial institutions in the colonies, Japanese authorities built exhibitions, museums, botanical gardens, and zoological gardens in cities from Manchuria to Singapore, often in cooperation with local elites. The zoos in Taipei (founded in 1908) and Seoul (founded in 1909) were especially popular. Nearly 370,000 people visited the Taipei Zoo in 1938, for example. More than 700,000 visited the Korean Royal Museum, Botanical Garden, and Zoological Garden the same year. The Korean institution, also known as the Shōkeien Gardens, was an expression of spatial politics on par with the Meiji-era creation of the Ueno Park complex in Tokyo on lands that were sacred to the early-modern Tokugawa regime. The Shōkeien took its name from the Shōtokukyū Palace (Ch'angdŏgung), a private residence of the Korean royal family partially opened to the public as a monument to the pursuit of imperial modernity under Japanese rule.[47]

Ecological modernity was thus often conveyed to colonial audiences as an explicit expression of cultural power. Nonetheless, millions of people, most of them non-Japanese, chose to visit colonial zoos, strolling through living tableaus of their own nation's ecology defined in terms of imperial progress. Local species were displayed alongside animals delivered from other colonies, protectorates, and client states within these gardens. Fauna from Taiwan's mountains and forests, for example, found its way not only to Tokyo and Taipei but also into collections from Seoul to Singapore. Korean animals were found in museums and holdings as far afield as Japanese-occupied Shanghai, the client state of Manchukuo, and Johor, where Tokugawa Yoshinari (1886–1976), a descendant of the founder of the early-modern Tokugawa Shogunate, and others went on safari with Sultan Ibrahim II in an effort to build sympathetic relations. The empire was described in natural terms in such institutions, rendered as a patchwork of animal habitats and species distributions that seemed to pay little heed to national boundaries even as they were made visible and meaningful through Japanese science.

As leaders of the empire's premier zoological garden, Ueno staff were called upon to consult on the construction and management of colonial cultural institutions, many of which they went on to lead.[48] Koga's arrival in Manchukuo, for example, was trumpeted in a 1940 article on the creation of the ambitious and well-funded Shinkyō Zoological and Botanical Garden, located in the center of the capital. Previously known as Changchun, the city was renamed Shinkyō, or "new capital," by Japanese authorities, who embarked on a grand program of modernist urban design. Parks and cultural institutions, as obvious markers of cultural achievement in a newly manufactured nation-state, were a centerpiece of these plans, and Koga directed the development of the Shinkyō complex.[49]

The garden was never fully completed—the war slowed construction—but it was conceived on a scale to "rival the largest institutions in the world," many times larger than Ueno. It was to be, then, the colonial apotheosis of Koga's metropolitan dreams. Botany and zoology came together in this "monument to culture," to borrow a phrase from the institution's first director, Nakamata Atsushi, to provide "views of nature previously unseen in other zoological gardens." Everything was to be on a grand scale, drawing on the latest technologies. "These gardens will allow visitors unprecedented access to the natural world of animals," Nakamata argued, "by combining botanical greenhouses with tropical animal environments" so that animals and plants "appear as they do in natural settings, as one." The gardens would do more than educate with these enclosures, he proclaimed, they would trump the climate of one of the world's "coldest nations," providing the people of Manchuria with a brightly lit hothouse for "comfort and escape" from the dark winters of Northeast China. An aquarium and heated reptile house were also planned.

In contrast to the enclosed microcosm of the tropical exhibits, the exterior portions of the Shinkyō gardens were envisioned as a "world without bars," an "ideal Manchurian landscape" modeled on Hagen-beck's most elaborate designs and exposed to the elements. Native fauna were the first to arrive in these fragments of "living ecology." "Six Manchurian tigers, four Père David's deer, two takin, twenty five deer, three red deer, and an assortment of other small animals and birds" inhabited the early exhibits along with Nero, a male lion bred at Ueno from Ali and Katarina, a pair of African lions that were delivered to Japan's Shōwa Emperor from Haile Selassie I, emperor of Ethiopia in 1931. The lion, Nakamata noted proudly, had "adjusted to the cold with a strength that he will now pass on to future generations of Manchurian lions."[50]

Both Koga and Nakamata place a premium on the exhibition of animals that seemed to be disappearing in the wild, a dynamic that they used to assert the particular importance of zoos in the colonies. "Invading armies often ignore local laws and drive animals to extinction," Koga wrote in an article published in the widely read Tokyo literary magazine *Bungei shunjū* the same year that he visited Nakamata in Shinkyō. Both men were determined that such would not be the case in Manchuria. "It is our hope," Nakamata concluded in his 1940 piece on Koga's visit and the Shinkyō gardens, "that the institution will preserve domestic species already on their way to extinction in addition to performing surveys [of animal resources] and pursuing technical research." Japanese intervention was framed as necessary—rather than contrary—to these conservation efforts because Japanese, unlike Chinese, Nakamata implied, understood how to "institutionalize scientific research."[51]

The economic importance of continental flora and fauna to the Japanese imperial economy was reflected in this focus on native species. It was further amplified in Shinkyō's special effort to acclimatize exotic species for possible husbandry and use. The most spectacular of these plans—unrealized—was framed as an answer to Koga's concerns about the ecological costs of colonial expansion and as a means of symbolically trumping Western nations. "The greatest example of animal extinction through human conflict," he wrote, "is the extinction of wild buffalo (baison) [bison]" along the United States' frontier.[52] In 1933, as relations with the United States were beginning to fray, William Randolph Hearst donated a small herd of bison to the Ueno Zoo. Brokered by Hearst's publishing colleagues at the conservative Yomiuri daily, the gift arrived with the hopes that the steppes of Manchuria, recently conquered by Japan, might offer refuge to North American fauna lost to the culture of manifest destiny. The animals were to be acclimatized and bred with an eye to transforming the ecology of Northeast Asia into a reflection of the North American plains, a move that was meant to reform the steppes into an even more prolific home for the breeding of military horses, among other things. In the end, the bison remained on display in Ueno, but their history speaks to the broad appeal of ecological modernity, notably as it connected to Japan's increasingly militarized vision of nature in the 1930s—the subject of the next chapter. The sense of loss and natural fragility identified by Koga was at work, in different ways and with distinct meanings, as far afield as San Francisco and Shinkyō.[53]

CONCLUSION

The culture of ecological modernity extended far beyond the institutional network that proclaimed imperial preeminence. Scientists, travelers, popular authors, reporters, and amateur natural historians chronicled the conquest of colonial ecosystems for diverse audiences, rendering the association between wilderness—and wildness—and the colonies as natural as the idea that Tokyo was the epicenter of Asian modernity. The exploits of big game hunters such as Tokugawa Yoshichika were recounted in newspapers and pulp magazines for adults and children alike. Widely known as the "duke of the tiger hunt," Tokugawa's travels and those of numerous other colorful explorers, hunters, and collectors lent an air of adventure to the facts of colonial conquest even as Japanese anthropologists, botanists, and zoologists were struggling to catalog the vast biodiversity of the country's new colonial holdings.

The five or six years immediately following the outbreak of war with China in 1937 were an especially heady time for Japan's scientists and collectors. Military expansion brought the diverse ecologies of China and Southeast Asia under Japanese control, and the period saw a flurry of cataloging and classification such as had not been seen since the nineteenth century, when natural-scientific nomenclature was refitted along Linnaean lines. Funded by a government eager to identify strategic and natural resources, scientists were often in the vanguard of the imperial advance. Carefully released to the press, their reports on the bounty of the Greater East Asia Co-Prosperity Sphere helped to reframe military conquest as scientific progress, as if the Japanese movement outward in physical space was also a step forward for civilization.

The period saw a boom in popular works that took readers along on natural-historical tours of the empire, which was rendered into a reservoir of unexploited resources, both physical and spiritual, waiting for Japanese discovery. "Our thirst for knowledge," wrote the geologist Fujisawa Takeo in one such report, "only grew as our scientific eyes [*kagaku no me*] took in everything from geological, zoological, and botanical specimens to the character and customs of the natives." It was as if the Japanese, with their scientific gaze, were the only ones capable of perceiving order in an environment that was otherwise chaotic. Adventure and development coincided in Fujisawa's account so that imperial exploration, the development of Japan's domestic economy, and the satisfaction of scientific curiosity became one and the same thing. Where "natives" saw trees, animals, and food in their environments, Fujisawa and his colleagues discovered "resources" (*shigen*). Fujisawa's "scientific eyes" were looking for raw materials and strategic assets.[54]

The pursuit of empire was thus framed as the satisfaction of curiosity, but such satisfaction, Fujisawa warned, did not come without risks. And these risks were not of the sort that one might expect. Wild animals did not concern the author—his team had military escorts. He was intimidated instead by the sensuous pleasures of colonial nature. Fujisawa reported being almost overwhelmed by the sensual onslaught of the south. It was as if nature welcomed the Japanese "penetration" of Southeast Asia, flooding the senses. "The climate enveloped our bodies," he wrote in the opening pages of his report, leading to "what we called 'southern stupor'" (*nanpō boke*). His team felt such an affinity with the "green jungle nirvanas" of the Malay Peninsula, Burma, Java, and Sumatra that they risked losing track of reason. "The smell of bananas" and the "sounds of wild animals," Fujisawa wrote, saturated the senses of these normally staid scientists so that he feared they might become incapable of reporting their findings back to the reading public.[55] Rationality and biology were once again at odds.

Fujisawa's report was an especially evocative summary of the contradictions that seemed to be at the heart of ecological modernity as Japan and its empire modernized together. The deep desire for contact with "real nature" that runs through his writing was framed as the antithesis of rational contemplation, as if the mind and the body were in opposition. It was a version of the same contradiction that concerned Koga and Inoshita. Modern consciousness seemed to demand a certain detachment from animals and the natural world, but in framing nature as a thing apart, ecological modernity generated its own culture of longing. To lose track of the distinction between oneself and the fecund world of the colonies, as Fujisawa feared he would, was to lose one's self just as surely as the absolute divorce of rationality from biology jeopardized what Koga called the "essence of humanity." Ecological modernity thus came to be characterized by a double desire, a wish for immersion in the "living world," as Nakamata called it, and the need to stand back and contemplate it. Under Koga and Inoshita the zoological garden was meant to answer the need for contact with nature without the risk of complete surrender or physical danger. The animal world was defanged as large predators were converted into "mascots." The new architecture allowed human beings to become the ones who lurked in darkened spaces, watching without being seen.

Not everyone was content to visit a zoo or sit at home and read about exotic jungles and colonial frontiers. Zoo attendance boomed across the early twentieth century, and Japanese travel agencies began to capitalize on the desire for contact with the "wild"—projected outward onto the colonies—as early as the turn of the century. By the 1910s the Japan Tourist Bureau and other agencies were offering package hunting and bird watching tours to Taiwan and Korea. The list of destinations expanded together with the nation's imperial reach. Ueno Zoo staff participated in a number of such expeditions. In 1939, for example, customers could join biologists and others on the twelfth Manchurian Hunt, which targeted big cats and bears.[56] Experts accompanied participants, who were often overwhelmed by the chaos of the natural world that confronted them overseas. A trip to the Shinkyō Zoo, the printed guide for the Manchurian Hunt suggested, might provide a welcome middle step between Tokyo and the colonial wilds.[57]

It is remarkable to think that the twelfth Manchurian Hunt took place in the context of a nation at war. Such blatant expenditures were unusual by 1939. The dreamlife of imperialism sponsored by the zoo began to waiver as the conflict that started in Manchuria in 1931 expanded into China proper in 1937 and then exploded across the Pacific and into Southeast Asia in 1941. Animal feed became scarce, trade with most foreign zoological gardens outside of the empire ceased, and zoo-keepers noted a decided drop in the number of young men visiting the Ueno Zoo as the draft redefined the institution's clientele. Several members of the zoo's own staff were themselves drafted after 1937, and the zoological gardens were redesigned once again, converted into a stage for the celebration of martial culture in the context of an imperial war. By the late 1930s the military culture once confined to the "animal war trophy" exhibits had conquered the entire garden. The core concern of the Ueno Zoo was no longer public education or imperial entertainment. It was the pursuit of total war. As we will see in the two chapters that follow, total mobilization at the zoo meant the mobilization nature and society alike.

PART TWO

The Culture of Total War

FIGURE 8. Animal veterans. "War hero military horse," reads the large white-and-red sign in front of a display for "military animals." Animal veterans were on display at the zoo from the 1890s. Here, a former Imperial Army soldier leads a warhorse out of its enclosure. A large placard explains the role of horses in the army's efforts on the Asian continent. The smaller frame underneath the description holds a military commendation for this particular horse. Similar commendations were found in front of other displays, including exhibits of "war dogs" (*gunken*) and "military pigeons" (*gunkyū*). Image courtesy of Tokyo Zoological Park Society.

CHAPTER 3

Military Animals

The Zoological Gardens and the Culture of Total War

MILITARY ANIMALS

Nature and the natural world—as a concept and a physical resource—played crucial roles in the articulation of Japanese wartime culture in the years between 1937 and 1945. Japanese military and political leaders used the country's limited natural resources as a primary justification for their aggressive actions overseas. Japan, the story went, was a "small island nation" beset by a group of more powerful aggressor states bent on restricting the country's prospects by limiting trade and monopolizing access to the natural bounty of the Asian continent and Southeast Asia in particular. Without access to the petroleum, timber, and ore of the region, ideologues and strategists argued, the country would never be able to experience freedom and national autonomy. The ongoing exploitation of weaker Asian states at the hands of Western colonial regimes provided Japanese propagandists with a powerful justification for the expansion into Manchuria in 1931, China proper in 1937, and Southeast Asia in 1941. Seen in these terms, Japan's national mission was to liberate the natural resources and peoples of Asia from corrupt Western exploitation and to "protect" them in the name of Asian brotherhood and future prosperity.[1]

Expansionist rhetoric was accompanied by broad changes in Japanese dealings with the natural world. The exploitation of natural resources—domestic and colonial—accelerated markedly in the late

1930s as the country geared up for and then executed total war. Total mobilization required the subordination of all energies to the war effort. Short-term military needs took precedence over other claims on resources, both ideological and material. As William Tsutsui points out, unilateral mobilization yielded enduring ecological aftereffects.[2] During the fifteen years of conflict between the invasion of Manchuria in 1931 and the surrender of 1945, the empire's natural resources, like its young men and women, were exploited and sacrificed in an escalating frenzy of consumption that came to encompass all sectors of the imperial economy, including the diverse animal resources under Japanese sway.

Nearly all aspects of Japan's war effort involved the mobilization of animals and animal products. New pressures were brought to bear on domesticated livestock at home and in the colonies. Cultivators and breeders were first urged and then required to increase output and to prioritize the needs of the state over their own. Everything was subject to military acquisition—from properly tanned cow and horse leather, which became infantrymen's boots, to the sheepskins that lined pilots' jackets—even in the face of pressing shortages on the home front. To a surprising degree, given the standard depiction of the Second World War as a consummately modern and therefore mechanized conflict, trained domesticated animals were an important military technology. Horses in particular were strategically irreplaceable. As one author put it in a 1943 article: "It is a great mistake to think that horses have no role in modern warfare. Weapons have become heavier as mechanization has progressed, and horse power has become more and more indispensible as a result." As "living weapons" (*ikeru heiki*), horses were so crucial to the war effort, the author wrote, that "the breeding of strong horses in greater numbers must be ranked alongside the manufacture of tanks or airplanes in military terms." The Imperial Army sought to deploy horses to the field at a ratio better than one horse for every three human soldiers, a stunning mobilization of human and animal biopower.[3]

Other species were enlisted as well. The war effort drafted an eclectic menagerie of animals including but not limited to elephants, camels, yaks, mules, donkeys, pigeons, dogs, and horses. These last three—dogs, pigeons, and horses—played the largest roles. The more exotic species of "military animals" (*gun'yō dōbutsu*)—elephants, camels, and yaks—were acquired as the army conquered new ecosystems and supplies of locally domesticated animals. Usually encountered by Japanese at the zoo or circuses, these species, together with their "native trainers" (*dojin kanrisha*), were put to work hauling ordinance and supplies, tasks that they often accomplished more efficiently in their native environments than imported horses and donkeys.[4]

This physical deployment was facilitated by a new rhetoric of animality. Just as officials attempted to diminish institutional and economic obstacles to state action—facilitating everything from rural administrative consolidation in villages to the creation of corporate cartels—the walls between the human and animal worlds that had been so carefully erected across the nineteenth century were attacked as impediments to victory. Alienation was no longer the central policy question at the zoo; the real issue was how to extract maximum support from all resources under Japanese control, human and otherwise. Mass warfare colonized life on the home front as leaders pursued efficient linkages between domestic production and distant battlefields. Originally framed as treasures whose protection justified violence overseas, families and individuals at home were increasingly asked to see themselves as "national resources" as the war situation worsened, an abstraction that reduced bodies to machines whose value could be measured in work and calories. As the pursuit of war tilted the home front into a "state of emergency," people also became, in a sense, "military animals," populations of physical bodies whose claims to privacy and autonomy were sacrificed in the "state of exception" that defined the fully realized culture of total war.[5]

The Ueno Zoo was a colorful oasis in the midst of this biopolitical gloom. Working with officials in the Ministry of the Army and the Ministry of Agriculture, Koga and his wartime replacement, interim zoo director Fukuda Saburō (1894–1977), who took over direct management of the gardens in August of 1941, endeavored to remake the gardens into a militarized playground, a place where animals turned public attention away from the brutal realities of the war toward stories of chivalrous soldiers and loyal animal companions. Even as life on the front was increasingly characterized by indiscriminant and impersonal death, the zoological garden gave form to a kind of martial nostalgia, urging people to connect their efforts at home with a style of warfare—defined by individual agency and soldierly gallantry—that was in the process of being destroyed on the modern battlefield. A series of popular festivals brought this vision of the war parading into the streets of the capital, where the animal world was made to seem to rise up, apparently of its own volition, in support of the Japanese cause.

As the conflict expanded from China into Southeast Asia and the Pacific, the Ueno Zoo became a funhouse mirror reflecting the utopian dreams of a nation at war. Administrators waged a two-front campaign as they sought to coordinate the activities of the gardens with the bipolar dynamics of imperial wartime: frenetic expansion overseas and countervailing contractions in the domestic economy. First, the representational world within the zoo was turned inward in an attempt to reframe the meaning of life on the home front. Administrators asked visitors to see something of themselves in the animal inhabitants of the zoo, connecting captive creatures with kith and kin rather than with the racialized others of the empire. Adventurous boys were like young warhorses, brave but in need of discipline; gentle giraffes became totems for adolescent girls, wide-eyed and graceful; housewives were asked to laugh in knowing solidarity as lionesses and even hippos tried to feed their young "rations" because raw meat and vegetables were in short supply; and everyone was called upon to recognize the loyalty and discipline of domesticated animals, especially those associated with the military. The zoo's three hugely popular Asian elephants—Tonky, Wanri, and John—were held up as natural exemplars, waving Hinomaru flags during elephant shows and genuflecting solemnly in front of the Animal Memorial (Dōbutsu ireihi), a large cenotaph erected in 1931 as a site for the propitiation of animal spirits lost at the zoo or in the war. It was the first such memorial built in the empire. By 1945 similar monuments were found at nearly all of the empire's major zoological gardens.

At the same time, administrators tried to bridge the streets of the capital with the frontlines, using "military animals" and mascots to connect visitors with the hardships of soldiers overseas. War itself led to a heightened awareness of animals' roles in modern everyday life—as food, labor, and companions—which in turn served to reframe the experience of soldiers overseas in deeply humanizing ways. Rather than linking to the transcendent vision of nature articulated in Kokutai no hongi and other exponents of what Julia Adeney Thomas has called "ultranational nature"—often the work of elite intellectuals and philosophers—the public culture of the war used animals in more humble ways, striving to elicit sympathy for men at war through detailed narratives of personal suffering and heroism. As embodied symbols capable of experiencing pain and feeling pleasure, military animals that had actually participated in the war were especially valuable in this regard. Certain of these "animal heroes" (gunkō dōbutsu) were shipped home, substitutes for the human soldiers who remained on the battlefield. Their celebration was used to create common bonds between those who lived alongside them overseas and those who cared for them on the home front.[6]

MOBILIZING THE ANIMAL WORLD

By the late 1930s the Ueno Zoo's primary mission had become the popularization of the war and the transmission of information deemed important to national victory. The institution had long used animal displays to facilitate the communication of state ideology into the realm of everyday metropolitan life, and these efforts accelerated and concentrated together with the crisis of war. Where diversity had once characterized the exhibitionary work of the gardens—the effort to address diverse audiences on an array of topics—the message was simplified and homogenized as the war deepened.

A policy statement on the management of cultural institutions during wartime, released by Inoshita Kiyoshi's Tokyo Parks Department and approved at the Fourth Annual Meeting of the Japan Association of Zoological Gardens and Aquariums (JAZA) in May of 1943, codified this mission for Ueno and other institutions throughout the empire. Most likely coauthored by zoo director Koga Tadamichi and Inoshita, the outline asked managers of zoological gardens, aquariums, and parks to commit themselves and their institutions wholly to the war effort; it argued that these institutions should be dedicated to achieving three interrelated goals. First, they should work to deepen knowledge of foreign lands—enemy, allied, and colonial. Second, their displays must serve the needs of wartime production by providing patrons with educational exhibits aimed at increasing agricultural production through the application of modern methods of animal husbandry (during the war these activities were carried out in urban backyards and vacant lots as well as in rural settings). And third, the memorandum contended that zoos and Children's Science Parks—Jidō Kagakuen, didactic outdoor play areas meant to introduce urban children to the pleasures of the natural world (there were five such parks in Tokyo in 1943)—were particularly well suited to the inculcation of "scientific attitudes" in the nation's children. This last task resonated with the wider belief—regularly conveyed in official, scientific, and popular media—that national scientific prowess would be a decisive factor in the war.

The Ueno Zoo, Koga argued, had an important role to play in these efforts to "mobilize wonder."[7] The zoo opened windows onto the world outside of Japan unavailable elsewhere in the capital. The report described the institution's activities as follows: "The Ueno Zoological Gardens has brought together a diverse collection of animals from various countries that provide a medium for the communication of complex information about conditions in foreign lands. This endeavor is aided by the posting of simple world maps and information about the distribution of various species. Special attention has been paid to the clear identification of animals from the Greater East Asian Co-prosperity Sphere, whose habitats and ranges are identified on maps as part of the effort to deepen knowledge of Japan's overseas territories."[8]

The zoo's role as a broker of colonial knowledge would be expanded in a variety of festivals and exhibitions outlined in the memo. They included the Southern Ecology Exhibition (Nanpō seitai ten) and an exhibition on animal distribution in South and Southeast Asia (Nanpō dōbutsu bunpu ten), which had already taken place by the spring of 1943. These were to be followed by an exhibition on animals of the Northern Territories (Hoppō dōbutsu ten) planned for the following autumn.[9] The physical extension of Japan's military and imperial reach was thus consciously reflected in the exhibitionary culture of the zoo, which sought to both make the conflict meaningful and to demonstrate the usefulness of the "animal resources" (dōbutsu shigen) now under Japanese sway.

The Northern Territories exhibition would include specimens gathered from Sakhalin and the Japanese-occupied Aleutian Islands. Several foxes and rabbits from the region found their way to Ueno just as Japanese positions on the island of Attu came under attack by Allied forces, an event that marked the inauguration of a new and bloodier phase of the conflict. Attu, a remote and strategically insignificant outpost where Japanese officers had eased their boredom by observing the island's lively bird population, also became home to the first publicly recognized instance of gyokusai, or the "shattering of the jewel," an archaic name for mass suicide in the name of emperor and nation. On this small, cold island an undersupplied Japanese contingent of roughly twenty-five hundred soldiers fought a hopeless battle against a well-supplied Allied contingent five times larger. Rather than surrender, they died nearly to the last man. These martyred soldiers became the standard bearers in what was increasingly characterized as a Manichean struggle against the overwhelming forces of darkness, savagery, and evil.[10]

By 1943 the Ueno Zoo already had a long record of service to this cult of martial sacrifice. Beginning in 1937 the zoo hosted a popular

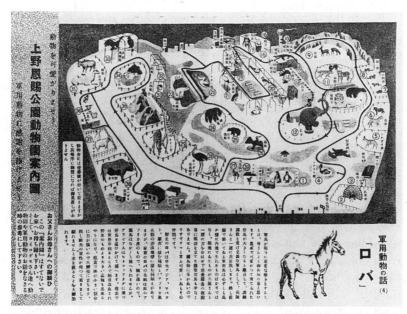

FIGURE 9. "About Military Animals (4): 'Donkey'" c. 1942. This special edition map, one of a series on "military animals," tells readers that it is "not just the well-known army horses" bred in Japan that work with soldiers at the front. They are also helped by a "cute breed with ears so long that it is called the 'rabbit horse:'" the donkey. Image courtesy of Tokyo Zoological Park Society.

series of festivals celebrating the heroism of Japan's "noble" military animals, "silent soldiers" (*mono iwanu senshi*) whose dedication to the war effort was touted as a model for all Japanese. The festivals were to "enhance the people's martial spirit and cultivate their interest in military animals."[11] To this end, a series of "military animal" maps explaining the place of animals in the war effort were provided to patrons free of charge. As these maps illustrate, when visitors set foot in the zoo, they entered a militarized fantasyland, a place where the war came to life in a congenial and sanitized form reminiscent of bedtime stories and fairytales. In a micropolitical expression of larger efforts at total mobilization, the maps encouraged fathers and mothers to take the zoo's militaristic message to their children's bedsides. "A request to fathers and mothers," the small box in the lower left-hand corner of each map asks, "Please do not throw this map away. Take it home and use it when you talk with your children about the zoo and military animals." Even bedtime stories were marshaled in the service of total war.[12]

Within the Ueno Zoo's walled grounds children and adults were encouraged to join in this symbolic enterprise and to celebrate the nation's expansion into new environments, conquest of foreign cultures, and the subordination of the natural world to Japan's imperial project. Troops mounted atop celebrated warhorses led parades, uniformed children saluted loyal animal soldiers, and government scientists explained the natural wonders of the Greater East Asian Co-Prosperity Sphere.

The 1943 memo showed that the zoological gardens were just one component of a network dedicated to making nature and animals appear to speak to the needs of a nation at war.[13] The mass media conscripted animals into ideological service: animals addressed the nation's children in radio programs, they acted as rhetorical proxies of children in everything from newspaper headlines to animated feature films, and they fanned the flames of martial ardor in public spectacles ranging from dog shows dedicated to cleansing impurity from newly codified "Japanese breeds" (Nihonken) to the elaborate parades and competitions of National Horse Day (Aiba no hi). Directing attention away from the deprivations and mass fatalities of modern mechanized warfare toward chivalrous soldiers riding on horseback, tropical hunting expeditions, and the timeless rhythms of a nationalized vision of nature, these depictions of warfare provoked a heightened awareness of the natural world through scarce natural resources, new and exciting flora and fauna, and the militarization of natural aesthetics such as the cherry blossom.[14]

THE EYE OF THE TIGER

According to the Chinese zodiac, 1938 was the Year of the Tiger, a bit of calendrical fortune that augured change for the Ueno Zoo's single captive Panthera tigris. The large male cat, purchased the previous May in anticipation of the event, was the centerpiece of the zoo's New Year's festival. Along with extra helpings of fresh meat, he received heaps of public attention. The creature's image appeared on postcards, in family photographs, and in the newspapers. Late December and early January witnessed a predictable boom in the public fascination with all things tigerish, a fact not lost on those concerned with harnessing public interest. Marketers had long been preparing to capitalize on the tiger image; they leveraged it to the advantage of a variety of products that had next to nothing to do with large, mainly solitary, carnivorous cats whose home range lay thousands of miles from downtown Tokyo. Propagandists did much the same thing, associating the tiger with various causes and groups in the hope that some of the feline's charisma would rub off on their chosen beneficiaries.

One group in particular stood out from the crowd of would-be tigers with its unusually persuasive claim to the beast's qualities of physical strength and rugged determination: the nation's soldiers, legendarily bold, rugged, and virile. The year 1938 also marked the first full year of conflict in the Second Sino-Japanese War (1937–1945)—soldiers and tigers alike were swept up in the celebration. Advertisers and ideologues focused attention on the troops and on mobilizing their families as potential consumers of a variety of goods to be used at home or shipped to fathers, sons, and brothers overseas. The zoo and its popular Tiger Festival served as a nexus for this convergence of politics and capital. The Morinaga Candy Corporation, which boasted a long record of participation in zoo events and regularly drew on the popularity of the zoo in print ads and product packaging, sponsored Ueno's New Year's festival in 1938. Events included an exhibit on tigers, their habitat, and their behavior, as well as a series of marketing opportunities. Banners strung above the zoo's walkways and a special-edition postcard created especially for the event by the well-known painter and member of the Imperial Fine Arts Academy Wada Sanzō (1883–1967) prominently featured the Morinaga name.

Printed in the national colors of red and white, the carefully designed cover urges customers to put the cards to patriotic use. "Let's send picture postcards (imon ehagaki) to our soldiers" reads the large text arrayed above a depiction of a bamboo and evergreen kadomatsu,[15] flanked by the national flag and the expansive radiating-sun standard of the Imperial Navy. If the front cover delivers a political message along the lines of "support our troops," the back cover gives a commercial spin to that support, placing the message "Thank you Mr. Soldier! Let's send the soldiers Morinaga Caramels" above a box of Morinaga Milk Caramels, available for five sen or ten sen, depending on how much one was willing to spend to satisfy a favorite soldier's sweet tooth. Morinaga's trademark cherub hovers in the upper left-hand corner of the frame. The bottom of the front cover states that the card was purchased at the Ueno Zoological Gardens, which itself had fostered the interbreeding of various species of commercialism, politics, and exotic animals since long before Morinaga arrived on the scene.

Wada's ink painting and its accompanying text make the connection between soldier and tiger. Printed in yellow and black and composed

FIGURE 10. "Tora" by Wada Sanzō, 1938. This commemorative postcard was distributed as part of a three-card special set to zoo visitors in 1938 to celebrate the Year of the Tiger.

with confident brushstrokes, the postcard tiger's powerful gaze—focused through pin-prick pupils—meets the viewer with assured strength. The animal's teeth, potentially fearsome, are covered by a faint smile, signaling perhaps that the cat's prey is nearby. Imperial chronology, Confucian classics, and martial rhetoric commingle in the text on the card's reverse side, which contains the following passage: "Tiger: Imperial year 2558 [1938] is the Year of the Tiger. The dauntless tiger crosses one thousand leagues, fearful of nothing. It is said that he topples all enemies. Thanks to our incomparably brave troops, ferocious like the tiger, an eternal peace is being established in Asia. We wish military success and long life to those troops who are being deployed this spring." Like the masterful tiger, Japan's troops subject time and disorder to their righteous control as they cross the vast territories of China.

The passage draws on the positive characteristics ascribed to *tora* (tigers) in East Asian culture and folklore.[16] These powerful animals were the subject of a great deal of literary and political reflection in early modern and premodern times. Writers and scholars made them into metaphors reminiscent of the rhetorical presentation of the lion—*Panthera leo*, the king of beasts—in certain Western traditions. Military leaders included the character for tiger in their names to the extent that *koga*, or tiger's fang, became a synonym for "general," or *shōgun*. The tiger's reign as the "king of beasts" in Asia was placed in jeopardy by Western discourses, which valorized the lion, after Perry's arrival in 1853, however. As Harriet Ritvo points out, for the British, the tiger "epitomized what man had to fear from the animal kingdom and from restive human subordinates."[17] Where the lion was a symbol of nobility and righteousness, a portrayal enhanced by its association with the British royal house, the tiger, viewed as a man-eater in the imperialist West, stood for the seditious inversion of the political and social status quo. The "lord of the hundred beasts" (hyakujū no ō) of the East was an "emblem of savageness and butchery" in the West.[18]

Seventy thousand sets of these cards, nearly all distributed one each to attendees, were printed for the New Year's festival, and a mobile post office was brought in to encourage patrons to send the cards immediately.[19] Such institutional maneuvers converted abstract discourse and propaganda into concrete action. A festively decorated post office, staffed by smiling uniformed attendants, sat within easy reach of the spot on which visitors were handed a neatly arranged postcard that greeted recipients with the message "send me to the troops," creating a sense of obligation. To keep the unusual and collectable gift would be a selfish act in a time when such behavior—even at this micropolitical level—was the target of extensive and well-funded government suasion campaigns.[20] The helpful staff and the actions of other patrons encouraged each recipient to follow his heart and send the card, thus continuing a circuit of gift exchange intended to knit together soldier and civilian, war zone and home front.

ANIMAL SOLDIERS

There was no clearer expression of the reorientation of the zoo's exhibitionary culture in the service of the war effort—and well beyond the walls of the zoo—than the multiyear series of events and festivals devoted to celebrating Japan's "animal soldiers." These were animals used by the military in their maneuvers, first on the Asian continent and later in the jungles and rice paddies of Southeast Asia, most notably horses, dogs, and messenger pigeons. Between 1937 and 1945 Ueno hosted eight highly publicized festivals dedicated to celebrating the contribution of "military animals" (gun'yō dōbutsu) and "animal heroes" (gunkō dōbutsu) to the war. More elaborate than the Meiji displays of animals associated with the imperial military or captured in the colonies, these festivals featured a wide variety of performances, exhibitions, ceremonies, parades, and choreographed demonstrations that allowed patrons to bear witness to the disciplined efficiency of the nation's "silent soldiers." Visitors could consult the schedule published in their daily newspapers to ensure that their visit to the gardens would include at least one performance.

The festivals reached beyond Ueno into other venues in the capital. The 1939 festival ran for ten days in early March and included activities in downtown Tokyo's Hibiya Park—adjacent to the former site of the Rokumeikan and the Yamashita Museum—exhibitions and demonstrations on the wide boulevard leading up to the Imperial Museum at the center of Ueno Park, and numerous events within the grounds of the zoo itself. The Tokyo Municipal Government, the Ministry of the Army, and the Ministry of Agriculture sponsored this free "Week of Gratitude to Army Horses and Animal Soldiers." Other sponsors included the Imperial Equestrian Society, the Japan Horse Racing Association, the Tokyo Horse Breeder's Association, and the record company Victor Japan.

Tokyo's mayor, Kobashi Ichita (1870–1939), kicked off the festival in Hibiya Park by introducing the evening's featured speaker, Fukutomi Hanzō, a lieutenant colonel in the Imperial Calvary. Fukutomi's lecture was followed by a series of speeches, a rousing musical performance, and a movie. While the title of the film shown on this occasion is uncertain, it was not uncommon to screen American Westerns in such festivals prior to Pearl Harbor. America's iconic rugged cowboy resonated with Japan's own imperialist mythology, providing an American counterpart to stock Japanese images of virtuous soldiers mounted on loyal steeds bringing justice to savage lands. The film was followed by a discussion of the place of animals in life at the front, a lecture on the bonds of affection between horses and soldiers, and a variety show put on by singers from Victor Japan's talent pool.

The zoo itself hosted an even more eclectic series of events, which were divided between the zoo grounds and the area in front of the gardens. Inside the zoo an award ceremony for "animal heroes" from the China War accompanied an exhibit of equipment used with military animals, a display explaining animal food and forage in the field, and a hands-on exhibition of veterinary instruments and horseshoe blacksmithing. Pamphlets describing the "Life of an Army Horse" (*gunba no isshō*) were distributed to attendees and a special commemorative stamp was created for the occasion, offering children the opportunity to record their participation in these unique events.[21]

The pamphlet recapitulated one of the primary functions of animal imagery aimed at children during the war: the association of children, typically boys, with the animal soldiers on display. The illustrated

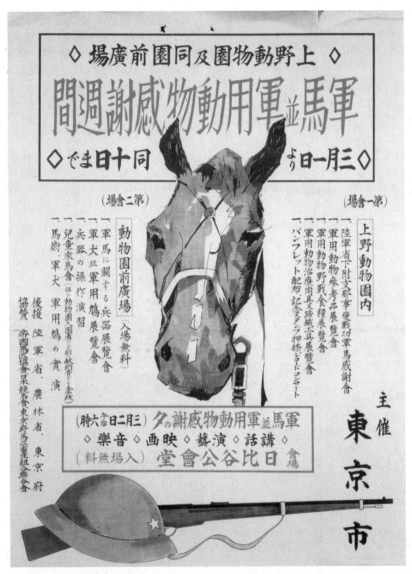

FIGURE 11. Military Spectacle: "Military Horse and Military Animal Appreciation Week." Sponsored by the City of Tokyo with support from the Ministry of the Army and the Ministry of Agriculture, festivities were split between the grounds of the Ueno Zoological Gardens and the central boulevard of Ueno Park. Horses were the main attraction at this event, but visitors could also watch military dogs in action as well as military pigeons. On the evening of the second day, the public was invited to Hibiya Park, where they could hear speeches, listen to live music, and watch a movie free of charge. Image courtesy of Tokyo Zoological Park Society.

booklet, designed to be read to children by compliant parents, tells the story of a war horse through drawings, photographs, and small snippets of text. The first three pages of the story show a young colt as he matures into a young adult, moving from suckling his mother, through his first encounter with a kind uniformed human trainer, a figure reminiscent of the schoolmaster, to running free through empty fields with his adolescent companion horses. The final pages show the horse boarding a transport ship bound for the continent and hauling heavy cannon at high speeds through clouds of billowing dust as soldiers wave rising-sun flags. The simple narrative closes by urging readers to express their gratitude to the horse soldiers, who have willingly given themselves to the Japanese cause. "This is how horse soldiers [gunba] aid our men at the front. We must thank these silent horse soldiers [mono iwanai gunbatachi] from the bottom of our hearts."[22] Not all events were so earnest or militaristic. The award ceremony was followed by a show featuring trained Japanese titmice, a traditional street entertainment used as festive punctuation to the day's events.

The wide area outside the zoo's main gates, where vivid red and white banners and a full array of national and military flags marked the occasion, was converted into a mock battlefield for the exhibition of equestrian heroes as well as their canine and columbine sidekicks. Children, encouraged by publications like the popular children's newspaper Tokyo Grade Schooler's News (Tōkyō shōgakusei shinbun) to wear military garb for the occasion, were offered rides on the backs of horses, a unique chance to play at soldier in an environment populated by "animal heroes."[23] While this youthful cavalry paraded in circles on horseback, impressive teams of Army draft horses hauled large cannon from place to place, and dogs trained to carry messages through enemy territory shot through an elaborate obstacle course to deliver fictional military intelligence into the hands of uniformed military officers. The explosive release of a flock of messenger pigeons said to be carrying children's notes to soldiers at the front capped off the spectacle, a columbaceous expression of the same effort to connect the home front with the frontlines seen in Wada's postcards.

The first military-animal festival, the China Incident Military Animal Memorial Service (Shina jihen gun'yō dōbutsu ireisai), took place over the course of a cool November week in 1937. As its rather unwieldy name indicates, the central event of this and subsequent military-animal festivals was neither the spectacle of trained horses and dogs, nor more innocuous events like the titmouse show, but rather the solemn memorialization of the nation's animal war dead. This funerary aspect contributed to the decision to reschedule the festivals to the early spring, the height of Tokyo's cherry blossom, or *hanami*, season. The traditional symbolism of cherry blossoms, whose transience is evocative of the evanescent life of the warrior, was effectively subordinated to the war effort, a move that affiliated fighting and dying for the state with the cosmic rhythms of nature.[24] Then, as now, zoo attendance during the flower-viewing season—Ueno Park being one of the country's most popular sites for flower viewing—was higher than at any other time. From 1939 until 1943, when the events were suspended, these festivals were scheduled for March and April, a move that effectively placed the military-animal festivals in prime time, guaranteeing large attendance numbers and increasing the chances that the stupa before which children, zoo staff, and Army officers alike bowed in gratitude during the ceremonies would be enclosed by a soft white frame of cherry blossoms redolent of military sacrifice and the romantic impermanence of the warrior's life.

Such events were nothing if not totemic rituals. Deceased military horses, dogs, and pigeons served as surrogates for those lost to the war, offering children and families the opportunity to mourn the death of their fathers, sons, and brothers. Moreover, as generic symbols of the war dead and the costs of conflict, military-animal martyrs offered abstract objects of mourning that appealed to a broad audience at an emotional level without becoming bogged down in specifics. These detached symbols provided a focus of emotive expression that could be shaped according to the needs of those who scripted their stories. These charismatic "silent soldiers" were voiceless icons who did not and could not have a say in the conditions of their military service, symbolic or otherwise. This dumb quality made them especially attractive to propagandists and war boosters.

The zoo, like the mass media, portrayed war animals as ideal soldiers: silent, strong, brave, obedient, and loyal unto death. The dead animals were said to have valiantly given their lives to protect their human soldier-masters, just as human heroes threw themselves into battle for the sake of emperor and country, sanctifying the nation with their blood. The animal heroes' stories, told in newspapers and recited by children or army officers during the memorial services, emphasized that their lives had been taken by the enemy. For their Japanese masters, these animal martyrs allegedly had given themselves willingly over to the war. This distinction was an important one rhetorically. To kill an innocent animal—and these animals were endowed with an innocence as pure as the pedigrees of the shepherds and thoroughbreds on display—was often presented as analogous to taking the lives of women or children. The enemy was brutish and savage because they killed guileless animals. The elaborate rituals dedicated to mourning the deaths of animal comrades cast the Japanese, conversely, as kind masters who shared a deep sympathy with nature even as it was the Japanese military who brought the creatures into harm's way.[25]

HORSE POWER

No animal was more effectively and comprehensively mobilized in the service of empire than the horse. Turning to the emperor illustrates how military horses, at the zoo and without, were used to project a romanticized empire. In his public persona, the Shōwa Emperor appeared in publicity photos and military reviews astride Shirayuki (White Snow), his magnificent thoroughbred Arabian stallion. Together with the emperor's two other most-prized mounts, Hanahatsu (First Bloom) and Fubuki (Snowstorm), Shirayuki was purchased from a breeder in Hungary's famed Babolna region, home of some of the world's most desired bloodlines. Known by name around the country thanks to numerous photo captions and news snippets, Shirayuki embodied the positive qualities associated with pedigreed horses and their noble masters. Each January, as the sovereign trotted Shirayuki past ranks of soldiers arrayed for New Year's inspection at the Yoyogi Review Grounds in Tokyo, Hirohito was at once the commander-in-chief of the nation's modern military and the living descendant of Japan's ancient, noble unbroken imperial line.[26] Modernity and antiquity melded in such depictions.

Unlike man's relationship with dogs, emblems of subservient domesticity, the elevation of this small bespectacled man over the raw physicality of Shirayuki—whose white coat not only signified noble purity but also displayed the animal's striking musculature—signaled a concord between man and nature, ruler and ruled. Shirayuki's willing obedience offered a romantic model for social relationships uniquely congenial to the totalitarian demands of the times. Commentators frequently noted the affectionate bond between Hirohito and his steed. Numerous photographs of the emperor offering treats to horses during inspection tours and the like reinforced this view.[27]

Such images both humanized and mythologized the emperor, and they were reenacted in countless representations of Japan's imperial troops. Depictions of life at the front, in both fiction and nonfiction, regularly featured horses. A disproportionate number of photographs and illustrations of the troops showed them riding on horseback rather than slogging through the mud or ducking fire in a foxhole.[28] Representations of the proud soldier erect on horseback recalled an imaginary age prior to the advent of mass mobilization and mechanized destruction, when individual agency, rather than technological superiority, could turn the tide. The men of such images were heirs to Japan's proud martial heritage (itself woven out of myth) of *bushidō*, the Way of the Warrior, and the cult of the sword. Narratives of this kind portray death as constitutive of character. Such fantasies denied and disavowed the impersonal and anonymous fatalities typical of what some commentators of the time called "scientific warfare," intentionally blurring the separation between man and animal in the effort to elicit voluntary support.

Ubiquitous in popular culture and state propaganda, representations of this kind mediated between the realities of war and its acceptance and support. The lyrics to the hit 1939 song "Beloved Horse March" (*Aiba shingunka*), among the most popular melodies of the war years, conveyed the texture and appeal of these images. The tune by middle school teacher Arashiro Masaichi and lyrics penned by a Shikoku resident named Kuboi Nobuo were the product of an effort by Agricultural Ministry's Bureau of Equine Management to popularize the role of horses in modern warfare. Brought together in Tokyo after a nationwide contest, Arashiro's music and Kuboi's lyrics struck a chord among soldiers and civilians alike, quickly becoming the favorite (and most lucrative) of the dozens of popular tunes that sang the praises of military horses and their masters.[29]

Periodicals advertised the vinyl release of the song. The Ministry of Agriculture and Forestry distributed a large number of scores during festivals and events and sent copies to schools. The song was also widely published in song collections. Its resonance can also be measured by the large numbers of scores and lyrics purchased. Thanks in large part to play on NHK radio broadcasts, over three thousand sets of sheet music for the song were sold by subscription within weeks of the song's release. Kuboi's lyrics were even more popular, with sales topping the forty thousand mark in the same period of time. The song imagines a bond based on shared mortality in an environment where death, falling like rain, is capricious and pervasive:

1. It has been months since I left home,
   Together with my loyal mount, willing to die with me
   I have passed over rivers and mountains
   Holding the reins with a tender touch

2. Snoring on a bunker captured only yesterday
   I catch some sleep today
   Did you sleep well, my horse?
   Tomorrow's battle will be fierce

3. Thanks to you I made it through
   A murky river and a rain of bullets
   Tears running down my face
   As I fed you at the end of that day

4. The charm sent from home
   I hang on this chestnut bay during battle
   How I've come to love
   This muddied whiskered muzzle

5. With a loud whinny calling victory
   Showing how fragile the enemy's ranks
   Charging straight ahead
   With this simple sword

6. I will never forget you
   Splendid bravery as great as any soldier
   Waiving the rising sun from your back
   Singing as we parade into the fortress[30]

Rather than painting a one-dimensional image of the valiant warrior, the song suggests a deeper companionship between human soldier and military horse, describing affection between two imperfect—and therefore more credible—characters. At the same time, the song orients the lonely soldier homeward—even textually, the horse is grammatically juxtaposed with the departure from home in the first verse. The horse has become a surrogate for the soldier's family.

Nothing evokes pathos as powerfully as the death of a loyal companion, and stories of animal fatalities were popular fare during the war. Imagawa Isao and Aaron Skabelund have uncovered the extent to which wartime media used stories of army guard and messenger dogs (*gunken, gun'yōken*)—German Shepherds, Doberman Pinschers, and Airedale Terriers—as a means for coming to terms with death, both animal and human.[31] School textbooks and youth magazines commonly employed such tales of bravery, loyalty, and self-sacrifice to expose children to tempered encounters with death. These encounters not only muted the impact of mortality and loss but also gave meaning to the deaths.

Stories of army horses were especially prevalent in publications aimed directly at soldiers. Reports on horses ranged from paeans to the bravery of stalwart army steeds in the face of certain death to advice on how to best care for one's mount. One adjectival phrase was so widely used that it became conventional in these depictions. Army horses were not simply "army horses" (*gunba*) or even "cherished" or "beloved horses" (*aiba*), they were "cherished horses who share the will to die," or *tomo ni shinu ki no aiba*. The first verse of "The Beloved Horse March" introduces the chestnut bay with this very phrase.

Encounters with animal death were deeply affecting experiences. "I cannot write through these tears," wrote Shirasaki Iwahide, a Pure Land Buddhist priest in the army recalling a scene he witnessed on the frontlines in China. Walking at sundown, Shirasaki came across a group of soldiers who were gathered around a dying horse, each of them weeping as they watched the creature, "an animal possessed of the great strength innate to all Japanese horses [*Nihonba*]," struggle for breath. The animal was too ill to walk to a veterinary officer, several miles distant, and his master, a special-services officer, sat crying with his arms draped around the horse's neck. "Sir," the priest urged the man, "please care for this animal until it passes, but know that when he dies he will certainly be reborn as the Horse-headed Kannon [Hayagriva] and safeguard our army's beloved horses." The priest recalled that the officer thanked him, saying, "He will certainly be reborn as a buddha. He has always fought bravely." As this conversation was coming to a close, a superior officer happened upon the group, scolding them. "Hey! What is this?! Crying? We don't cry!" To which the horse's owner replied, "Sir, the horse is dying," a response that directed the reproachful officer's eyes to meet the horse's gaze just as its body began to slacken and its breathing weaken. He, too, began to sob as the horse died.[32] This community of tears, shared among even the most battle hardened of soldiers upon the death of an animal comrade, was a standard trope in war stories. It provided an outlet for the feelings of sorrow experienced by soldiers whose codes of masculinity frowned upon weakness and explicit emotion. The stories also allowed readers at home to join vicariously in this fraternity of grief.

The message that the priest Shirasaki took away from the tearful episode shows how these stories also funneled assertions of Japan's moral exceptionalism. "How full of human feeling [ninjō] that scene was," he wrote. "I thought to myself, 'This is it!' This is the reason why Japan's troops surpass all others in the world. Isn't this compassion that pours out for a single horse the same compassion that they express for the entire world? The sentiment of 'Peace for Asia' which has been focused on China for so long is a manifestation of the same state of mind that I saw expressed over that single horse. These two things are in fact one, coming from the same caring spirit [aijō]."[33]

Army priests regularly performed rites for army horses, dogs, and messenger pigeons, which were used extensively in place of less reliable and more costly radios. These memorial services responded to the need of soldiers to come to terms with the deaths of dear animals. As one correspondent put it, "Horses and soldiers who battle together become as one [jinba ittai]. Just as many soldiers have given their lives for peace in Asia, tragic tales of horses who have fallen in this foreign land are too numerous to count. Man and horse—the battlefield is red with stories that bind these two spirits together. Such accounts bring tears to a soldier's eyes."[34] The walls between species seemed to collapse in the heat of battle, forging emotional connections that were used to rally troops and metropolitan crowds alike.

As we saw in the case of the 1937 China Incident Military Animal Memorial Service at Ueno, such commemorative proceedings were reproduced as grand spectaculars on the home front, offering thousands, and in some cases tens of thousands, the opportunity to share in the national community of gratitude and grief. 1939's National Horse Day (Aiba no hi), which took place on April 7, was perhaps the most impressive display of ideological horse power during the war. Celebrations took place throughout the empire. The national Buddhist Union (Bukkyō Rengō) mobilized all fifty-six of Japan's major Buddhist sects to host China Incident War Horse Festivals at thousands of temples, large and small, in Japan proper and overseas. As with the festivals at Ueno Zoo, the centerpiece of the program was the mourning of the nation's animal war dead. In this case, however, the celebration was centrally choreographed and performed on the same day at temples throughout the empire, including venues in Seoul and Taipei.

The directors of the Buddhist Union, in consultation with officials in the Ministries of the Army and Agriculture, established the basic program for events at temples. In addition to ritual observances of the war dead, both animal and human, which were to be carried out in accordance with the standard practices of each sect, priests and their lay supporters were to organize "China Incident Army Horse Festivals, services to comfort the restless souls of horses which have nowhere to rest, and venues for the celebration of equestrian heroes" at each participating temple.[35] The Buddhist Union urged zealous cooperation from all individuals, arguing that the events offered an ideal opportunity for the public demonstration of "Buddhist patriotism" (*Bukkyō hōkoku*).[36]

Each major temple nationwide received a comprehensive program of events. Special guests included the standard assortment of local politicians and soldiers in addition to the most honored human guests, those who had either raised or trained horses drafted into the army, a group consisting of thousands (perhaps tens of thousands) of individuals. A listing of such persons was to be obtained and formal invitations were to be mailed to them. On the festival day every temple bell in the nation would ring eighteen times at high noon. Events would include public recitations of poetry devoted to horses, most notably a poem by the Meiji emperor distributed to affiliates together with the program, lectures by soldiers, games of various sorts, and rousing songs about army horses, including "The Cherished Horse March." Crowds on the 7th, already certain to be significant, were augmented by the large number of kindergarten pupils educated on the grounds of the Union's temples. Then, as now, Buddhist temples were among the most prominent sites for preschool education.[37]

The observance of National Horse Day was not limited to Buddhist temples. In Tokyo alone tens of thousands of spectators turned out to take part in celebrations. On the morning of the 7th a grand cavalcade of some fifteen hundred horses, many in full military regalia, paraded across the city accompanied by an even larger number of imperial troops and members of various riding groups. The display constituted a spectacle of raw horsepower not seen in the capital since the elaborate processions of feudal lords from their regional holdings to the shogunal capital of Edo. Events, reviews, competitions, and exhibitions were held in venues across the city, including the imperial review grounds in Yoyogi, Hibiya Park, and Ueno Park.[38] Similar events took place in other major urban centers.

Parade participants in Tokyo began to assemble at the Yoyogi Review Grounds early on the morning of the 7th, growing in number as branches of the Military Horse Training Association began arriving from cities and villages across the Kantō Plain. They were soon joined by members of various youth riding groups, all carrying banners and flags announcing their group's name and proclaiming their allegiance to the war effort or their reverence for the sacrifices made by the nation's brave horses. Colonel Kuribayashi Tadamichi (1891–1945), chief of the Ministry of the Army's Equine Affairs Section, and his troops arrived by midmorning.[39]

Taking up the head of the retinue, Kuribayashi led the procession of "invincible riders" (*muteki kigun*) out of the Yoyogi grounds and into the capital at 11 A.M. Their entrance into the city was celebrated by cannon shot and an enthusiastic version of "The Cherished Horse March," sung by a choir of boys and girls pulled from the city's schools. As the slow-moving procession jangled its way through the warm spring day, it was met by spirited renditions of the March. The parade's route snaked through the center of the city, past the ministry buildings of Kasumigaseki, around the outer edges of the Imperial Palace, through Ginza, the commercial heart of the capital, and across Nihonbashi Bridge. A thirty-minute break at Uchisaiwaicho allowed throngs of children and adults to display their gratitude to the "brave" horses by offering them water and fresh carrots. Thus fortified, the formation marched on to its ultimate destination, Kudanzaka, the location of the Yasukuni Shrine, center of the nation's cult of war dead. There, they dedicated prayers and speeches to soldiers lost to the war, human and otherwise.[40] This solemn event was repeated regularly, though in less grandiose form, at Yasukuni. A statue to martyred horses, dogs, and pigeons still stands prominently within the shrine grounds today.

Events on the 7th did not end in Kudanzaka. At 3 P.M. crowds at Yoyogi cheered an exhibition of military tactics featuring precision drills, exhibitions of strength and speed, and mock cannon fire, events that had been rehearsed at the zoo during earlier festivals. The festivities at Yoyogi were followed by a full-scale "Horse Night" in Hibiya Park on the other side of the imperial palace. The Minister of the Army and the Minister of Agriculture appeared as special guests, where they joined the crowd of several thousand to watch performances by dance troupes, storytellers, comedians, a children's drama company, and singers after a set of formal speeches.[41]

These events, which recurred in various forms throughout the war years, were designed to meet concrete political and military goals even as they stoked the fires of patriotism. In addition to projecting romantic images that belied the brutal realities of modern warfare, horses were essential to the execution of the Japanese military command's tactical agenda. National policy makers concerned with increasing the nation's equestrian population envisioned that such spectacles would generate support for the country's vast horse breeding programs. Much of the conflict was fought on terrain that was too damp, too rough, or too mountainous for motorized vehicles; horses provided a source of transport well adapted to use in such difficult conditions. As one official put it, the nation's pronatalistic policy of "bear children and multiply" (*umeyo fuyaseyo*) applied to mares as well as mothers.[42]

CONCLUSION

War brings death, and death was given a formal place at the Ueno Zoo in November 1931, on the cusp of the nation's long descent into total war. Two months earlier a group of Japanese military officers had detonated a small quantity of explosives along tracks owned by Japan's South Manchuria Railway Company. Blamed on Chinese elements, the explosion provided a pretext for the invasion of Northeast China, the area commonly known as Manchuria, home to the Japanese client state of Manchukuo from 1932. It was in this heightened context, as newspapers began to fill with photographs of troops overseas mounted on horseback, that the gardens unveiled the first public Animal Memorial (Dōbutsu ireihi) built at a Japanese zoological garden. The unveiling was presided over by Buddhist nuns from Nagano's Zenkōji Temple and attended by dozens of officials and visitors. The monument marked the public acknowledgement of a simple fact of life at zoological gardens everywhere: death. Dedicated to the conservation and celebration of living creatures, zoological gardens tend to sequester death, hiding it behind the walls of animal hospitals, managing it through careful press releases or, for less well-known animals, silence. Even today, only the most charismatic animals draw enough public recognition to require more than the collection of mortality information for legal, accreditation, or conservation purposes. To publicly recognize mortality in an environment defined by captivity—and thus almost total animal subordination to human agents—is to risk community criticism, reduced attendance, and unwelcome curiosity about the world behind the exhibition.

Until well into the post–World War Two era most zoological gardens were lethal places for animals. "Surplus" fauna was regularly culled; husbandry and exotic animal veterinary medicine were in a provisional state. It was only warfare that brought sustained medical (as distinct from scientific) attention to exotic animals in Japan. Former zoo director Kurokawa Gitarō had been trained in veterinary medicine, and nearly all zoos kept a veterinarian on contract or on staff, but exotic animal treatment was not systematized until the Imperial Army took an interest in the 1930s, when the tactical potential of such animals became clear. Elephants, yaks, and camels, among other species, were discussed and studied at the Army Veterinary Hospital, where zoo director Koga Tadamichi trained in the years after his graduation from Tokyo Imperial University, and to which he returned at the rank of colonel when he was called up in 1941.[43]

The public recognition of death—its mobilization as ritual and spectacle—is one of the things that sets Japanese zoos in general and the Ueno Zoo in particular apart from gardens in other places. According to a 2002 survey of sixty-nine Japanese zoological gardens by Daimaru Hideshi of Hiroshima's Asa Zoo, 69.6 percent of gardens had monuments for deceased animals. Most of these monuments, like the zoos that held them, were created during the postwar high-growth decades from the 1960s to the 1990s, but monuments also spread within the prewar network of the Japan Association of Zoological Gardens and Aquariums. Memorials were built as military culture became normalized at gardens from Seoul (Keijō) and Taipei to Kyoto and Sendai, and by 1945 more than half of the zoos in the empire housed permanent public memorials. Several others hosted memorial services for deceased zoo animals on a regular ritual calendar, most often in synch with national Animal Appreciation Week in the autumn, but occasionally in line with Ueno's springtime schedule for military-animal propitiation rites, designed to make the most of the familiar association between cherry blossoms and fallen soldiers.[44]

The appeal of such monuments was manifold. It extended beyond military matters into the broader culture of ecological modernity wherein monuments and ceremonies offered ritual surety in the midst of an increasingly industrialized society. It is a central irony of modern everyday life that a sense of alienation from animals and the natural world has developed within an economic system that has brought unprecedented efficiency to the exploitation of natural resources, animal and otherwise. Meat eating and pet keeping both became more prevalent as the archipelago industrialized, and Ueno's Animal Memorial has been used to address losses in both of these practices as well as to propitiate the spirits of dead zoo and military animals. Even today the Ueno Zoo remains as much defined by death as it is by life. All creatures die, of course, but death has become a central pillar of the zoo's institutional folklore in the decades since 1945, when the bombings of Hiroshima and Nagasaki gave blinding form to the threat of extinction (*zetsumetsu*)—human and animal—that slowly emerged as the institution's most dependable claim to relevance in a changing postwar world.

It is tempting to cast the creation of these memorials and monuments in the most positive terms, and they are rich reflections of a Japanese willingness to recognize animals in ritual practice, especially when viewed in comparative perspective. Militaristic or not, the staff at Ueno chose to recognize the loss of the animals under their care. Records and common sense tell us that the zoo's keepers often developed deep emotional bonds with the animals under their care, and even today zoo staff can be seen laying flowers at the Animal Memorial as they offer quiet, personal prayers, often after hours or when crowds are not present. But rituals and monuments do more than simply recognize lost lives; they can, as Barbara Ambros argues, offer validation for the exploitation of animals. Rites of propitiation, Nakamaki Hirochika observes, can function as validation for the exploitation of animals as well as an admonition against it.[45] Indeed, by addressing the tensions between ought and is, between the facts of how animals actually are treated and how many people believe they should be handled, such rites may, under certain circumstances, ease the killing of animals. They can help to reframe slaughter as sacrifice.

CHAPTER 4

The Great Zoo Massacre

As I see it, the relationship between the potential victim and
the actual victim cannot be defined in terms of innocence
and guilt. There is no question of "expiation." Rather, society
is seeking to deflect upon a relatively indifferent victim, a
"sacrificeable" victim, the violence that would otherwise be
vented on its own members.

—René Girard, *Violence and the Sacred*

Sacrifice fortifies social borders—between kin and non-kin;
animal and human; man and God—by its very staging of
their threatened collapse.

—Susan L. Mizruchi, *The Science of Sacrifice*

THE CULTURE OF TOTAL SACRIFICE

The most disturbing thing that ever happened at the Ueno Zoo was the
systematic slaughter of the garden's most famous and valuable animals
in the summer of 1943. At the height of the Second World War, as the
Japanese empire teetered on the brink of collapse, the zoo was transformed from a wonderland of imperial amusement and exotic curiosity
into a carefully ritualized abattoir, a public altar for the sanctification of
creatures sacrificed in the service of total war and of ultimate surrender
to emperor and nation. The cult of military martyrdom is often recognized as a central component of Japanese fascist culture, but events at
the zoo add a chilling new dimension to that analysis.[1] They show that
the pursuit of total mobilization extended into areas previously unex-
amined, suggesting how the culture of total war became a culture of
total sacrifice after 1943. In staging the collapse of the zoo's symbolic

society—the figurative disintegration of ecological modernity—Japanese leaders used the spectacular charisma of the garden's animals and the ritual mechanisms of animal propitiation to promote a cult of martyrdom on the home front meant to encompass the human and the animal worlds alike.

The killings were carried out in secret until nearly one-third of the garden's cages stood empty, their former inhabitants' carcasses hauled out of the zoo's service entrance in covered wheelbarrows during the dark hours before dawn. By early September twenty-seven specimens representing fourteen different species had been killed, most with poison, some by starvation, and a few by strangulation or with bloody hammer blows and sharpened bamboo spears wielded by the same keepers who had nurtured the animals with care just days before. The creatures that were killed included nationally famous animals such as Ali and Katarina, Abyssinian lions sent to Emperor Hirohito from the emperor of Ethiopia; Hakkō, the leopard mascot famously captured by Japanese troops during the invasion of Manchuria; and, most memorably and most tragically, John, Tonky and Wanri, performing elephants known to children throughout the empire thanks to starring roles in school textbooks, children's stories, and magazine feature articles.[2]

The slaughter was a cruel process made particularly sickening by the sense of betrayal that permeated each step. When keepers arrived with piles of poisoned raw meat and fresh vegetables rarely seen during the lean war years, many of the creatures dived in with gusto; ursine species grunted with satisfaction as they ate horsemeat laced with massive doses of strychnine; big cats purred with relish as they tore into lethal cuts of meat. Only the elephants, intelligent and sensitive to human emotional cues, demurred entirely, perhaps responding to the misgivings of their trainers, perhaps repelled by the strychnine that oozed from the fresh potatoes and carrots used to tempt them. When animals took the bait, their caretakers watched in horror as hungry satisfaction turned to panic; many of the men turned away in revulsion as the chemical agents triggered an escalating series of muscle spasms that usually culminated in cardiac arrest. Strychnine works slowly and has no anesthetic or sedative properties. It was, as one keeper put it, "a terrible, pathetic way to die."[3]

Orders from the highest echelon of the Tokyo government said that rifles, kept at hand for use in cases of escape, were not to be used in the killings. Public disorder was the paramount concern, and anxiety about secrecy took precedence over animal suffering. Strychnine was brutal but quiet; rifle shots were impossible to conceal given the zoo's proximity to a densely populated neighborhood.

The men who carried out the killings felt betrayed themselves. Most of the zoo's professional staff did not agree with the orders dictating how the slaughter was to be carried out. In a dynamic that belies facile assertions of an easy match between official wartime doctrine and actual social practice, employees showed remarkable creativity as they resisted harming the animals at all. Citing (and sometimes manufacturing) plans for food substitution, animal evacuation, and emergency euthanasia, the zoo's staff, led by interim zoo director Fukuda Saburō, urged a reasoned approach to the problems of zoo keeping during wartime rather than the zealous pursuit of "holy war." If limited feed was an issue, guidelines called for the investigation of food substitutes before euthanizing irreplaceable animals. If escape during bombardment was a concern, arrangements could be made to evacuate the animals to rural holding pens or regional zoos, which were eager to show the high-profile animals kept in Tokyo. And finally, if bombing was imminent or cages were in fact damaged in a raid, zoo staff was trained in the use of Winchester rifles. Training exercises showed, Fukuda claimed, that the most dangerous animals could be dispatched in the time between the first air-raid siren and the likely arrival of aircraft overhead. Seen in this light, the entire episode provides a microhistory of fascism's contested emergence during the war, showing how the discourse of martyrdom for the nation—as a particular kind of death—moved to center stage at the zoological gardens and in the broader culture.

There was, Fukuda and others asserted in a variety of letters and memos, no need to carry out most of the executions as ordered, and staff sought at each step to stall, divert, or simply stop the killings. These acts of resistance were met with rebuttals from the office of the capital's governor general or his parks commissioner, Inoshita Kiyoshi. Indeed, this entire bizarre episode of animal slaughter, what I have chosen to call the "Great Zoo Massacre" following Robert Darnton's rich analysis of the "Great Cat Massacre of Rue Saint Severin" in eighteenth-century Paris, was orchestrated by a man with little knowledge of the zoo's day-to-day administration, Ōdachi Shigeo (1892–1955), the imperially appointed governor general of Tokyo. Ōdachi followed up the secret killings with a spectacular public pageant reframing the deaths as acts of martyrdom in the service of the nation. One of the most powerful and influential men in the Japanese empire, Ōdachi became home minister slightly more than a year after ordering the massacre.[4]

That the animals would be killed when food was scarce or in anticipation of Allied bombs that might lead to escapes was not surprising. Similar killings had recently taken place in London and Berlin, and the zoo's staff knew of them.[5] Just as in those cases, food was short and loss of control over the animals was a possibility in the event of an air raid. In consultation with Director Koga Tadamichi and Commissioner Inoshita, Fukuda and his staff developed elaborate plans to answer these and related questions. These plans and the deteriorating war situation explain the timing of the events; the war had entered a "critical phase" in 1943—*jikyoku* in the parlance of the time—and the animals could not be kept as they always had been. The plans are less helpful, however, in explaining the peculiar details of the massacre. That someone of Ōdachi's importance—one of the empire's most important technocrats, the man most directly responsible for managing the imperial capital—would take such an active role in the public *staging* of the slaughter is something of a riddle. He could have ordered the killing with the stroke of a pen.[6]

At first blush, the killing of creatures captured from the wild or carefully bred in captivity and selected for exhibition due to their ecological, scientific, cultural, or political value seems to run entirely counter to the mission of the zoo, and Ōdachi's participation only exacerbates one's sense of confusion. Why did someone of Ōdachi's stature get involved in such questions so soon after his promotion to Governor General of Tokyo, a new position created by the Home Ministry to rationalize control over the imperial capital at a critical moment? As the empire threatened to shatter, why would Ōdachi, a man who had also been special mayor (tokubetsu shichō) of occupied Singapore—the top civilian administrator—and who knew more than nearly anyone about the state of affairs at the edge of empire, concern himself with such an ostensibly marginal matter?[7]

It is a moment much like the one that inspired Darnton's exploration of artisanal culture under the *ancien régime* in France. Darnton's investigation started with a singularly unfunny joke, the riotous slaughter of a shop master's cat by workers in Paris and its subsequent parody in mocking puns and performances. "Where is the humor," Darnton asks, "in a group of grown men bleating like goats and banging with their tools while an adolescent reenacts the ritual slaughter of a defenseless animal? Our own inability to get the joke is an indication of the distance

FIGURE 12. Tokyo governor general Ōdachi Shigeo and members of the Youth Society for Buddhist Tradition (Shidō Bukkyō Seinen Dentō Kai) leading the procession to the Memorial Service for Animal Martyrs on September 4, 1943. Crowds of youngsters from the surrounding neighborhood can be seen following the procession. The Elephant House stands in the background of this image, shrouded in red-and-white curtains, or *kōhaku*, sometimes used to mark ceremonial space. Courtesy of Tokyo Zoological Park Society.

that separates us from the workers of pre-industrial Europe." That recognition of distance can provide a starting point for fruitful investigation. "When you realize that you are not getting something—a joke, a proverb, a ceremony" that is particularly meaningful to those on the ground at the time, he finishes, "you can see where to grasp a foreign system of meaning in order to unravel it. By getting the joke of the great cat massacre, it may be possible to 'get' a basic ingredient of artisan culture under the Old Regime."[8] Similarly, by decoding another puzzling ceremonial slaughter—the massacre of a number of well-known and valuable animals at Tokyo's Ueno Imperial Zoological Gardens in 1943—we may grasp some of the central dynamics of life on the Japanese home front in the context of imperial collapse.

For many of those living in Tokyo at the time, Ōdachi's involvement was just as puzzling in 1943 as it is today. This makes it all the more intriguing for historians. Even in the midst of total war, it was a moment marked by an appalling rupture of the imperial quotidian, the shocking irruption of the bloody war and its irrational sacrifices into a landscape of leisure, curiosity, and conquest, one of the few places that might have seemed insulated from the real-world complexities and costs of imperial life, a retreat where one could still imagine taking one's children for a day of fun and distraction. This sense of disruption and change appears to have been the intention of Ōdachi's involvement. The war entered a new and particularly lethal phase in 1943. Henceforth there could be no haven from the demands of the conflict, no private life exempt from the needs of the nation, and no escape from mobilization, no matter how temporary or seemingly inconsequential.[9]

A STRANGE SORT OF CEREMONY

Only when all of the killings were completed were they made public, and then in a carefully choreographed religious pageant. The centerpiece of the governor general's involvement was an elaborate memorial service staged on the grounds of the zoo on September 4, 1943. On that day, as afternoon temperatures climbed into the mid-eighties and newspapers celebrated Japan's war against the Allies, hundreds of officials and spectators followed Governor General Ōdachi and a group of formally costumed Buddhist monks, led by Ōmori Tadashi, chief abbot of Asakusa's Sensōji Temple, out of the tree-lined central promenade of Ueno Park, under the gates of the zoo, and down into the gardens. The solemn parade wound through the eerily hushed grounds past empty cages. As they walked, officials found themselves shadowed by a second, less organized sort of pageant; dozens of children from the surrounding neighborhood had heard that something unusual was happening in the zoo. Typically curious and eager for news of their favorite animals or strange goings on, the children had snuck in by a variety of routes known to those who grew up in Nezu, the neighborhood of narrow streets and tightly packed houses that bordered the zoo to the east. After a few short moments, the processions arrived at their destination: a large white tent hung with banners announcing the "Memorial Service for Martyred Animals."[10]

Abbot Ōmori and his monks entered the tent first, heads bowed as they shuffled past lines of chairs to the dais at the front of the large enclosure. They were followed by Ōdachi and then, after a short but meaningful distance, by Prince Takatsukasa Nobusuke (1889–1959), chair of the Japanese Association of Zoological Gardens and Aquariums and father-in-law to the Shōwa Emperor's daughter. Like the Shōwa

FIGURE 13. Abbot Ōmori Tadashi leads the Memorial Service for Animal Martyrs at Ueno Zoo. Certain of the animals were eventually buried under the ground occupied by Ōmori, who kneels facing a cenotaph dedicated to the spirits of dead animals. It is worth pausing to consider this image in its immediate context. At a time when thousands of soldiers and civilians were dying each day in the war overseas, hundreds of officials and select members of the public were asked to break with routine and visit the zoological garden for an animal memorial service sponsored by one of the capital's most powerful civilian administrators. Image courtesy of Tokyo Zoological Park Society.

Emperor himself, Takatsukasa was part of a long tradition of aristocratic naturalists and outdoorsmen. He became particularly well known in the prewar years for his ornithological surveys, even garnering the nickname "Bird Prince" (Kotori no kōshaku).[11] He served in the House of Peers before moving on in 1944 to become the chief priest of Tokyo's Meiji Shrine, the complex of beautiful buildings built to honor Japan's first modern monarch.

Many of the fine details of the ceremony are lost, destroyed in the chaos of the war years, but we do know that it included some five hundred formal participants, including dozens of municipal and national politicians and elite bureaucrats, as well as an array of imperial military officers and representatives of the Kenpeitai, the Japanese military police. Behind these men came a carefully selected collection of Tokyo residents perhaps believed to represent the ceremony's intended audience: women and children on the home front who had become the garden's primary clientele in the years since the beginning of the war with China in 1937. This group included representatives from the recently formed Greater Japan Women's Association (Dai Nihon Fujinkai), young women from the capital's women's colleges, and a selection of boys and girls from the Tokyo school system.[12]

Once inside the tent, the group was welcomed by Abbot Ōmori and asked to sit quietly as the monks began to intone a sutra in memory of zoo animals "sacrificed to the critical war situation" (*jikyoku sutemi dōbutsu*). As the monks solemnly read the sutra and dozens of news reporters took notes, one person after another moved forward to offer incense and bow before a funerary tablet inscribed with the words "animal martyrs" (*jun'nan mōjū*), an appellation that drew on language long used to sanctify human sacrifice in the service of war. Resonant and respectful, the term *jun'nan*, or martyr, was ubiquitous in a wartime discourse centered on a cult of sacrifice for the sake of nation, emperor, and family. The same term is used by many Japanese Christians to describe Christ's sacrifice on the cross. Before the war's frenzied final phase, however, such "martyrdom" tended to be reserved for the sacrifice of soldiers on the front.

Governor General Ōdachi and Prince Takatsukasa were the first to approach the dais. They were followed by an array of officials beginning with the deputy governor general and ending with the school principals from throughout the city. Next came Aoyama Hiroko and Hanasawa Miyako, teenagers in their first year at Takedai Girls' Higher School, equivalent to boys' middle school. When the young women finished making their offerings and bowing their heads before the memorial, a pair of younger children, Satō Sadanobu and Waki Takako, came forward. Sixth-graders at the Shinobugaoka National Elementary School in Tokyo, Satō and Waki recited quick words of mourning and made their offerings with heads bowed. The Office of the Governor General made certain that news reporters had the correct information for each of the participants: their names, schools, and ages.

An article published in the nation's largest daily the morning after the ceremony described the scene:

> A young boy and a young girl stood with their hands clasped and heads bowed before a small mortuary tablet of unfinished wood inscribed with the words "Animal Martyr Mortuary Tablet" (*jun'nan mōjū reii*). A memorial service for zoo animals martyred for our nation took place at 2 o'clock on the afternoon of September 4 at the Ueno Zoological Gardens. The service was held in front of the Memorial for Deceased Animals located between the Elephant House and the Nilgai Enclosure. Written in ink at the entrance: "Memorial Service for Animal Martyrs." Incense floated through the air before a new stupa, light flickered across an altar surrounded by mountains of the animals' favorite raw meats and sardines, carrots, and fruits. Bouquets of

flowers were even personally laid before the altar by Governor General Ōdachi and Prince Takatsukasa Nobusuke, Chairman of the Japanese Association of Zoological Gardens and Aquariums.[13]

Parks Commissioner Inoshita, the article relates, brought the formal ceremony to a close, ending his remarks with this caution: "We want people to give serious thought to the dire circumstances that demand these extraordinary measures." The article finishes with a melancholy flourish. The formal service may have been over, "but smoke from new incense continued to rise for many hours, put there by the small hands of neighborhood children who heard rumors of the funeral and crowded in one after another, anxious to say good-bye to the lions and tigers they had loved so long and known so well."[14]

The killings took place in secret to preserve the impact of this public event and to prevent any spontaneous expressions of dissent. The representation of the deaths, rather than their actuality, mattered most to Ōdachi. This carefully choreographed spectacle appears to have been addressed to two audiences. The first and most obvious audience was the millions of Tokyoites and others who read about and visited the zoo each year and identified with its famous animal inmates. The second included elite bureaucrats, politicians, military leadership, and technocrats in the Home Ministry. In each case, it was Inoshita's appeal that people "give serious thought to the dire circumstances" of the war that best expressed the governor general's intended message.[15] Such a statement implied (but was carefully phrased so as not to directly assert) a change in the course of the war and asked people to consider what such a change might mean.

Ōdachi used the zoo killings—and the intervening media of the animals themselves—as a way to address one of the great taboos of official speech in Japan at the time: defeat. When the governor general and his subordinates such as Inoshita referenced the "critical war situation" (*ji-kyoku*), they were in effect asking people to look down a road toward possible defeat and even greater personal sacrifice. The public spectacle of men, women, and children processing into the zoo to mourn "animal martyrs" that had to be sacrificed because of the deteriorating war situation was the beginning of the governor general's campaign to shift the terms of public discourse and inure the people of Tokyo to the demands of a failing empire. It might also be seen as a small but important step toward the tragic mass suicides and hopeless unarmed charges that brought the war to a gory crescendo in 1945.

Prior to being posted in Tokyo in 1943, Ōdachi served as governor general of occupied Singapore, and in that capacity he watched the Japanese empire expand and then, with terrifying speed, begin to contract as the weight of American industrial power swung behind the war effort. Already by 1942 the Japanese Navy had suffered its first defeats at the Coral Sea and Midway, and Ōdachi, as the man ultimately responsible for mobilizing the capital's population to resist an invasion, was looking for a way to cut through the white noise of official propaganda. The anonymous mass death and brutal hardships of the frontlines would soon be visited upon the capital's populace, he believed, and the triumphalist narratives of Japanese victory that filled newspapers and official pronouncements had allowed some to grow woefully out of touch with the real war situation.[16] Similarly, and perhaps even more importantly to a technocrat like Ōdachi, certain policy decisions in the capital were being made based on the official narrative of continued conquest. In the wake of the strategically insignificant but symbolically humiliating Doolittle Raid of April 1942, the Imperial Army had promised that "not a single enemy plane" would ever again darken Tokyo's skies. Such assertions continued into 1943, even as the empire began its cascade. To prepare for bombardment was to put the lie to the military's pledge, and Ōdachi moved carefully as he began the process.

The governor general was dealing with powerful political forces when he ordered the sacrifices. Even for someone of his stature, the question of defeat was not easily broached in public discussion. In private, people had been talking of such things freely for years by 1943, but the boundaries of permissible public speech were still carefully policed, and he was a civilian administrator dealing with military questions.[17] As often happens with the mythology of war in times of military failure, by 1943 a significant gap had developed between the realities of Japan's war situation and the orthodox image of the conflict recognized in the state-monitored public media. Ōdachi apparently saw the sacrifice of zoo animals as a way to bridge this gap without provoking censure from those who monitored the acceptable frontiers of expression.[18]

By addressing the issue via the zoo animals, Ōdachi gained a large audience and avoided interference from the military or others in the government. The zoo massacre could be framed as a simple act of expediency rather than a major policy decision. And the actual killings were easily justified to anyone who might question Ōdachi's motives. As Fukuda argued when visited by concerned police officials and members of the military police in the closing days of August, at a time when many human beings could not secure enough calories to sustain themselves it was increasingly difficult to justify keeping large carnivorous animals in the zoo. And furthermore, the killings could be said to have been carried out in order to keep public order. Citing the zoo's emergency plans, Ōdachi suggested that killing the animals was prudent given the chaos that would erupt in the event of a cage breach. "A single bomb might kill dozens or even hundreds of people," he is quoted as saying, "but human beings instinctually fear a single tiger far more than any bomb."[19] As for Ōdachi's particular flourish, he made certain that the public memorial service was recorded and broadcast via the mass media. It was painted as an act of compassion aimed at children. Who would deny Tokyo's children the opportunity to mourn the poor animals they had "loved so long and known so well"?[20]

This public ritual was an early rip in the fraying fabric of wartime official culture, a culture that would, within two short years, call upon all imperial subjects to be ready to sacrifice themselves and their families in a Manichean struggle against the overwhelming power of the American military. In 1943 the ethos of total sacrifice was just moving to center stage, the ethos that would lead hundreds of young men to fly stripped-down aircraft into American warships and inspire women and children to begin training with bamboo spears in the hopes of holding off heavily armed Allied soldiers.[21] This ideal of absolute self-surrender to the emperor and the nation—the dark heart of what postwar Japanese scholars have labeled the "emperor system"—had long been present in Japanese discourse. It was the *scope* and *subject* of Japan's wartime cult of martyrdom that were changing in 1943. By the summer of 1945 official culture would celebrate the conviction of mothers to offer their lives and those of their children for the country, a merciless echo of the massacre of these "animal martyrs." In the early years of the war such status was generally reserved for soldiers at the front. The Great Zoo Massacre, then, is also a potent reminder of the necessity of treating warfare as an evolving—and contingent—process rather than a single, coherent event.

Ōdachi's policy choices indicate that he was concerned first and foremost with public order in the capital. His second concern seems to have been to prepare the people of Tokyo for possible violent resistance in the event of invasion rather than warning them in the hopes of saving lives. He was charged with preparing the city for bombardment, and this was one rather small—though perhaps uniquely telling—aspect of those preparations. No longer would the cult of martyrs be limited to

soldiers on the frontlines. As the empire collapsed, so did the humanizing logic of ecological modernity. Families on the home front were now
called upon to prepare themselves for acts of bodily heroism and martial sacrifice. In 1943 what had long been a question for soldiers *elsewhere* in the empire, whose sublimated sacrifice was mourned by those
at home, was in the process of becoming an issue for men, women, and
children *at home* in Japan. The entire nation—with the crucial exception of the emperor himself—would now be called upon to play the role
of martyr.[22] And indeed, in the full expression of this logic the whole
nation might theoretically be sacrificed to preserve the exceptional status of the emperor.

As was shown in the previous chapter, eulogizing soldiers' hard lives
and valiant sacrifice had long provided the central focus for a wartime
ideology aimed at spurring productivity and discipline on the home front;
bringing the practices (rather than the ideal) of heroic self-destruction
into the households of the imperial capital was something new. With
the fall of the Japanese-occupied Aleutian island of Attu in 1943, in
which a contingent of twenty-five hundred soldiers sacrificed their lives
rather than surrender, the term *gyokusai*, literally the "shattering of the
jewel," or the sort of death-before-dishonor suicide missions that American GI's branded "banzai charges," had begun to appear in Japanese
newspapers. What remained uncertain in the summer of 1943 was
whether or not such behavioral exemplars should be incorporated into
efforts to mobilize civilian society for similar sacrifices rather than in
support of the troops. There was no predetermined descent into the lethal final months of the war. Without taking an explicit public stance on
this question at the time of the sacrifice, Ōdachi made it clear that he
believed those on the home front had to be prepared for the next phase
of the conflict, and the zoo massacre was one of the first public steps in
this campaign.[23]

The dramatic news of a slaughter at the zoological gardens would
carry this message to the metropolitan audience in a way that was not
possible in stories about human combat casualties on distant battlefields. Director Koga, who took leave from the zoological garden in July
1941 in order to join the faculty of the Army Veterinary College, recalled after the war how he had learned of the massacre and how Ōdachi intended to use it:

> I was called to the office of the Parks Commissioner [Inoshita Kiyoshi], and
> I rushed there together with Fukuda Saburō, my replacement during the war.
> When we arrived we were informed that the Governor General had decided

that the zoo's big animals had to be put down. I said to myself, "Ah, the moment has finally come." It seems that there was quite a debate over taking things this far at the highest levels of the municipal government, and there was nothing we could do but bow our heads to the decision. I heard that the decision was made because many people believed we were still winning the war. But Governor General Ōdachi was the mayor of Occupied Singapore, or Shōnan as we called it then, before coming to Tokyo, and he knew the real situation. He disapproved mightily of the way people on the home front were behaving. When he became Governor General he was determined to wake the people up to the fact that war is not so sweet a thing. So Ōdachi chose to use the zoo's animals rather than simple words as a way to chastise the people. Some argued that herbivores such as the elephants could be evacuated to the countryside, where they would survive on grass and plants, but Ōdachi stubbornly refused to allow it because his real concern was not the animals at all.[24]

But of course Ōdachi *was* concerned with the animals, just not the way Koga might have hoped. Ōdachi seems to have understood that the killing of the zoo's animals, which were uniquely popular and nearly universally liked, offered a means of cutting through the chorus of official blandishments. It would draw on deep emotional affiliations in a way that a more human story could not, especially after so many years of mass human casualties. This point is crucial: it was not so much the killings that mattered for Ōdachi but rather their public ritual celebration.

MASS-MEDIATED SACRIFICE

Perhaps the most productive way to think about the events at the zoo that summer is to consider them as a distinctly modern form of animal sacrifice. It is an odd idea, and the Japanese terms for sacrifice, *kugi*, or *kyōgi*, were not used in wartime descriptions of the massacre. Much like cannibalism, *kugi* was beyond the pale in imperial Japan, a marker of the darkest sort of primitive behavior associated with those either far away in time or lurking in the "uncivilized" corners of the empire.[25] Folklorists such as Yanagita Kunio argued that Japanese had sacrificed animals in ancient days or distant places, but in the contemporary moment sacrifice was attributed to the "barbarian" peoples of the imperial periphery. When *kugi* and its synonyms did appear in literature, it was often in the pulp fiction of empire that offered readers tantalizing glimpses of primitive rites still performed in the jungles of Southeast Asia and the like, areas beyond the reach of Japanese civilization and populated by people said to have evolved little beyond the brute culture of the animals being sacrificed.

And yet, Ōdachi's overriding interest in the animals to be killed was their symbolic value as sacrificial victims. As Henri Hubert and Marcel Mauss argue in their classic study on sacrifice, the success of a sacrificial ceremony hinges on the socially recognized value of the victim. The victim must be of a special status; it must stand apart from its surroundings by virtue of some defining characteristic or characteristics.[26] A proper sacrificial victim is particularly precious in symbolic terms, and the impact of the sacrificial rite—in the case of the zoo, the Buddhist rituals carried out by Abbot Ōmori and their subsequent rehearsals in the popular media, not the killings themselves—increases in direct proportion to the symbolic value attached to the object sacrificed. The zoological garden provided a stock of animals already endowed with the extraordinary surplus value necessary to a successful sacrifice in the context of an industrialized mass society. The economy of the zoological garden is premised on the notion that the animals held in its cages are distinctly (and sometimes uniquely) valuable, and few institutions spoke to such a wide audience in 1943, when the Ueno Zoo was in all likelihood the most popular zoo in the world.

The zoological garden provided Ōdachi with a powerful amplifier through which to broadcast this message. The flood of new animals that followed Japan's military expansion brought zoo attendance to new heights. Official gate numbers peaked at 3,270,810 in 1942, the same year that the tide of Japan's imperial expansion crested. Attendance in early 1943, prior to and immediately following the sacrifice, was similarly impressive. Well over two million people visited the gardens that year even as the conflict entered a new and particularly brutal stage. Attendance plummeted, however, in the two years following the killings as the tolls of war soared. Just over half a million people visited the zoo in 1944, and in 1945 attendance hit a twenty-two-year low, with only 290,000 visitors, less than a thousand per day on average.[27]

The sacrifice came during the heyday of the Ueno Zoo, a time that Director Koga would later recall as a "golden age," when the institution was flooded with hoards of visitors and so many new specimens that it had run out of exhibition space. Largely detached from the realities of naval defeats and attenuated lines of supply, the overpopulated zoo remained a center for celebration until the memorial service itself. Press coverage was always strong at the zoo because, among its other attractions, the institution delivered information in prepackaged narratives that fit neatly into newspaper columns, replete with eye-catching images. The place was a news magnet. Patrons and reporters alike went there to escape from the oppressive realities of the war, and the killing of such charismatic captives—many of them icons of imperial acquisition—furnished the kind of sensational event that was certain to garner attention. Press coverage was carefully coordinated by the Office of the Governor General, which offered reporters a surprise press release on September 2 announcing that certain of the animals in the collection had been "put down" for fear that they might escape during possible bombings. Many papers ran the short announcement verbatim on September 3. The following ran in the *Mainichi News* that day:

> Given the critical state of the war, the city of Tokyo has decided to prepare for the worst by ordering that the most dangerous animals kept in the collection of the Ueno Zoological Gardens be put down. A memorial service conducted by Chief Abbot Ōmori Tadashi of the Asakusa Temple will be held at the zoo at 2 P.M. on the 4th in front of the Deceased Animal Monument. Because even the tamest animals can become frenzied in violent bombings, every large animal from the lions on down must be put down. We ask for understanding on the part of the people of Tokyo who have loved these animals for so long.[28]

Over five hundred formal invitations were printed on fine paper (something of a rarity during the war) and sent to the homes of officials that same day. Similar invitations were delivered to the offices of the city's major media outlets.

The Office of the Governor General took care in managing the event because the slaughter of popular animals held in the empire's premier zoological garden was an act fraught with ambivalence. Like all acts of sacrifice, it was at once an act of sanctification and "a crime, a kind of sacrilege."[29] This is the fundamental contradiction of the sacrificial act; it assumes two opposing aspects, appearing, as the anthropologist René Girard suggests, at times as a sacred rite and at other times as a sort of criminal activity, an appalling act of violence.[30] Abbot Ōmori offered a series of rites intended to negotiate this contradiction carefully, channeling the violent emotions released by the slaughter. As with other sacrifices in other contexts, the zoo massacre "released an ambiguous force—or rather a blind one, terrible by the fact that it was a force. It therefore had to be limited, directed, and tamed."[31] Modern priests conducting rites of sacrifice scripted by elite university-educated bureaucrats in the context of one of the twentieth century's most popular cultural institutions, Ōmori and his monks sought to parlay ancient techniques for dealing with death into the service of the total war.

The evident innocence and massive charisma of the animals themselves impeded such management. The highly anthropomorphized performing elephants Tonky and Wanri, to take the most obvious examples, were known to millions of adults and children in midcentury
Japan, and Ōmori and the press labored to render their deaths as a
self-sacrifice performed for the Japanese people; these endearing trained
beasts were recast as innocent victims who gave their lives to protect
the very nation that kept them caged. The memorial service offered
both participants and the reading public alike a ritual in which the
spiritual value embodied in these national pets was consumed in a rite
that framed the killings as acts of public protection even as it implied
that many more sacrifices were to come, and that the audience itself
might soon assume the martyr's role sanctified in the ceremony.

Japan's mass media, and especially newspapers, provided the means
by which most people became aware of the sacrifice. Jingoistic and
carefully monitored by the Home Ministry and other agencies, the press
presented the memorial service as a yet another spectacle of nationalist
sacrifice, albeit an exceptional one. Nested alongside dozens of related
articles about such things as young pilots saying goodbye to their
mothers before heading overseas or the heroic exploits of soldiers as far
off as New Guinea, the sacrifice echoed the accelerating tempo and
darkening timbre of an empire in decline, adding new dimensions (and
new victims) to ongoing efforts at mass mobilization.

The massacre was a compelling story, and it ran in many of Tokyo's
major dailies as well as several other periodicals with wide circulation.
Rather than extrapolating to broad analysis of the war situation through
the news of the massacre or writing stories about the animals themselves, feature reporting on the event nearly always took the form of
heartrending tales focused on human children and zookeepers, such as
Fukuda Saburō, who assumed the mantle of "Mister Zookeeper" previously inhabited by directors Kurokawa and Koga. Much as it had been
for decades, the quality of the relationships between keepers and the
animals described by reporters took on a domestic cast, mimicking the
dynamics of familial relationships.

With the killings those domestic metaphors assumed a darker hue,
turning the murderous actions of the interim zoo director, the avuncular
"Mister Zookeeper," into a kind of metaphoric filicide. When Fukuda
described his experience of the killings to a reporter in an interview published on September 4, the day of the memorial service, his grief was
palpable, and he presented the massacre as a kind of mass infanticide:

We will hopefully be forgiven by the little boys and girls who have loved these animals. It has been twenty-two years since I started working at the Ueno Zoological Gardens. I raised all of the animals that were killed with tender care (*teshio ni kakete kita*). Many of them were born and died right here at the zoo. If they were humans, it would be as though I was the first to put them in diapers. They were truly darling to me. Even though it hasn't been said openly, the animals died to let the people know that bombings are unavoidable.[32]

The slippage in Fukuda's words between human children and animal innocents is conspicuous, illustrating the powerful ambiguities that radiate from all aspects of the massacre. It is difficult to imagine a more horrifying metaphor than the slaughter of one's own children, and it speaks to the terrible predicament of the zoo staff, caught between the demands of their professional roles and the emotional realities of working day in and day out with living animals, feeling creatures with lives of their own. The relationships that develop between keepers and their animal charges are often as powerful as those that unite pet owners with their companion animals, a relationship so intimate that nearly three-quarters of American dog owners today consider their pets to be "like a child or part of the family."[33] Similar feelings characterize pet ownership in contemporary Japan, as they have since at least Meiji times, when "pets" (*aigan dōbutsu*) became markers of middle-class status.[34]

Important differences do emerge, however, in the reporter's depiction of Fukuda's feelings, which include a putative vow of revenge. Fukuda himself conveyed one portion of the official message in the interview, pointing out that the animals died to deliver a point. The reporter suggests a more violent and active reaction, describing Fukuda as a father who has sacrificed his children, and whose grief has taken the form of a vendetta in the service of war.

Fukuda sits at his desk staring blankly out of the window. He must be thinking of the beloved children he has killed with his own hands—cherishing his memories of the animals. "It couldn't be helped, given the war situation," he says as if speaking to himself. But even as he turns to look outside, a fiercely cold determination to win the war flashes in the zoo director's eye.[35]

In this rendition of the sacrifice, Fukuda, a man who privately risked censure and possibly worse by resisting direct orders from his superiors to kill animals, is made to perform the emotional response solicited by the ritual. The article offers readers his story as a script whose plot line is one of revenge. The sacrifice was meant to offer a lesson communicated through "the zoo's animals rather than simple words," to borrow a phrase from Koga's postwar recollections. The ritual attempted to press the spectacular shock produced by the killings into the service of the state, to manage interpretations of the killings so as to produce a greater degree of dedication to the defense of the nation. They were framed as necessary acts that required vengeance on the part of the nation in whose name they had been carried out. Much of this management took place in press reports on the ritual, which sought to direct the anger and frustration of the deaths away from the zoo's managers toward a distant enemy. The zoo managers were instead to be pitied for their grief, like the government, which claimed to be acting in the people's best interest. The "sacrifice of so many animals so beloved to the people of Tokyo," one reporter claimed, "has caused feelings of unwavering determination for the final battle to boil up in people's hearts."[36]

Reception is the bogey of cultural history, and there is, of course, no way to know precisely how each member of the public interpreted the sacrifice. But the zoo's rich collection of wartime documents offers some tantalizing clues. The zoological gardens hold a small and surprisingly unedited cache, a rarity perhaps attributable to the seemingly apolitical nature of the institution itself or maybe even active intent on the part of Koga and others. Regardless of the origins of this little documentary treasure, the gardens hold thousands of pages of material from a period that is often an archival lacuna, a happy find for historians concerned with daily life during the war.

Quite literally folded in between the pages of this archive are a series of letters to the zoo director that arrived in the wake of the sacrifice. One of the most striking of these letters, addressed to Fukuda himself, exhibited the desired conversion of grief and shock into anger and determination:

> I saw the evening paper last night and I couldn't believe my eyes. Since I was little the lions, tigers, and elephants of picture books and magazines have called to me. And then one day, my mother took me to the zoo, and there right in front of my eyes, weren't those the very same lions, tigers, and elephants from the books moving around right in front of me? But then I saw last night's paper, and I couldn't bear to look. I feel so sad. I can't imagine what it is like for those who have cared for the animals for so many decades. Even though it is for the war it is really pitiful. We must destroy the Americans and British who killed these animals. I can't wait to become a soldier, so that I can avenge these animal martyrs. Perhaps that would satisfy the animals who made me so happy.[37]

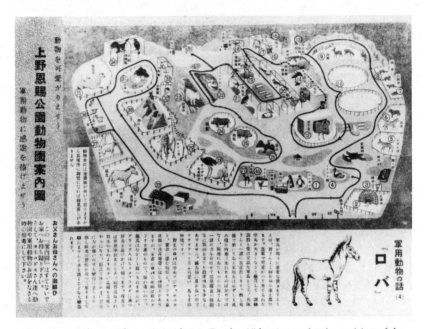

FIGURE 14. "About Military Animals (4): 'Donkey,'" late 1943. A grim revision of the 1942 map seen in the previous chapter. Water buffalo fill the elephant house (12), wild boar stand in for slaughtered bears (24, 25), and the large animal house (11) is disturbingly blank. The text on the map remains unchanged, urging parents to "Take this 'guide map' home with you so may use it to tell your children about military animals and the zoo." Image Courtesy of Tokyo Zoological Park Society.

The anger expressed in the last three sentences of the letter is striking, and much like the resolve attributed to Fukuda in the *Yomiuri* interview, the jump from grief to martial determination has a manufactured feeling. And yet, as Emiko Ohnuki-Tierney has found in her research on young, well-educated Kamikaze pilots, such statements were hardly unusual in wartime Japan.[38] The letter was simply signed "a young patriot" (*shōkokumin*), a generic term used during the war to refer to anyone of high school age or younger.

But reactions to the sacrifice were not as homogenous as officials might have liked. Nor were they as uniform as stock portrayals of inhuman Japanese "ultranationalist" fanaticism would have it. Those who chose to send letters were hardly a brainwashed horde of bloodthirsty emperor worshippers intent on sacrificing themselves at all costs. The letters reveal a deep, sad current of humanity running through wartime culture, a sense of helplessness in the face of grand events that is doubled against the patriotic bromides of the "young patriot" and kindred writings in the press. The call for vengeance against the Americans and British cannot be said to be typical. Just as often, the letters simply professed deep regret or sadness, sharing feelings of loss that extinguished any vengeful motives. "Dear Mr. Zookeeper," read the uncertain and carefully penned characters of a first-grader writing to the zoo director, "It is so sad that you killed the animals. Up until now I have always loved the zoo. I liked the elephants the most. I liked the tigers, lions, and polar bears, too. But now the animals I like aren't there anymore. How sad."[39] Such letters tell a very human story of lost innocence and fading hope in the context of dying empire. They imply that hopelessness and grief, in addition to (or perhaps in most cases rather than) burning martial conviction or mindless emperor worship, should be given voice in our attempts to comprehend the Japanese culture of fascist martyrdom, especially as it encompassed the home front in the final years of the war.[40]

The letters were limited neither to children nor to simple prose. An older writer crafted a somber *haiku* dedicated to the "animal martyrs" that illustrates a distinctly Buddhist approach to human–animal dynamics: "When you are reborn, may you return as human, on the autumn breeze."[41] In these cases, the ritual appears to have been effectual only to the extent that it made the senseless realities of the zoo massacre available to readers as a trigger for mourning, an event that gave emotional structure to the imperial collapse that they witnessed in myriad small happenings around them. For those who took the time to write the zoo director at least, the ceremony was emotionally evocative. It was not, however, sufficient to the task of transforming these emotions into "a feeling of unwavering determination for the final battle" in every case. The ambiguities built into the ceremony allowed for a variety of responses to the Great Zoo Massacre, many of them directly counter to the intended effects of the ritual. As Japan entered the postwar period, the unpropitiated spirits of these slaughtered animals would return to haunt popular memories of the war and its cruelties, allowing for a different kind of mourning and a new kind of forgetting. While the war raged, however, with press controls in place, the ambiguities inherent in the sacrifice—the ambivalence produced by the ritual "drawing together of the sacred and the profane"[42]—were largely suppressed from public view.

Performed by a Buddhist abbot and witnessed by grade-schoolers and elite politicians alike, the strange act of animal consecration that

was the Great Zoo Massacre was also an act of inversion and dehumanization. It was a ritual mechanism designed to elevate the slaughtered animals as exemplars of righteous death even as it facilitated the
reduction of their human counterparts to what philosopher Georgio
Agamben might call "bare life," or "life exposed to death." Where the
protection and well-being of those on the home front had long been
held up as the very reason for the war, the men, women, and children of
Tokyo were incrementally reduced to a population of biopoliticized
bodies as the conflict deepened, into creatures valued for their brute
contributions to the war effort but ultimately expendable.[43] This shift
could only take place once the killings were made public. In the hidden
world of the killing floor, the zoo's animals remained just that, animals.
"Martyrs" in public, they were mere objects in the taxonomically conditioned world of slaughter.

The full historical import of this event only becomes visible when
that hidden world is brought into the story. The pageant of martyrdom
forced a meaning upon the public that had been concocted by the
bureaucratic leadership, yet in the long term that meaning rebounded
upon its sponsors, largely because the squalid processes of the killing
floor awakened the public imagination in the aftermath of national defeat. Arriving at that fuller account requires that we return once again
to the world within the zoo, and the conceptions and commitments that
ordered life—and death—behind the walls.

THE TAXONOMY OF A MASSACRE

Much as it had in the formation of the zoological gardens in the nineteenth century, taxonomic knowledge played a critical part in its symbolic destruction in the 1940s. In the summer of 1941, six months before the attack on Pearl Harbor brought the United States into the war,
a new and particularly unfortunate systematics was developed at
Ueno.[44] Like many other men at the time, Director Koga left his civilian
position to rejoin the military in 1941, taking the rank of colonel in the
Imperial Army. Four days after Koga's departure, a directive arrived
from the Eastern Command Veterinary Division, within which Koga
was an officer, instructing Fukuda and his staff to draw up emergency
plans to be used if the zoological garden was bombed or raided. In consultation with Koga, Fukuda developed the *Zoological Garden Emergency Procedures*, a plan for the extermination of the collection in the
event of emergency. Forwarded to the Eastern Command on August 11,

the document reclassified the entire collection according to the danger posed by each species in the event of cage break. It was a road map for the slaughter that followed two years later.[45]

The *Procedures* distributed all of the zoo's animals into four classes, or *shu*, the same term used for biological "species" in Japanese coined by Itō Keisuke in the nineteenth century. Here, though, the nomenclature was one of fear and hazard rather than place of origin, physiological affinity, or evolutionary descent. Distinctions were not made between carnivores and other animals in the distribution of species into the new taxa. Class One species, termed "extremely dangerous," included all of the zoo's ursine and large feline specimens, as well as canines such as coyotes, poisonous reptiles, and nonhuman anthropoid primates such as baboons. The class further encompassed elephants, hippopotamuses, bison, and the zoo's sole hyena. Class Two animals, "relatively less dangerous," included a menagerie of wild medium-size mammals such as badgers, raccoons, and foxes. It further included emus, ostriches, and all raptors, in addition to ruminants such as giraffes and various deer species. Eighteen crocodiles and a pair of seals were also ranked in this class. Class Three, or "common domesticates," was comprised of barnyard species such as rabbits, goats, and pigs, as well as geese, pheasants, chickens, and a variety of other fowl. Forty mountain goats, four Bactrian camels, four mules, three donkeys, and several other sizable ungulates rounded out the less threatening category of "general domesticates"—these included most of the "military animals" discussed in the previous chapter. The final class, simply lumped together as "other," was populated by more than six hundred canaries, an aviary of other songbird species, turtles, and an unspecified number of "small animals."

The *Zoological Garden Emergency Procedures* was structured by two interrelated concerns: physical threat and attitudes about wildness. It was further shaped by the assumption that the category of biological species was the appropriate analytical unit for such a document. When they wrote the procedures, Fukuda and the other authors assumed that what held true for the generic species also held true for all members of that class in the gardens. They did not make distinctions based on the behavioral or life history of individual creatures: one elephant was as dangerous as another in the classificatory world laid out in 1941; a cub was as dangerous as an adult. It was a habit of mind and notation that would return to haunt Fukuda and his staff two years later, when the generic categories written into the hastily assembled bureaucratic memo would provide the governor general with easy justification for the extermination of individual animals that the zoo staff sought to save.

Assumptions about wild animals versus domesticated animals are most evident in the differentiation of "relatively dangerous" animals from "general domesticates," classifications that draw on the cultural binary of wild and tame rather than any measure of physical strength or threat.[46] The categorization of the zoo's raptor population in the "relatively dangerous" category illustrates the point. It is difficult to imagine birds of prey posing as much of a public threat as large mammals such as the herd of water buffalo, donkeys, mules, and camels that were classed as "general domesticates," and therefore less likely to be put down. One can imagine the pandemonium that would result from a group of water buffalo running amok in the heavily trafficked streets surrounding Ueno Station. The physical threat or public disruption from an uncaged raptor seems rather less pressing than four scared Bactrian camels weighing up to fifteen hundred pounds each.

The "extremely dangerous" animals posed the greatest concern. Risk, value, and human curiosity are closely linked at the zoo, which features carefully buffered encounters with physically imposing creatures and draws on the promise of safety and the thrill of danger to bring in patrons. In 1941 one implication of this taxonomy was inverted. Where danger and human fascination with ferocious creatures had previously ensured that many more threatening animals received greater care, it now sealed their fate, placing them at the top of the list of executions. Recognizing that animals in the first class were also the most significant in the zoo's collection, the authors were at pains to emphasize to the Eastern Command that the zoological gardens were taking a wide array of extra precautions to guard against the "unlikely event" of an animal escape. Koga and others knew that zoos in Europe had seen escapes, and they installed reinforced concrete barriers at great cost. Steel was used in the latest cage designs, and further efforts were underway to develop the safety procedures. Targeted for extermination in 1943, these animals were not all killed, but the deaths that did occur meant the destruction of nearly all of the zoological garden's most popular animals.

Zoos throughout the archipelago marketed danger and the threat of escape. They made a spectacle of their emergency escape drills by publicizing "escape days" during which patrons could watch (and sometimes join) staff as they trained in various methods of capture ranging from lassoing deer to netting bear. In some cases, keepers would enter enclosures with animals. Pulling deer and other relatively tame animals to the ground, they tie-down roped them rodeo-style as onlookers cheered. In other instances, human beings would play the part of rogue animals, roaring in mock ferocity at screaming children before being netted and tackled by several of their colleagues. Such festivities often ended with a bang and a burst of smoke as gun-toting keepers fired blank cartridges into one cage or another.

The business of the 1941 document was more serious. The *Procedures* outline a series of escalating measures to be taken in response to air raid warnings, when metropolitan Tokyo was under attack, and when the zoo itself was threatened. At "stage one," reached when an air raid warning was broadcast, zoo staff were ordered to prepare "extremely dangerous" and "relatively dangerous" animals for execution. All animals were to be placed in their sleeping cells and patrons were to be informed of the heightened status via announcements over the garden's public address system.[47] All preparations, like the killings, were to be "carried out so as to avoid shocking the general populace," a phrase that recurs in institutional documents from this period. The zoo kept loaded rifles on hand for use in case of an escape. Poison, which was judged to be "no less lethal than gunshots," was the sanctioned means of killing because it was quiet. The report included a rough appendix estimating lethal dosages of hydrocyanic acid and nitric strychnine for each type of animal.[48] It also provided a budget for the purchase of extra nets and other items to be used to capture animals if an escape occurred but did not demand lethal action.

Stage two measures, which basically amounted to stand-by status, were to be taken when it was confirmed that the Tokyo metropolitan area was under attack. The zoo's main gates were to be chained, and patrons within the grounds were to be ushered off of the premises or escorted to designated air raid shelters. By this time zoo keepers should have completed preparations for the "disposal" of all Class One and Class Two specimens. If the situation was particularly threatening, employees were to prepare for the extermination of the entire zoo collection, including the horses, mountain goats, and ducks classified as "common domesticates." Only the canaries, turtles, and doves of Class Four were exempted.

Bombings or other threats such as fire that directly jeopardized the zoological garden triggered "stage three." Animals were put to death in the order designated in the *Procedures*, beginning with Class One and working through each of the subsequent categories. Deemed the greatest threat, various species of bear filled the first seven spaces on the list. They were to be followed by the zoo's large cats and canines such as hyena and coyotes. The last spaces in the "extremely dangerous" category were filled by hippos, American Bison, elephants, and three species of primate, including a family of six baboons.

As events unfolded in 1943, the hippos, primates, and bison were not included in the official listing of animals slated for death submitted to Ōdachi's office in late August. Ultimately neither the hippos nor the primates were slaughtered in 1943. Only at the last minute were the American bison put to death, killed in an apparent act of symbolic revenge against a species associated with the enemy. Randolph Hearst donated these animals to Ueno in 1933. They were bludgeoned to death with hammers only three days before the memorial service, the last animals to be killed other than the elephants and a young leopard cub. Rumor at the zoo had it that the head of the first bison to die was handed over to a taxidermist to be mounted trophy style. We know for certain that the creature's skull was kept.

THE KILLING FLOOR

Press portrayals of determination and organized precision notwithstanding, the 1943 killings were a messy, disorganized affair fraught with dissension. Their grim history serves as a reminder of the complexities that enter the historical field when we try to account for the reality that human beings are not the only creatures whose stories matter in historical terms. Elephants and other large mammals are neither fully self-conscious agents in the human sense nor affectless objects.[49] If we hope to understand events like the Great Zoo Massacre, we must begin to pay closer attention to these historical actors, creatures who influence the course of events both through cognitively and instinctually conditioned action and through the complex emotions that they can induce in people. That rich emotional bonds (as well as dislikes) can develop across species boundaries suggests the necessity of a more delicate methodology. We cannot fully understand the human experience of this resonant cultural event without paying close attention to the role of animals, including recognition of the physical pain and emotional trauma that shaped the actions of people and animals alike. This section and the following one attempt to render such complexities into the stuff of history. Together, they constitute a microhistorical analysis focused on affect and the conditions of possible political action in a time of military emergency.

On August 16, 1943, Koga and Fukuda were called to Park Commissioner Inoshita's office where they were told that the big game (*mōjū*) in the zoo's collection were to be killed under orders of strict secrecy. The killings began the following night. Koga and Fukuda each later recalled that, though saddened, they were not surprised by the decision to kill certain zoo animals. What surprised them were the urgency of the orders and their own lack of agency in the process.

Neither Koga nor Fukuda were opposed to killing animals per se. Zookeepers had started the process of culling animals in response to the war as much as two years before Inoshita gave them the bad news. The first wartime killings took place under Koga's direction before he joined the military and before the emergency procedures were committed to paper. In February 1941 Koga's staff shot several animals deemed "surplus." Even today when the conservation mission of zoological gardens has been strengthened through public scrutiny and binding international conventions, zoos can be lethal places for animals. Before the implementation of such agreements as the Convention on International Trade in Endangered Species of Wild Fauna and Flora (CITES) in 1975, species of all kinds were routinely slaughtered as part of the day-to-day work of the zoo.[50] In the early 1940s, as the zoo was caught at the intersection of plummeting food availability and skyrocketing acquisitions from a swelling empire, the zoo culled a number of animals.

These "surplus" animals were routinely shot after operating hours, and their carcasses were dealt with in a number of ways. Some were rendered into taxidermy specimens. If the slaughtered animal was less charismatic or in poor physical condition, it might have simply been buried in the yard behind the zoo hospital alongside dozens of other specimens. In less common instances, the creatures traveled the well-worn path between the zoological garden and any number of veterinary or biology classrooms. The lack of publicity sets the 1941 killings apart from those in 1943. These animals were killed in a manner that was not designed to put their deaths to public use. They were killed as a matter of course, neither in secret (the gunshots would have been clearly audible to hundreds of nearby families) nor as a part of a staged spectacle. Their deaths received little attention or public comment.

The status of such animals was more akin to those held in less pleasant "total institutions" such as the laboratory or the slaughterhouse, where killing was the norm rather than the exception. Death is a regular part of life in zoological gardens, though it is usually kept sequestered behind the scenes. Patrons may understand that the zoological garden's animals must die like other living creatures, but they tend to ignore this less seemly side of zoo culture unless it is made explicit by outside critics or the institution itself. This unreflective, almost willful ignorance is reinforced by the zoo-going public's lack of general knowledge. In most cases, our curiosity is ephemeral. For most spectators one Manchurian bear is much the same as another, and indeed each brown-coated bear is in many ways indistinguishable from all of the others regardless of species, sex, or even age once the animal has grown into adolescence and ceases to play on our sympathy for "cute" creatures. In a world of largely anonymous and interchangeable specimens or spectacles, the death of many animals is easy to ignore. Only in the case of such highly charismatic individuals as performing elephants or species such as the panda do individual animal deaths register with the broader public.

Emotion can cut both ways, however. Killing an animal that is compliant and docile is heartrending. Animals that fail to conform to our needs and expectations are quite another matter. As with millions of pets expelled from households in Japan (or the United States, for that matter) each year, zoo animals that misbehave or go so far as to attack their human minders easily slip into categories of being that are not only denied moral consideration but which can seem to demand slaughter. Such was the case with the male Asiatic elephant known as "John." The decision to kill John came during a meeting on August 1, 1943, between Inoshita and Fukuda, approximately two weeks prior to Ōdachi's intervention at the zoo. John had been a problem since 1927, when the tremendous creature injured his trainer during a public performance.[51] For the next four years, until 1931, the zoo's only male elephant was excluded from participation in any performances. In that year, Ishikawa Fukujirō, a brash, confident young animal trainer who had experience in one of Japan's circuses, arrived in Tokyo eager to prove himself. He immediately took to working with John early each morning, usually with supervision from Director Koga or another of the zoo's more experienced keepers.

His attempts were short lived and ended in tragedy. Ishikawa was fatally gored by John three days after he arrived at the zoo, his chest ripped open by the elephant's tusks during a morning training session as Koga looked on in horror. The young man died in a local hospital two hours after the incident, thanking the nurse for her care as he bled internally and struggled to breath with a punctured lung and several fractured ribs.[52] John, an animal whose colorful image as a friendly behemoth was ubiquitous in youth-oriented print culture, quickly found his legs shackled in heavy chains. The large, intelligent animal's irritation was evident to zoo visitors. While the female elephants Tonky and Wanri performed in the yard outside, John rattled the thick chain on his legs and swayed back and forth in the dim interior of the garishly decorated Elephant House.

John was a difficult animal, and the zoo was confronted with a decision about what to do with an unmanageable "wild" elephant who had been rendered into a popular storybook character. Public image was at odds with the institutional reality, and zoo administrators sought to resolve this contradiction by using the crisis of the war as an alibi. He was "unmanageable" and therefore dangerous, or so the logic went. In fact, his death might be seen as a kind of revenge killing, only required because he had taken a human life. Where decisions about killing animals later that same August caused a great deal of emotional turmoil among the staff, neither the archival record nor postwar memoirs show much hand wringing over the "man killer's" execution. Fallen from grace and no longer deserving of protection, John could be put down with a clear conscience.[53] Fukuda's diary entry on the meeting with Inoshita in which the decision to kill John was made simply states, "Told to shoot male elephant, John."[54]

Since the multiple gunshots required to kill the male elephant would cause a commotion in the areas surrounding the zoo, it was decided that that the best method to deal with the giant pachyderm was starvation. The elephant's access to food and water was stopped on August 13, 1943, just three days before orders came down to dispose of the entire class of "extremely dangerous" animals. The tremendous elephant died, chained in place, on August 29, seventeen days after keepers stopped providing sustenance. Within those seventeen days the entire world of the zoo turned upside down. By August 29 twenty-two other animals had been poisoned, strangled, or stabbed to death, and John's more charismatic female companions, Tonky and Wanri, were well on their way to death as well.

Staff from the Veterinary College and various members of the Tokyo University science faculty had been eagerly awaiting the large elephant's death, and they arrived at 11 A.M. the following morning to begin dissecting the tremendous body. Anticipating that the elephant's corpse would be too large to move for the long-awaited dissection, the team had begun bringing the necessary chemicals (to preserve the elephant's hide) and tools to the zoo several days before he collapsed for the last time (he had fallen and struggled to his feet repeatedly as his strength waned). The dissection took four hours. Professor Ogawa Sansuke of Tokyo University's Brain Research Center led the dissection, taking possession of John's skull and brain, which remain preserved in a large jar in one of the university labs to this day. John's lethal tusks, the larger of which was measured at 57 centimeters, were sawed off and weighed. At least one of the tusks stayed in the zoo's possession until well into the postwar period. After his massive hide was removed and coated in preservatives, John's flesh and bones were hacked into pieces and deposited in a hole dug for the purpose in front of the concrete Monument to Deceased Animals together with remains from other slaughtered animals, the same monument before which Tonky and Wanri once bowed in memorial services for other deceased animals. The hide was delivered to Captain Ujie Kōno, who handled clothing requisitions for the Imperial Army, in the hopes that John's huge skin might be put to use in soldier's uniforms. Captain Ujie's business card is lodged in between the pages for September 9 and 10 in Fukuda's grim wartime diary, annotated in Fukuda's hand with the captain's home phone number and a notation that the "elephant's skin will be donated to the Imperial Army."[55]

Though his death was sanctified in the September 4 memorial service, John's death was in some ways a separate event, showing us how the institution's staff might have dealt with such matters in the absence of Ōdachi's intervention. His slaughter illuminates the complex moral economy of the zoo. Koga and Fukuda were willing to slaughter animals in response to the cruel circumstances of war, but they acted with attention to the institutional logic and local knowledge of the zoological garden. They were far less concerned with the dynamics of imperial collapse and mass mobilization. Fukuda recalled the day of the order as follows:

> August 16 was a day that I will never be able to forget. On that morning I received a call from the Parks Commissioner asking me to come to his office immediately. I had a feeling that this was about the disposal of the big game, and I drew up a list of the animals that had to be killed. Koga had already arrived from the Army Veterinary School when I got there. My prediction had been right on target, but we were told that the poisonings had to take place within a single month. And that we couldn't use rifles because the gunshots would cause public unrest.[56]

With the decision to starve John, it is clear that Fukuda and Koga were capable of killing animals in response to the crisis of war. Only the speed, scale, and purpose of the killings changed with Ōdachi's intervention on August 16. Both Fukuda and Koga were shocked that so many animals were to be killed within such a short period of time, and they were at a loss as to how to accomplish such a slaughter without the use of rifles.

The two men quickly moved to circumvent aspects of Ōdachi's orders, working feverishly to save dozens of animals deemed innocent or harmless. Both men had repeatedly expressed their emotional attachment to wildlife under their care—Koga in particular had built a gracious public image through the authorship of various books in which he expressed affection for "his" zoo animals, including essays on the rich emotional lives of animals—and they were torn between their duty to the state and their obligations as zoo keepers. In the immediate period following the orders from the governor general, the men's attachments to their animal charges won out, and they set their minds to saving as many animals as possible. It is a moment that shows how tactics of everyday resistance meant to preserve autonomy were employed as individuals adjusted to a political field tilting toward mass martyrdom.

The institution of the zoological garden is premised on a moral contract under which it is assumed that captive animals will received a degree of care deemed "civilized" or "enlightened." As the animal protection advocate Watanabe Waichirō put it in an interview in 1942, "The treatment of animals in a given society is a barometer of how far that society has progressed culturally. Countries where the love of animals is weak are clearly culturally inferior."[57] Imperial zoological gardens such as Tokyo were the most obvious national barometers. Men like Koga and Fukuda constantly negotiated the terms of the contract in the course of their everyday labors, and Ōdachi's orders pushed at the limits of their sense of moral correctness. Starving John, a confirmed man killer, was one thing, but what about the more docile and affectionate female Asiatic elephant, Tonky? She regularly performed tricks for her trainers and generally behaved as a hefty pet for the zoo staff. Tonky was a favorite of both the zoo staff and the throngs of visitors who lined up to see her perform with her happy companion, Wanri.

Much as notions of personhood—understandings of who should (and who should not) receive full moral consideration within a given community—are crucial in determining the distribution of medical care within human populations, certain animals within the zoo often receive disproportionate allocations of resources thanks to the emotional ties that bind them to the humans who are responsible for their care. This particular principle was clearly expressed in the efforts of Koga and Fukuda on behalf of particular zoo animals in the late summer of 1943. Tame and affectionate, Tonky received far greater consideration than did the "wild" and dangerous John.

Orders were in place, however, and even as the two men sought to save certain animals, others began to die. The first victim of the zoo massacre was killed on the night of August 17. Probably captured or purchased during a hunting expedition to the client state of Manchukuo, this bear had been part of a group of Manchurian bears given to the Ueno Zoo by Prince Takamatsu. In the final report on the killings, the animal's age was estimated at six years, and its value at approximately eighty yen. Like almost all of the executions, the bear was killed in the evening after the zoo's gates had closed behind the departing crowds.

The poisoning was an atypically smooth operation. Because regular feeding schedules had been interrupted on the 16th in order to increase the animals' appetites, the bear was eager to eat the sweet potato its handler passed through the bars that evening. It immediately consumed the proffered morsel, which had been injected with three grams of nitric strychnine, the dosage dictated by the appendix attached to the 1941 *Emergency Procedures*. Standing outside the cage, keepers kept detailed records of the bear's death, paying close attention to the effects of the poison on the 273-pound animal.[58] Absorbed quickly, strychnine passes into the animal's system through all mucous membranes, especially the stomach and small intestine. The alkaloid extract obtained from the dried ripe seeds of *Strychnos nux vomica*, a small tree native to the East Indies, does not kill quickly and has no anesthetic or narcotic effects. The victim is acutely conscious as the poison takes hold.

Within three minutes of eating the potato the female bear's legs began to shake, threatening to buckle under her as the strychnine started to work on her central nervous system, inducing an escalating series of spasms that quickly came to affect all striated muscles. Within ten minutes she was exhibiting classic signs of strychnine poisoning, eyes open unnaturally wide, teeth exposed in a terrible smile as muscle spasms pulled at her lips. The bear's body contorted with painful convulsions that were interrupted by periods of complete muscle relaxation and rapid, panicked breathing. The poison acts on the nervous system: the senses become excruciatingly enhanced such that any amount of stimulation can bring on another series of convulsions. The bear experienced almost uninterrupted spasms for nearly twenty minutes. Twenty-two minutes after eating the potato, she lay dead on the floor of her cage, probably asphyxiated when a particularly strong series of spasms shot through her respiratory muscles. A male bear was also killed that same night. As the slaughter progressed, keepers placed signs saying "under construction, animals may not be visible" on cages left empty when their inhabitant's bodies were hauled away, hidden under tarps. Eventually, large signs were placed at the entrance to the zoo itself. Even as the massacre progressed, zoo attendance during the daytime hours was quite large, averaging several thousand patrons per day. We have no records of what the patrons thought as they moved past one empty cage after another or found peccaries or other species in cages still labeled for the larger ursine or feline species that, unbeknownst to them, were being slaughtered.

The first two killings were exceptional in that the animals succumbed to the poison with "relative ease," as the diary recording the killings makes clear. In his semi-confessional 1968 book, *The Real Story of the Ueno Zoo* (*Ueno Dōbutsuen no jitsuroku*), Fukuda describes the squalor:

> It should be noted that the animals were not killed by poison alone. Or more honestly, that relatively few animals died from just the poison. Most of them refused to eat the poisoned feed or were given too small a dosage (we were completely inexperienced at this, and we weren't able to estimate the weight of many of the animals accurately, so all we could do was give it our best guess). So most of the animals did not die peacefully. We had to kill them using all sorts of methods. It was unconscionably cruel.[59]

The manner of each animals' death mattered to Fukuda and his colleagues, and it shaped how they recounted the killings after the war. Inexperienced and undersupplied with strychnine, staff were faced with a gruesome task as the killings accelerated in order to meet Ōdachi's August 31 deadline. The animal's feed may have been stopped in an attempt to increase their appetites, but many animals slated for execution, most notably the enviably diverse collection of ursine species, were naturally able to forego food for extended periods of time in the wild, and they refused to eat bait tainted with the scent of poison. Other animals eagerly bit into the meat or vegetables, only to spit it out when the poison hit their tongues.

Under pressure from superiors, keepers resorted to a collection of spears, wires, ropes, and hammers to complete their grisly task. In some instances, these weapons were almost certainly the more humane option. Though not as quick as rifles, hammers and spears had the virtue of eliminating guesswork. The drawbacks of the strychnine were evident early in the process, but they became too obvious to ignore when the time came to dispatch Katarina, one of a pair of lions gifted to the Shōwa Emperor by the emperor of Ethiopia in 1931. Katarina had given birth to numerous cubs in the years since her arrival, providing the institution with a dependable series of newsworthy births and feeding young animals into the system of zoos.[60] By Fukuda's count, it took one hour and thirty-seven minutes to kill the lioness. When keepers could no longer bear to stand by and watch the animal suffer, they stepped in and stabbed her with an improvised spear.[61] Ali, the large male lion that was Katarina's companion and the closest thing to a "real lion" Fukuda says he ever saw, was dispatched much more quickly, swallowing a full dose of poison in a single bite; the male lion died thirty-two minutes after he swallowed the horse meat.[62]

Like many of the animals slaughtered at the zoo, the lions' carcasses were hauled out of the zoo under tarps and brought to the dissection tables of the Army Veterinary College very early in the morning on the day they were killed. Once they arrived at the school the animals were subjected to full dissection. Each specimen was carefully weighed and photographed before being opened up by the students and their teachers. Every care was taken to preserve the coats of the animals so that they could be passed along to the taxidermist who had been hired— under the condition of absolute secrecy—to preserve and sculpt the corpses. Reports on the dissections show that the interests of the scientists and instructors at the school largely mirrored those of the zoogoing public. They were more concerned with exotic big game species than they were with domestic species that might have been more readily available. Domestic bears (as opposed to exotic foreign species) in particular were not included in the final report on the dissections sent to Ōdachi and Inoshita by the staff of the veterinary college.[63]

AND THEN THERE WERE TWO

Let us return to the image with which we started our journey: Governor General Ōdachi leading a thin procession through the zoo grounds on September 4. At his side are two young boys in elementary school uniforms. Behind them, against a striped backdrop of a large piece of fabric hung over the Elephant House, stands a larger group of adults and children watching as the monks and other invited guests process toward the Memorial for Deceased Animals in order to mourn the eradication of all of the zoo's "extremely dangerous" animals, from lions and bears to tigers and elephants.

It is a chilling image that holds an even more chilling secret. Tonky and Wanri, the performing elephants who were the zoo's main attraction, were not dead on September 4, 1943. They sat starving behind the red and white striped fabric in the background of the image, kept quiet by their obedient respect for their keeper's orders. The ceremony celebrating the sacrifice of the "animal martyrs" took place five days after John's death. Since keepers had held out hope for a transfer of these favorite animals, strict orders to deny the pair food had only come down on August 25, a mere ten days before the ceremony. There was not enough time to starve the animals, and they refused to eat poisoned forage. Obedient to the end, they followed their keepers orders to stay quiet so well that records indicate that Ōdachi and the entire procession walked past on their way to the celebrate the death of the two elephants—who would be singled out during the memorial service as particularly virtuous martyrs—without any hint that the huge animals lay dying just a few feet away.

Early in the process, the keepers were not alone in attempting to save the animals. The same day that Koga, Fukuda, and Inoshita discussed Ōdachi's orders, they also penned letters to several other zoological gardens asking if they might be able to take possession of certain animals from Tokyo's collection. One such letter, addressed to zoo directors in Sendai and Nagoya, reads as follows:

> Please excuse this sudden solicitation, and please keep these communications strictly private. I know that we all share hearty salutations in celebration of our ongoing progress in the war which is doing so much for our national glory. However, it has become necessary to put in place certain safety measures here in response to the enemy's reprisals since one imagines that this area will almost certainly be their first target. Because we are located in the center of the capital, we have decided to evacuate animals. Since your gardens are in relatively safe areas, if you would like to take custody of these animals we would be pleased to either present them to you as gifts or as part of an exchange. We would ask to revisit these arrangements once peace has come. Our shipping budget is very tight at the moment. We ask that if interested you contact us immediately with your response.[64]

The letter, which makes no mention of the ongoing massacre, closes by offering two spotted leopards and two black leopards to the Nagoya

Zoo and one female elephant, Tonky, to the Sendai Zoo. Similar communications were sent to other zoological gardens.

For a brief moment, it seemed as if Tonky might escape the slaughter and be removed to the relative safety of Sendai, a regional city in northeastern Japan. Ezawa Sōji (1906–1972), the director of Sendai Zoo, responded to Fukuda's letter immediately, writing that he would be thrilled to take possession of Tonky, and that a member of his staff would arrive in Tokyo on the 23rd or 24th of August.[65] The response from Nagoya was somewhat more guarded. Nagoya's collection did not contain black leopards, and the director stated that he would be very pleased to add the pair offered by Tokyo to his collection. However, the acquisition would have to receive approval from the city administrators, as that city's zoo was in the process of reevaluating the size of their collection in response to food shortages and safety concerns.[66]

When Ezawa's assistant, a man named Ishii, arrived from Sendai on the 23rd, he offered not only to take possession of the elephant but also to trade several baboons for Tokyo's male spotted leopard. Enlivened at the prospect of saving at least two animals, Fukuda went immediately to meet with his superior, Inoshita, and started making preparations for the transport of the two animals. These dealings were abruptly cut short a few hours later by a call from Inoshita's office ordering a stop to all preparations for the "evacuation" (sokai) of the elephant and any other animals. Inoshita, it seems, had received a phone call from an infuriated Ōdachi. The scheduled killings were to take place in absolute secrecy and as ordered, and a memorial service was to be arranged within the grounds of the zoological garden as scheduled. Ishii returned to Sendai empty handed.[67]

Given his apparent motives, Ōdachi's anger is understandable. The zoo sacrifice was designed to inspire a greater degree of dedication and determination among Tokyo's residents in preparation for the arrival of American bombers and troops. The "evacuation" of the institution's most popular elephant, an animal endowed with personality and character in the wider media, hardly delivered the sort of message that Ōdachi desired. Large-scale evacuation programs were, in fact, enacted once the capital came in range of Allied bombers in 1944, and Ōdachi supported them so long as they did not in his estimation weaken the war effort, but it is crucial to remember that the sacrifice occurred just as the nation's leaders were struggling to come to terms with the altered military situation. Ōdachi may have forecast the arrival of American bombers, but in 1943 his plans did not extend to animal "evacuations," or *sokai*, the same term that would be used for the removal of children from the capital once bombers began to appear with regularity the next year.[68]

The governor general was also concerned that the movement of so large an animal through the streets of central Tokyo would cause public unrest. Tonky was sure to draw crowds. This was precisely the sort of spectacle that the military police hoped to avoid. Not only would it send the wrong message to the capital's population, it would almost certainly draw people into the city's streets, and the wartime state was acutely allergic to any large gathering not dedicated to the celebration of the war effort. In fact, when word of the elephant's potential removal reached the Public Safety Division of the Tokyo Police, an inspector was immediately dispatched to the zoo to confirm that no suspicious activities were taking place. This inspection came in addition to inquiries from the head of the military police stationed in Tokyo and the chief of the Ueno Park police station. Fukuda's actions were closely monitored by a coterie of interested agencies, then, and his diary is filled with their name cards and notations on their visits.

Each of the agencies was concerned that rumors of something strange happening at the zoo were beginning to spread throughout the capital. By the time the police inspector arrived at the zoo, the killings had already passed through their first phase. The slaughter was brought to a halt for a single day on August 23rd while police consulted with Inoshita and Fukuda, but they resumed again on the 24th, the same day that orders arrived sealing Tonky's fate.[69]

Inoshita's office kept the governor general's staff much more accurately informed of events as they unfolded after this direct inspection. In one of his formal reports to Ōdachi's office on the sacrifice, Inoshita notified the governor general that zoo staff were scheduled to kill twenty-two animals through strychnine poisoning in the days between August 17 and August 31. Among the animals scheduled for death, the report stated, were several specimens that deserved special note. These included a pair of lions presented to the zoo by the Imperial Household Ministry, a Korean bear donated by Prime Minister Tōjō Hideki (1884–1948), and a Malaysian bear donated by the Sultan of Johore through the good offices of the "Tiger Hunting Duke," Tokugawa Yoshichika. The list also noted a pair of Manchurian bears brought to the zoo by Prince Takamatsu and an elephant donated to the children of Japan by the Boy Scouts of Thailand, Wanri. The listing may have been an effort by Inoshita to impress upon Ōdachi that these were not just any animals.

But lineage and pedigree did not protect the animals, and their remarkable value may, in fact, have made them even more appealing as ideological media. Each of them was dead before the end of September.[70]

Inoshita's report outlined more than simply which animals were to die. It also addressed the ways in which the zoo administration would manage information surrounding the sacrifice. Mindful of Ōdachi's concern for secrecy, Inoshita stressed that all information regarding the killings would be kept strictly secret, and that all the public announcements would come from the governor general's own Office of Information, which would be kept abreast of events as they unfolded. He also confirmed that a large number of monks from the Youth Society for Buddhist Tradition (Shidō Bukkyō Seinen Dentō Kai) would join in the memorial service, which was to be modeled on celebrations of animal war dead that had taken place at the zoological gardens each year since the war began in 1931. In a notable departure from past ritual practice, however, Inoshita emphasized that the flesh and bones from these animal martyrs would be carefully maintained and interred alongside the zoo's current Memorial to Deceased Animals (in past years carcasses had been disposed of elsewhere). Plans for a new cenotaph commemorating the unique sacrifice of these martyred animals were drawn up with the idea that the monument would be constructed soon after the early September ritual.[71]

Inoshita further emphasized, with no apparent irony, that the slaughter was being carried out in accordance with the zoo's own commitment to rational scientific principles. The report stipulated that the scientific value of all animal carcasses would be evaluated in consultation with the staff of the Army Veterinary College, "an institution with which the zoological garden maintains strong ties," and that the value of a particular specimen would dictate the ways in which it was handled. Regardless of their rarity, all animals would be put to use in support of "scientific research" (gakujutsu kenkyū), providing dissection opportunities for faculty and students from the school. Following dissection, coats and skins would be removed from the carcasses and prepared for preservation. In the case of particularly rare exotic animals, the specimens would be rendered via taxidermy into natural-historical specimens that were to be put on display within the zoo in the months following the sacrifice, as in fact they were. In the days following the ceremony on September 4 the signage in the Taxidermy House was amended. The exhibit was dedicated to the zoo's "animal martyrs." But, of course, not all of the "martyrs" were dead. The elephants remained alive for well over two weeks after Abbot Ōmori and his monks sanctified their deaths.[72]

When firm orders arrived demanding that the pair of female elephants be killed, keepers began to explore ways to put the animals to death. They set about trying to poison the pair. When even the tender skin behind the animals' ears proved too thick for needle injections of cyanide and strychnine, keepers saturated potatoes with massive doses of strychnine and offered them to the elephants. Keepers put the animals at ease by offering them several untainted morsels, which the elephants eagerly consumed, occasionally showing thanks by caressing the keepers with their soft trunks. Once the keepers believed that the animals had relaxed, they would slip the elephants a poisoned potato. Each time they substituted a tainted potato, however, the animals would spit the offending tuber out unchewed. Undeterred, the keepers continued to offer potatoes injected with various doses of poison, hoping that the elephants would eat one if the dosage were lowered or they relaxed enough. This continued for quite some time, and the elephants eventually lost their tempers with the small crowd who had gathered to offer them tainted treats. When a small pile of poisoned potatoes accumulated at the feet of the animals, they began throwing the discarded food across the room at a group of military officers and zoo administrators who stood monitoring the proceedings. Apparently, their aim was rather good, and the keepers stopped trying to feed the animals potatoes.[73]

As heartening as this small act of defiance is, it did not alter the animals' fate. To borrow Fukuda's words, "the decision was made" once the funeral procession marched past their cage and abbot Ōmori performed rites for the two elephants.[74] This realization was slow in coming to the elephants' keepers. The two men had each protested loudly when Fukuda ordered them to starve Tonky and Wanri. Like Fukuda himself, they did not support the governor general's decision, and they risked censure by voicing their concerns openly. As Fukuda soon found out, their protests did not stop at words. Both men started quietly slipping their elephants untainted vegetables and potatoes when the attempt to poison them failed.

Tonky in particular was hard to refuse. Brought to Tokyo when she was only four years old, zoo staff had seen Tonky grow into a beautiful, docile, affectionate adolescent. The genial giant would greet keepers with a salute of her trunk as they walked past her cage each morning, and she regularly begged treats from staff by performing tricks as they approached. Keepers used to take her out of her cage each morning before the gardens opened for a stroll around the grounds, where she would nuzzle staff with her trunk and trumpet playfully at men and women as they hustled into work. For the first week or so after her feed had been cut, Tonky continued to perform tricks as Fukuda and other staff passed the Elephant House, occasionally sounding her trunk in a high-pitched appeal. As she weakened, however, the tricks became fewer and fewer, and eventually she no longer even raised her trunk. Still, fortified by the small amounts of food and water that had been secretly delivered, Tonky outlived her larger, more robust companion Wanri.[75]

Poisoned by her own body when unevacuated waste products reached toxic levels and were absorbed into her bloodstream, Wanri finally succumbed at 9:25 P.M. on September 11. Fukuda's diary entry for the day describes how Tonky, the smaller of the two females, caressed the prostrate body of her longtime companion as Wanri lay dying on the floor of the Elephant House. Once Wanri had passed away, Tonky continued to caress Wanri's corpse in the manner of grieving elephants in the wild. Tonky only left the dead elephant's side when her keepers pulled her away so that the dissection team could commence their work. As with John, Wanri's hide was donated to the army. According to zoo records, the rest of her remains were interred with the other animals' in front of the memorial, where they remain to this day.[76]

When Tonky did not immediately follow Wanri it became apparent to Koga, who was part of the dissection team, that someone was slipping food to the younger elephant. Calling Fukuda aside, Koga sternly instructed the interim director to inform the elephant's keeper, Sugaya, that the animal was now military property and continued feeding was absolutely unacceptable. Tonky had to be killed. He further ordered Fukuda to attempt to poison the pachyderm again, since her hunger would no doubt be greater and her resistance perhaps lower. On September 13th the elephant, noticeably thinner, was offered poisoned potatoes once again. This time, rather than throwing the poisoned vegetables at onlookers she simply let them drop to the ground, still refusing to eat them. Hoping that cyanide would work where strychnine had failed, keepers offered Tonky a pail of water laced with the poison. Whether because of scent or because she sensed something was amiss, she refused the liquid. On the 14th, Fukuda informed Koga that continued starvation was the only option. Nine days later, at 6:30 A.M. on September 24, Fukuda received a call at his home from the keeper on night watch informing him that Tonky had died at 2:42 A.M., watched over by her loyal keeper, Sugaya. With Tonky's death, imperial Japan's modern animal sacrifice came to a close, at least at Ueno.

In point of fact, the killings had only just begun. Ueno set the stage for institutions at home and overseas. Zoological gardens and circuses throughout the empire destroyed the core of their collections in the two years after Ueno's Great Zoo Massacre, usually as a hedge against cage breaches in the event of bombings, and often in response to direct orders from Home Ministry authorities. In each case, the reasons for the orders were clear: the course of the war had shifted decisively. The protocols of self-sacrifice were now inescapable. Japan's special attack forces—popularly known as *kamikaze* in the West, but inclusive of a host of operations, from submarine units to airplanes—came together between late 1944 and early 1945, and news media amplified the grim innovation.[77]

The majority of the captive animals killed in the home islands were dead before Allied aircraft began bombing Japanese cities in November 1944. Osaka's Tennōji Zoological Garden and Ueno's sister institution in Tokyo, the Inokashira Nature Culture Park, were the first to follow Ōdachi's lead, enacting emergency measures immediately following Ueno's ceremony for animal martyrs.[78] The empire's three large colonial zoos—the Taipei Zoo, the Seoul Zoo, and Shinkyō Zoo—were among the last to follow suit, instituting their own liquidation policies only as the conflict reached its final phase in late 1944 and 1945. In many cases propitiation rites (private and in some cases public) were performed at gardens, and in each case records of the killings radiate the same surreal ambiguities as the event at Ueno. Japan's animal kingdom was now being used to close the circuit of human biopolitical reduction in the context of total war. Some three hundred large mammals, raptors, and reptiles were killed between September 1943 and August 1945. By 1946 only two elephants remained alive in Japan. In 1940 there had been more than twenty.

CONCLUSION

It matters how the animals died at Ueno. It matters in ethical terms to the extent that animals merit moral consideration, even in the most trying times. It matters in historical terms as well. The manner of the elephants' deaths opened up a space not only for the pursuit of total mobilization—the elevation of a cult of personal sacrifice in the domestic sphere—but also for the repudiation of war as fundamentally counter to the realization of true human dignity in the postwar era. Summoned by the need to make sense of the war and the enduring legacy of their strange deaths, the ghosts of the zoo's sacrificed elephants returned to haunt postwar Japan. Neither Abbot Ōmori and his coterie of monks nor Governor General Ōdachi and the wartime media managed to overcome the sense of betrayal generated by the Great Zoo Massacre in 1943, sentiments and emotions that I have tried to evoke at points in this chapter as a means of bringing this historical moment—the "riddle" of wartime culture with which we began—more forcefully into the present. We cannot, I think, understand the "dark valley" of Japan's imperial nadir without accounting for the powerful emotions of the time, and the story of Ueno's "animal martyrs" offers us a connection with that world.

We are not alone in making use of that connection, a fact that makes it all the more valuable in historical terms. The events of the Great Zoo Massacre returned to public consciousness soon after the war ended. It is impossible to say whether the spark for this return to memory came from postwar children eager to see "real elephants," newspaper reporters interested in a story, or Koga himself, who sought to redefine his role in the slaughter without denying it, but by 1949 a nationwide chorus rose up demanding the undoing of the trauma at Ueno via the return of the elephants to the zoo. Tonky and Wanri and John began to appear in kamishibai (picture stories narrated for an audience by a storyteller) and in popular short fiction. The postwar version of the massacre reached its canonical form in "The Pathetic Elephants" (Kawaisōna Zō), a short story by the award-winning children's author, Tsuchiya Yukio (1904–1999).[79] Tsuchiya had written several jingoistic stories of Japan's imperial heyday, children's adventures in the context of empire, but it was Ueno's elephants that cinched his fame. The story was first published as a part of a collection of essays approved for the grade school curriculum by both the U.S.-led Supreme Command Allied Powers (SCAP), which ruled the country for seven years after 1945, and the Japanese Ministry of Education.

The story became a perennial favorite of conservative Ministry of Education bureaucrats and left-leaning grade school teachers alike. Half a century after the war ended, an expanded and illustrated version of Kawaisōna Zō ranked among the best-selling children's stories in the country. Reframed as a fairy tale of popular victimization and national suffering aimed at the nation's youngsters, the fascist spectacle led by Governor General Ōdachi was transformed into a pacifist parable.

Much like wartime "Military Animal" commemorative zoo maps, which suggested that parents use them as bedtime stories, such readings helped to usher generations of children into the national community of selective war memory and postimperial amnesia. The analysis of such micropolitical acts can tell us many things, but in the context of this chapter and the next they serve to underscore the zoological garden's role as a broker between not just the natural and the social worlds— which were strategically collapsed in the sacrifice and then rebuilt to suit Ōdachi's agenda—but also between mass culture and social practice. The culture of spectacle did more than entertain passive patrons; it facilitated changes in thought and action through the manipulation of emotion and curiosity, drafting children and their parents first into the wartime culture of self-abnegation and later into the service of a new consumer-oriented, politically pacifist postwar order.

The imaginary blood of the Great Zoo Massacre runs through the circulatory system of postwar Japan's memory industry, and it became more important over time. *The Pathetic Elephants* sold well over one million copies between 1970 and 1998, and topped two million by 2005. As of 2007 the book had gone through more than one hundred and fifty reprintings and spawned dozens of alternate versions, counternarratives, and television and stage dramatizations. Doraemon, the well-known animated robot cat, offered a version of the story. Radio networks carried the voice of Akiyama Chieko, a conservative voice of folksy common sense akin to Paul Harvey in the United States, throughout the country each August 15—the date of Japan's 1945 surrender—as she recited the full text of Tsuchiya's story live over the air.[80] Her photo, rather than Tsuchiya's, appears on the cover of several versions of the book, and she released a popular record album of her rendition. Begun in 1967 as the Japanese economy matured and discontent with the Vietnam War fed postwar Japan's growing pacifist consensus, Akiyama's readings continued into the twenty-first century, slowly taking on the patina of tradition in the fast-paced media landscape of late twentieth-century Japan.

The Pathetic Elephants is so widely recognized that the critic Hasegawa Ushio has identified it as a defining "myth" for the postwar nation.[81] Like all myths of any consequence, this one carries multiple meanings, not all of them acknowledged. The zoo's slaughtered animals are now fixed in the master narrative of postwar Japanese "victim consciousness," wherein the Japanese people are cast as victims of the rapacious Japanese military. In the case of the sacrifice, people were encouraged to identify with the animal victims rather than those who ordered the killing, an ironic appropriation of Ōdachi's own logic. As martyrs to the war, the animals have allowed people to satisfy the compulsion to return to and mourn the trauma of conflict without necessarily considering its historical lessons.[82] For generations of children growing up in a country where even limited education about the war is a problem of intense national debate and international controversy, the forced starvation of the zoo's elephants may rank among the most familiar events of the conflict.[83] This is almost certainly the case in the realm of sentiment, where the emotional resonance of a story about the heartless starvation of helpless animals has often eclipsed nonfiction accounts of stories about adults. Innocent and untarnished, children and animals are disproportionately prominent in postwar mediations on the war and its meaning.

Even as the pathetic sacrifice of the zoo's animals has been aestheticized into an object of ongoing mourning, the garden's (and the nation's) historical connections with colonialism and imperialism have been actively erased and then forgotten, an act of institutional amnesia that remains in effect to this day. "War" and "empire," as the next chapter shows, were decoupled in the postwar zoo—as they were in works such as Tsuchiya's story, which rendered Governor General Ōdachi (a civilian bureaucrat) into a uniformed officer in the Imperial Japanese Army. The "war" was mourned at tragedy; the "empire" was forgotten, and it was in part the intense suffering of these strange "animal martyrs"—delivered to children at their bedsides and in their school textbooks—that facilitated that postimperial amnesia.

PART THREE

After Empire

FIGURE 15. The Children's Zoo ("Kodomo Dōbutsuen"). Reprinted from Koga Tadamichi, *Kansatsu ehon: Kindaa bukku, kodomo dōbutsuen* (Tokyo: Fureburukan, 1949). Image courtesy of Froebel-kan Publishing.

CHAPTER 5

The Children's Zoo

Elephant Ambassadors and Other Creatures
of the Allied Occupation

I consider early childhood events as most essential to a man's
scientific and philosophical development.

—Konrad Lorenz, Nobel autobiography

When I visit the zoo, I see the bars of the animal's "cage" as
a mirror that reflects each of you. That is because when you
face the animal on the other side of the bars we can see
whether you are a good or bad child as clearly as if it were
reflected in a mirror.

—Okamatsu Takeshi, "The Zoo as Mirror" (*"Dōbutsuen*
no kagami")

BAMBI GOES TO TOKYO

"Bambi," a diminutive white-tailed fawn, arrived at the Tokyo's Ueno
Imperial Zoo on May 19, 1951, with great fanfare. The first of his species (*Odocoileus virginianus*) exhibited at the Ueno Zoo, the fawn was
a gift from Walter Disney himself to the children of Japan in celebration
of the end of the war and the Japanese premiere of the animated film.
Old warhorses—the stallions ridden into battle by Japanese officers at
the height of the nation's imperial glory—were pushed aside to make
way for the cute, wide-eyed mascot of American corporate interests and
sentimental environmentalism.[1] In the early 1940s, as Japan's empire
expanded, these warhorses had been media stars, celebrated at zoos, in
parades, in popular music, and in feature films and newsreels.[2] By the
time *Bambi* premiered in Japan in 1951, the erstwhile champions were

emblems of an empire in ruins, reminders of a conflict that many wanted to forget. The demobilized horses (sometimes called *fukuin dō-butsu,* or "demobilized animals," a play on the term *fukuinhei* used to described demobilized soldiers) were enlisted as labor, transferred to the farm section of the gardens' new Children's Zoo, or, rumor had it, eaten.

A commercial failure when originally released in the United States in 1942, the film opened in New York as Americans were struggling to come to terms with the realities of the war.[3] It was the height of the U.S. retreat in the Pacific: fathers, brothers, and sons were being shipped to far-off lands and the newsreels that preceded Disney's sentimental elegy to lost innocence were often filled with images of fiery destruction that echoed in the film. Five years in production, and costing more than $5 million to produce, *Bambi* lost more than $1 million in 1942. After the war Disney attempted to recoup his losses with the Tokyo release and an American rerelease. In commercial terms, the film represented the expansion into Asia of what Victoria DeGrazia has called the "irresistible empire" of American-style mass consumer capitalism. In cultural terms, it illuminates the nexus that I have called "empire after empire," the arrival of triumphant America in a Japan suddenly bereft of empire.[4]

A captive market under the U.S.-led Allied Occupation (1945–1952), postwar Japanese, like postwar Americans, were transfixed by *Bambi.*[5] In the United States, *Bambi* resonated with the vision of the home as an endangered paradise that drove anxious Cold War Americans out of cities and into suburban enclaves. In Japan, laid waste by nuclear weapons and napalm, this coming-of-age story in a fire-scorched landscape struck a different chord, echoing the ongoing occupation of the country by Disney's own countrymen, drawing attention to the war's traumatic end. The film joined with a host of other media to augment the growing sense that the Japanese people—as opposed to their leaders—had been innocent victims of the war.[6]

This chapter explores the historical conjuncture represented by this ambassador of American mass culture. The orthodoxies of sentimental war commemoration and imperial amnesia that characterized postwar Japanese attitudes about the conflict were already ingrained in the zoo in 1951. After defeat, Japan's history of popular jingoism and imperial sacrifice, given grim form in the bloody procedures of the Great Zoo Massacre, was renarrated to cast the Japanese people as innocent children beguiled by a small military clique and slaughtered by a merciless alien foe. The American occupation also invested in the re-presentation of the Japanese as innocents: the supreme commander, U.S. general Douglas MacArthur, once likened the conquered nation's level of psychological development to that of a twelve-year-old child.[7]

Rebuilt into a monumental celebration of the future under American hegemony, the zoo became a spectacular rejection of the past, a theme park focused on the figures of the uncorrupted child and the blameless animal.[8] Animals and children were reframed together as part of the difficult process of "de-imperialization"—the deconstruction of empire—and national reconsolidation. Once presented as totems of empire and marked as future soldiers, Japan's zoo animals and children were now given roles meant to illustrate the convergence of the postwar United States and occupied Japan.[9] Tokyo's Ueno Zoo, like the manicured suburbia of the American dream, became a conservative paradise: a carefully controlled, sanitized, and brightly lit landscape managed in the service of national unification and economic transformation.[10] Children took on unprecedented importance in this setting. "The zoo must be an oasis for children," wrote Director Koga Tadamichi, who returned to the gardens in October 1945 after resigning his positions as an officer in the Imperial Japanese Army and instructor at the Army Veterinary College. Under Koga's renewed leadership the institution became a device for taming the nation's "wild" postwar children (*susanda kodomo*) in the service of peace and productivity.[11]

Where the wartime zoo was hammered into a ritual altar intended to generate consent and spur personal sacrifice, the postwar gardens were converted into a "leisure cultural education institution" designed to mobilize children's "instinctual" fascination with animals in the pursuit of their own "humanization," a pursuit that implied the dehumanization of older generations under the wartime regime. The institution sought to marshal kids both as actors and audience in the years after 1945—not only working *for* children but also working *through* them—and as a result this chapter is particularly attendant to the role of children as historical actors. The idea that children—unacculturated and uncorrupted—shared innate qualities with animals had a long history at the zoo, but the connection took on new salience under American occupation, where kids could often act in ways that adults could not. At the same time, Koga and his colleagues understood the simple fact that anyone who could claim to speak in the service of children could also lay claim to a powerful moral and political position.

As he struggled to make a place for the zoo in postwar Japan, Director Koga refined his earlier ideas on the importance of animal encounters.

"There can be no questioning the fact that human beings are a special kind of animal," Koga argued at the beginning of his 1959 book on *Animal Affection*. "When seen in this way it becomes clear that animal lives [*seikatsu*] and human lives [*seikatsu*] are fundamentally the same." Animals were simply more honest, "completely naked" of pretention, and therefore both restorative and instructive to watch. "The more we watch them, the better we understand ourselves." The purpose of the zoo was to frame—and thus define—such acts of self-recognition.

Koga sought to mobilize this process of interpellation—forcing visitors to ask themselves, in a sense, who they think they are—in the pursuit of a "New Japan" (*Shin Nippon*). The zoological garden, he argued in his savvy pursuit of funding and public support under foreign occupation, offered a means of accelerating the peaceful humanization of the "nation's future leaders." "The cultivation of the spirit of kind treatment of animals . . . is in a sense a short-cut to the attainment of true humanity [*jitsu no hyumanichī*]. The construction of a good zoo for the younger generation is, we believe, the most satisfying act that a peace-loving educated people can do for their country."[12] The postwar zoo sublimated the shame of military defeat and the anxiety of occupation into a celebration of national revival in the name of the country's kids, fusing exhibition and social action around a figure—the "child," a category every bit as abstract and ideologically useful as the "animal"—that few could reject. Rebuilt and illuminated against the backdrop of a bombed-out capital, the occupation-era zoo sought to reinforce the new order of things in the guise of staging a childish escape from it.[13]

EMPIRE AFTER EMPIRE

This reorientation away from sacrifice and conquest toward childlike innocence took place in a context of institutional and national decolonization.[14] Japan not only lost the war in 1945; it also lost an empire built over the course of more than fifty years. The formal components of the Greater East Asia Co-Prosperity Sphere were dismantled through forced decolonization—a process that included changes in the former homeland (*naichi*) as well as in former colonies (*gaichi*)—completed under Allied command in less than eighteen months. As Lori Watt argues in her work on colonial repatriation in the wake of defeat, the rapidity of this formal process belies a longer, far more complicated history of postimperial disentanglement that has been overlooked by historians and the general public.[15] The pervasive and intentional *absence* of empire is easily ignored in institutions less overtly associated with Japan's imperial project, but it cannot be dismissed at the zoological gardens, where decolonization played out in the concrete work of reconstruction.[16] The specific history of the zoological gardens offers us a means of addressing the more general problem of decolonization under occupation and illustrates how Japan's well-known history of postwar redevelopment and trans-war modernization was also a story of empire's creation and destruction, followed by the quest to regain sovereignty on economic and political terms palatable to an occupying army.

Koga and his staff registered the loss of empire with particular concern. They worried that decolonization would mean the end of access to desirable species found in the colonies and the loss of a key component of the gardens' institutional mission.[17] When the Allies disassembled the Japanese empire, the zoological garden's reach was also reduced.[18] Once the nexus of a network of cultural and scientific institutions that could reach into habitats and private holdings from the Malay Peninsula to Manchuria, the Ueno Zoo was now, in the starkest terms, a second-rate zoological garden serving the ruined capital of a diplomatically isolated American protectorate.

The first Americans arrived at the zoo's gates less than a week after Allied forces landed in Japan. SCAP officials wasted little time putting the zoo, along with the capital's other large cultural institutions, to work in support of their agenda.[19] Koga, conversant in English and a savvy political operator, moved with alacrity to incorporate Allied purposes. He even announced a new motto suited to the demands of "peaceful Japan" (*heiwa Nippon*): "The zoo is the peace" (*Dōbutsuen wa heiwa sono mono*).[20] As John Dower has shown, "demilitarization and democratization," rather than sacrifice and conquest, were the order of the day.[21] Phrased in awkward English and often reprinted without accompanying Japanese translation, Koga's slogan addressed at once the nation's occupiers and a domestic population exhausted by war and desperate for renewal. The occupation-era zoo brought both groups together.

GIs received free admission and were a common sight at the zoo. American families sat among the mostly Japanese crowd when *Bambi* was first shown at the garden's new outdoor movie theater, the Kamoshika-za, in 1946. The theater was built, in part, to compensate for the absence of megafauna slaughtered during the war. Without access to foreign species and funds for the development of new immersion exhibits,

Koga wrote in 1947, "only movies and photos can show [animals in] a completely natural setting" to crowds who longed for encounters with "real animals."[22] He feared that the loss of the colonies would exacerbate the nation's ongoing alienation from the animal world.[23] This was especially true of young children, who did not have a memory of the zoo during its imperial heyday. The loss of empire, then, was associated with the loss of an authentic self through the disappearance of animals, but it was perceived as a particular threat to the development of the nation's youth. Koga, like his contemporaries in the United States examined by Gregg Mitman, turned to movies as a means of addressing this deficit, hoping that motion pictures could offer a substitute for the authentic motion of living animals.[24]

Film, however, could never completely replace the real thing. The ultimate goal was the creation of a "true zoo" (dōbutsuenrashii dōbutsuen) filled with "real animals," and that could only be accomplished through "the progress of civilization," by which Koga meant technical and material development directed by scientific knowledge. "Zoological gardens evolve as civilization develops," he wrote after the war. "The zoo offers an unadulterated image of the human being's natural desire for nature, a natural reflection [of civilization]." He continued, "To put it a bit more clearly, the ideal situation is to be able to look at animals, which are natural objects [shizenbutsu], surrounded by flora [from their native habitat] and other animals."[25] This microcosm of nature could only be accomplished in a "large setting" and "without caging the animals" so that they could be seen to move freely. Koga continued to believe, as he had before the war, that the development of such an institution was not only possible, it was essential to a healthy, functioning society. Technology and trade could manufacture a "real ecology," a source of spiritual revival. This ecology could in turn lubricate the gears of progress, spurring the kind of material advances that made the zoo possible in the first place.[26]

In the early years of the occupation, when Japan was diplomatically isolated and even food was difficult to come by, such arguments appeared to be little more than a postimperial fantasy. Much as it was built up through the physical expansion of empire, the zoo was slowly emptied by imperial atrophy. Many of the animals at the center of the collection before the war were killed, starved to death, or simply allowed to die following the sacrifice of 1943. By 1945 the collection was reduced to one-third of its wartime heights. "Only the giraffes remain," Koga wrote dejectedly, and when the largest of them, Nagatarō, died in 1947, he had to resist calls that the animal be butchered and fed to the hungry public. "I couldn't imagine offering children the image of people eating their beloved Nagatarō."[27]

In these "lonely" times keepers bred pigs in the lion cages, ducks in the flying cages, and began auctioning rabbits for meat in order to raise funds. The younger zoo staff titled their satirical in-house magazine "The Sons of Pig [*sic*]" to comment on the absurdity of a culture where little pigs pranced behind bars that once held lions.[28] Feed was so short in 1946 that children visiting the gardens, perhaps on their way to the zoo's Pig-Chicken-Duck Lottery or Rabbit Spot Sale, could barter their way in with a bucket full of pumpkin seeds from gourds grown in Tokyo's burnt-out vacant lots.[29]

Like the kids who paid their way in with seeds, Koga struggled to turn hardship into a virtue. He successfully lobbied SCAP officials for increased funding as part of an effort to convert the zoo—once a spectacle of imperial success, now a summary of the costs of war—into a beacon of healthy recovery for the country's youth.[30] Gone were the empire, its animal totems, its vision of boys as colonial adventurers and girls as the mothers of future soldiers. In their place emerged the stuff of this chapter: a future-oriented conglomeration of amusement park rides, the Kamoshika-za Theater, the nation's first children's zoo, and a profitable "Monkey Train" operated by a trained Crab-Eating Macaque named "Chico" purchased from an American GI.[31] A flood of American animals followed Chico into Ueno's cages and attendance surged. Gate numbers grew by more than one thousand percent in the four years after surrender. Total attendance quickly surpassed wartime heights that Koga and Inoshita, who retired in 1946, had thought unapproachable. Over three and a half million customers visited the Ueno Zoo in 1949.

Economic development supplanted imperial expansion as the nation's driving mission during these years, a trend that accelerated as Japan's postwar became embroiled in the Cold War contest between the United States and the Soviet Union. This geopolitical transformation was reflected in the world of the zoo: former colonies were rendered as independent nations, displays no longer charted species distributions within the outlines of the Greater East Asian Co-Prosperity Sphere, and British and American intervention opened Africa (long inaccessible and idealized as the most authentically "wild" continent) to collecting expeditions. Animals were similarly reframed: New acquisitions no longer arrived as military trophies. Instead, such distinctively "American" fauna as pumas, porcupines, and alligators arrived as gifts from U.S. zoos, corporations, and the United States Army. Dozens of monkeys and snakes arrived as presents from American GIs who picked up pets during the Pacific campaign. And a state-of-the-art "African Ecology Diorama" dedicated to the "conservation" of African fauna opened in 1955, the same year that the government officially pronounced the "postwar" period finished.[32]

The formal empire may have unraveled in 1945, but aspects of imperial culture were rewoven into the new fabric of postwar institutional life. "Zoos are the barometer of a civilization," Koga argued in reference to Africa and Asia at the end of the occupation in 1952. It was the duty of "civilized nations," defined as those with zoological gardens, to "protect" rare fauna from "uncivilized" countries by putting the animals on display.[33] Increasingly portrayed as victims of diffuse global environmental degradation after the war, wild animals became endangered emblems of a shared global inheritance. As such, acquisition by economically powerful nations (including Japan in 1952 by Koga's reckoning) could be framed as a scientific necessity. Thus were the old dichotomies of empire—the "civilized" imperial center and the "natural" colonies—reconfigured to suit the new age and to allow the continued movement of fauna (and natural resources more broadly) from the underdeveloped periphery to the developed economies of the metropole. Indeed, by the 1950s Koga was surprised to discover that while the disappearance of empire did limit direct access to certain Asian environments, Japan's incorporation into the American Cold War order led to increased access to more plentiful and more diverse fauna through amplified global trade.

This reconfigured empire was expressed in both institutional and cultural terms. During the postwar years, Japanese zoos began to use conservation (rather than conquest) as the primary justification for their operation.[34] The "preservation of wild animal [populations] on the edge of destruction has become an important new mission for [Japanese] zoological gardens," Koga wrote in 1957. This anxiety about disappearing nature manifested in broader cultural realms. In Japan and around the world, the question of extinction became suddenly more pressing. The pursuit of endangered species was most often justified in the name of the world's children, who were seen as at once insatiable in their desire to see unusual animals and pitiable as they lost access to the vanishing wild.

But "animals" and the "wild" never entirely disappeared in the zoo. They simply became more valuable and desirable.[35] Specific animals were killed and entire species went extinct, but the broader dynamics of ecological modernity remained in place. In the acquisitive logic of midcentury conservationism, the extinction of a given species in the wild could offer a convincing justification for the further collection of other "threatened" wild animal populations, which were to be brought to the zoo for attempted breeding and study. "When we fear a species may go extinct in the wild, we must act to conserve it," Koga wrote in an essay on the purpose of the zoological gardens. "Conservation" was here synonymous with "collection."[36] The postwar zoo was sustained by this sense of nature's retreat, which came into being as the dream of imperial bounty faded. The term "extinction" (*zetsumetsu*)—referenced only rarely in prewar times, most often as a criticism of enemy military action or colonial exploitation by "natives"—became increasingly prominent in the Ueno Zoo's public relations materials as the occupation ended and Japanese culture became entangled with the atomic anxieties and neo-Malthusian fears of global human "overpopulation" in the 1950s and 1960s.[37]

This rhetoric was part of a rising global chorus of loss and anxiety that developed together with the atomic Cold War and the global processes of decolonization that shaped the second half of the twentieth century.[38] After returning in 1956 from an around-the-world tour of zoological gardens that included meetings of the International Union of Directors of Zoological Gardens (IUDZG; formed in 1946), the International Union for Conservation of Nature (IUCN; created in 1948), and the International Society for Museums, Koga remarked that the words "preservation" and "extinction" seemed to be on everyone's lips.[39] In 1948 Fairfield Osborn (1887–1969), president of the New York Zoological Society, which administered the Bronx Zoo, gave voice to this broadly shared sentiment in his influential book *Our Plundered Planet*. Koga had a copy in his library. Begun midway through the Second World War, the book spoke eloquently of another war: "This other world-wide war, still continuing, is bringing more widespread distress to the human race than any that has resulted from armed conflict. It contains potentialities of ultimate disaster greater even than would follow the misuse of atomic power." "This other war," Osborn concluded, "is man's conflict with nature."[40] The dynamics of ecological modernity had become the stuff of apocalypse.

NEOCOLONIAL POTLATCH

For some, the barren landscapes of the country's zoos reflected the grim outlook of postwar ecological modernity. For others, the empty cages offered a stage for the dramatization of renewal. Few large exotic animals were left alive in Japan after the war. Following the Great Zoo Massacre in 1943, zoos and circuses were ordered to "liquidate" all "dangerous animals," a class that included most of the large mammal species that visitors expected to see. More than three hundred lions, tigers, bears, and elephants were slaughtered. Many of these killings were sanctified in rituals akin to those performed at Ueno by Abbot Ōmori and his Buddhist monks, but just as often the killings were left unpublicized and undiscussed. Troops stationed in the northern city of Sendai, where Fukuda had hoped to send the docile elephant Tonky for safe keeping in 1943, for example, believed they were fed polar bear meat following the decimation of the Sendai Zoo's collection in 1944, but the source of the unfamiliar meat was never confirmed. Sendai and many smaller zoos simply closed. Others, like Ueno, labored on, transformed by food shortages and air raids into condensations of the broader culture of national suffering.[41]

Faced with the prospect of a zoo where pigs outnumbered patrons, Koga decided early in the occupation to focus his energies on the creation of a collection of domestic animals "suitable to Tokyo's role as the nation's capital." The reorientation underlined the fact that Tokyo was a *national* capital for the first time in more fifty years through the exhibition of "distinctly Japanese" fauna. Japanese brown bears, Japanese pheasants, Japanese serows (*Nihon kamoshika*, the namesake of the Kamoshika-za Theater), Japanese wild boar, Japanese deer (portrayed as Bambi's "cousins"), and Hokkaidō bears were purchased or sometimes captured by volunteers. Groups of school children waded into streams in pursuit of Japanese giant salamanders, which they proudly shipped off to Tokyo, care of "Mr. Zookeeper."[42]

Despite such efforts, the new "Japanese-style zoo" (*Nihonrashii dōbutsuen*) was unsatisfying for just about everyone. "Where are the animals?" Koga recalls being asked as he stood in the middle of the gardens. "What is this, a pig garden!?!" griped another visitor. The zoological garden was associated with the overseas exotic and the colonial wild in the popular imagination. Neither the trauma of war nor appeals to natural-historical patriotism could dislodge the idea that a "real zoo collection" must include lions, tigers, and elephants, at the very least. Such creatures were out of reach in postimperial Japan. "When people think of the zoo," Koga wrote in the travel magazine *Tabi* in 1949, "they think of foreign species." But, he lamented, "very few really large animals are left available to a Japan that has lost Taiwan, Korea, and

Sakhalin."[43] Old collection networks were gone. SCAP maintained a monopoly on formal economic and diplomatic exchange.

Koga's clever response to the problem of formal isolation was to shift his efforts into the informal economy of the gift, less carefully policed by SCAP. Zoological gardens, especially those associated with governments and royalty, are embedded in multilayered systems of exchange that trade in more than money. Animals are sometimes assigned monetary prices, but as the events of 1943 illustrate so clearly, cash can hardly capture their full value. Gardens work instead in a system of hybrid exchange that is often carried out as real barter but characterized in the language of gift giving, cultural diplomacy, or conservation. This shared logic of exchange produces common understandings of institutional status and collective notions of capital—cultural capital that is objectified in living creatures and institutionalized via professional organizations such as the IUDZG and IUCN. Individual and institutional prestige—recognition as a "good zoo" or as an innovative zoo director, for example—are built and lost through such networks.

It is a system that, like the potlatch practiced in certain communities in the northwestern United States, builds solidarity through reciprocity in which both the honor of the giver and the recipient are engaged.[44] In this case we might call it "neocolonial potlatch," since the system was activated in response to and conditioned by American neocolonial rule. Koga understood the protocols of this modern potlatch. He knew that zoological gardens, like museums and other kinds of cultural institution (or even nation-states themselves), are partially sustained and defined through mutual recognition.[45] He also understood that zoo directors, himself included, were loath to leave a gift unanswered. In a fully realized potlatch system the failure to match a gift with a return of equal value could lead to a loss of prestige, social censure, or worse. Matching a gift would create a system of stable statuses; overmatching a gift, however, could produce an escalating contest for honor, and beginning in 1948 Koga sought to spark a series of escalating gift cycles with zoos in the United States.

He did this by sending letters of inquiry and small (at times unsolicited) gifts to such places as the National Zoo in Washington D.C. and the Honolulu Zoological Gardens. His efforts were successful. By the end of the occupation in 1952 the Ueno Zoo, formerly a summary of Japan's imperial reach, was repopulated with gift animals, most of them from the United States. The institution offered visitors a satisfying map of Japan's cultural and diplomatic reintegration into a U.S.-led international order. Koga did this, in part, by using the very "native species" that zoo-goers in Tokyo found so unsatisfying. When, for example, a relatively modest delivery of eight turtles arrived via military airmail from the Hogle Municipal Zoological Garden in Salt Lake City, Utah, in April 1949 in response to Koga's gift of a giant salamander to Salt Lake City Mayor Earl J. Glade, Koga responded with a veritable deluge of Japanese fauna—a disproportionate response that was all the more impressive given Ueno's depleted state. Within a few short months a menagerie of Japanese macaques, pheasants, cranes, salamanders, badgers, and bears found its way to Salt Lake City and an equally sizable collection of coyotes, macaws, (de-scented) skunks, pumas, and lions arrived in Tokyo. These were the first lions to set foot in Japan after the war. They were celebrated in news articles and happy advertisements from Lion Brand Toothpaste, among others. SCAP officers visited to bask in the animals' public relations glow.

The gifts were framed as hopeful signs of normalization; they were a boon for the Ueno Zoo, of course, but they were also treated as indications of growing affiliation between former enemies. The entire exchange—approved by SCAP at Mayor Glade's urging and likely with support from the Church of Latter-Day Saints—was presented as an act of "animal diplomacy." "We pray that these animals will carry out their duty as ambassadors of peace," read a September 1949 article in *The Zoo News* (*Dōbutsuen shinbun*), invoking a Christian vocabulary that was increasingly prevalent in occupied Japan. The animals, the article concluded, would "bring America and Japan together in understanding through the affection of the many people who care for them." Innocent and charismatic, the creatures were instruments for the political mobilization of human emotions; they lent a distinctive face to the occupation. At the same time, Salt Lake City's small zoo itself took on an imperial aspect: it contained what may have been the largest collection of Japanese fauna available anywhere outside of Asia.

"ANIMAL KINDERGARTEN"

Even as Koga was manipulating the levers of American sentiment, he also sought to "protect" Japanese children from many aspects of the occupation. This conservative impulse was most clearly expressed in the opening of Japan's first children's zoo (*kodomo dōbutsuen*) in April 1948. Japan's zoos had always cultivated children as a segment of their audience, but the opening of Ueno's new "Animal Kinder Garten," as it was identified on the gate, marked the first time that a domestic zoo offered kids a distinct space of this kind, a segregated area specifically designed to nurture children's "human instinct" for moral behavior through direct encounters with uncaged animals.[46] Built alongside the new Monkey Train at the center of the gardens, the Children's Zoo offered children of middle school age and younger (and their parents) a series of enclosures defined by low fences and a feed stand, where they could purchase food to feed to a variety of free-roaming "gentle animals." The Children's Zoo was meant to help create a new child for a new Japan: a peaceful, productive, and above all disciplined child capable of sustaining the nation's postwar recovery.

The Animal Kinder Garten sought to instill compassion, diligence, and peacefulness, values that bespoke gentle docility rather than obedience to military orders. Such ideas were not new at Ueno—before the war Koga and others had argued that similar attitudes were central to the development of good imperial administrators—but they were devoted to a different disciplinary task as economic development supplanted military conquest at the center of national life, and therefore they received greater attention and institutional support. Built over the wreckage of the wartime Elephant House—destroyed by an American bomb in 1945—and loosely modeled on an idealized farm, Ueno's Children's Zoo offered patrons a carefully curated, intensively managed vision of a world at peace, a small utopia where kids were safe, change was muted through appeals to the rhythms of a rural setting, labor was aestheticized as entertainment, and behavior was carefully regulated in the name of moral development. Ironically, given the modern desire to seal childhood off from politics (a desire expressed in the construction of the Kodomo Dōbutsuen itself), the Children's Zoo may have been the most ideological space in the occupation-era zoo.

Expressing deep concern about the degenerating moral character of Japanese children, "the nation's future leaders," Koga designed the Children's Zoo to address those worries.[47] In the aftermath of total war, the bright, wholesome vision articulated in the area stood in sharp contrast to the dark, pessimistic anxieties that gave it form. "Quite some time has passed since the creation of peaceful Japan [heiwa Nippon kensetsu] became the defining purpose of the new Japan," Koga wrote in 1948. "But as I read about all of the trouble in the newspaper each

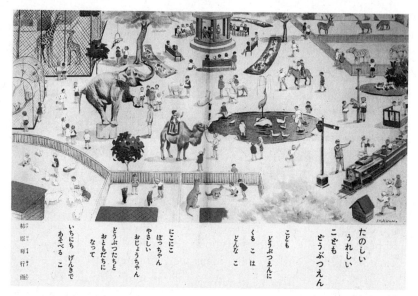

たのしい
うれしい
こども
どうぶつえん

こども
どうぶつえんに
くる
こは
どんな
こ

にこにこ
ぼっちゃん
やさしい
おじょうちゃん
どうぶつたちと
おともだちに
なって

いちにち
げんきで
あそべる
こ

柿原喜市行画

FIGURE 16. "Fun and Happy Children's Zoo" ("Tanoshii Ureshii Kodomo Dōbutsuen"). An idyllic depiction of the Children's Zoo from 1949, this image collapses the space between the area and the Monkey Train, seen stopped at the miniature train signal on the right side of the illustration. Children were encouraged to enter enclosures holding barnyard animals, kangaroos, and even baby bears (shown here drinking milk from a bottle). Goats, rabbits, and other domesticated species roamed free in the Children's Zoo, where the bars and barriers that characterize most zoo exhibits were removed or reduced to their minimum possible size. Image courtesy of Froebel-kan Publishing.

day or look at the behavior of youngsters in the zoo, I cannot help but feel that our goal is farther away than ever."[48]

Like many adults at the time, Koga had grown accustomed to the clear lines of authority that developed during the war. He was also reacting to the sense of dislocation that arose when the ideological imperatives of total war—which required all to accommodate change in the name of national survival—were peeled away from a social landscape that had been fundamentally transformed through those same wartime policies. As Sonya O. Rose suggests, "War, especially total war, transforms the everyday in unparalleled ways." Thus, she argues, "war's liberating potential threatens the very unity that the nation is supposed to represent."[49] The resulting moral panic, which developed as such anxieties were taken up into public discourse and policymaking, was shared by societies around the postwar world (notably in 1950s America) as they pursued reintegration. It reached a particularly fevered pitch in Japan, where the legitimacy of the nation's ruling class was undermined by defeat and compromised by foreign occupation. "In such times," Koga observed in a dejected tone in 1947, "it can seem as if the world is filled with nothing but guile [akudoi]."[50] The loss of empire and war was thus felt individually by many, especially men such as Koga whose codes of masculinity and hierarchy were called into question.

Koga's writings on the Children's Zoo showed that he understood the moral treatment of animals and the production of moral human beings to be part of an intertwined process. "I don't just want to create human beings who are not cruel to animals," Koga said of the decision to create Ueno's Kodomo Dōbutsuen. "I want to create human beings who are *unable* to be cruel to animals."[51] Compassion and control worked hand in glove in such statements, which were given urgency through Koga's public observations on the "general deterioration of national moral standards after the war, particularly the increasingly dissolute nature of our children."[52]

The director's writings during the early occupation are replete with examples of "wild children." In a 1947 essay on the Children's Zoo for parents participating in the country's new network of American-style parent-teacher associations (PTA), Koga wrote:

> [A] group of about ten children [at a school in Tokyo] cut into cages with wire cutters in an attempt to steal baby rabbits and make off with cute pigeons. Such behavior is entirely new since the end of the war. If you try to control these kids when they are goofing off, making a ruckus or throwing rocks at the animals, they are completely dismissive. These are the same children who must carry the burden of a building a Peaceful Japan. It would be too much to say that wholesome childrearing is the only path to the establishment of a Cultured Japan, but nobody can think that we should just let such wild children go.[53]

After a lengthy list of other misdeeds at the zoo Koga argued: "Not once did I witness such activities before the war," despite records indicating that numerous similar infractions occurred during the 1920s and 1930s. When viewed from a postwar zoo decimated by war, sacrifice, and starvation the period "before the war," as Koga called the years prior to the massacre of 1943, appeared as a golden age. Even 1941 and 1942, he wrote, were times when the "mood ran high" and "the people's morals" were in good order. Threatened by the uncertainties of the early occupation, Koga was nostalgic for the heady days of empire.[54]

Koga struggled nonetheless to master the practical challenges. "The administration of the Children's Zoo is quite difficult," he told the PTA.

"In actuality, we are bringing animals out to play with children and putting children into the displays with the animals. When there, they are made to take care of the animals and pet them [*aibushitarisaseru*]." Koga's use of the causative verb form—*saseru*—is telling: such close encounters required careful stage directions. "An extremely accomplished guide who knows animals very well and who understands children" is indispensable, he argued. "It would not be an exaggeration to say that the entire success or failure of the Children's Zoo hinges on . . . such a person." Children could neither be left to their own devices nor in the sole care of their parents. In occupation-era Ueno, these "guides," often costumed in American-style overalls, were invariably men, avuncular keepers near the end of their careers at the zoo.[55] Such gentle caregivers in American costume carried a strong message about reconciliation.

The carefully constructed idyllic scene included calves, donkeys, rabbits, monkeys, squirrels, goats, sheep, pigs, kangaroos, chicken or duck chicks, cockatoos, small birds, and gold fish. Koga also wrote of his desire to include bear cubs and the like "when they are small and docile." And as though invoking the Biblical dream of a peaceable kingdom, where the "the lion will lie down with the lamb," Assistant Director Fukuda was particularly fond of exhibiting groups of infant predators (literally lion and tiger and bear cubs) and prey species together.[56]

All of the animals in this playful menagerie were chosen for docility and vulnerability. Administrators were understandably concerned about the safety of children and animals, but they were also focused on the moral lessons that could develop. "When entrusted with a vulnerable animal, children exhibit one of two diametrically opposed reactions," Koga told the PTA. "They either love the animal or they torment it." Such behavior, he continued, may be a manifestation of the child's natural sentiments, but "it is our duty to do our utmost to nurture the compassion in the child's heart and suppress such malice."[57] The purpose of the Children's Zoo, he wrote, was "to slowly nurture, bit by bit, a sense of compassion for the weak, a quality that is extremely lacking in today's world."[58]

OCCUPIED JAPAN'S ELEPHANT MANIA

Young Japanese mattered to the postwar operation of the gardens in countless ways, especially as they became important players in the broader public sphere. As an "oasis for children," the Ueno Zoo was a focus of youthful political action, though not always in the ways that

Koga might have hoped. When zoo workers joined other city employees in a general strike in March 1948, for instance, children led successful counterprotests against labor. "Today at the Ueno Zoo bars kept people out rather than holding animals in," read an article in the generally conservative *Yomiuri News*. "A group of more than one hundred angry children and adults climbed the zoo's closed gates and crowded into the grounds, only to be chased by zoo keepers. The kids seemed to be having great fun running around while a Malaccan Cockatoo sang out 'Hahaha, strike, strike' ['hahaha, sutoraiki, sutoraiki']."[59] Koga doubtless saw these children as "wild," but they got their way: the zoo was opened to the public free of charge the following day.

The implausibly eloquent cockatoo invited *Yomiuri* readers laugh and dismiss the protest as a colorful embellishment on the grander events of the day, but Koga and his staff saw an opportunity in youthful energy, and they worked hard to draw children into the service of the zoo. Indeed, one of the most impressive examples of organized political action by children during the Allied occupation developed at the zoo under Koga's hopeful eyes, just a few weeks after the "invasion of the zoo." In late 1948 and early 1949 tens of thousands of Japanese children took to the streets in a series of events that deserves to be called an elephant mania. The kids' goal was simple—the return of elephants to the Ueno Zoo—but when the media framed their efforts as an apolitical and spontaneous "craze," neither revolutionary nor reactionary, they offered perfect cover for the zoo's staff, who leveraged the children's determined pursuit of "real live elephants" against aspects of SCAP policy that impinged on the institution's own ability to act.

As we will see, the initial spark for the elephant mania came out of Koga's own unsuccessful attempt to bring elephants back to Ueno. Amplified by the nation's three major dailies—the *Asahi*, *Mainichi*, and *Yomiuri*, each of which bid for the rights to sponsor the spectacle—and pursued by thousands of eager children, the zoo director's efforts to undo the ritualized horror of the Great Zoo Massacre via the return of elephants developed into one of the occupation's most highly publicized efforts in cultural diplomacy. By October 1949 the elephant mania had come to involve Japanese Prime Minister Yoshida Shigeru, Indian Prime Minister Jawaharlal Nehru, and Thai Field Marshal Plaek Pibulsongkram, as well as a host of SCAP officials, several large corporations, and the national rail service. In the midst of global decolonization and regional tumult, this diverse group converged around the figures of two large pachyderms—Indira, who arrived as a "gift to the children of

Japan" from Nehru, and Gajah (quickly renamed Hanako), proffered by Pibulsongkram in the name of the Boy Scouts of Thailand—and they did so in the name of Tokyo's children.

Only two other elephants were alive in Japan when Indira and Hanako arrived: a pair of retired circus performers kept at the Higashi-yama Zoological Gardens in Nagoya, some 220 miles southeast of Tokyo, where zoo director Kitaō Eiichi had successfully resisted war-time orders to "liquidate" them.[60] Soon after resigning his military commission, Koga tried to persuade Kitaō to exchange one of the pair for one of Ueno's giraffes. Kitaō refused, citing the animals' "deep emo-tional bonds." Though the refusal was no doubt in part practical—the elephants were Higashiyama's main draw at a time when money was short—it was also rooted in careful observation of the animals' behav-ior.[61] When Kitaō and his staff separated the two elephants as a test in 1946, the pair went "wild," ramming the walls of their cages and injur-ing themselves as they panicked and struggled to reunite. They were, Kitaō diagnosed sadly, traumatized by the war and the recent loss of two fellow elephants who did not survive 1945. Kitaō's logic is confirmed by the biologist Joyce Poole's recent fieldwork on the elaborate mourn-ing rituals of elephants in the wild. It is indeed likely that the pair were traumatized and grieving.[62]

This recognition of the elephants as *both* complex social animals— "real live elephants"—*and* symbols may help to account for postwar Japan's mania.

In a dynamic not unlike the mobilization of children to serve agen-das buoyed by sentimental ideas about the meaning of childhood, the elephants, as living creatures, could lend substance to the ideas and emotions they were felt to represent. Not only were the Ueno Zoo's wartime elephants martyred as loyal innocents by representatives of the state (a fate that rendered them into ready surrogates for postwar Japa-nese who wished to see themselves as innocent victims of the conflict), they were also highly intelligent, emotionally complex mammals whose physical characteristics and social attributes aroused human curiosity and emotional attachment. There is, as Gregg Mitman's research sug-gests, little objectivity when it comes to these giant mammals. They are the definitive "charismatic megafauna," and this embodied charisma may have facilitated an escapist empathy—the imaginary occupation of the animals' affective world—that rendered them into an appropri-ate refuge from the nation's poisoned imperial past.[63] "Even for some-one like me who can't trust people anymore," wrote one misanthropic zookeeper traumatized by the war, "I can pour my feelings into these animals."[64]

Natural history catalyzed history in this case, stimulating a growing popular fascination with elephants in postwar Japan, and Tokyo's children wasted little time in giving voice to their "need" for an elephant when they learned through news reports that Koga was unable to procure one of Nagoya's animals. Urged on by editorials in each of the capital's major dailies, children joined a series of letter-writing campaigns engineered by the papers as part of an intense postwar contest for market share. Cards and notes bemoaning the absence of elephants began to arrive at the zoological garden, the mayor's office, and the newspapers themselves, which forwarded them to the Indian and Thai embassies as part of a lobbying effort to rebuild Japan's international connections and newspaper readership through the charisma of captive animals and the voices of children. The absence of elephants was, some suggested, a form of "child cruelty," and the frenzy only increased when Koga (who leveraged the children's covetousness in support of budget requests) argued that the impoverished institution could not afford to keep an elephant.

"I love the zoo," wrote young Kondō Kōichi in a letter to the *Mainichi Shinbun* written before elephants or lions returned to the zoo. "Before the war," he continued, "when we lived in Tokyo, my father always used to take me to visit the Ueno Zoo, but when I recently visited the zoo on a school trip, I was disappointed that there weren't any elephants or lions. My little sister turns nine this year, so she doesn't even remember elephants or lions from when we visited the zoo together [during the war] because she was too small. When I show her a picture of an elephant and tell her that elephants are bigger than cows, she says she can't believe it." Kondō concludes by urging all of the people of Tokyo to each send "a little bit of money" to Director Koga so that Ueno can afford to keep an elephant. "I'm sending money I got from my dad because my little sister wants to see a real elephant."[65]

Inspired by such letters and spurred on by Koga, who suggested that he would be "delighted" to see elephants return to Ueno if only funding could be found and the SCAP ban on animal imports lifted, the Taitō Ward Children's Congress (Tōkyō-to Taitō-ku Kodomo Gigai) decided to address the problem. The group, made up of children from the section of the capital that includes Ueno Park and the Ueno Zoo, was established after the war as part of SCAP efforts to nurture a democracy rooted in the purity of the nation's kids. Similar organizations (along with the aforementioned parent-teacher associations) were created across the country with varying degrees of success and durability. The Taitō Congress, which included representatives from each elementary school in the district, took the return of elephants to the Ueno Zoo as its particular mission. It was a purpose that resonated with adult corporate and institutional agendas, and it illustrates how the children's field of social action was conditioned—not defined—by the broader culture. The Children's Congress was more than a simple mouthpiece for adults. Its members—urged on by Koga and others to be sure—pursued their cause with enthusiasm and originality; they issued a formal public statement asking for the delivery of one of Nagoya's elephants to the Ueno Zoo in early May.[66]

Addressed to the "Children of Nagoya," the statement expressed the "keen desire" of Tokyo's children to "see a genuine living elephant."[67] The formal declaration asked "our friends, the children of Nagoya to hear our voices, the children [of Tokyo]," to "realize our dream even one day sooner by allowing us to borrow an elephant to display before the jubilant children of Tokyo."[68] Envy, the quest for authentic experience, and the assertion of a certain kind of subjectivity, a right to be heard—all revolving around the figure of the "real live elephant"—were woven into the statement, which was carried aboard a night train bound for Nagoya by two young Taitō representatives, Harada Naoko and Ōhata Toshiki, a girl and a boy.

When Ōhata and Harada stepped off the train with accompanying adults in Nagoya at 5:55 A.M. the next morning, they quickly made their way to a specially convened meeting of the Nagoya Children's Congress at Nagoya City Hall. It was an institutional connection sanctioned by SCAP, and its use in this manner speaks to the savvy pursuit of autonomy by Japanese under the neocolonial system arranged by the Americans. Both the children and their adult sponsors were engaged in a delicate but playful political improvisation that balanced cautious resistance *against* and calculated conformity *with* American hegemony.[69] They were bending the rules in pursuit of an object understood to be divorced from formal, adult politics. It was a politics enabled by the presence of children—innocent and therefore harmless within the cultures of postwar sentimentalism—and set in motion by the zoo, "a place that most people assume has no connection to real society," as Koga put it.[70] Once in the hall, Harada and Ōhata presented their petition to the assembled children, only to see parliamentary democracy in action: the Nagoya Children's Congress failed to reach a resolution, perhaps intentionally.

The Taitō representatives were discouraged but undefeated when they returned to Tokyo. Ōhata and Harada were probably the first children to present a petition to Japan's postwar National Diet. Three days after returning to Tokyo, the pair took their petition to the Diet building, where they presented it to Matsudaira Tsuneo (1877–1949), the first president of the newly created House of Councilors (Japan's Upper House) and former Ambassador to Great Britain and the United States. Father-in-law to the Shōwa Emperor's younger brother, Prince Chichibu, and head of the Imperial Household Ministry throughout the war, Matsudaira accepted the revised petition, which asked the Diet to allow the importation of an elephant for display at Ueno. Such actions were beyond Matsudaira or the government's powers in 1949 since SCAP maintained control over diplomacy and trade at the time, but the president promised to do his best for the children. It is unclear whether or not Matsudaira did, in fact, act on behalf of Taitō's kids, since events took an unexpected turn: a mass pilgrimage of Japanese children to the city of Nagoya.[71]

Though they were unsuccessful in their attempts to "borrow" one of Higashiyama's elephants, the Taitō Children's Congress petition did reach Nagoya's mayor, the auspiciously named Tsukamoto Zō (1889–1952; "zō" is a homonym for "elephant"), who joined together with Koga and Kitaō to lobby SCAP officials for permission to bring Tokyo's children to Higashiyama to see the Nagoya elephants. If the elephants could not be brought to the children, they reasoned, the children should be brought to the elephants.

Over the course of the following months as many as fifty thousand children from Tokyo and around the country climbed aboard a series of special "Elephant Trains" (Zō ressha) bound for Nagoya. The "Elephant Engine" (Erefuantō-go) eventually became the subject of a best-selling children's book; it was a fifteen-car special charter jointly sponsored by the Japan Travel Bureau (JTB) and the *Mainichi Shimbun*, the newspaper that printed young Kondō's plea for his sister. The first Elephant Train arrived in Nagoya carrying more than one thousand children, most of them from Tokyo's downtown Shitamachi area, home to Taitō Ward. Visitors were welcomed with an exuberant Festival for Tokyo's Children, and the trip proved so popular that Japanese National Railways added another "elephant train" route between Osaka and Nagoya.[72]

ELEPHANT AMBASSADORS

This was the context into which Indira and Hanako arrived. Overwhelmed by the children's crusade, SCAP officials offered a special dispensation for the importation of elephants for Ueno, and delegations from both Thailand and India moved to send animals. When "Gajah" arrived from Thailand on September 4, children lined the railway tracks to welcome her to the zoo. A "naming ceremony" was held on September 10 to officially rename the Thai animal "Hanako," but it was Indira, "a messenger of affection and goodwill from the children of India," who garnered the most attention. At fifteen, the Indian elephant was much larger than the two-year-old Hanako, and the Indian embassy staff, together with the *Asahi News*, which brokered the gift, did an excellent job of drumming up public interest.

During a nationwide radio broadcast in India, Nehru announced the gift as a demonstration of generosity toward a fellow Asian nation laid low by a Western power, shaping the animal into a "mascot" for the Indian nation itself.[73] "The elephant is a noble animal much loved in India and very typical of India," he wrote in a letter that accompanied Indira. "It is wise and patient, strong and yet gentle." This particular animal was taken from the forests of Mysore when young, Nehru said, and it was selected in part because it was well trained and in part because it exhibited "all the auspicious signs," most notably eight toenails each on its front and back legs (four on each foot), an unusual quality that associated the animal with the eight auspicious signs of Buddhism, a gesture to one of the cultural strands connecting the two nations.[74]

Nehru, one of the originators of the nonaligned movement and hopeful of Japan's future role in that effort, described the contribution with a combination of pacifism and pan-Asianism addressed to the children of Japan. "Children all over the world are in many ways like each other," Nehru wrote. "It is when they grow up that they begin to differ and, unfortunately, sometimes they quarrel. We have to put an end to these quarrels of grown-up people and I hope that when the children of India and the children of Japan will grow up, they will serve not only their own great countries, but also the cause of peace and cooperation all over Asia and the world."[75] Reproduced as part of a series of commemorative postcards and blown up for display next to Ueno's new Elephant House, Nehru's letter attempted to revitalize inter-Asian connections threatened by American intervention through the medium of the animal gift. The animal, deployed as a bridge to between children rather than an expression of formal diplomacy, was framed as part of a shared adult effort to protect "childhood" as a time severed from the wartime past and distinct from the concerns of adults. Nehru speaks *for* and *to* children here, using them to shift the transaction into a less formal register. "You should treat this elephant as a gift, not from me, but from the children of India to the children of Japan," Nehru wrote. The prime minister added a personal touch to the gift. The elephant was named after his only daughter, a future prime minister herself: Indira Nehru Gandhi.[76]

The elephants were welcomed by a smiling Yoshida Shigeru. Yoshida, who later became the president of the Japan Association of Zoological Gardens and Aquariums, reveled in the popular diplomacy of Indira's arrival. On October 1 he joined Tokyo Mayor Yasui Seiichirō for the playfully named "Ms. Indira's Presentation Ceremony" (Indira Musume no Zōteishiki), a coming-out festival for the animal. Elevated into an answer to the Great Zoo Massacre by members of the zoo staff, the ceremony dwarfed its wartime ancestor.[77] Child representatives arrived from more than sixty elementary schools in Tokyo, and more than forty thousand people crowded into the gardens. Where small piles of food had been offered before a memorial altar in the rituals of 1943, Prime Minister Yoshida, smiling for photographers, offered the fifteen-year-old Indira a banana flown in for the purpose. The crowd erupted in applause when Harada Naoko, one of the young Taitō representatives, gave a formal speech.[78]

By the close of the Allied occupation in 1952 Indira and Hanako had been seen by more than ten million people at the Ueno Zoo alone (millions more in photographs). Their mass appeal was so striking that the *Asahi* and *Mainichi* newspapers entered into a competition for the right to cosponsor with the City of Tokyo a "Traveling Zoo" that would bring elephants "to the children of regional Japan whose desire to see an elephant is so palpable."[79] In the end, the *Asahi*, the original sponsor of Indira's delivery, was selected by city officials. The Indian elephant set off in the spring of 1950 with a selection of other animals, taxidermy specimens, and a modified Monkey Train on a tour of eighteen regional cities from northern Hokkaido, where they were welcomed by Ainu in traditional garb, to Mito, just north of the capital. The taxidermied animals included Ali and Katarina, lions offered to the cult of wartime sacrifice in 1943. Katarina was posed in order to make "the holes in her hide less visible."[80] Trumpeted as an ambassador of peace, Indira's arrival sanctioned the emerging sense that Japan was "recovered" from the

Fukuda→ many

war. She was, in the evaluation of one local official, a medium for "the consolation of children through enjoyable entertainment and practical animal education." For others she was something else, a transitional object that seemed to return the trauma of the Great Zoo Massacre from the postwar present back into the wartime past. "I saw that elephant," assistant zoo director Fukuda Saburō recalled long after he administered the starvation of Indira's predecessor, "and I knew that peace had finally come to the zoo."[81]

CONCLUSION

The sound of camera shutters swept through the crowd of reporters gathered at the Ueno Zoo when a middle-aged man, dressed in a businessman's conservative suit and tie, reached out to shake eight-year-old Suzie's hand. The press had been waiting all day for such an opportunity, and there was a palpable sense of relief as it passed onto film. Photographers stopped grumbling to zoo staff about the lack of good photo opportunities as soon as Suzie stepped back from the handshake. They had their shot, and it ran in several newspapers the following morning, April 21, 1956. The image captured an unexpectedly candid moment, coming when Suzie—a charismatic youngster who often asked for coins to buy candy at a nearby kiosk—rode her bicycle up to the man and extended her open hand, palm up, her usual way of asking for money. She was dolled up in a matching bonnet and shirt set and plaid skirt. Disarmed by her frank openness, the man misunderstood her gesture and did what he had been trained to do: he reached out and shook her hand. Suzie turned his hand over to look inside for a coin. Finding none, she offered him a wide, toothy smile. He laughed quietly as she continued to hold his fingers, perhaps amused by the unexpected encounter, perhaps somewhat troubled by the sight of Suzie's inch-long canines.[82]

"Suzie" was the Ueno Zoo's famous bicycle-riding chimpanzee. The maxillary canines of *Pan troglodytes* can grow to intimidating size, but the chimp was hardly a threat. She was an affectionate creature with impeccable table manners (she could use a spoon and fork) whose single vice was her sweet tooth; she took sugar with her tea. The amiable chimp was more likely to do a standing back flip in an attempt to earn candy than to threaten the man standing alongside Director Koga. Koga knew the young chimpanzee well—he was usually the one to give her coins—and she would never have gotten so close if he believed she was dangerous. The man standing next to him was too important.

The gentleman who shook the chimp's hand that afternoon was Hirohito, Japan's Shōwa Emperor, and it was the juxtaposition of emperor and chimpanzee that so entranced the gathered crowd.

The emperor and Suzie were both performing that day: she in an attempt to earn money to buy chocolate from a nearby kiosk, he in an effort to expand his public role after the American occupation.[83] They made an odd couple. He was the embodiment of Japanese civilization, a symbol maintained by SCAP in an effort to stabilize the defeated nation.[84] She was trained to ape that civilization; she defined its limits when she failed to recognize the emperor as anything other than a man in a suit. But the pair also shared a certain status, occupying opposite poles of the human spectrum, both of them at once within and beyond the normal confines of what it meant to be a person. Hirohito, the Shōwa Emperor, was legally recognized as the descendant of gods for the first forty-six years of his life, until the American-authored Constitution of Japan was ratified in 1946, redefining him as a human "symbol of the state and of the unity of the people." Both Hirohito and Suzie were, in a sense, learning how to be human. Both were living symbols.[85]

Although the meeting with Suzie was unscripted—another small reminder that animals can shape the course of events—the encounter was, in a sense, intentional. Hirohito made deliberate use of the dynamics of ecological modernity—the juxtaposition of animals and humans—in his pursuit of a more humane postwar image. He was, in a sense, returning to the mechanism at work in Georges Bigot's 1887 print, discussed in chapter 1. But where Bigot mocked Japanese elites, who were shown primping before a mirror that revealed them to be monkeys mimicking civilization, Hirohito used the country's mass media to show himself in a new light. When he visited the zoo he stood with the Japanese people, taking in the humanizing spectacle of captive animals. Zoo going was a widely shared experience during the late 1940s and 1950s—before the advent of television—when yearly attendance at Ueno consistently exceeded 3.5 million people and the number of zoos nationwide began to grow again. Such encounters were meant to underline Hirohito's own assertion of humanity, presented in a 1946 radio broadcast widely known as the "declaration of humanity" (*ningen sengen*).

Hirohito was deeply familiar with the Ueno Imperial Zoological Gardens. He had enjoyed private and public visits when he was a child, and he was aware of the numerous animals held in the prewar zoo in his name. And of course the institution maintained its formal imperial connection into the postwar era because of him: the term "onshi"

FIGURE 17. When Suzie met Hirohito. The Shōwa Emperor smiles down at Suzie the chimpanzee, 1956. Image courtesy of Tokyo Zoological Park Society.

(Ueno Zoo's full title is Tōkyō-to Ueno Onshi Dōbutsuen), signals an imperial gift, in this case in celebration of Hirohito's marriage. But he walked into a place at once very familiar and very different in 1956. The basic structure of the zoological gardens remained intact, but the politics of the institution had changed. Ueno had once claimed to represent a vast ecological empire reaching from Sakhalin to Sumatra. It was now developing into a themed space on the American model. Even Suzie bespoke a new geopolitics. Though her species was native to Africa, the personable chimp was born in the United States, trained as a circus performer, and brought to Japan with her companion, "Bill," in 1951.

The humanizing dynamics of ecological modernity were at the center of the broader campaign to redefine the emperor—and thus in a certain sense the nation—in the postwar years. Under SCAP management, Hirohito was transfigured from a stern military leader—the figure astride the alabaster purebred Shirayuki at the Yoyogi Review Grounds in 1942—into an avuncular biologist defined by his curiosity about the natural world. Indeed, from 1946 forward, Japanese were told that the general on horseback was not, in fact, "the real Shōwa Emperor." That emperor was an "anachronism" dreamed up by "the old military clique," in the words of *Yomiuri* reporter Ono Noboru.[86]

Ono's popular book, *Tennō no sugao* (*The Emperor's True Face*), was one of the first entries in the effort to reframe Hirohito as a "scientist" or "biologist." The very first line of the book sets the driving theme in motion: Hirohito is a man at once with the people but distinct from them. "Since I don't drink or smoke," says the emperor in the midst of a "chance interview" with Ono, "the only hobby for me is biological research." Ono goes on to track the emperor's "long history of scientific accomplishment" back into his prewar youth, arguing that he only set it aside at the request of military officials, who urged him to "avoid such mundane human activities" (*ningenteki na zokuji*) because they would undermine his "sense of divinity" among the people. Like those who fought in his name, the emperor, too, was duped by the military. "When we think about such ideas now," Ono asserts, "they are obviously nonsense [*nansensu*]."[87]

The "biologist emperor," as Ono called him, was created through his encounters with the living world. When photographers showed him looking through his microscope at the hydrozoa that occupied most of his academic time—he published at least eighteen articles and research reports over the years—he joined Japan's long tradition of "gentleman scientists," an intellectual lineage that linked him to the world inhabited by Tanaka Yoshio, Itō Keisuke, and other Tokugawa-era natural historians, specifically the feudal lords trained by those nineteenth-century specialists. It was a status defined by curiosity and leisure rather than the pursuit of profit or even useful knowledge, and it is clear as one reads through the dozens of intellectual hagiographies dedicated to the emperor's research that the purpose of his work was to illuminate the sovereign's inner life rather than to serve the military and industrial programs carried out in his name. In this sense, Hirohito's retreat to the Imperial Laboratory constructed within the grounds of the Imperial Palace in 1926 was akin to the ancient retreats of "cloistered emperors," sovereigns who entered the Buddhist monastic community, a symbolic (and at times genuine) abdication of concern with this world in favor of the effort to understand another. The Shōwa Emperor's pursuit of science, then, like the protection of childhood or the exhibition of animals, marked a public renunciation of politics that was, in itself, deeply political. The imperial retreat into nature, like the spectacular culture of the zoo under Allied occupation, was an effort to reinforce the new order of things by dramatizing a way to withdraw from it—in this case, into a domain of innocent, indeed childlike, curiosity and wonder.[88]

CHAPTER 6

Pandas in the Anthropocene

*Japan's "Panda Boom" and the Limits
of Ecological Modernity*

"The Battle for Panda Profit"

It used to be said that things go together
like tigers and bamboo,
Now the fashion is pandas and bamboo.

That's it! A panda pattern!
That's it! A panda brand!
Try to be the first to register that
trademark.

Panda, pandas why do they get us so
excited?
Panda, *pandane*, panda's seed.

Oo! This is Japanda!

—Inoue Hisashi[1]

All animals are equal, but some are more equal than others.

—George Orwell

THE "PANDA BOOM"

When two giant pandas arrived at Tokyo's Ueno Imperial Zoo from the People's Republic of China (PRC) on October 28, 1972, it signaled diplomatic normalization between former foes in a brutal colonial war. It also marked the apex of human fascination with the world of the zoo in Japan. Few animals so clearly encapsulated the workings—and limits—of ecological modernity as these bears. At once objects of intense global cultural, scientific, and political attention and subject to relentless ecological marginalization in the wild, the giant pandas illustrated the conflicted status of wildlife in the modern world. Tensions between conservationism and consumerism often remain hidden beneath the surface of public life in Japan, even within the zoological garden, but the histories of these diplomatic tokens—at one point the most-viewed animals on the planet—show how the creatures' bodies registered the impact of basic human fascination as amplified through cultural diplomacy and the institutions of mass culture.

China and Japan were formally estranged for twenty-seven years following the collapse of the Japanese empire in 1945. The delivery of Kang Kang (Kan Kan) and Lan Lan (Ran Ran; paired names are a form of diminutive often used with pandas delivered outside of China) marked a geopolitical watershed and the expansion of Chinese "panda diplomacy" into East Asia.[2] Fueled by a culture industry eager to extract maximum profit from the alluring *Ailuropoda melanoleuca*, annual attendance at the zoological gardens climbed above seven million in 1973, where it hovered for more than a decade. Patrons waited in lines nearly two miles long for a thirty-second glimpse of the slow-moving pair. "Panda goods" (*panda guzzu*) flew off zoo shelves, legal battles erupted over the right to trademark images of naturally occurring species, and commentators breathlessly explained grainy video footage of the animals' mating attempts on the nation's television news and talk shows.

Japan's "panda boom" (*panda buumu*) lasted for more than thirty years. The Ueno Zoo held nine giant pandas between 1972 and 2008, when the so-called last panda, a twenty-two-year-old male named Ling Ling, died childless, despite the investment of millions of yen in breeding efforts and flights to Chapultepec Zoological Garden in Mexico City, home to the only three breeding-age females not owned by the PRC available anywhere. After 1984 the Chinese instituted a "panda monopoly" in which it leased most giant pandas in complex financial transactions rather than giving them away as tokens of diplomatic goodwill. These "rent-a-pandas," to use panda expert George B. Schaller's phrase, have been effective tools of cultural—and environmental—diplomacy for the PRC.[3] Across the decades between 1972 and 2008, well over 130 million people laid eyes on Ueno's pandas during visits to the zoo, and many times that number participated in what former Ueno Zoo director Nakagawa Shirō has called, in a telling characterization, the "mass-media phenomenon" of the panda boom, when "the pandas' media value outstripped their worth as physical animals."[4] The boom was sustained by the energy of Japan's bubble economy of the 1980s and early 1990s and intensified by the birth of a pair of panda cubs in the mid-1980s. It slowly dissipated as Tong Tong—conceived through artificial insemination in the operating theater at Ueno in 1986—and Ling Ling failed to produce offspring at the start of the new century.

Postimperial mascots and, from 1984, postcommodity treasures, the history of Ueno's pandas shines a light on the social, political, commercial, legal, and technological aspects of ecological modernity in Japan. These broadly interacting processes, each addressed in this chapter and all centering on the charismatic panda, make a distinctive statement about the nature of the beasts at the climax of modernity. The natural world itself, which had formed the merciless and nurturant context in which human striving still sought to make a home in the nineteenth century, now strangely comes to resemble a zoo, in which human actions establish the terms on which living creatures—human and otherwise— live their lives. Ueno Zoo, situated in the heart of the world's largest city, became a theater of the ecological modern, where the panda mania dramatized in microcosm the eerie reversal of natural and social realities that has yielded up the Anthropocene, the global "age of the human" defined by the Nobel-laureate atmospheric chemist Paul J. Crutzen. This chapter uses history of the charismatic giant panda to explore the connections between mass culture, diplomacy, and conservationism at the Ueno Zoo. The goal is to show how individual people and animals participated in these abstract processes in the course of their everyday lives in pursuit of something so common as a trip to the zoo. The purpose is to help us to take stock of our own desires, actions, and beliefs as we participate—wittingly and unwittingly—in the development of the Anthropocene, a dynamic so large in scale that it often seems to have little connection to daily life in Japan and elsewhere.

THE SCIENCE OF CHARISMA

The scale of the panda boom was so unprecedented that it inspired Nakagawa Shirō, director of the Ueno Zoo from 1987 to 1990 and chief keeper (*Shiiku kachō*) when Kang Kang and Lan Lan first arrived in Tokyo, to look for origins beyond the scope of human thought and conscious agency. The allure of these bears, he argued in a blurring of natural and cultural causes that harkened back to the theories of

Ishikawa Chiyomatsu and other Meiji-era advocates of social evolution, was such that it could not be explained through reference to human history alone. Nakagawa believed that the panda boom developed thanks to a double trick of biology and history. Innate human curiosity and natural animal charisma combined, he wrote, to "tie the masses to the animals." *Homo sapiens*, he reasoned, have an inborn attraction to animals that share morphological and behavioral qualities with human children. This natural attraction coincided with the giant pandas' inherent capacity to convert such curiosity into emotional attachment, and the two were fused in a crucible offered by history: the "epoch-making event," in the zoo director's words, of postcolonial diplomatic reconciliation between two former enemies. The panda boom, Nakagawa wrote, was the product of these three "overlapping" determinants—human evolutionary predisposition, animal charisma, and political context—each essential to the outcome.[5]

Nakagawa's arguments remind us of what can happen when begin to see the zoological garden—and historical settings in general—as something more than a passive stage for independent human actions, as a living environment rather than a landscape of purely symbolic dominion. In such settings, people are never the only actors. As we saw with the recalcitrant elephants Tonky and Wanri in chapter 4, animals may not be fully self-conscious agents in the idealist sense, but they can certainly engage in considered actions that shape the course of events. Nakagawa's observations take us yet another step toward a blending of natural history and human history.[6] In his reading, the panda boom requires us to reconsider how we think about human agency, even in a context so thoroughly acculturated as the zoological garden. Were the people who lined up at the zoo in 1972 entirely free of what the philosopher R.G. Collingwood called their "animal nature"—their evolutionarily conditioned appetites and impulses—especially in the presence of such charismatic animals as Kang Kang and Ran Ran? Nakagawa's answer, as I show below, was an emphatic "no." The "natural appeal" of the pandas was simply too powerful. It is an argument that asks us to bring the concerns of environmental history and the history of science into conversation with those of diplomatic history and the history of the media. It suggests that the common metaphor of "media ecology" should be taken more literally in some cases. There are important environmental dimensions to popular culture in mass-culture societies such as Japan.[7]

Pandas, Nakagawa observed, were not just any animals. They seemed designed—through a quirk of evolutionary fortune—to play on human psychology. Drawing on work by the Austrian "father of ethology" Konrad Lorenz, cowinner of the 1973 Nobel Prize in Physiology and Medicine, and the 1966 book *Men and Pandas* by the British naturalists Desmond and Ramona Morris, Nakagawa identified the development of a uniquely powerful "charm" (*miryoku*) in the space between the bears and the people who came to see them. "Since even before the birth of the zoo, certain display animals—peacocks, parrots, camels, and elephants—have been very popular with the masses," he wrote in a manual on panda captivity published by the zoo in 1995. "But the panda is something more; the physical animal we call the panda elicits a tremendous 'feeling of wellbeing' in human beings."[8]

Nakagawa suggested that *Ailuropoda melanoleuca* was unique in its embodiment of physical characteristics that "trigger" (*shigeki*) what Lorenz called "releasing mechanisms" in human beings.[9] In a famous 1950 article Lorenz identified "species-preserving" qualities—expressions, gestures, physical attitudes, and characteristics—that elicit impulses toward self-protection or the care of young. These characteristics perform an evolutionarily advantageous function because they systematically dispose human beings to respond to signs of need and of danger; however—and this is the key point—these qualities can become "erroneous[ly]" attached to animals and even physical objects. "The most amazing objects can acquire remarkable, highly emotional values by [the] 'experiential' attachment of *human* properties," he wrote. "Steeply rising, somewhat overhanging cliff faces or dark storm-clouds piling up have the same, immediate display value as a human being who is standing at full height and leaning slightly forward"—that is, they appear threatening.[10] This anthropomorphism, rooted for Lorenz in the deep time of evolutionary physiology and psychology rather than the changeable realm of history and culture, is even more pronounced in human responses to nonhuman animals, especially animal faces. Camels and llamas, he points out, are commonly seen as "looking haughtily at the observer" because the nostril is located higher than the eye, the angle of the mouth is slightly downward, and the head is normally carried just above the horizontal.[11]

Releasing mechanisms help us to become attached to children and to sustain those attachments over the course of juvenile maturation. The emotional effects of these "biologically relevant stimulus situations," Lorenz argued, are most pronounced when associated with the human response to small children. "A relatively large head, predominance of the brain capsule, large and low-lying eyes, bulging cheek region, short and

FIGURE 18. The biology of "cute." Konrad Lorenz's releasing schema for human parental care responses. Left: "head proportions perceived as 'loveable' (child, jerboa, Pekinese dog, robin)." Right: "related heads which do not elicit the parental drive (man, hare, hound, golden oriole)." Konrad Lorenz, *Über tierisches und menschliches Verhalten, Band II* © 1965 Piper Verlag GmbH, München.

thick extremities, a springy elastic consistency, and clumsy movements represent the major character[istics] . . . combining to give a child (or a . . . doll or an animal) a loveable or 'cuddly' appearance." People respond to these distinctive features, he argued, with nurturant affection. To demonstrate this point and its relation to animals, Lorenz offered an illustration of "releasing schema for human parental care responses," which shows how certain physical characteristics whether of humans *or* animals combine to "elicit the parental drive" in human beings.

Stephen Jay Gould used Lorenz's theory to argue that the visual "evolution" of Mickey Mouse from a pointy-nosed sharp to the rounded host of the Magic Kingdom suggests the "unconscious discovery of this biological principle by Disney and his artists," and he summarizes Lorenz's logic as follows: "We are, in short, fooled by an evolved response to our own babies, and we transfer our reaction to the same set of features in other animals."[12] It is an argument that suggests a fundamental blurring between biological and cultural impulses, or perhaps more striking, the biological beginnings of even the most trivial-seeming modern cultural phenomena.

Nakagawa emphasized the process described by Lorenz. The pandas' "potent symbolic appeal," he wrote, was mainly derived from their "neotenous," or infantile, appearance (*yōjisei*). Like Gould, neither the Morrises nor Nakagawa chose to take explicit sides in the debate over whether such attachments were biologically "innate" or "learned from our immediate experience with babies and grafted upon an evolutionary predisposition for attaching ties of affection to certain learned signals." They did, however, show that *Ailuropoda melanoleuca* embodied a host of characteristics that might be added to Lorenz's list of "releasing schema for parental care responses"—giant pandas were even "cuter" than the model.[13] The bears have a flat face, as do humans relative to other primates; we have bred this quality into many "toy" dog breeds. Yet pandas also have no or little tail, sit up vertically like children, and can manipulate small objects in a human-like way. The panda's "thumb," in fact an exaggerated wrist bone, provides a unique anthropomorphic feature, allowing it to eat as we do. Pandas appear rounded, harmless, playful, and sexless ("human beings keep their sex organs covered; so does the panda," the Morrises observe), qualities that facilitated their acculturation as the very embodiment of "cute" (*kawaii*), perhaps the definitive commodity quality in late-modern Japan.[14]

Possessing a unique catalog of neotenous traits, pandas projected an unrivaled charisma that cut across lines of age and gender. "Zoos that exhibit giant pandas," Nakagawa wrote, "not only see an increase in numbers, but they also see an increase that does not skew according to old or young, male or female." Where other popular zoo species such as elephants or peacocks might appeal more strongly to a particular age group or gender, pandas elicited "good feelings" in all who encountered them. "There can be no doubt that one experiences the same feelings of affection when standing in front of a panda as one does when looking at a child," he argued. "It is akin to the maternal instincts experienced by women."[15]

There can be no doubt that a host of social dynamics augmented the pandas' physical appeal in Japan. They were rare, scientifically mysterious, and representative of China, a foreign country at once historically familiar and politically alien. Like the okapi and the pygmy hippopotamus—with pandas, the "three great animal rarities" (*sandai chinjū*) regularly cited by Japanese zoo professionals—pandas appealed to those fascinated by rare objects. This curiosity was only increased by the unsettled question of the species' classification.[16] Even DNA analysis has failed to settle the issue of placement once and for all, but the preponderance of evidence suggest that giant pandas are in fact members of the bear family (Ursidae), despite energetic efforts to place them with the raccoons (Procyonidae).[17] This debate, which reaches back to at least the nineteenth century, is reflected in the animal's equivocal nomenclature. The Latin name, *Ailuropoda melanoleuca*, literally means "black-and-white cat foot," and the Chinese characters used for the animal (大熊猫, *dàxióngmāo*) mean "large bear-cat." Following precedent set in the Meiji period, when Chinese characters were often seen as signs of older, potentially superstitious attitudes toward animals, the Japanese have generally opted for a transliteration of the common English "panda" (パンダ, *panda*), a choice that has fueled the proliferation of puns and word play around the creatures, including such questionable turns of phrase as those found in this chapter's epigraph. More recently, the discovery of fossils including a "false thumb" similar to the panda's has allowed some to label the species a "living fossil," a designation that associates the creature with dinosaurs, that other "totem animal of modernity," to use W. J. T. Mitchell's expression.[18]

Seen in this way, the "panda boom" was neither purely natural nor entirely social, but a hybrid that reflected the logic of the zoological gardens specifically and ecological modernity more broadly. The surge in public curiosity about the bears resulted from a triangular convergence among the morphology and behavioral characteristics of the animals, the desires and dispositions of human subjects conditioned to respond to those factors, and the institutions and processes that led to the bears' removal from the fading forests and bamboo groves of Western China and their delivery into the concrete and glass air-conditioned Panda House at the Ueno Zoo, a specially designed building completed in 1973.[19] Over three decades, diplomats and politicians, the mass media and toy manufacturers, conservationists and the zoo's agents stimulated, amplified, and mobilized the "good feelings" induced by these slow-moving, evolutionarily "peculiar" black-and-white creatures in the service of political and economic agendas that were often at odds with strict environmental or ecological concerns. Though framed as "visitors" or "ambassadors" from foreign nations or, more often, a nature apart from (if often threatened by) the motors of industrial development, the material history of the bears demonstrates that by the 1970s such clear distinctions between the natural and social worlds had become truly illusory, social fictions useful in the pursuit of further profit, prestige, and political advantage or, more optimistically, wonder, curiosity, and environmental conservation.

PANDA DIPLOMACY

Politics, conservation science, and consumer fascination converged on the bears, but to Nakagawa's way of thinking, the creatures that arrived in Tokyo in 1972 were first and foremost "political animals" (*seijiteki dōbutsu*). The most basic "meaning of this is that the animals move—especially when they move internationally—through the actions of the Chinese government, which controls their habitat, rather than through the commercial animal trade that is normally used by zoos."[20] This definition was born of direct experience with trying to gain access to and information about this most endangered and most desired species. For all of their global appeal, the entirety of the world's dwindling population of wild giant pandas falls within the borders of the PRC. Attempts at captive breeding are neither successful enough to sustain the species nor are they any longer possible without the intervention of the PRC government, which holds rights to nearly all bears of breeding age.[21] These tensions between desirability and scarcity, on the one hand, and conservation and politics, on the other, were the defining characteristics of "panda diplomacy" in the late twentieth century.

Zoo attendance and mass media attention indicate that giant pandas were hugely popular diplomatic symbols, but as the PRC government discovered when their conservation efforts were criticized as anemic, the knit between the animal's image and the specific content of its intended political message was loose and open to multiple readings or even counterreadings. The bears were, not to be too cute about it, fuzzy symbols, emotionally resonant signs that opened the way for what Emiko Ohnuki-Tierney, following Pierre Bourdieu, has called *meconnaissance*, or the absence of communication that results when different parties do not share a meaning but instead derive different meanings from the same symbol.[22] To choose the most obvious example of the phenomenon, for officials in the PRC, the giant panda is a national mascot, a symbol of China's unique ecology and the nation's commitment to its preservation. For members of the World Wildlife Fund (WWF), who chose the creatures as their mascot, however, the bears were meant to represent wildlife and the wild as finite and threatened entities. Seen through this optic, China emerges less as a unique and beautiful environment than as a source of mismanagement and menace. "The world's" panda population is endangered, and for many critics China—rather than a subset of the people who call that country home—emerges as the threat.

This lack of representational surety helps to account for the care taken by PRC officials in their symbolic and physical management of the bears, and later, as we shall see, for the care that Japanese managers took with their own captive mascots. Giant pandas may generate "good feelings," as Nakagawa argues, but the association between those feelings and any specific referent beyond the bears themselves is complex. Panda diplomacy was a human endeavor, but it was carried out in constant relation to creatures that refused to always act or affect as intended.

Japan's panda boom was just one front in the broader use of giant pandas in the diplomatic sphere, a global phenomenon that has mapped the foreign concerns of the PRC across the last half of the twentieth century. Panda diplomacy was a kind of national branding. To be more specific, it was what advertising professionals might call an attempt at "brand endorsement," wherein the government sought to enhance the symbolic equity surrounding the pandas and transfer it to the Chinese nation. Through the careful use of these creatures, officials and diplomats in the PRC attempted to create symbolic connections between giant pandas and China among various foreign publics and their leaders. As a result, the association between the abstract, imagined community of "China" and the visually specific image of the giant panda is now global.

Playing on the mass appeal and physical rarity of the giant panda— fewer than twenty were seen alive outside of China before the Second World War—panda diplomacy began with a pair of gifts to the Soviet Union in the late 1950s. Ping Ping and An An were the communist vanguard of one of the world's best-known (and perhaps most successful) efforts at modern cultural diplomacy. Ping Ping arrived at the Moscow Zoo as an expression of cordial relations between the two nations in 1957, and An An arrived two years later. Gifts to the Democratic People's Republic of Korea began six years later, in 1965. Five animals were given to the North Korean government between 1965 and 1980.[23]

The new phase of panda diplomacy began with U.S. President Richard M. Nixon's surprise visit to China in February 1972. Nixon's visit was a brilliant diplomatic move in the context of an increasingly "hot" cold war, and the president returned to Washington with his diplomatic credentials significantly enhanced. His wife, Pat, returned with a promise from Chinese Premier Zhou Enlai that two giant pandas would soon arrive in the American capital. The normalization of relations between the United States and China was thus bracketed by cultural gestures on the part of the PRC, prefaced by so-called ping-pong diplomacy and concluded with the first extension of panda diplomacy outside the Communist sphere. It remains unclear exactly how Zhou reached the decision to send the animals—some stories, in all likelihood apocryphal, chalk it up to a translation mistake involving a packet of Zhou's Panda Brand cigarettes: "I would like one of those," the First Lady, a private smoker, is said to have remarked—but Mrs. Nixon was by all accounts delighted, and the president recognized the symbolic value of the gift. When Ling Ling and Hsing Hsing arrived at the National Zoo in Washington on April 16 the First Lady was on hand to welcome them along with twenty thousand others (her husband did not attend). Annual attendance at the National Zoo climbed to 1.1 million following the pair's arrival, and the bears' delivery was closely reported in the Japanese press. Nixon sent a pair of musk oxen to the PRC in return.[24]

The diplomatic use of *Ailuropoda melanoleuca* reached its pinnacle as part of the PRC's broader diplomatic rapprochement with the West in the 1970s, when animals were strategically distributed in zoos across North America, Western Europe, and Asia. Their arrival in mass-consumer societies such as the United States, Japan, and the United Kingdom sparked international fascination with the animals, which in turn led to the species' reclassification under the Convention on International Trade in Endangered Species of Wild Fauna and Flora (CITES), the international agreement that regulates international trade in rare and endangered plants and wildlife. In a shift that underlines the proliferation of unintended meanings and consequences around the bears, in 1984 the species was moved from the relatively unregulated CITES

Appendix III to Appendix I, "species threatened with extinction," the most closely regulated class of fauna. The move was due in part to a series of surveys supported by the WWF that suggested the species was in greater peril than many had thought. These surveys were inspired by the arrival of giant pandas in Washington, D.C., and other Western cities, and it is because of them that the giant panda is now widely assumed to be the most endangered ursine species in the world.[25]

Over the subsequent decades, as the animals gained notice in the international arena, giant pandas evolved into symbols for China itself. Given the international dimensions inherent in the idea of the modern nation-state (always a part of a system, always bounded by other states), the animals became Chinese icons in their travels, both visual and physical, abroad. This reclusive species, which has been marginalized by the Chinese people over several millennia through expanded cultivation of lowland bamboo areas and intensive logging of upland mountainous habitat, has in the last fifty years developed into a "national treasure." In China, as elsewhere, modernity—in this case state-administered capitalism—has produced conditions conducive to fascination with *dàxióngmāo*, and pandas are the largest draw at the Beijing Zoo.

The panda's threatened and then endangered status has added to its value even as it has, in recent years, opened the PRC to criticism from foreign nongovernmental organizations and governments over the failure to adequately protect panda habitats from human encroachment.[26] Before the development of extensive legal protections for the species, the claims of PRC officials on the pandas superseded those of conservation biologists, others in the scientific community, or local officials. As Nakagawa notes, in the 1970s and early 1980s the approval of three separate government agencies was necessary for the release of a single bear overseas. The ministries of Forestry, Construction, and Foreign Affairs all played a role, and final approval could only come through the State Council, the chief administrative authority of the PRC. Only the giant panda required such special approval, unlike other animals on the PRC's official list of most-endangered species, such as the golden (or snub-nosed) monkey, which may be as endangered as the panda.[27]

Officials released bears only sparingly, and on particular kinds of occasions, creating a culture of scarcity that augmented the bears' efficacy and profile. This tension between cultural ubiquity and physical rarity was one motor of the species' global popularity, and Chinese diplomats and foreign politicians alike exploited it. Gifts tended to be made during official diplomatic visits by foreign heads of state, when the story-lines attached to the bears could be defined and when their symbolic impact would be augmented by prominent media exposure on front pages or in the political-news sections. The visual attraction of pandas also seemed ready-made for televised news.

Such gifts between individual leaders were also assumed to generate domestic goodwill for foreign leaders. While Nixon did not go to Beijing asking for a giant panda, those who followed in his wake often did. Japanese Prime Minister Tanaka in 1972, French President Georges Pompidou and British Prime Minister Edward Heath in 1974, Japanese Prime Minister Ōhira Masayoshi in 1979, and Japanese Prime Minister Suzuki Zenkō in 1982 all arrived in Beijing on state visits under popular pressure to "bring a panda home," and each of them was able to announce the successful completion of agreements securing pandas for their countries. The display of pictures of giant pandas alongside a politician, what we might call "diplomatic neoteny," is akin to the stereotype of the politician holding a baby. The gifts were always framed as exchanges between the "people of China" and their counterparts overseas, but in each case diplomatic staff handled the transactions as affairs of state.

While Ling Ling and Hsing Hsing gave a soft face to U.S.-PRC relations, the initiation of panda diplomacy between the PRC and the United States generated considerable anxiety for Japan. The country remained fixed in the United States' diplomatic and military orbit after the end of the Allied Occupation and the enactment of the first in a series of security treaties in 1952 (renewed amid massive protests in 1960), and the Japanese followed the U.S. lead in refusing to recognize the government of the PRC. Despite the delicate nature of the Japanese situation, neither Nixon nor Kissinger's State Department chose to warn their Asian allies of his decision to visit China (announced in July 1971; carried out in February 1972). Improved U.S.-PRC relations had the potential to isolate a dependent Japan—the opposition Socialist Party (JSP) and Communist Party (JCP) had long argued for normalization with the PRC as a means of asserting Japanese autonomy—so Prime Minster Tanaka Kakuei (1918–1993) and his Liberal Democratic Party (LDP) colleagues were left scrambling after Nixon's announcement. Officials in the Ministry of Foreign Affairs eventually arranged for Tanaka to visit Beijing in September, six months after Nixon.

The U.S. president's decision to visit Beijing was the first of two so-called Nixon shocks, moves by the White House that redefined Japan's global role in the space of a few short months. The second came in August 1971, when the president announced that his government would impose a 10 percent surcharge on imports and abandon the gold standard in response to a deteriorating balance of payments. This move, which essentially ended the Bretton Woods system that structured global capitalism after the Second World War, skyrocketed the value of the yen—previously pegged at a favorable rate of 360 yen to the dollar—to almost 300 to the dollar. Japan's American-oriented export-driven economy went into a temporary tailspin.[28] Kang Kang and Lan Lan arrived in the period between these events and the global "oil shock" of 1973, when access to Middle Eastern oil was called into question. The "cute" pair of "VIP guests of state"—the latest and most popular in the zoo's long line of such popular diplomats—were welcomed by the press and the public alike as a much-needed distraction and a sign that fears over national isolation were unfounded.[29]

Japanese newspapers latched onto the panda story even before Tanaka departed for Beijing. The media frenzy surrounding the pandas was, to some, more noteworthy than diplomatic normalization, in part because many took normalization for granted in the wake of Nixon's visit. Pandas also fed the culture of denial that surrounded the nation's imperial past. While diplomatic questions may have required consideration of the conflict that led to division between the two countries in the first place—the taboo topic of war responsibility—the delivery of clumsy, fuzzy, apparently harmless bears was another matter altogether. Speculation ran wild. "Will Japan get its own panda?" asked an article in the *Yomiuri shinbun* on the eve of Tanaka's departure, one of many that pondered the question.[30] Live pandas, rather than cold documents, came to be viewed as signs of genuine rapprochement and diplomatic success. The United States and the USSR, the Cold War world's superpowers, received giant pandas, but did postimperial Japan, a rising economic force but faded colonial power, merit such a gift?

Politicians and bureaucrats recognized the symbolic importance of the gift—a mark of international stature and parity with the United States as well as a sign of postimperial amity with the PRC—and Nakagawa and his colleagues at the zoo did their best to prime the potlatch pump, just as Koga had after the war in his efforts to repopulate the Ueno Zoo. The zoo's staff, in consultation with government officials, pursued a very public version of Koga Tadamichi's occupation-era tactics with Salt Lake City's Hogle Zoo: they used the semaphore of the public gift to signal their desire for the bears. Ueno sent two pairs of animals—a pair of chimpanzees and a pair of black swans—to the Beijing Zoo on the eve of the prime minister's visit. The Beijing Zoo returned a species of stork historically found in both countries but which was on the cusp of extinction in Japan and a pair of black cranes.[31]

The signal from Nakagawa and his zoo director, Asano Mitsuyoshi, was read clearly in Beijing, but the bears' arrival in Tokyo was not so smooth. As uniquely valuable creatures and popular symbols, Kang Kang and Lan Lan were claimed by multiple constituencies within Japan, each eager to draw value from the bears' cache of symbolic charm.

The gift was a mass media spectacle from the beginning. The diplomatic talks in Beijing were a rare "live television" event—*namachūkei*—broadcast from a country at once off-limits and historically familiar to the public, and it garnered a large television audience. The early seventies were a time when the simultaneity of live international television continued to hold a spectacle value of its own, so when Cabinet Secretary Nikaidō Susumu (1909–2000) announced the decision to send pandas during a live broadcast immediately following the eagerly awaited declaration of diplomatic normalization, it generated considerable excitement. "In recognition of diplomatic normalization between Japan and China," Nikaidō pronounced, "it has been decided that a pair of pandas, one male and one female, will be delivered as a gift from the people [*jinmin*] of China to the people [*kokumin*] of Japan."[32] Phone calls poured into the Ueno Zoo asking whether the bears would be housed in Tokyo or in some other location. Large regional zoos in Osaka, Kyoto, and elsewhere made aggressive bids to house the animals, suggesting that it would be a sign of evenhandedness on the government's part. Gardens in smaller cities focused on the prospect of a traveling "Panda Show," a late-modern version of the Traveling Zoo that carried Nehru's elephant Indira hither and yon across the Japanese countryside. Okinawa Prefecture, a former protectorate of the United States only returned to Japanese control in June, sent sugar cane and invited the bears to "visit beautiful Okinawa."

Speculation ended on October 6 with the formal announcement that the Ueno Zoo would house the animals. "Because the pandas are a gift from the Chinese people to the people of Japan," zoo director Asano said in an *Asahi* interview, "our goal is to locate the bears where they are most likely to be seen by the largest number of people." He argued that Ueno, as the country's largest (in terms of collection) and most visited zoo, was the best choice for this reason.[33] It was an important victory for the Ueno Zoo at a time when the garden's urban location and relatively small enclosures were increasingly criticized in the media and by organizations such as the Japan Society for the Prevention of Cruelty to Animals (JSPCA). Koga Tadamichi and other members of the Tokyo Zoological Park Society (TZPS)—along with several prominent occupation-era foreigners, including Jean MacArthur, the supreme commander's wife—had helped to create the JSPCA in 1948. The organization was built on foundations laid by the Nihon Jindōkai, or Japan Humanitarian Society, founded in 1915 by the writer Nitobe Inazō, his wife, Mary, and others as an umbrella organization addressed to questions of cruelty to children and animals. Asano and Nakagawa were important members of the JSPCA in 1972. Nakagawa remained chairman of the board until 2010.[34]

The JSPCA board was split over the question of location. Several members of the society, including the prominent children's author and Mainichi News editor Togawa Yukio (1912–2004), who sat on the board, argued that while Ueno might be suitable for the surge in viewers immediately following the animals' arrival, the newer Tama Zoological Park, opened in 1958 on a sizable wooded lot in the city's less populated western suburbs, offered a superior environment for long-term exhibition. "Convenience only matters so much," Togawa argued in an October 11 *Asahi Shinbun* article entitled "Spectatorship or Conservation, Which Will Take Priority?" "If they die it will be a tragedy. Tama is larger and has better air, and it would be best for the pandas." Minamimura Rika, a ten-year-old girl from Yokohama, concurred in a piece on the pandas for the widely read front-page "Vox Populi" (*Koe*) column in the *Asahi*. "I'm against putting the pandas, cared for in China, where the air is so good, in a place with such terrible air [as Ueno]. They will get sick." Rika's voice was not taken as representative of the opinions of children as a whole, however, and consistent with the pattern where notions of childhood and children's interests mediated adult political and social contests, the decision to leave the pandas in Ueno was formulated as a response to the needs of youth. "Whatever we say," argued Uchiyama Norihisa, a member of the JSPCA board and professor at Tsurumi University, "Ueno is best because it is most easily accessible to the greatest number of children. The children have already chosen Ueno."[35]

The bears arrived on October 28, less than a month after the gift's announcement in Beijing. They were welcomed at Tokyo's Haneda International Airport by zoo staff and more than two hundred reporters, who snapped photos of the animals in their green delivery containers, posed in front of the specially chartered Japan Airlines (JAL) DC-8 that carried them from China. Like Ueno, JAL fought for rights to the bears. All Nippon Airways (ANA), the country's second-largest airline, mounted a public campaign with the Ministry of Foreign Affairs; they made the case that, having carried the chimpanzees and other gifts to the Beijing Zoo only a few weeks earlier, they were better prepared. This publicity "air war" (*kūchūsen*), as the papers called it, was serious business. Japanese foreign tourism and airfreight traffic were growing together with the country's GDP, and both airlines viewed diplomatic normalization with China as an opportunity to expand their networks into a potentially profitable new area. JAL, the nation's flag carrier, was eventually chosen for symbolic reasons, but not before the center-right *Yomiuri shinbun* offered the provocative suggestion that delivery could be carried out by the Air Self-Defense Forces, postwar successor to the Imperial Japanese military.[36]

The bears were officially welcomed at Ueno on November 4 by a cross-section of the Japanese political elite. Cabinet Secretary Nikaidō was joined by the secretary general of the LDP and prominent representatives of most major political parties. These national politicians were joined by the mayor of Tokyo and the head of the Municipal Assembly. Director Asano read a speech and a smiling representative of the People's Republic stepped forward to express his "hope that this pair of pandas, symbols of the deep affection between the Chinese people and the Japanese people, will grow strong and live long, just as the feelings between our two nations must."[37] "Miyo" an orangutan pulled a string on a piñata (*kusudama*) unfurling a banner that read "Welcome to the Giant Pandas, Kang Kang and Lan Lan," and the curtain was pulled away from the panda's temporary lodgings—a hastily renovated tiger cage.[38] The bears "appeared nervous" according to Honma Katsuo, the keeper directly charged with the bears' care, by all accounts a sensitive interpreter of animal emotion. Meanwhile lines were already forming outside of the zoo's new "Panda Gate" (Pandamon) as patrons (including the media personality Kuroyanagi Tetsuko, who claimed to be the "pandas' biggest fan") eagerly awaited a turn in front of the bears.[39]

Prime Minister Tanaka and other politicians quickly deployed the panda in support of their reelection bids. Panda images proliferated on political posters and other paraphernalia as each party and individual politicians struggled to lay claim to the bears' charismatic power. When the LDP used pictures of Kang Kang and Lan Lan on a twenty-five-thousand-unit run of campaign buttons, they were flooded with requests for more from across the country—"panda politics" was a national business as well as a question of foreign relations. The Clean Government Party (Kōmeitō) and the Socialists quickly followed suit with their own badges, posters, and panda slogans.[40] Despite the Socialists' stronger claims on the "China question," the LDP took control of the panda storyline. It projected a clear narrative that trumped the ambiguity at the heart of panda politics—namely, the complicated nature of the association between the bears held in Ueno and China proper.[41]

This symbolic promiscuity confounded the categories within which political reporters sought to describe Prime Minister Tanaka's visit. "This is not a normal zoo exchange," an editor for *Nihon keizai shinbun* (*Nikkei*), the nation's largest economic newspaper, noted. "It is a state-level question" (*kokka-reberu mondai*). But it was a state-level question that refused to confine itself to one site or to answer to the standard techniques of political reporting. "No matter how many times our reporters visit the Ueno Zoo they get the same answers: 'Giant pandas belong to the order Carnivora and the family Procyonidae . . .' or 'The panda's menu will be . . .' and so on, but the answers to such important questions as 'When will they arrive?' and 'What sorts of animals will be chosen?' are all held by the [Japanese] government or the Chinese. We've had to use Inada, our special correspondent in Beijing, and our political reporters on this job." The result was the "birth of the *panda kisha*," or "panda reporter." Those "unlucky (?)"—the question mark is theirs—enough to land this new beat were called upon to combine the sensibility of a cultural affairs (*shakaibu*) reporter with the more highly valued skills of a "serious" political correspondent (*seijibu*). They were required, in other words, to accommodate the complex hybridizations of ecological modernity.[42]

"Panda reporting" was competitive business. Good images and exclusive news yielded immediate sales increases. "More than 120 newspapers, television and radio stations, magazines, and international wire services applied to Tokyo officials" for slots at Haneda Airport and the zoo on the day of the animals' delivery, the *Nikkei* editor remarked. In the end, the number of participants was limited according to each organization's status within the capital's various correspondents' clubs (*kisha kurabu*) and by circulation. The *Nikkei*, as an elite and widely read daily, was allowed to send the maximum: two reporters and a photographer each to the airport and the zoo. "The same number we sent when Prime Minister Tanaka completed negotiations [in China] and returned home," the editor remarked, seemingly in wonder at the popularity of the beasts.⁴³ The paper would have chosen to send more, he continued, but the numbers were strictly limited, as were the terms of their participation. Photographers "were not allowed within seven meters of the pandas, and we were told the event could be canceled at any moment for health reasons. It was exactly like covering a formal state visit."

The pandas, in the flashbulb heat of their arrival, bent journalistic norms and the gendered assumptions that underwrote them. Because there was not much preparation time ahead of the unveiling at Haneda, the *Nikkei* editor wrote in his editorial on the "birth of the panda reporter," photographers were left scrambling for spots, and when the covers were pulled from Kang Kang and Lan Lan's crates at 8 P.M., "the media-types all yelled out 'waaait!' like petulant children." Sarcastic reporters "were heard to mutter 'they're just animals' [*tada no dōbutsu da*] and so on," the editor reported, but "everyone really just wanted a better view"—no less the men than the women. "Female reporters from the women's weekly magazines kept calling out 'How cute!' [*Kawaii wa!*] but exclamations of 'Oh, cute' [*Oo! Kawaii*] could also be heard from [male] reporters one might expect to be a bit more calm."⁴⁴ Even "level-headed" veteran reporters at the *Nikkei*, a self-consciously somber paper sometimes called "Japan's *Wall Street Journal*," were swept up in the emotion of the moment. It was a "strange feeling" for many of the men, who found themselves "asking questions as if they worked for a women's weekly:" "When will they mate" and "Is Lan Lan-chan fertile" and "How long is a panda pregnancy?" As the reporters fell victim to their own media frenzy, a sense of disorientation found expression, as though the symbolic promiscuity at the heart of panda politics had led to uncertainty and, in some cases, self-doubt. Did these odd creatures really have anything to do with the political reality of Japan's relation to China?⁴⁵

"LIVING STUFFED ANIMALS"

The pandas may have arrived as "political animals," but the "panda boom" was defined by consumer culture. The species' neotenous fascination was amplified and organized through the work of industrialized consumer capitalism, which saturated the space between the animals and their viewers with purchasing opportunities. "We cannot represent the cuteness of these animals," Nakagawa recalls being told by an executive from a toy manufacturer in the early 1970s. "When it comes to stuffed animals, we can always make something that is more loveable than any kind of real animal," the executive continued. "Only pandas are different. No matter what we do, we can't match the real thing."[46] Pandas inverted the normal order of things in the commercial world that encompassed the zoo. They were "living stuffed animals" (*ikite iru nuigurumi*) or "stuffed animals made by nature" (*shizen ga tsukutta nuigurumi*), and as such they were uniquely desirable, but for those who paid close attention their very naturalness seemed to highlight the inability of commodities to fully comprehend natural phenomena. All copies would fail to "match the real thing."[47]

In 1972 the weekly magazine *Shūkan asahi* estimated that there were approximately one hundred different kinds of "panda toys" on the market in Japan before Kang Kang and Lan Lan's arrival, a somewhat surprising number since the species had never before been seen alive in Japan, but a drop in the bucket when measured against the marketing tsunami that washed over the nation following Cabinet Secretary Nikaidō's announcement. Japanese toy manufacturers sold upward of 10 billion yen in panda-related goods—mainly stuffed animals—in the first three months after the delivery of Kang Kang and Lan Lan, and the number goods for sale has only proliferated in the decades since.[48]

"They were so cute!" exclaimed one of the first people to see Kang Kang and Lan Lan on their first day of public exhibition. "Just like a stuffed animal!" The young woman had camped out overnight with about forty others, sleeping through a light rain in order to be one of the first to see the animals.[49] "What did they dream of? Why, pandas, of course," read the headline of an article in the *Yomiuri shinbun*.[50] There were five thousand people in line when the zoo's gates opened at 9 A.M. Five hundred police were deployed to the park, including a contingent of riot police. By mid-morning nearly twenty thousand people had gathered to "pay respects" (*ogamu*) to the pandas, as a reporter from the *Tokyo shinbun* put it, citing popular temple unveilings (*kaichō*) of relics and other rare objects that have taken place in Ueno's temples and shrines for centuries as historical precedent for the "pilgrimage" to see the pandas. It was an apt metaphor in one sense—early-modern *kaichō* were both spectacular *and* spiritual—but in this case the pilgrimage was to a state-run institution serving up several seconds of "face time" (*taimen*) with exceedingly rare foreign animals whose images were circulating in a swirl of commodities and commentary unimaginable in early-modern Edo.[51] For all its vibrant popular culture, Tokugawa Japan could match neither the scale nor the amplitude of the late-modern consumerism embodied in the "panda boom."

Children lined up to look at the pandas with stuffed animals already in hand.[52] A female plainclothes police officer used a bullhorn to urge patrons to "please keep moving" and, ironically, to "remain quiet." "Photographs are not allowed," yelled another. The line snaked its way over two kilometers to the bottom of Ueno Hill, "under the eyes of Saigō Takamori," as one article put it, citing the statue of the revolutionary hero and his dog that overlooks the park's main entrance.[53] The announcements were repeated, verbatim, every six seconds. When patrons attempted to stop in front of the cage, one of ten specially chosen officers wearing white gloves would step forward and gently push them along, quietly suggesting that they "continue forward." A police official noted that they were using techniques created for dealing with "sit-in protesters and the like."[54] The line moved "like a conveyor belt," another official happily remarked, using the machinery of mass production as a metaphor for the movement of spectators.[55] "I waited in line for three hours," said one patron, "and saw them for thirty seconds." "I only saw its butt!" declared another. "It was hiding in the shadows," complained a third. "I waited in a long line and saw them for a brief moment," said a man who brought his wife. "What we really saw were lots of people." Most agreed with the father of several disappointed young children, who vowed that they would "return at another time, when we can see them more easily."[56]

What did people think they were buying when they bought tickets to look at the pandas? Almost certainly, some made the purchase for simple reasons of company and social cachet. They may have come to look at the people, or in order to tell friends they had been there. Others, however, came to see the animals, and this is the act that concerns the critic John Berger, who argues that trips to the zoo are attempts to answer a fundamental thirst born of the impoverished relationship with animals that is endemic to modern societies. For him, the central question is this: "Why are the animals less than I believed?" It is a question that is buried in some of the comments above. Berger's answer to the question is startling and stark. The reason, he suggests, is that when you are looking at zoo animals, "you are looking at something that has been rendered absolutely marginal." For Berger, the motor behind this change is capitalism itself. "Zoos, realistic animal toys and the widespread commercial diffusion of animal imagery, all began as animals started to be withdrawn from daily life. One could suppose that such innovations were compensatory. Yet in reality the innovations themselves belong to the same remorseless movement as was dispersing the animals."[57]

The exhibition of giant pandas in Tokyo, one could argue, marked the pinnacle (or nadir) of this dynamic. The animals were so visually consuming that they seemed to require firsthand witness, and when the conditions of that witness were unsatisfying, they resulted in criticism of the conditions of the moment rather than the condition of modern life more generally. Viewers vowed to return again, to find a time when their hopes and expectations might be met. This is a point on which Berger's view could be taken a further step. Modern life not only marginalizes animals physically, but it also produces conditions within which the pursuit of a satisfying encounter with the animal world becomes more desirable for many. Whether that desire is born of some biological instinct—an assumption that Berger hints at sharing with Lorenz—or from a logic internal to the cultural moment is not the crucial point. What matters most for us, in our focus on animals *and* humans in the zoo, is the acceleration of the cycle. "The reproduction of animals in images—as their biological reproduction in birth becomes a rarer and rarer sight—was competitively forced to make animals ever more exotic and remote," Berger writes.[58] To which we might add, "and thus ever more desirable." The pandas embodied this dynamic, exhibiting an irreducible appeal—the inability of toy manufacturers to "match the real thing," which only spurred more creative attempts to do so— that pushed the motors of production and the conveyor belt of exhibition to the breaking point.

In the end, it was the animals' bodies that registered the stress of the cycle. Tokyo's giant pandas were subjected to unprecedented human attention, and that attention took a physical and psychological toll. Welcomed at the airport by more than two hundred newly minted *panda kisha*, the bears were tracked through the Tokyo night by the swirling yellow lights of patrol cars as they made their way past curious onlookers and crowds of children holding stuffed toys and into the zoo. There, they were allowed several days of adjustment—"Animals are most vulnerable when they first arrive," Honma noted—before the official unveiling on November 4 and the surge of visitors the following day. The noise and chaos of exhibition weighed on the animals—not to mention the lack of appropriate food, as Nakagawa and Honma discovered that giant pandas only eat particular kinds of bamboo. By November 8 headlines had changed from "Nihao, Everyone, Welcome, Panda" to "Panda Down!" ("Panda daun!").[59]

Lan Lan collapsed from stress or exhaustion on November 7, a physical casualty of mass fascination. By the afternoon of the first day of exhibition it was clear to Honma and Nakagawa—both unfamiliar with the species and therefore especially vigilant—that the female bear was experiencing difficulties breathing. Foam began to form around her mouth, and her behavior became increasingly erratic. She started pacing back and forth across her cage, an action that delighted visitors, who applauded when the animals moved. Patrons were dismayed when the bears stayed still or hid—sometimes calling out over bullhorns carried into the zoo to rouse them—and so what Honma saw as "irritated pacing," others understood as playful energy.[60] Exhibition hours were shortened day by day. By the end of the second day of full-scale public exhibition the situation had worsened, and exhibition was halted altogether.

The *Mainichi shinbun* reported the closure as if reporting on an exceptional case of overwork, a common news topic in the self-sacrificial culture of bubble capitalism, where "death from overwork" (*karōshi*) was an officially recognized ailment. "After trying to please everyone for several days in a row, the pandas at the Ueno Zoo, Kang Kang and Lan Lan, have crashed from too much work. They have grown tired due to non-stop labor since their welcome gala on the 4th, as loudspeakers have continued to sound, and they've been seen by more than 30,000 noisy people." After listing more of the difficulties faced by the bears, the reporter informed readers that the zoo was "halting 'exhibition' in order to care for the pair."[61]

The zoo instituted a series of measures that were framed in generally sympathetic human terms by the press. Beginning on November 9, papers began to report that the pandas would be taking a "two-day weekend," pulling the pair into ongoing debates over work and leisure in a country where salaried employees (and many others) worked a six-day workweek. Exhibition time was further limited to only two hours (10 A.M. to noon) on days when the bears were not "on vacation." The newspapers *Sankei* and *Tokyo shinbun* were vaguely critical of the decision, implying that exhibition time was not sufficient, but other papers simply reported the news or portrayed it in a positive light, suggesting that the bears were "enjoying their weekends together" and that they would be more fun to watch thanks to the limited stress.[62] The *Yomiuri* suggested that "the pair has enjoyed their first 'day off' since the two-day weekend was instituted." Adding that Kang Kang, the male, "struck a pose" like a rugby player while rolling a basketball around his cage while Lan Lan "relaxed in the 'panda pose,' leaning up against the wall with her legs out in front of her." Both had a marvelous time, according to the reporter, especially when they were handed a bunch of Okinawan sugar cane.[63]

The systems instituted to protect the bears from human attention became themselves the focus of media commentary. The plans to open a new Panda House were widely discussed. Descriptions of the planned structure in the nation's newspapers read like an upscale real estate ad: "The pandas' new 'sweet home' [suiito hōmu] . . . will include full climate control, air conditioning and heat, glass all around, an extra room, and an interior garden." It also included a glass-encased "birthing room." The new facility was built next to the Elephant House in the space left by the Monkey Train, which was removed in 1973 over concerns that it violated the terms of the country's first comprehensive Animal Welfare legislation, passed the same year.[64] Total area, including the professionally designed "bamboo garden," was approximately seventeen hundred square meters. "It will look like heaven," reported the *panda kisha* from the *Sankei shinbun*, "when seen through the eyes of a salaryman living in a 2DK [two-rooms plus dining and kitchen] high-rise apartment."[65] Once opened, the space allowed more views of the bears and limited the cacophony that surrounded them. The bears' keepers noted that each seemed to "settle in" to the new space with ease.[66]

The cost of the new lodgings was the subject of considerable public debate. "A radio quiz show caught my attention the other day," wrote 52-year-old Tōjō Mitsuko, a housewife from Aichi Prefecture, in a letter to the editor of the *Mainichi shinbun*. "It asked listeners to guess how much it cost to build the pandas' new house: (1) 10,000,000 yen, (2) 20,000,000 yen, (3) 40,000,000 yen." The answer, Tōjō was "shocked" to discover, was 40,000,000. How could the country justify such expenditures "when there are elderly people who need care, and so many others living at the edge of their means," she asked.[67] She was not alone in her criticism. A high school student from Kanagawa Prefecture wrote to the *Sankei* asking why the bears "should be allowed to live in conditions better than most human beings."[68] Others replied that such arguments missed the point by drawing misleading financial connections between animal welfare and human welfare. Yamawaki Yaichirō, a twenty-nine-year-old company employee from Tokyo, wrote to the *Sankei* suggesting that the money being spent on the Panda House was not likely to be taken from needy people. He continued, "And furthermore, we should address the needs of disabled people and others through legislation regardless of whether or not we decide to spend substantial amounts on the panda cage."[69]

THE NATURE OF COPYRIGHT ·

The reproduction of "living stuffed animals" meant big profits, and efforts to make claims on the pandas extended into the realm of copyright law, where the distinction between nature and artifice was written into judicial precedent thanks to a contest over the ownership of panda images and panda dolls. The case in question developed when the owner of the Sakuragitei concession stand located outside of the zoo's main gates filed suit against the Tokyo Zoological Park Society (TZPS) and the Sun and Star Corporation for trademark infringement. The owner of the stand, which sold a variety of panda-related goods, including a popular "panda-yaki," a bun filled with bean paste and stamped into the shape of a panda, had filed legal papers in 1977 to trademark a stuffed "family panda" (*fuamirī panda*) doll that showed an adult panda hugging a baby panda. The claim was brought in June 1983 in reaction to TZPS plans to begin marketing a "parent-child panda" doll (*oyako panda*), manufactured by Sun and Star, that shared a similar pose and nearly identical markings.[70]

When notified of the suit, TZPS temporarily stopped display of the dolls, which had already received coverage in the popular "Blue Pencil" (Aoenpitsu) editorial section of the *Asahi shinbun*. Asahi editors suggested that the creation of the doll might presage the arrival of a real baby, fanning the flames of a growing national obsession with panda reproduction.[71] Zoo leadership was eager to avoid negative public attention in this connection—they had failed to produce a cub in the decade since Kang Kang and Lan Lan arrived—and after consultation with legal counsel, the "parent" and "child" portions of the doll were clipped apart and sold separately at the zoo store. Clerks were instructed to avoid displaying the larger doll holding the smaller, to place items between the "parent" and the "child" when arranging shelves, to avoid referencing them as a "set" or "pair," and finally to enter separate prices and item descriptions when selling the two dolls to the same customer. That is, instead of simply noting "stuffed animal," sales people were told to handwrite "parent" and "baby" (as opposed to "cub") next to the separate entries. The "baby" doll sold for 600 yen and the larger "parent" doll cost 3,800 yen.[72]

Sakuragitei's counsel, Akao Naoto, was not satisfied that the separation of the two items answered the contents of the original claim, and when the two sides were unable to reach an accommodation out of court he proceeded with the suit. The suit, however, revealed that TZPS and Sakuragitei might, in fact, both be guilty of trademark infringement. The concessioner had failed to renew its original 1977 trademark application, and it lapsed in August 1980. A company in Kawasaki had filed papers to trademark the name "parent-child pandachan" in the interim and begun selling a doll of the same general description as those involved in the suit. TZPS and Sun and Star pursued a judgment annulling the original Sakuragitei claim while Sun and Star negotiated a transfer of the trademark from the company in Kawasaki.[73] The company then moved to void Sakuragitei's original trademark application by arguing that a photograph of a toy resembling the Sakuragitei's "family panda" set was published in the pages of *Asahi Graph* magazine as early as 1972, thus invalidating the original application for trademark in any event.[74]

The squabble reached a new stage when Akao appealed again, this time to the Tokyo High Court (the region's circuit court of appeals), arguing that there were substantial differences between the item in the photograph and the "family panda" sold at Sakuragitei. When the Court denied this claim on the basis that, "while there is notable difference between the items in question, the extent of those differences is not enough to justify their consideration as distinct entities" in intellectual property terms, Akao appealed again. The case proceeded to the Supreme Court of Japan, where it was handled with unusual speed. On June 23, 1989, six years after the original claim by Sakuragitei but only a few weeks after the case's submission to the court, the Supreme Court issued a curt statement upholding all previous judgments in the case without elaboration.[75]

The real legal import of the case is not immediately apparent in the language of the judgments involved, according to Iwataki Tsuneo, a lawyer whose work concerns trademark and intellectual property questions. Iwataki argues that the case defines nothing less than the distinction between nature and art, creativity and mimicry in relation to animals and other natural phenomena. The key issue, he writes, is the boundary between "products that simply imitate natural items [*shizenbutsu*]" and those that accentuate their features or otherwise alter their appearance to such a degree that they may be called human creations and trademarked. The ruling made it impossible to trademark images or representations of animals striking a pose or engaged in behavior that "may be found in nature," and nature in this case included the animals in the zoo. In order to merit legal protection, a depiction must have proportions, coloring, or other alterations that are "only possible with human intervention." He offers the examples of Dumbo and Mickey Mouse, creatures whose neoteny is so exaggerated that they could only be seen as products of the human imagination.[76]

Iwataki, writing for an audience of designers concerned with their ability to depict naturally occurring species and to protect those depictions from uncompensated imitation, discerns the core issue: that a line between nature and culture can be essential to certain kinds of marketing—and to capitalism more generally. It is, as Marx and others have argued, crucial to the division of the world into marketable commodities.[77] In the context of our history, the Sakuragitei case may also be seen a continuation of the Meiji-era effort to clarify distinctions between products of "human manufacture" (*jinkō*) and things that were "made by nature" (*tenzō*) in the Yamashita Museum—itself built in an effort to "promote industry" (*shokusan kōgyō*). But where Tanaka Yoshio and Machida Hisanari debated the location of silkworms and domesticated animals within a taxonomy that wished to draw clear lines between natural objects and manufactured artifacts in an agrarian age, lawyers for Sakuragitei and the Ueno Zoo disputed the free use of images and likenesses, especially those of pandas, in an age of mass media. The political-economic context had changed radically, but the proper relationship between nature and culture remained an open question in the discourse surrounding the zoo.[78]

TZPS leaders were, of course, pleased to win the case, but they immediately recognized that the verdict had broad ramifications for the institutions under their control. They could now produce a "parent-child panda" doll without reference to trademark and copyright limitations so long as the image was sufficiently "true to life," but so could any other business or entity in Japan. The same freedom of reproduction applied to depictions of all of the animals in the zoo, present and future, and the Ueno Zoo's ability to lay proprietary claim to representations of its own animals—now legally defined as "natural" even if the species was no longer extant in the wild—was clearly circumscribed. Zoo animals were "natural" according to legal precedent, and so the complex marketing apparatus of the Ueno Zoo, traditionally built around a monopoly on depictions of animal "stars" (*sutaa*)—the performing elephants Tonky and Indira, for example—was threatened with collapse.[79]

Officials took comfort in the fact that the creatures' names, at least, remained proprietary, but Nakagawa suggests that the legal shift sparked a debate about the "Disneyfication" of the zoo's visual culture

Disneyfication vs. fading biodiversity + exotic animal trade

at a time when the institution was striving to address such grim issues as fading biodiversity and the costs of the exotic animal trade. Even in the most serious of times the Ueno Zoo had struggled against associations with sideshows and circuses, staff argued. If images were now remade—caricatured—in order to maintain copyright, the institution risked becoming a theater of the absurd, a place where the contradictions between conservation and consumerism would begin to define the Ueno Zoo's image at home and, more important to some, in the international community of zoo professionals. In the end, the institution's leadership chose a middle path, pursuing selective trademarks on specific animal caricatures (so-called "character goods") while, for the most part, they did their best to "match the real thing" in their depictions of pandas.[80]

This species alone required no further characterization in order to maximize its public appeal, and that made it uniquely desirable for zoo professionals and zoogoers alike. In the case of the giant pandas, we might say that desire was amplified through the failure of commercial representation. The fact that there was no way to out-cute the real pandas—sans quotations marks—only further concentrated attention on the real animals. And if adult "living stuffed animals" that "tricked" people into emotions associated with babies were desirable, how much more so an actual baby—a real reproduction—of the species? Letters from throughout the country and overseas flooded the zoo with the same question: where were the children? After all, Kang Kang and Lan Lan were male and female and they were said to be of breeding age. As the zoo's marketing staff and designers at Sun and Star confronted the limits of their abilities, Nakagawa and the Ueno Zoo's technical staff redoubled their efforts to reproduce the real thing.

THE BIOTECHNOLOGY OF CUTE

There was pressure on the zoo administration to breed the pandas from the moment that Kang Kang and Lan Lan arrived in Tokyo. The Noachian structure of the Chinese gift—a male-female pair rather than a single bear or animals of the same sex—is conventional in zoo exchanges, and it is commonly taken as a signal that the giving institution would like to see the animals bred. That was how Kobayashi Seinosuke (1920–), a noted nature writer and member of the JSPCA board, interpreted the Chinese gift. Since the PRC "chose to deliver a male and a female, one each," Kobayashi remarked in an October 1972 interview with the *Asahi shinbun*, the animals "arrived carrying an important message: 'please make these animals breed.'"[81] The reproductive theme was echoed in Director Asano's November speech welcoming the bears to Tokyo and thanking a delegation from the PRC. "We welcome these greatest of gifts [*saikō no okurimono*] marking diplomatic normalization between Japan and China. In recognition of the goodwill of the Chinese people, we will do our utmost to breed a second generation of pandas."[82]

Perhaps inspired by Nixon's musk oxen, Prime Minister Tanaka sent a pair of homely Japanese serows to the Beijing Zoo in answer to the panda gift, and Director Asano, inspired by comments from T. H. Reed, director of the National Zoo in Washington, promised a new generation of pandas. The announcement sparked a friendly competition between Washington and Tokyo to see who could breed the animals first, but it was met with mixed feelings by Honma and Nakagawa, who learned from the Chinese keepers who accompanied the bears to Tokyo that the species was "poorly suited to breeding in captivity" and that Kang Kang, the male, was still an adolescent at two years old.[83] Neither had Lan Lan, at four, ever given birth. Furthermore, there appeared to be no properly documented scientific reports on panda behavior in the wild, as related to mating or any other behavior. What they had was the book by the Morrises, an outdated Japanese natural-historical account based on information gleaned from historical texts, and Dwight D. Davis's detailed 1964 study, *The Giant Panda: A Morphological Study of Evolutionary Mechanisms*, which was entirely based on knowledge gained through dissection.[84]

The incentive to breed the animals grew as restrictions on traffic in the species developed due to increasingly stringent national and international regulations, the start of the "rent-a-panda" lease system by China in 1984, and a shift in relations between the WWF and the PRC in the mid-1980s that saw the prominent conservation organization take a more proactive role in limiting the movement of its mascot species.[85] Following Japan's formal entry into the CITES convention in 1980 (delayed by debates over whaling and sea turtle harvests, among other issues),[86] members of the Japanese Association of Zoological Gardens and Aquariums (JAZA), which included all of the country's major gardens, also vowed in 1986 that they would "no longer purchase animals" and that "conservation would take precedence over [diplomatic] goodwill."[87] The statement signaled JAZA's decision to join other elite zoological gardens and aquariums in a move away from the exotic-animal trade and toward greater efforts at collaborative breeding. It was a choice that allowed Japanese zoos to continue to trade with gardens in North America, Western Europe, and Australia, and which limited dealings with noncompliant institutions for legal and ethical reasons.[88] It also promised to accelerate the circulation of new species through the gardens as animals were moved about for breeding purposes. "Animal exchange will become more and more prominent as we move from the singular focus on expressions of goodwill to a multifaceted focus on species conservation," a JAZA representative told the *Yomiuri*.[89] More animals and greater diversity in the collection were good for gate receipts and breeding, officials reasoned.

The breeding drive was aided by an intuition of changing ecological realities among zoo professionals, their growing sense that human impact on the natural environment required something new of the zoo. In the context of "environmental destruction caused by humans," the *Yomiuri* article stated, zoo directors around Japan now agreed with William G. Conway, director of the Bronx Zoo, that "gardens must move from being consumers to becoming producers" of animals.[90] It was a remarkable statement on at least two levels. First, it reversed the normal vector that moved animals from the wild to the zoo and illustrated an awareness of the links between consumerism (even in this limited sense) and ecological degradation. Second, and more pertinent to the case of the pandas, it redirected the zoo's economic and bureaucratic energies away from the purchase of animals recently acquired by capture and onto the bodies of individual animals already in its cages. This shift had obvious benefits for dealings with exotic animal dealers, but it also led to unprecedented technical and medical manipulation of the animals already in captivity at zoological gardens. In the long run, the turn inward sped the implementation of salutary animal husbandry techniques, most notably "enrichment," or the recognition (born of the ethology championed by Lorenz and others) that animals in captivity need stimuli in order to remain psychologically and physically healthy.[91]

To this end, Ueno began the slow, contentious, and still incomplete process of bending intuitional efforts away from "recreation" and toward "nature conservation" (*shizen hogo*).[92] This alteration marked the single largest change in the garden's mission in the postwar period, and it began in earnest in the last decade or so of the twentieth century. As the zoo's own in-house history (published in 2003) put it, "Zoological gardens are often said to have four main functions. Recreation, education, research, and conservation. Be that as it may, until as little as ten years ago, recreation was the only function given importance by the zoo or by visitors."[93] Nevertheless, the recent emphasis on conservation, science, and breeding may also be seen as an amplification of older trends, however transient or marginal.

As early as the 1880s, Ishikawa Chiyomatsu championed the zoo's role as a site for the propagation of scientific consciousness. Koga Tadamichi, Ueno's longest-serving director, was eloquent in his discussion of environmental degradation after the war. He was also instrumental in founding the Japanese branch of the WWF in 1971.[94] As we saw in the previous chapter, the gardens actually increased their role in the global exotic-animal trade after 1945, but Koga also devoted significant resources to captive breeding. He was internationally recognized for his success in breeding large bird species, especially cranes, symbols of the Japanese nation and the imperial house. He pioneered the use of artificial insemination in bird breeding, and in 1986 JAZA established the "Koga Award" to mark his passing and recognize outstanding accomplishments in captive breeding at the country's zoos. The garden's veterinarians, keepers, and affiliated scientists—many of whom also actively urged the government to become party to CITES at the time of its initial enforcement in 1975—thus had long focused on breeding programs (both unaided and artificial) as a means of growing species stocks and building institutional prestige, but it was only in the 1990s that those piecemeal efforts were consolidated and given significant funding by the city and national governments.[95]

From Ishikawa to the present day, arguments in favor of the gardens have always sought to push the institution's agenda forward by focusing on the problems of the past. This is not to say that conditions have not improved over time for many of the animals held in Ueno's cages. They have, as the reduction in stereotypical behavior measured by former Ueno Zoo director Komiya Teruyuki indicates.[96] But the history of Ueno's pandas also shows us how turbulent and indeterminate such developments can be. The costs of progress have been exacted from the bodies of the zoo's own animals, and they have tended to lead to a narrowing of ecological vision suited to the status quo rather than opening up broader discussions about the nature of modernization and the place of animals and the natural world in it. One of the goals of this book has been to defamiliarize the zoo, to uncover what is often unrecognized in this most popular of cultural institutions. Often that has meant seeing politics in a landscape devoted to playful education—the Children's Zoo as a site of disciplinary dystopia? Bambi as a neo-colonial mascot?—but it can also mean turning our eyes away from ideology and discourse and toward the bodies through which they have been enacted, whether those bodies were human or not.

Nowhere were these tensions more evident than in the pursuit of panda breeding. It was, in fact, panda sex that sparked the Sakuragitei lawsuit. After considerable frustration on the part of the impatient ranks of panda reporters, Kang Kang and Lan Lan mated for the first time on April 24, 1974.[97] Freud is supposed to have said that people go to the zoo to see animals with their clothes off, and the dramatic increase of interest in the zoo in the spring and summer of 1974 leaves little doubt that sex is good for the zoo business, especially panda sex.[98] The details of the bears' "courtship" and the eventual "marriage" were laid out in detail in the pages of newspapers and recounted with relish on the evening news. Photographers beseeched zoo administrators to share more explicit images. The large department stores in Ueno's busy Hirōkōji section, where the lines for the panda exhibit ended, inflated a huge blow-up panda and unveiled a series of "Panda Festivals" aimed at zoogoers.[99] The single-day record for paid zoo entrance was set on May 5, 1974, National Children's Day, when 125,000 people lined up hoping to catch a glimpse of neotenous bears having sex behind glass. The British BBC and the American network ABC sent camera crews, and newspapers turned to the task of speculation about the possibilities of babies.[100] Perhaps somewhat tired of seeing the adult bears, merchandisers and the public alike were eager for a new animal attraction.

But as Nakagawa and Honma had been warned, giant pandas do not breed well in captivity. Nor do they conform to the norms of the nuclear family. In the wild, a female panda may mate with several males while in estrus (a fact that may help to explain the poor reproductive record in captivity), and newborn cubs are often left untended and alone for extended periods while the mother forages for food or is otherwise engaged. Mass media characterizations of Kang Kang and Lan Lan's mating focused on the romantic ideal of "love" between a pair of monogamous "married" animals, and the habit of leaving cubs was treated as "abandonment" in the scientific community since it seemed to increase mortality. Alert to this problem, China collected cubs as part of its captive-breeding programs, which developed as part of China's growing system of panda reserves and research stations. These stations were partially funded through leasing fees gathered from foreign zoos such as the San Diego Zoo, which could then justify the loan as an act of "conservation" or "education" rather than a purely commercial action, thereby circumventing the CITES prohibition against the transfer of Appendix I fauna for commercial reasons.[101]

On November 14, the zoo's new director, Iwauchi Nobuyuki, called a news conference in the Zoo Hall. Over one hundred reporters crammed into a space designed for sixty people, and the director announced "Lan Lan-chan is not pregnant" into a bank of microphones. It was a moment of irony that points toward deep-running contradictions of ecological modernity. Instead of becoming mascots for the success of conservation efforts and captive-breeding programs, pandas figure as reminders of the limits of human progress and the costs of our enduring (commercial) fascination with animals and the wild. We want them more than any other creature, but attempts to facilitate reproduction fail more often than they succeed, and failure only seems to breed more desire and redoubled effort. This, in turn, can justify an even a greater degree of technological manipulation in pursuit of baby icons of biodiversity. Such attention is not necessarily unjustified in conservationist terms, but as Japan's "panda boom" illustrates, it is naïve to believe that conservation is the sole—or perhaps even primary—driver of our efforts.

This conflicted nexus comes together in the ubiquitous WWF icon of the roly-poly black-and-white panda. A real bear sold for profit inspired a generic image. In 1958 a young bear named Chi Chi was bartered out of the PRC by the Austrian wild-animal dealer Heini Demmer, who eventually sold her to the London Zoo for a rumored price of 10,000 pounds. London had its own "panda boom" when Chi Chi arrived, and the animal became a muse for the ornithologist and conservationist Peter Scott, who was looking for a logo for the new organization he helped to create, the WWF, formally established in Switzerland in 1961.[102] The bear was so popular that Prime Minister Edward Heath, following in Tanaka's footsteps, returned to China to request a second specimen in 1974. He then went back again (this time in a semiofficial capacity) in 1988 to request another.[103]

The embracing irony emerged on May 25, 1979, when Kang Kang and Lan Lan mated for the last time. The entire captivity regime at Ueno had been redesigned to increase the likelihood of a pregnancy in the years since the pair arrived, and this fourth and final mating attempt was, in that sense, successful. It was also the end of Lan Lan. The new "Ueno Zoo System" for panda husbandry was the product of intensive comparative study by Nakagawa and the team of keepers devoted to the giant pandas' care and breeding. After close examination of the systems used in Beijing, Shanghai, and Basel, Nakagawa's team opted for a modified version of the "Basel System," which attempted to manipulate the animals' desire in the hopes of inspiring copulation at the moment of greatest receptivity. Kang Kang and Lan Lan were both let into the glass-enclosed "garden" until the onset of estrus or, if keepers were able to identify it through observation or urine samples, proestrus. They were then separated until Lan Lan was judged most fertile, at which point they were reunited in the hopes that pent up ardor—or instinct—would lead to pregnancy.[104]

It was a successful innovation, or so it seemed to be. The final observation notes from the event give a sense of the backstage dynamics of the panda boom. "4:53 P.M. – 6:23 P.M.: Female elevates hindquarters and presents, male assumes mounting posture. When male retreats, female follows, presenting. Situation continues for extended period. Copulation from 6:19 P.M. for 1 minute and 42 seconds. Male and female both give affectionate calls." The episode, one of three that day, was recorded by still camera and video for later observation. Although it was clear to everyone—including the reading public—that the bears had mated, it was not certain that Lan Lan was pregnant until she died several months later, on September 4. X-rays of the carcass revealed a fetus, which was confirmed by dissection. The cause of death was listed as pregnancy-induced toxemia. The bear's liver had failed.[105]

The pent-up desires of the bears' human audience would have to wait for the arrival of a new set of pandas. Kang Kang died the following June, but not before Prime Minister Ōhira Masayoshi requested a replacement for Lan Lan during a 1979 diplomatic mission to China. Ōhira was followed to Beijing in 1982 by his successor, Suzuki Zenkō, and a replacement for Kang Kang arrived in October 1982 to mark the first decade of normalized relations between Japan and the PRC. The new pair, Fei Fei and Huan Huan, were installed in the Panda House and the garden area was expanded. Fei Fei was a more robust-looking animal than Kang Kang, and Huan Huan showed signs of having given birth while still in the wild. Speculation about the arrival of a panda baby began to elevate again. But it quickly became clear that the two animals could not abide each other's company.[106] They were uncharacteristically ferocious with one another, a dangerous development given the strength of panda jaws, evolved to cut through tough bamboo.

In June 1985 Huan Huan became only the third panda in the world to give birth to a cub conceived through artificial insemination. Ueno's pandas were, in this sense, a kind of biotechnology: organisms artificially shaped by human beings to serve human ends.[107] In this case, rather than

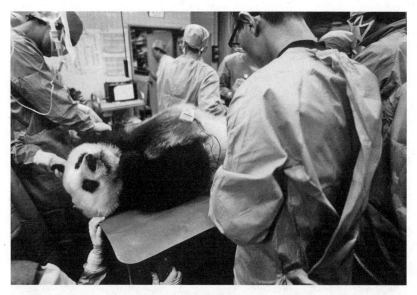

FIGURE 19. Huan Huan in the operating theater, 1985. Both Huan Huan (the female, shown here) and Fei Fei were sedated for these procedures. Huan Huan gave birth to three cubs conceived through artificial insemination, Chu Chu (male, b. 1985), Tong Tong (female, b. 1986), and You You (male, b. 1988). The Tokyo team was so successful that it began to train technicians from other zoos. Image courtesy of the Tokyo Zoological Park Society.

breeding hearty warhorses for use in wartime, as described in chapter 3, the zoo was motivated by the combination of ecological scarcity, national pride, and "unfathomable cuteness" to invest tens of millions of yen in the project of reproduction. Huan Huan's pregnancy was a tremendous success for the zoo's technical staff, but everyone was soon disappointed when the infant Chu Chu, as the 5-ounce, 6.5-inch cub was posthumously named, was crushed under his mother less than forty-three hours after birth.[108] Such deaths are common. Of the 120 giant pandas born in captivity between 1963 and 1992, only 47 survived the first month.[109]

Trapped in these multiplying contradictions, the country had to wait another year. Tong Tong (the name was copyrighted by TZPS before being made public) was born via the same process on June 1, 1986, and another cub, You You, followed two years later. These animals were bred with semen harvested from the sedated male Fei Fei through electro-ejaculation in a state-of-the-art operating theater. The animal's sperm was stored in sterile tubes and kept in refrigerators with redundant power supplies until it was injected into Huan Huan, who so intimidated

FIGURE 20. The weight of history—Tong Tong on a scale. Born at the Ueno Zoo on June 1, 1986. This female cub was the second giant panda conceived through artificial insemination in Japan and the first to survive for public viewing. Attendance at Ueno hit new records as thousands lined up to see the shy young creature. Shown here on October 26, 1986. Image courtesy of Tokyo Zoological Park Society.

Fei Fei that "natural breeding proved impossible."[110] The timing of the injection was dictated by on-the-spot chemical analysis of urine samples gathered by staff members who stayed on twenty-four-hour rotations in the spring weeks when female giant pandas tend to go into estrus. The tiny animal that resulted—panda cubs typically weigh less than four ounces—was not merely an animal image reproduced as "compensation" for the withdrawal of animals "from daily life," as Berger has argued. She was a living creature, yet an artifact, created through careful technical intervention in order to maintain a species that had found a home in the modern system of consumer desire, politics, and professional science.[111]

CONCLUSION

This, then, marks the endpoint of our story: the artificial reproduction of animals that refused to breed in captivity carried out in the service of a popular fascination with "cute" creatures but justified as a proper scientific response to the crisis of extinction, a crisis generated by the same processes of modern development and consumption that fed the popular obsession with the species in the first place. It was an inversion and confirmation of the process of animal marginalization identified by Berger, a process that I take as emblematic of ecological modernity in Japan and elsewhere. Berger has famously argued that zoo animals "constitute a living monument to their own disappearance."[112] The case of the pandas illustrates the extension of the processes identified by Berger into the bodies of living animals and the return of those dynamics into the realm of the social via the work of exhibition. Put differently, it reminds us that zoo animals are more than just objects of display. They are living creatures *and* objects of display, what Japanese law calls "display animals" (*tenji dōbutsu*).[113] The case of Ueno's giant pandas underlines this interplay between representation and the natural world within the zoological gardens, the fungible roles that animals play in mediating that process, and the ways in which human cultural choices can impact individual animals and the broader natural world.

Epilogue

The Sorrows of Ecological Modernity

When an unnamed 144-gram giant panda cub died at the Ueno Zoo on July 11, 2012, it gave form to the enduring paradoxes of ecological modernity.[1] The story of this tiny furless animal illustrates at one and the same time the mass appeal of animals and nature within Japanese society and an unfulfilled longing for those same things. It shows how politics have penetrated nearly every aspect of life at an institution that has, since the end of the Allied occupation in 1952, sought to define its mission in terms of apolitical recreation and education. And it demonstrates the tensions between the global realities of a changing natural world—the dynamics that I have tagged, following Paul Crutzen and others, as the Anthropocene—and everyday life in an industrialized, mass-culture society such as Japan's. Born through "natural breeding" in an environment crafted by and for human beings, the cub was a hybrid of the natural and the artificial whose existence—had it survived—was dependent on continued human intervention.

The newborn was entangled in politics from the start. Its parents arrived at the Ueno Zoo on February 21, 2011, three years after the death of Ling Ling, who had for years been famous as Ueno's "last panda." Ling Ling was not in fact the last giant panda to walk the paths of Ueno's state-of-the-art Giant Panda House, but he was the last of the species owned by a Japanese organization or government. Indeed, eight giant pandas remained in Japan when Ling Ling died in 2008, six at Adventure World in Wakayama Prefecture and two at the Kobe Municipal

Ōji Zoo. All of those animals, however, were the property of the People's Republic of China (PRC). The PRC uses costly leases—cast as conservation and breeding agreements—to manage the overseas careers of giant pandas and to fund the Wolong National Nature Reserve in Sichuan Province, the controversial conservation area meant to protect panda habitat. As the PRC's economy has shifted from state-centered socialism to a "socialist market economy," so too has the nation's panda policy evolved into a striking blend of monopoly capitalism and bureaucratized conservationism in the service of the state. The Chinese government is exploiting the simple fact that giant pandas become more desirable globally as their numbers and habitats shrink.

Ling Ling's death left a hole in the Ueno Zoo's exhibitionary landscape that could be filled by no other species. Ueno was home to at least one giant panda from 1972 until 2008, and for many the association between the black-and-white bears and the Tokyo zoo was definitive. The health and identity of Tokyo's premier zoological garden, the nation's de facto national zoo, was understood to be contingent on access to one or two of the world's dwindling supply of nineteen hundred or so giant pandas, creatures held in a Chinese monopoly. "It simply is not Ueno Zoo without a panda," one official remarked in public comments, but as a subsidiary of the Tokyo city government, the zoological garden had no direct means of securing another bear. Panda leases typically span a full decade and cost at least U.S.$1 million per year. Such large commitments are a special expenditure for the zoo, despite an annual budget of several billion yen, and the costs of political exchange were at first too high for Tokyo's notoriously bellicose mayor, Ishihara Shintarō (1932–), who dismissed the idea of "borrowing" pandas from the Chinese as a diminution of Japanese national prestige. "No pandas" for Tokyo ("Nō panda"), he pronounced loudly, echoing the title of his infamous coauthored 1989 book, The Japan That Can Say No ("Nō" to ieru Nihon), a neonationalist assertion of Japanese autonomy in the context of twentieth-century American hegemony. This time his target was twenty-first-century China.[2]

In the absence of giant pandas, zoo director Komiya Teruyuki and his staff began to lobby Ishihara behind the scenes and to look for other ways to sustain attendance. "Ling Ling made a great contribution to the zoo by attracting lots of visitors," Komiya told a reporter. "From now on, I hope other animals will play his role."[3] Komiya's efforts were creative: sloths traversed thick ropes stretched above walkways, constrained only by their instinctual refusal to drop from heights; a rescued Steller's Sea Eagle stood entirely uncaged on a small island in Shinobazu Pond, held in place by injuries sustained in the wild (and treated by veterinarians); and the elephant enclosures were remodeled and expanded, part of an effort to restore the giant creatures to the center of the zoo's exhibitionary culture. But people still wanted to see giant pandas. Surveys showed that *Ailuropoda melanoleuca* were the zoo's single largest draw.[4] Kiosks and gift shops continued to sell "panda goods," and patrons continued to snap photos next to the giant panda statue stationed just in front of the institution's main exit.

Finally, a male-female pair of bears, Ri Ri and Shin Shin, arrived in Tokyo from the Wolong Reserve. Panda flags were once again unfurled throughout Ueno's busy shopping districts, news crews set up shop in familiar spots near the Panda House, and zoo staff set to work helping the animals adjust. "They seem to like Japanese bamboo and apples," Komiya told the assembled reporters.

For his part, Mayor Ishihara started with apathy and ended with aggression. When asked why he had changed his stance on the lease, the mayor answered testily, "Because there was strong demand from local groups." Reporters pressed: "Which local groups in particular?" To which Ishihara replied, "Preschoolers."[5] Laughter rippled through the crowd at the thought that Ishihara might capitulate so easily, but it was clear that the zoo had lobbied hard, leveraging children and adult nostalgia in a manner that echoed director Koga's strategy under American occupation fifty years earlier. "I don't really care about pandas," Ishihara remarked. "Aren't they really just expensive commodities?"[6] But the animals and the mayor were locked in a mass-media embrace, and Ishihara, a former playwright with a knack for dark comedy, made the most of it. Reporters and editors knew that Ishihara could be counted on to say something pithy and dismissive when asked about the Chinese bears, and the mayor used the creatures to draw attention to his controversial attitudes toward China, turning "panda diplomacy" on its head in the process.

By the summer of 2012 Shin Shin was pregnant and Ishihara was in heated negotiations for the City of Tokyo to buy one of the Senkaku Islands (Ch. Diàoyú Islands), a small archipelago in the East China Sea claimed by China, Japan, and Taiwan. The purchase appears to have been intentionally provocative, a tool for the mayor to use Tokyo's traditional control over dozens of tiny outlying islands in order to galvanize nationalist sentiment at home in support of Ishihara's run for higher office. The mayor resigned in November 2012 to lead the conservative Sunrise Party of Japan, but before he left he made the most of the media attention surrounding the pregnant panda, tying the Chinese mascot to the incipient conflict over uninhabited islands claimed by the PRC. "I think we should name the cubs *sen sen* or *kaku kaku*," the mayor remarked in June, invoking the island's Japanese name and perhaps playing with the fact that the two halves of "Sen-kaku" are homophones for "war" and "nuke." "Whatever we call them," Ishihara argued the following day, "the fact that they are Chinese possessions won't change." It was a sarcastic reversal of official diplomacy phrased in the idiom of panda politics. PRC spokesman Hong Lei had remarked two days earlier, "The Japanese can call the islands whatever they wish, but the fact remains that they are Chinese possessions."[7]

Birth and death brought détente in the realm of panda politics. Shin Shin's cub was welcomed as good fortune in the wake of the disaster of March 11, 2011, when tens of thousands of people lost their lives to a massive tsunami and the nuclear facility at Fukushima tripped into meltdown, threatening Tokyo and northeastern Japan with radiation contamination. "The giant pandas are messengers of friendship," Chinese foreign ministry spokesman Liu Weimin told reporters, and Ueno staff celebrated the success of "natural breeding," a noninvasive breeding program designed to stimulate ursine desire through staged separations and timed reunions. It was a tremendous success for the team at the zoo, but celebrations were as short-lived as the cub itself. Six days after birth the tiny creature died of pneumonia. Komiya's replacement as director, Doi Toshimitsu, wept as he announced the loss. An autopsy revealed that the cub probably died because it was breast-fed rather than bottle-fed. Natural nursing is less controlled, and the creature seems to have inhaled a small amount of its mother's milk.

It is a loss that underlines the contradictions at work in the zoo. "Natural breeding" was justly celebrated as a step forward for Ueno's captive-breeding program. It implied not only a less invasive approach to the animals but also a more fully developed understanding of what drives pandas to mate. The cub was the first giant panda born in Japan conceived through sexual intercourse. At the same time, it may have been the preference for "natural" feeding that led to the animal's death, and the simple fact remains that cub mortality in zoos outside of the PRC is high. In an interview with the Xinhua news agency immediately after the death at Ueno, Zhang Hemin, director of the Chinese Conservation and Research Center for the Giant Panda at Wolong, suggested that 15 percent of giant panda cubs born outside of China died, as opposed to a survival rate of "nearly 100 percent" at Wolong and its sister preserve in Chengdu.[8]

Zhang tagged the animal's death to "inexperience" on the Japanese side. "The relatively low survival rate of baby pandas abroad is rooted in inexperience in dealing with emergencies," he said. Zhang continued, further asserting Chinese technical superiority, that an expert from Wolong had flown to Tokyo to share Chinese "know-how and methods." He said he suspected that the local staff may have failed to spot possible danger or take proper rescue measures. "The baby panda could have survived if they had more practice." Zhang's colleague, Wu Kongju, from the Chengdu Research Base of Giant Panda Breeding, echoed this sentiment: "Chinese zoologists have spent dozens of years developing related technology and skills. Our foreign peers should try hard to learn as well in order to raise the survival rate of giant pandas abroad."[9] Neither man questioned the wisdom of flying bears to zoological gardens as far away as Madrid, Tokyo, and Washington, D.C.

All of these particulars were canvassed intensively in the media, building the sad little story of a lost cub into a larger reality that embraced giant pandas from their advent in Japan, their role as objects of public spectacle. Breeding was an important but ultimately secondary concern. The species embodies this central tension at work in the zoo: they are uniquely attractive as visual objects yet poorly suited to life in captivity, especially captive breeding. This tension between visual appeal and physical needs is crucial not only for giant pandas but throughout the zoo. People visit zoos, like museums, to look. But in the case of the zoo, unlike the museum, the objects on display are alive. This liveliness can be a boon—the sensory recognition of an animal's presence contributes to our own sense of wonder—but it can be at odds with the reality of the animal's physical needs, and when the sense of wonder feels inauthentic there follows a powerful sense of disaffection. The pandas mark an extreme example of this phenomenon. Due to their spectacularization in various mass media, they are, as former director of the Ueno Zoo, Nakagawa Shirō, has argued, "a species whose visual worth outstrips their value as physical animals."[10] Sorrow at the newborn's death speaks to this inevitable moment of disenchantment.

The charismatic panda has paradoxical features as a political emblem, and as an emblem of consumer culture, features that are also visible in the drama which now centers on its biological reality. The effort to breed pandas in captivity, like the other stagings of this drama, exemplifies what Timothy Mitchell calls the "metaphysics of capitalist modernity." That is, the capacity of modern culture to designate a set of images and signs as representations of a realm of reality beyond themselves. In this case the dramatization within the zoo of an authentic "nature" lying beyond its walls, a domain framed by the edge of human culture itself, sequestered as the province of science but which ultimately serves social ends. The process creates a gap, akin to that Nakagawa identified between the physical and media value of the panda, but which also serves in the designation of "natural resources" and other products of modern commodity culture.[11]

In the service of modern systems of politics, economics, and rationalization, Mitchell argues, objects were collected and arranged to stand for something else, somewhere else. Exhibitions, department stores, and museums are contrived to evoke a larger truth: nation and progress, empire and industry, orient and occident, nature and society. Everything is set up as a picture or exhibition of some encompassing idea or order. Through their techniques of display these institutions produced a sense of certainty about representation and its referents, creating the feeling that there is in fact an external reality somewhere "out there" that was merely being referenced or summarized within the museum or the exhibition. This structure spread globally across the nineteenth and early twentieth centuries, moving together with the institutions that gave it form and the economies that reaped its profits. The creation of the Ueno Zoo and the National Museum were early steps in its Japanese development.

The payoff of such representations is the affirmation of authenticity: not within the artificial world of the exhibit itself, which is assumed to be manufactured, but in the imagined or implied world that it claims to represent.[12] Yet these systems are haunted by intimations of self-defeat. The real thing—the orient or nature, for example—is always somewhere else. The scale and accuracy of these representations—thousands of natural-history specimens, dozens of display cases—serves the illusory feeling that there must exist some original of which the exhibition is merely a summary or sketch, that there is a more pure reality out there, untouched by the forms of displacement, mediation, and reproduction that render the image merely an image.[13] Zoological gardens such as Ueno trade on the promise of bringing that external world into the realm of the exposition itself, of overcoming the ontological instability of this system of representation through the brute (or sublime) physicality of the animals themselves. The pandas were so adorable that they seemed to offer the possibility of canceling out the alienating effects of modern culture by offering a real thing that was so appealing, so satisfying, that it was sufficient unto itself. At the same time, the sideshow aspects of the zoo, the focus on spectacle rather than science that has characterized the place since the first decade of the twentieth century, suggests that visitors don't need to take things so seriously. People are there, the logic goes, for the simple act of looking. But looking is rarely as simple as it seems.

Ueno's planning staff played on this dynamic when they submitted an outline detailing plans for a zoo expansion, inspired by the popularity of the giant pandas, in 1975. The committee suggested that "exhibits of animals elicit a nostalgia for nature" in visitors, and that properly displayed animals would facilitate a "recuperation of the humanity" that was lost in the "separation from nature that has developed together with machine civilization in the city." It was a plan indebted to previous discussions of the zoo by Koga Tadamichi and others, but those earlier efforts, the authors argued, were "insufficient." They did not provide a "doorway for the introduction of correct knowledge about nature," and they "failed to support conservation." The zoological garden, the report suggested under the section on "new social needs," was different from the museum because it could provide an "oasis" of "real nature" in the city. On this point it was "fundamentally different from the museum" and "more in-line with the needs of the times," which were increasingly dictated by environmental change.[14]

But no matter how lavish the cages and enclosures became, Nakagawa pointed out in 1995, the zoo's animals always remained what Japanese law calls "display animals."[15] The animals in the zoo have been disembedded from (or bred outside of) their native ecologies and, in the case of Ueno, relocated into the heart of the largest urban environment on the planet. The resulting sense of contrast is part of what makes zoo visits enjoyable. But it is also in part because of this process that, rather than answering the nostalgic hopes identified by planners, the zoo instead cultivates them and thus perpetuates a longing that cannot be fulfilled, either in the zoo or in the natural world. The recurring effort to reform and reshape its landscape suggests that the zoological garden is engaged in a constant and unavailing struggle to overcome that insufficiency. The life and death of Shin Shin's cub asks us to recognize the costs of the pursuit of "real nature" even as we recognize its powerful appeal. It is a process born of the global alienation from nature—what Koga invoked when he urged a "return to true humanity" in the 1930s—that began to develop in Japan from at least 1822, when Udagawa Yōan finished his *Botany Sutra*.

Over the course of the century or more encompassed by this book, the pursuit of that other world has been reflected in the changing culture of the zoological gardens. When the zoo was created in 1882, it was designed, in part, to hold nature at bay. "Civilization" was the ordering principle of the gardens. Each and every cage or enclosure was contrived to underline the separation of humans from animals, Japanese from savagery. Today, as we look at Ri Ri and Shin Shin kept captive in a multimillion-dollar facility filled with state-of-the-art equipment and manned by highly educated keepers, veterinary scientists, and media professionals, we are made to see a natural world that has been enclosed for its own protection. The humanity that was imagined into being in the nineteenth century has become nature's greatest threat. Where the Ueno Zoo once walled nature out to "protect" Japanese claims to civilization, it now walls animals in as part of a broader effort to protect wild nature from human depredation, and the zoo converts this defensive struggle into the stuff of spectacle.

Humanity itself has somehow been lost in the triumph of mankind. The stunning objective of modernity, that of liberating humanity from its subjection to a natural order, has incarcerated human beings in a disorienting hall of mirrors, where nearly everything in our field of vision looks like a reflection of ourselves. Very large natural phenomena (earthquakes, tsunami, typhoons) still defeat the controls that humankind has asserted, as do the very small (retroviruses, prions). But creatures on the scale of zoo animals, earlier bespeaking immediate physical danger or the living mystery of the natural world, have now become emblems of a precarious and destructive human sovereignty.[16] It is a new global reality that asks us to think against the grain of modern culture, to see connections where we have been trained to find difference and to see interrelationships in places that we have been taught to dismiss.

If the world has indeed entered the "Anthropocene," the "age of humanity," then there may be no better place to study its cultural meanings than the zoological gardens, a consciously designed middle ground between human society and the natural world.[17] The hybrid institution of the zoo—a stage for diplomacy, marketing, education, and entertainment—is a microcosm of Japan's broader engagement with these dynamics. It shows us that environmental questions need to be asked in the realms of culture and consumerism as well as politics and economics, and that none of those worlds can be properly said to be separate. They all have their being within the complex ecology of modern life.

Notes

INTRODUCTION

1. My approach to the problem of ecological modernity—the emergence of a new culture across the nineteenth century—shares a great deal with William R. Leach's analysis of capitalist modernity in America over much the same time period. See *Land of Desire: Merchants, Power, and the Rise of a New American Culture* (New York: Pantheon, 1993). On the transformation of attitudes toward the natural world in the United States, see Linda Nash, *Inescapable Ecologies: A History of Environment, Disease, and Knowledge* (Berkeley: University of California Press, 2006). For a similar treatment of related dynamics, see Ruth Rogaski, *Hygienic Modernity: Meanings of Health and Disease in Treaty-Port China* (Berkeley: University of California Press, 2004). Though it is not framed as such, it is worth noting that Rogaski's book can be read as an environmental history along the lines of Nash and Brett Walker. Brett L. Walker, *Toxic Archipelago: A History of Industrial Disease in Japan* (Seattle: University of Washington Press, 2010).

2. In an important sense, I am arguing that modernity is always "ecological," but I use the term "ecological modernity" here to designate a particular aspect of the broader modern culture. I use the terms "modernity" and "modernization" in specific ways. By "modernization" I mean the bureaucratic, economic, technological, and especially industrial developments that have rationalized production since at least the nineteenth century. I outline the meaning of "modernity" in the pages that follow, but it must be noted at the outset that I have chosen the term "ecological modernity" in order to distinguish my approach from the debate among sociologists and other social scientists over "ecological modernization." Much of that work is valuable, but it has often been informed by a set of progressive assumptions—the notion that societies tend to select increasingly environmentally beneficial policies over time for rational

reasons—that are not born out in the events at the center of my study. As I argue in the third section of this introduction, "ecological modernity" at the zoological garden has been characterized as much by dissention, contradiction, and displacement as it has by improvement or rationalization. As I argue in the next section, the preponderance of empirical data on climate change, biodiversity, and pollution in Japan (and elsewhere) suggests that this is also the case well beyond the institution at the center of my account. Brendan F.D. Barret, *Ecological Modernization and Japan* (New York: Routledge, 2005); Arthur P.J. Mol, *The Ecological Modernization of the Global Economy* (Cambridge, Mass.: MIT Press, 2001); Arthur P.J. Mol, David A. Sonnenfeld, and Gert Spaargaren, eds., *The Ecological Modernization Reader* (London: Routledge, 2009).

3. As Raymond Williams, William Cronon, and others have made clear, few ideas are so complicated as that of "nature." This was also the case in Japan, as Julia Adeney Thomas has shown. The idea of "nature," commonly rendered as *shizen* or *tennen*, is itself a human fabrication deeply enmeshed in cultural, political, social, and scientific dynamics. Throughout the text I have sought to maintain a distinction between "nature"—this complex and contested idea—and the "natural world," used to signal flora, fauna, and environmental elements. These things and creatures were, of course, used, influenced, and made meaningful by human beings. But they also *influenced* people and culture. It is along this axis of action that I have drawn the distinction between "nature" and the "natural world." "Nature" is a human idea. The "natural world" is a category of things that can reach out and touch (or bite) you. Raymond Williams, *Keywords: A Vocabulary of Culture and Society* (New York: Oxford University Press, 1976); William Cronon, "A Place for Stories: Nature, History, and Narrative," *Journal of American History* 78, no. 4 (1992): 1347–1376; Julia Adeney Thomas, *Reconfiguring Modernity: Concepts of Nature in Japanese Political Ideology* (Berkeley: University of California Press, 2001); on animals and agency, see Brett L. Walker, *The Lost Wolves of Japan* (Seattle: University of Washington Press, 2005). A note on chronology is also in order. Although I do parse ecological modernity's development for smaller shifts in use and meaning, it is important to note the relatively consistent character of these dynamics over the course of the 120 years or so covered in this book. When viewed against the deeper history of humanity's long presence in the Japanese islands, modernity reads as the rapid amplification of earlier regimes of resource exploitation and environmental impact. The mid-level chronological punctuations that tend to concern modernist historians can obscure as much as they reveal in our focus on distinction over continuity within the modern era. I do not argue for radical discontinuity from early modernity to modernity. As I show in chapter 1, the intellectual connections between Tokugawa Japan and Meiji Japan were subtle and multifaceted. The ecological effects of these changes, while certainly complex, were often far less subtle. On long term environmental dynamics in Japan see Conrad Totman, *Green Archipelago: Forestry in Pre-Industrial Japan* (Berkeley: University of California Press, 1989) and Yumoto Takakazu, *Kankyōshi to wa nani ka* (Tokyo: Bun-ichi, 2011).

4. I am drawing here on Carol Gluck's work. As Gluck suggests, such cultures find distinctive expression according to place and time, but they were characteristic of most modernizing states in the nineteenth century. For Japan see Carol Gluck, "Meiji for Our Time," in *New Directions in the Study of Meiji Japan*, ed. Helen Hardacre and Adam L. Kern (New York: Brill, 1997), 13–16. See also my "Didactic Nature," in *JAPANimals: History and Culture in Japan's Animal Life*, ed. Gregory M. Pflugfelder and Brett L. Walker (Ann Arbor: University of Michigan Center for Japanese Studies, 2005). Michel Decerteau makes similar arguments in his *The Writing of History* (New York: Columbia University Press, 1992). For the United States see "The Trouble with Wilderness; or, Getting Back to the Wrong Nature," in *Uncommon Ground: Toward Reinventing Nature*, ed. William Cronon (New York: Norton, 1995) and Richard White, "Are You and Environmentalist or Do You Work for a Living?" in *Uncommon Ground*. For France see Michael Bess, *The Light-Green Society: Ecology and Technological Modernity in France, 1960–2000* (Chicago: University of Chicago Press, 2003). For a salutary effort to look beyond the idealization of "wilderness" in the American case, see Aaron Sachs, *Arcadian America: The Death and Life of an Environmental Tradition* (New Haven, Conn.: Yale University Press, 2013). Japan was also home to traditions other than ecological modernity, many of them associated with aesthetic practices such as poetry or with the close cultivation of highly stylized environments such as temple gardens and cemeteries. Ecological modernity, in contrast, has tended to emerge from institutions associated with popular and research science and engineering such as the zoo, the science museum, the laboratory, and the schoolhouse. We can also see related dynamics in the abattoir and the supermarket, the commodities trading system, and the modern discourse on "natural resources." On "natural resources" as a modern idea see Satō Jin, *'Motazaru kuni' no shigenron: jizoku kanō na kokudo wo meguru mō hitotsu no chi* (Tokyo: Tokyo Daigaku Shuppan Kai, 2011). On the Japanese discourse of seasonality: Haruo Shirane, *Japan and the Culture of the Four Seasons: Nature, Literature, and the Arts* (New York: Columbia University Press, 2013). Julia Adeney Thomas shows how such aesthetic ideas were transported into ultranationalist discourse in Japan in her "Ultranational Nature," in *Reconfiguring Modernity*, 179–208.

5. The clearest and most influential statements of this sort in Japan Studies came out of the seminal Hakone Conference in 1960, where leading Japanese and American scholars gathered to debate the nature of Japanese modernization. The crucial discussions on this point focused on the role of inanimate energy sources in modernization and the role of secularization in building a modern nation-state. For a summary of the proceedings, see John W. Hall, "Changing Conceptions of the Modernization of Japan," in *Changing Japanese Attitudes toward Modernization*, ed. Marius B. Jansen (Princeton, N.J.: Princeton University Press, 1965). On the conference in general see J. Victor Koschmann, "Modernization and Democratic Values: The 'Japanese Model' in the 1960s," in *Staging Growth: Modernization, Development, and the Global Cold War*, ed. David Engermann, Nils Gilman, Mark Haefele, and Michael E. Latham (Amherst: University of Massachusetts Press, 2003).

6. See, for example, Koga Tadamichi, "Dōbutsu no shiiku kōza," *Kōen ryokuchi* 3, no. 1 (January 1939).

7. The phrase is Alfred W. Cosby's. See his *Children of the Sun: A History of Humanity's Unappeasable Appetite for Energy* (New York: Norton, 2006). See also Oliver Morton, *Eating the Sun: How Plants Power the Planet* (New York: HarperCollins, 2009). For a seminal study of human bodies in urban environments see Gregg Mitman, *Breathing Space: How Allergies Shape Our Lives and Landscapes* (New Haven, Conn.: Yale University Press, 2007). The literature on urban ecology is vast. For a summary of international work on the topic see John M. Marzuluff, Eric Shulenberger, Wilifried Endlicher, Marina Alberti, Gordon Bradley, Lare Ryan, Ute Simon, and Craig ZumBrunnen, eds., *Urban Ecology: An International Perspective on Interaction between Humans and Nature* (New York: Springer, 2008). See also Emma Marris, *Rambunctious Garden: Saving Nature in a Post-Wild World* (New York: Bloomsbury, 2011).

8. I am drawing most directly here on Bruno Latour, *We Have Never Been Modern* (Cambridge, Mass.: Harvard University Press, 1993). See also Timothy Mitchell, *Rule of Experts: Egypt, Techno-Politics, Modernity* (Berkeley: University of California Press, 2002) and Donna Haraway, *A Cyborg Manifesto: Science, Technology, and Socialist-Feminism in the Late Twentieth Century* (New York: Routledge, 1992). As Tessa Morris-Suzuki has shown, the argument that Japan—almost always in contradistinction to a rather simplistic idea of the "West"—lacked the concept of "humans as subject and nature as object" is both common and deeply suspect. I further follow Morris-Suzuki in a refusal to identify a single unitary "Japanese view of nature." Close attention to the events surrounding the zoo—rather than "theories of Japaneseness" (*Nihonjinron*), for example—shows that no single tradition encompassed the full culture at any point. For a treatment of various "natures" in Japanese thought, see "Nature" in Tessa Morris-Suzuki, *Re-Inventing Japan: Time, Space, Nation* (New York: M.E. Sharpe, 1998). Ecological modernity was one culture among others in a contested ideological and institutional field. It was, as I show, a culture of considerable influence and scope, but I make no assertion of universality despite the claims of many of my actors along these lines. Julia Adeney Thomas also addresses a closely related set of issues, and while our analysis and arguments differ at times, most often due to divergent focus (elite intellectual discourse versus a cultural institution aimed at the broader population), I have found her work to be tremendously helpful at each stage. See, Julia Adeney Thomas, *Reconfiguring Modernity*; see also, Julia Adeney Thomas, "'To Become as One Dead': Nature and the Political Subject in Modern Japan," in *The Moral Authority of Nature*, ed. Lorraine Daston and Fernando Vidal (Chicago: University of Chicago Press, 2004), 308–330.

9. Buddhist theology, for example, located the "beastly realm" (*chikushōdō*) below that of the human (*nindō*) in the six states of existence, or "six paths" of samsara (*Rokudō rinne*). When possible, I use the term "beast" in reference to these older discourses rather than "animal," or *dōbutsu*, intentionally. "Dōbutsu" took on a new meaning early in the nineteenth century, as I show in chapter 1. On Buddhism's relationship with the animal world in Japan see Barbara Ambros, *Bones of Contention: Animals and Religion in Contemporary Japan*

(Honolulu: University of Hawaii Press, 2012). Arne Kalland addresses related issues in his *Unveiling the Whale: Discourses on Whales and Whaling* (New York: Berghan Books, 2009). See also John Knight, *Waiting for Wolves in Japan: An Anthropological Study of People-Wildlife Relations* (Honolulu: University of Hawaii Press, 2006).

10. Available on the Keio University Library website, accessed May 1, 2012, http://project.lib.keio.ac.jp/dg_kul/fukuzaw a_title.php?id=3. On the early history of the museum complex, see Alice Yu-Ting Tseng, *The Imperial Museums of Meiji Japan: Architecture and the Art of the Nation* (Seattle: University of Washington Press, 2008); and Shiina Noritaka, *Meiji hakubutsukan kotohajime* (Kyoto: Shibunkaku shuppan, 1989).

11. Albert M. Craig, *Civilization and Enlightenment: The Early Thought of Fukuzawa Yukichi* (Cambridge, Mass.: Harvard University Press, 2009). Ōkubo Toshimichi, "Ōkubo Toshimichi bunsho," reprinted in *Nihon kagaku gijutsu shi taikei*, ed. Nihon Kagaku Kyōkai (Tokyo: Daiichi Hōki Shuppan, 1964). Tessa Morris-Suzuki, *The Technological Transformation of Japan: From the Seventeenth to the Twenty-First Century* (Cambridge: Cambridge University Press, 1994).

12. Michael Sorkin, "See You in Disneyland," in *Readings in Urban Theory*, ed. Susan S. Fainstein and Scott Campbell (Malden, Mass.: Blackwell, 2001), 208.

13. Those who would prefer a detailed institutional and financial history of the organization should first consult the official history of the Ueno Zoo, the *Ueno Dōbutsuen hyakunen shi*, two volumes, totaling more than fourteen hundred pages. Further work on these questions can be found in various articles listed in the bibliography by Ken Kawata, former general curator, Staten Island Zoo.

14. Jody Emel and Jennifer R. Wolch, introduction to *Animal Geographies: Place, Politics, and Identity in the Nature-Culture Borderlands* (New York: Verso, 1998). See also Lorraine Daston and Gregg Mitman, *Thinking with Animals: New Perspectives on Anthropomorphism* (New York: Columbia University Press, 2005). And most especially, see Harriet Ritvo, *The Animal Estate: The English and Other Creatures in the Victorian Age* (Cambridge, Mass.: Harvard University Press, 1989).

15. On reclassification of the natural world in the imperial age, see Harriet Ritvo, *The Platypus and the Mermaid, and Other Figments of the Classifying Imagination* (Cambridge, Mass.: Harvard University Press, 1997), 10. In important ways, time and culture worked differently in the Japanese case. The flood of species came, in a sense, all at once when the country "opened" its libraries to the full array (rather than a small selection) of Western natural-historical texts in the mid-nineteenth century. See also Richard Drayton, *Nature's Government: Science, Imperial Britain, and the 'Improvement' of the World* (New Haven, Conn.: Yale University Press, 2000).

16. In describing the institutional network of the zoo, I am drawing on Latour's approach as outlined in his "Drawing Things Together," in *Representations in Scientific Practice*, ed. M. Lynch and S. Woolgar (Cambridge, Mass.: MIT Press, 1990). See also Richard H. Grove, *Green Imperialism: Colonial*

Expansion, Tropical Island Edens, and the Origins of Environmentalism (New York: Cambridge University Press, 1995).

17. On the history of zoos around the world, see Vernon N. Kisling, *Zoo and Aquarium History: Ancient Animal Collections to Zoological Gardens* (Boca Raton, Fla.: CRC Press, 2001); Nigel Rothfels, *Savages and Beasts: The Birth of the Modern Zoo* (Baltimore: John Hopkins University Press, 2002); and Bob Mullan and Garry Marvin, *Zoo Culture* (Urbana: University of Illinois Press, 1999). According to Kisling, the Calcutta Zoo opened in 1876. The Melbourne Zoo was the first built outside of Europe. It opened in 1872, the same year as the Yamashita Animal Hall in central Tokyo.

18. Elizabeth Hanson, *Animal Attractions: Nature on Display in American Zoos* (Princeton, N.J.: Princeton University Press, 2002). There are nearly ninety accredited zoos and dozens more monkey parks, animal safari parks, and other animal attractions in Japan today. For up-to-date listings, see the Japanese Association of Zoos and Aquariums (JAZA) website, accessed 2011, www.jaza.jp /z_map/z_seekoo.html. For accreditation information worldwide, see the World Association of Zoos and Aquariums website, www.wasa.org.

19. I have chosen to use the relatively unfamiliar term "Anthropocene" because I believe that it is empirically accurate and also, in part, to defamiliarize the ideas of "modernity" and "modernization" at work in so much writing on Japan. The point here is not to engage in a debate over nomenclature, but to focus our attention on aspects of modernity that may have been previously overlooked. For an accessible summary of the idea of the Anthropocene, see Paul J. Crutzen, "Geology of Mankind," *Nature* 415 (January 3, 2002). On "globalization," see Arjun Appadurai, *Modernity at Large: Cultural Dimensions of Globalization* (Minneapolis: University of Minnesota Press, 1996). For a study of globalization in Japan, see Andrew Gordon, *Fabricating Consumers: The Sewing Machine in Modern Japan* (Berkeley: University of California Press, 2012). See also Michael Hardt and Antonio Negri, *Empire* (Cambridge, Mass.: Harvard University Press, 2000). On writing the history of "deep time," see Daniel Lord Smail, *On Deep History and the Brain* (Berkeley: University of California Press, 2008). On the Pleistocene and the Holocene see Lydia V. Pyne and Stephen J. Pyle, *The Last Lost World: Ice Ages, Human Origins, and the Invention of the Pleistocene* (New York: Viking, 2012). As a nonspecialist, I have made some basic assumptions about the science of climate change and contributions from Crutzen and others. Following work by historians such as Dipesh Chakrabarty and Naomi Oreskes as well as reports from the United Nations Intergovernmental Panel on Climate Change, I have chosen to accept the basic scientific consensus on these matters. Dipesh Chakrabarty, "The Climate of History: Four Theses," *Critical Inquiry* 35 (2009): 197–222; Naomi Oreskes, "The Scientific Consensus on Climate Change," *Science* 306 (December 3, 2004).

20. I am drawing here on the contribution from Will Steffen, Jacques Grinevald, Paul Crutzen, and John McNeill, "The Anthropocene: Conceptual and Historical Perspectives," *Philosophical Transactions of the Royal Society* 369 (2011): 842–867. See also Stuart Chapin III, Erika S. Zavalta, et al., "Consequences of Changing Biodiversity," *Nature* 405 (May 11, 2000): 234–242.

21. Some scholars argue that the beginning of the Anthropocene must be marked far earlier, at the dawn of the agricultural age, for example. This is a reasonable argument. I have chosen to focus on the industrial era because of the amplified human impact rather than out of any sense that humans did not influence global climate in earlier eras. Industrialization within the frame of the nation-state—rather than the slower paced change of agricultural development or long-term population growth, for example—is the crux of the matter to my way of thinking. See Chakrabarty, "The Climate of History," 209–210. See also William F. Ruddiman, *Plows, Plagues, and Petroleum: How Humans Took Control of Climate* (Princeton, N.J.: Princeton University Press, 2010).

22. Lippet, *Electric Animal*, 3. For a critical engagement with Lippet, see Nicole Shukin, *Animal Capital: Rendering Life in Biopolitcal Times* (Minneapolis: University of Minnesota Press, 2009). On a distinct but related discourse of loss and longing in modern Japan see Marilyn Ivy, *Discourses of the Vanishing: Modernity, Phantasm, Japan* (Chicago: University of Chicago Press, 1995).

23. "IUCN—What Is Diversity in Crisis?" accessed July 8, 2011, www.iucn.org/what/tpas/biodiversity/about/biodiversity_crisis/.

24. Steffen et al., "The Anthropocene"; Chapin and Zavalta, "Consequences of Changing Biodiversity."

25. The OECD Environment Programme, "Environmental Performance Review of Japan," OECD, 2002, accessed June 26, 2012, www.oecd.org/env.

26. Walker, *Lost Wolves*; Mike Danaher, *Environmental Politics in Japan: The Case of Wildlife Preservation* (Saarbruken: VDM Verlag, 2006).

27. Chakrabarty, "The Climate of History"; Julia Adeney Thomas, "Using Japan to Think Globally: The Natural Subject of History and Its Hopes," in *Japan at Nature's Edge: The Environmental Context of a Global Power*, ed. Ian Jared Miller, Julia Adeney Thomas, and Brett L. Walker (Honolulu: University of Hawaii Press, forthcoming).

28. I am drawing here on Sheila Jasanoff's sustained discussion of related dynamics. See Sheila Jasanoff, "A New Climate for Society," *Theory, Culture & Society* 27, no. 2–3 (2010): 233–253. She deals with related issues in "Testing Time for Climate Science," *Science* 328, no. 5979 (2010): 695–696.

29. Chakrabarty, "The Climate of History," 221, 207; on the distinction between "nature" and "culture" in the Western scientific tradition, see Bruno Latour, *We Have Never Been Modern* (Cambridge, Mass.: Harvard University Press, 1993).

30. Naomi Oreskes, "The Scientific Consensus on Climate Change," *Science* 306 (December 3, 2004).

31. Jasanoff, "A New Climate for Society," 250.

32. Ibid.; The parallels between the emergence into consciousness of climate change and arguments on the nature of the European Enlightenment made by Max Horkheimer and Theodor W. Adorno are striking. On the enlightenment as "disaster triumphant," see their *Dialectic of Enlightenment* (New York: Herder and Herder, 1972), 3.

33. Nyhart's elegant formulation of the "biological perspective" differs from my approach in its closer focus on the history of science. Because my history is

focused on a site rather than a body of discourse, I have chosen to use the term "ecological modernity" rather than, say, "biological modernity" or the "biological perspective." The events described in *The Nature of the Beasts* took place in lived interactions among people and animals as well as in the realm of academic discussion. The key transition in Nyhart's *Modern Nature*, however, also holds in the broader Japanese case. The shift from a university-based elite science focused primarily on taxonomy into the civic realm of museums, schools, zoos, and other public enterprises can be seen in Japan in the first decades of the twentieth century, when the number of zoos expanded and the scientific community entered a period of diversification and specialization. As I argue in chapter 2, it was during this period that the Ueno Zoo became separated from the main currents of elite scientific research in modern Japan. See Lynn K. Nyhart, *Modern Nature: The Rise of the Biological Perspective in Germany* (Chicago: University of Chicago Press, 2009), especially "Introduction: The Biological Perspective and the Problem of a Modern Nature," 1–34. On opening the field of environmental history to new methodological approaches, see Sverker Sorlin and Paul Warde, "The Problem of the Problem of Environmental History: A Re-Reading of the Field," *Environmental History* 12, no. 1 (2007): 107–130. Julia Adeney Thomas suggests a similar move in the epilogue for our coedited volume, *Japan at Nature's Edge*.

34. Of course, zoos were not alone in making symbolic claims on the natural world. Gardens, botanical gardens, and even farms made similar efforts. The Ueno Zoo simply tended to do it on a larger scale.

35. Koga Tadamichi, "Dōbutsuen no fukkō," *Bungei shunjū* 27, no. 3 (March 1, 1949).

36. R.G. Collingwood, *The Idea of History* (Oxford: Oxford University Press, 1946), 216.

37. I am drawing here, in part, on David Blackbourn's "Introduction: Nature and Landscape in German History," in *The Conquest of Nature: Water, Landscape, and the Making of Modern Germany* (New York: Norton, 2006). See also Andrew Pickering, *The Mangle of Practice: Time, Agency, and Science* (Chicago: University of Chicago Press, 1995), 15.

38. For a similar read on the relationship between real and imagined landscapes, see Blackbourn, "Introduction," 15.

39. See, for example, Timothy S. George, *Minamata: Pollution and the Struggle for Democracy in Postwar Japan* (Cambridge, Mass.: Harvard University Press, 2001); Jun Ui, *Industrial Pollution in Japan* (Tokyo: United Nations University Press, 1992); Norie Huddle, Michael Reich and Nahum Stiskin, *Island of Dreams: Environmental Crisis in Japan* (New York: Autumn Press, 1975); and especially Brett L. Walker, *Toxic Archipelago*. In Japanese, the various works of Miyamoto Ken'ichi are representative of a strong tradition of critical social scientific and humanistic research. For works coming out of the young field of "environmental history," see Mototani Isao, *Rekishi toshite no kankyō mondai* (Tokyo: Yamakawa, 2004); Matsuda Hiroyuki and Yahara Tetsukazu, eds., *Kankyōshi to wa nanika* (Tokyo: Bun ichi, 2011).

40. Hiraiwa Yonekichi, "Ori no jū," *Dōbutsu bungaku* 82 (1941): 25; Koga Tadamichi, "Dōbutsuen no fukkō," *Bungei shunjū* 27, no. 3 (March 1, 1949).

41. On CITES, see Rosalind Reeve, *Policing International Trade in Endangered Species: The CITES Treaty and Compliance* (London: Royal Institute of International Affairs, 2002). To be sure, participation in CITES is not the same as compliance. While the staff of the zoo have sought to negotiate the tensions between conservation regulations and institutional needs—specifically, the pursuit of growing attendance amidst budget limitations—Japan as a whole has a far more checkered history. As of 1989 Japanese had registered more exceptions than any other nation to CITES rulings. The majority of these exceptions concerned cetaceans and other marine mammals. For an overview of these issues and a survey of Japanese attitudes toward the natural world, see Stephen R. Kellert, "Japanese Perceptions of Wildlife," *Conservation Biology* 5 (1991): 297–308.

42. See, for example, Kawabata Hiroto, *Dōbutsuen ni dekiru koto: shu no hakobune* (Tokyo: Bungei Shunjū, 1993).

43. Blackbourn, *Conquest of Nature*, 8–19.

44. Jasanoff makes this same point in her analysis of the climate crisis. Jasanoff, "A New Climate for Society," 233–253.

45. I am drawing here and elsewhere on Timothy Mitchell, *Colonizing Egypt* (New York: Cambridge University Press, 1988). See also, Martin Heidegger, "The Age of the World Picture," in *The Question Concerning Technology and Other Essays* (New York: Harper & Row, 1977), 115–154.

46. On the new regimes of knowledge and especially sight, see Timon Screech, *The Lens within the Heart: The Western Scientific Gaze and Popular Imagery in Late Edo Japan* (Honolulu: University of Hawaii Press, 2002). On the pursuit of professionalization in the Japanese scientific community, see Hiroshige Tetsu, *Kagaku no shakai shi: sensō to kagaku* (Tokyo: Iwanami Shoten, 1973) and *Kagaku no shakai shi: keizan seichō to kagaku* (Tokyo: Iwanami Shoten, 1973). See also Murakami Yōichirō, *Nihonjin to kindai kagaku* (Tokyo: Shinōsha, 1980) and Murakami Yōichirō, *Kagakusha to wa nani ka* (Tokyo: Shinchōsha, 1994). Both Hiroshige and Murakami suggest the success of this nineteenth-century process of professional distinction. By the close of the Meiji era in 1912, the figures of the "scientist" (*kagakusha*) and the "engineer" (*kōgakusha*) were widely accepted, as was their unique status in relation to the study and transformation of the natural world. Indeed, the pursuit of professional distinction by scientists across much of modern Japanese history was not in relation to claims on knowledge of the natural world, but rather vis-à-vis a somewhat idealized "Western science" and scientists, who were often perceived as more advanced. It is interesting to note that the social status of scientists and engineers in Japan was often subject to less critique or doubt than it was in the United States and many of the other Western societies idealized by many in Japan. In part, the framing of Japanese science as "behind" may have helped to secure the status of the nation's scientific community. See Suzuki Jun, *Nihon no kindai 15: shin gijutsu no shakai shi* (Tokyo: Chūō Kōronsha, 1999). Hiromi Mizuno, *Science for the Empire: Scientific Nationalism in Modern Japan* (Stanford, Calif.: Stanford University Press, 2010). For a related history of professionalization in the United States, see Mark Barrow, *A Passion for Birds: American Ornithology after Audubon* (Princeton, N.J.: Princeton University Press,

2000). On the sciences and claims to political authority, see Andrew Jewett, *Science, Democracy, and the American University* (Cambridge: Cambridge University Press, 2012).

47. "Shinto" was not consolidated until later in the nineteenth century. See Helen Hardacre, *Shinto and the State, 1868–1988* (Princeton, N.J.: Princeton University Press, 1991). Historians of science specializing in Western culture have identified a similar co-evolution of professional distinction and epistemological innovation. See, for example, Sheila Jasanoff, *The Fifth Branch: Science Advisers as Policymakers* (Cambridge, Mass.: Harvard University Press, 1998). See also, Pierre Bourdieu, "The Specificity of the Scientific Field and the Social Conditions of the Progress of Reason," in *The Science Studies Reader*, ed. Mario Biagioli (New York, Routhledge, 1999), 12–30. Sheila Jasanoff, "The Idiom of Co-production," in *States of Knowledge: The Co-production of Science and the Social Order*, ed. Sheila Jasanoff (New York: Routledge, 2004).

48. On the question of savagery in modern Japanese history see Robert Tierney, *Tropics of Savagery: The Culture of Japanese Empire in Comparative Frame* (Berkeley: University of California Press, 2010). A wide array of factors conspired to elevate the social status of technicians, engineers, and scientists across the nineteenth and early twentieth centuries. For the best synopsis of these dynamics in English, see Tessa Morris-Suzuki, *The Technological Transformation of Japan: From the Seventeenth to the Twenty-First Century* (Cambridge: Cambridge University Press, 1994).

49. Latour, *We Have Never Been Modern*.

50. Mullan and Marvin show how the institution of the zoological garden has become global in *Zoo Culture*. For a critical reading of the zoo, see Malamud, *Reading Zoos*. As I show in chapters 3 and 4, those who focus on the prevalence of *kuyō* and other propitiation rites within Japanese society as a sign of more or less enlightened attitudes toward animals miss the role of those rites in *facilitating* the process of animal use, exploitation, and slaughter. For a related argument, see Arne Kalland, *Unveiling the Whale*. For a provocative but ultimately unconvincing counterargument regarding Japan as a "post-domestic" society, see Richard Bulliet, *Hunters, Herders, and Hamburgers: The Past and Future of Human-Animal Relations* (New York: Columbia University Press, 2007). Bulliet's overall argument is certainly worth consideration, but his analysis of Japan is empirically flawed. Japanese worked with domesticated animals for centuries prior to modernity, most notably the millions of ungulates that were bred, used for labor, and, more often than Bulliet or many of the Japan specialists that he cites allows, consumed for calories. The relationship between so-called "outcastes" or "polluted ones" (*eta* or *hinin*) and this culture of domestication is remarkably under-studied in Japanese- and English-language scholarship. On the consumption of meat and meat-eating in Japanese history, see Hans Martin Krämer, "'Not Befitting Our Divine Country': Eating Meat in Japanese Discourses of Self and Other from the Seventeenth Century to the Present," *Food and Foodways* 16, no. 1 (2008): 33–62.

51. Kawamura Tamiji, "Dōbutsuen no kaizensaku," *Hakubutsukan kenkyū* 13, no. 1 (January 1940): 3.

52. Timothy Mitchell, *Colonizing Egypt*, xiii; see also Homi Bhabha, *The Location of Culture,* especially 86.

53. Lippet, *Electric Animal*, 1. Julia Adeney Thomas makes a related argument about the use of "nature" (*shizen*) in her *Reconfiguring Modernity*. By 2006, for example, the majority of the protein in the average Japanese citizen's diet came from beef, chicken, and pork (much of it imported from abroad) rather than from vegetables and seafood for the first time in history. Ministry of Agriculture, Forestry, and Fisheries, *Visual: Japan's Fisheries* (Tokyo: Fisheries Agency, 2009), 4. Andrew Gordon, *A Modern History of Japan: From Tokugawa Times to the Present* (New York: Oxford University Press, 2003).

54. Martin Heidegger, "The Age of the World Picture," in *The Question Concerning Technology and Other Essays*. I am drawing on Timothy Mitchell here as well. See his *Colonizing Egypt*.

55. See Karl Marx, *Capital*, vol. 1. See also Walter Benjamin, "Paris, Capital of the Nineteenth Century," in *Reflections* (New York: Schocken Books, 1978), 146–162. Leo Marx, *The Machine in the Garden* (New York: Oxford University Press, 1964).

56. On the meaning and uses of pets, see Yi-fu Tuan, *Dominance and Affection: The Making of Pets* (New Haven, Conn.: Yale University Press, 1984). For a discussion of animals in contemporary Japan see Suga Yutaka, ed., *Hito to dōbutsu no Nihonshi: dōbutsu to gendai shakai* (Tokyo: Yoshikawa Kōbunkan, 2009).

57. Morio Watanabe, "Media toshite no dōbutsuen," in *Dōbutsuen to iu media*, ed. Morio Watanabe (Tokyo: Seikyusha Raiburarī, 2000), 46.

CHAPTER 1

1. As Barbara Ambros notes, the characters "動物" were used together centuries earlier in Japan and millennia earlier in China. They appear in the Chinese *Rites of Zhou* (*Zhouli*), first identified in the second century CE and in various Heian-period poetic dictionaries in Japan, notably the *Kigoshō* (*Notes on Poetic Words*) compiled by Fujiwara no Nakazane (1056–1118) and the *Iroha jiruishō* (mid-twelfth century). The point here is that the term was given new significance in 1822. Barbara Ambros, *Bones of Contention: Animals and Religion in Contemporary Japan* (Honolulu: University of Hawaii Press, 2012). While it is reasonable to think that Yōan knew of these precedents, he made it clear that his intention in the *Botanika kyō* was to find a Japanese equivalent for the Western notion of "animal." See also Roel Sterckx, *The Animal and the Daemon in Early China* (Albany: State University of New York Press, 2002), especially 16–19; and James Bartholomew, *The Formation of Science in Japan: Building a Research Tradition* (New Haven, Conn.: Yale University Press, 1993). On Buddhism's relationship with animals, see Hirabayashi Akihito, "Bukkyō ga oshieta dōbutsukan," in *Hito to dōbutsu no Nihon shi: shinkō no naka no dōbutsutachi*, ed. Nakamura Ikuo and Miura Sukeyuki (Tokyo: Yoshikawa kōbunkan), 102–125.

2. I am grateful to Federico Marcon for introducing me to Yōan's work. Yōan expanded on the *Sutra* in his 1835 *Principles of Botany* (*Shokugaku*

keigen) and in his 1840 *Introduction to Chemistry* (*Semi kaisō*), which established many of the terms used in modern chemistry. For the classic overview of these issues, see Nishimura Saburō, *Bunmei no naka no hakubutsugaku: Seiyō to Nihon*, vol. 1–2 (Tokyo: Kinokuniya, 1999). See also Togo Tsukahara, *Affinity and shinwa ryoku: Introduction of Western Chemical Concepts in Japan* (Amsterdam: J.C. Gieben, 1993). *Shokugaku keigen* has been reprinted: *Shokugaku keigen/Shokubutsugaku*, ed. Ueno Masuzō and Yabe Ichirō (Tokyo: Kōwa Shuppan, 1980).

3. Nishimura, *Bunmei no naka no hakubutsugaku*, 483–486. Yōan would eventually add "fungi" (*kin*) to his taxonomy. Full text of Udagawa's *Sutra* is available online: Waseda University Library, accessed June 28, 2012, http://archive.wul.waseda.ac.jp/kosho/bunk008/bunk008_a0208/bunk008_a0208.html. See also Ueno Masuzō, "Udagawa Yōan no shokugaku" in *Hakubutsugaku no jidai* (Tokyo: Yasaka Shobō, 1990), 102–109. Ueno Masuzō, "Udagawa Yōan: kindai Nihon dōshokubutsugaku no kusawake," in *Hakubutsugakusha retsuden* (Tokyo: Yasaka Shobō, 1991), 130–134.

4. The phrase used, "如是我聞" (*nyoze gamon*), is standard in Buddhist sutras. According to tradition, the Buddhist canon was compiled during the first Buddhist council after the Buddha's death. His disciple and cousin Ānanda, who had served him for twenty-five years, was said to have perfect recall, and he recited all of the Buddha's sermons for recording. "Thus I have heard that" was Ānanda's reference to his act as a faithful conduit of correct teachings. I am grateful to Barbara Ambros for this insight.

5. Tsukahara offers a summary of the relevant literature on Udagawa and the *Botanika kyō*. See especially "Shift of Yoan's Interest to Chemical Studies," in *Affinity and shinwa ryoku*, 117–146.

6. Nishimura, *Bunmei no naka no hakubutsugaku*, 483–486. In the absence of expressed intent, Udagawa's real purpose is a riddle whose final answer must remain elusive. Although the tone of the *Sutra* and later work suggest otherwise, Udagawa could also have meant the *Botanika kyō* as a parody of other scholars' piousness or as a critique of Buddhism more broadly. It seems more likely, however, that he was drawing on Buddhism's rich theorization of death and rebirth across realms. People were located above beasts in the six domains of Buddhist rebirth. Beasts were distinguished from people largely because they were subject to untrammeled desire. Yōan seems to have substituted reason and intelligence for the Buddhist concern with desire and appetite while maintaining the heirarchy between people and animals.

7. Ueno traces the beginnings of this transformation to the writings of Ono Razan (1729–1810) and others working with the *Honzō kōmoku* , a translation of the Chinese natural historian Li Shizhen's (1518–1593) influential *Bencao gangmu* (Systematic material medica). See also, Endō Shōji, *Honzōgaku to yōgaku—Ono Razan gakutō no kenkyū* (Tokyo: Shibunkaku Shuppan, 2003). On the introduction of Western systematics by Udagawa's colleague, Itō Keisuke, see Ueno Masuzō, *Hakubutsugakusha retsuden*, 134–137; Ueno Masuzō, *Seiyō hakubutsugakusa retsuden: Arisutoteresu kara Dauin made* (Tokyo: Yushokan, 2009). See also, Doi Yasuhiro, *Itō Keisuke no kenkyū* (Tokyo: Koseisha, 2005).

8. As Pamela Asquith and Arne Kalland note, "sei" can also be translated as "nature," as in the "essential quality and character of something." Kalland and Asquith, "Japanese Perceptions of Nature: Ideas and Illusions," in *Japanese Images of Nature: Cultural Perspectives*, ed. Pamela J. Asquith and Arne Kalland (New York: Curzon, 1997), 8. Udagawa expanded this discussion in *Shokugaku keigen*. On the representation of animals in Edo Japan, see Nomura Keisuke, *Edo no shizenshi: 'bukō sanbutsu shi' wo yomu* (Tokyo: Dōbutsusha, 2002).

9. Morris-Suzuki makes similar point about neo-Confucianism and nature. Tessa Morris-Suzuki, "Concepts of Nature and Technology in Pre-industrial Japan," *East Asian History* 1 (1991): 81–96. See also Pamela Asquith and Arne Kalland, "Japanese Perceptions of Nature," 1–35; Arne Kalland, "Culture in Japanese Nature," in *Asian Perceptions of Nature: A Critical Approach*, ed. O. Bruun and Arne Kalland (London: Curzon, 1995), 243–257. Stefan Tanaka and Julia Adeney Thomas both approach this dynamic through the broader frame of "nature," each offering convincing analysis of intellectual discourse as social theorists and philosophers struggled with these questions. In both works, Katō Hiroyuki is taken as emblematic of the broader projection of time into nature through the work of Charles Darwin, Ernst Haeckel, and Herbert Spencer. See Julia Adeney Thomas, "Katō Hiroyuki: Turning Nature into Time," in *Reconfiguring Modernity: Concepts of Nature in Japanese Political Ideology* (Berkeley: University of California Press, 2002), 84–110, and Stefan Tanaka, "Naturalization of Nature: Essential Time," in *New Times in Modern Japan* (Princeton, N.J.: Princeton University Press, 2004), 85–110.

10. I am drawing here on Georgio Agamben's critical response to Michel Foucault. Georgio Agamben, *The Open: Man and Animal* (Stanford, Calif.: Stanford University Press, 2003). See also, Nicole Shukin, *Animal Capital: Rendering Life in Biopolitical Times* (Minneapolis: University of Minnesota Press, 2009), 9.

11. Ambros, *Bones of Contention*, 33–40. On the relationship between caricatures of Buddhist thought and "Western" attitudes toward animals and nature, see Arne Kalland, *Unveiling the Whale: Discourses on Whales and Whaling* (New York: Berghan Books, 2003), especially 166.

12. On the ideological uses of *shizen*, see Thomas, *Reconfiguring Modernity*; Terao Gorō, *"Shizen" gainen no keisei shi: Chūgoku, Nihon, Yoroppa* (Tokyo: Nobunkyo, 2002), especially pp. 233–246; Yanabe Akira, *Honyaku no shisō— "shizen" to NATURE* (Tokyo: Chikuma Shobō, 1995).

13. For Latour's account of the separation between "nature" and "culture" or "science" and "society," see Bruno Latour, *We Have Never Been Modern* (Cambridge, Mass.: Harvard University Press, 1993). I have also found Thomas's "'To Become as One Dead': Nature and the Political Subject in Modern Japan" useful. See Lorraine Daston and Fernando Vidal, eds., *The Moral Authority of Nature* (Chicago: University of Chicago Press, 2004), 308–330.

14. On the "anthropological machine," see Georgio Agamben, *The Open*.

15. Komori Atsushi has suggested that the Deer-Cry Pavilion derived its name from actual deer (*Cervus nippon*) held in the Yamashita yard. The Rokumeikan was planned while the Yamashita Museum (also known as the Yamashita Monnai Hakubutsukan and the Uchi Yamashita Hakubutsukan after

its location inside the Yamashita Gate) was still in use. Komori Atsushi, *Mōhitotsu no dōbutsuen shi* (Tokyo: Maruzen, 1997).

16. Michael Dylan Foster, *Pandemonium and Parade: Japanese Monsters and the Culture of Yokai* (Berkeley: University of California Press, 2008), especially pp. 30–35; Ueno Masuzō, "Jobun: Edo hakubutsugaku no romanchishizumu," in *Edo hakubutsugaku shūsei*, ed. Shomonaka Hiroshi (Tokyo: Heibonsha, 1994), 12–15. The development of modern veterinary medicine (*jūigaku*) was also significant; it marked the medicalization of the human–animal separation. Udagawa played a crucial role in this conversion as well. In his *Shokugaku keigen* he argued that botany could only be fully understood once separated from the pursuit of *materia medica*. See his *Shokugaku keigen*.

17. On status and its trans-Restoration history, see David L. Howell, *Geographies of Identity in Nineteenth-Century Japan* (Berkeley: University of California Press, 2005).

18. See Tanaka Yoshio, *Dōbutsugaku* (Tokyo: Hakubutsukan, 1874). See also *Dōbutsu kinmō*, ed. Tanaka Yoshio and Nakajima Gyōzan (Tokyo: Hakubutsukan, 1875). And, *Kyōiku dōbutsuen* (Tokyo: Gakureikan, 1893). For a related piece that cites Tanaka's work, see also Shima Jirō, *Hakubutsu kyōjūhō* (Tokyo: Hokuō Saburō, 1877). See also Brett L. Walker, *The Lost Wolves of Japan* (Seattle: University of Washington Press, 2000), especially 24–56.

19. Sasaki Toshio, *Dōbutsuen no rekishi: Nihon ni okeru dōbutsuen no seiritsu* (Tokyo: Kodansha, 1987), 106–114. See Peter Kornicki, "Public Display and Changing Values in Nineteenth-Century Japan: Exhibitions in the Early Meiji Period and Their Precursors," *Monumenta Nipponica* 49 (1994): 167–196.

20. The Boshin Civil War, or *Boshin sensō*, was modern Japan's war of consolidation. It pitted supporters of the ruling Tokugawa Shogunate against insurgent forces mainly from powerful domains in Western Japan, Satsuma, Chōshū, Saga, and Tosa, who fought in the name of the emperor. The conflict carried over from 1868 to 1869 and was followed by dozens of smaller skirmishes. The forces of imperial restoration were eventually victorious. The young emperor Mutsuhito, the future Meiji Emperor, was placed on the thrown in 1868.

21. Tokyo Kokuritsu Hakubutsukan, ed., *Tokyo Kokuritsu Hakubutsukan hyaku nen shi* (Tokyo: Dai Ichi Hōki Shuppan, 1973), 87–114.

22. Machida Hisanari, "Hakubutsukyoku dai san nenpō," in *Tokyo Kokuritsu Hakubutsukan*, 632. Stefan Tanaka, "Naturalization of Nature: Chronological Time," in *New Times in Modern Japan*, 111–142.

23. Hakubutsukyoku, "Dai ichi go reppinkan," in *Tokyo Kokuritsu Hakubutsukan hyakunen shi—shiryō hen*, ed. Tokyo Kokuritsu Hakubutsukan (Tokyo: Dai Ichi Hōki Shuppan, 1973), 208.

24. The layout and number of buildings changed in the years that Yamashita was in use. For a basic map, see Tokyo Kokuritsu Hakubutsukan, *Tokyo Kokuritsu Hakubutsukan hyakunen shi*, 208.

25. Hakurankai Jimukyoku, "Mokuroku," 184–193. A larger collection of butterflies was also taken to the expo in Vienna, where it garnered much attention from collectors and specialists interested in the unusual species. Iida-shi

Bijutsu Hakubutsukan, ed., *Tanaka Yoshio* (Iida: Iida-shi Bijutsu Hakubutsu-kan, 1999), 16–18.

26. For an insightful reading of this early "developmentalism," see Federico Marcon, "Inventorying Nature: Tokugawa Yoshimune and the Sponsorhip of *Honzōgaku* in Eighteenth-Century Japan," in *Japan at Nature's Edge*, ed. Ian Jared Miller, Julia Adeney Thomas, and Brett L. Walker (Honolulu: University of Hawaii Press, forthcoming).

27. On the Taiwan intervention, see Robert Tierney, *Tropics of Savagery: The Culture of Japanese Empire in Comparative Frame* (Berkeley: University of California Press), especially pp. 33–77. On the "rabbit craze," see Pieter S. de Ganon, "Down the Rabbit Hole," *Past & Present* 213 (2011): 237–266, and Sasaki Toshio, *Dōbutsuen no rekishi: Nihon ni okeru dōbutsuen no seiritsu* (Tokyo: Kodansha, 1987), 108–110.

28. On parks and greenspace, see Maruyama Atsushi, *Kindai Nihon kōenshi no kenkyū* (Tokyo: Shibunkaku, 1994), and Thomas R.H. Havens, *Parkscapes: Green Spaces in Modern Japan* (Honolulu: University of Hawaii Press, 2012).

29. "Imperial Ueno," in *Parkscapes*. On the emergence of the idea of the "public" and the political ramifications of the nation's new public conscious-ness, see Carol Gluck, *Japan's Modern Myths: Ideology in the Late Meiji Period* (Princeton, N.J.: Princeton University Press, 1985); Sheldon M. Garon, *The State and Labor in Modern Japan* (Berkeley: University of California Press, 1990); Andrew Gordon, *Labor and Imperial Democracy in Prewar Japan* (Berkeley: University of California Press, 1992). On the history of the police in modern Japan see Obinata Sumio, *Kindai Nihon no keisatsu to chiiki shakai* (Tokyo: Chikuma Shobō, 2000).

30. On the politics of museums in Meiji Japan, see Tanaka, *New Times in Meiji Japan*. See also my "Didactic Nature," in *JAPANimals: History and Cul-ture in Japan's Animal Life*, ed. Gregory M. Pflugfelder and Brett L. Walker (Ann Arbor: University of Michigan Center for Japanese Studies, 2005). On the museum and time, see Tanaka, *New Times in Meiji Japan*.

31. Keio University, "Seiyō jijō," accessed May 1, 2012, http://project.lib .keio.ac.jp/. On the exhibitionary complex, see Tony Bennett, *The Birth of the Museum: History, Theory, Politics* (New York: Routledge, 1995).

32. Ibid.

33. On the process and politics of "tranlsating the West," see Douglas How-land, *Translating the West: Language and Political Reason in Nineteenth-Century Japan* (Honolulu: University of Hawaii Press, 2001). On the origins of "dōbut-suen" in particular, see Sasaki, *Dōbutsuen no rekishi*, 7–36. It should be noted that Sasaki and most other scholars writing on this dynamic have overlooked the innovative character of "dōbutsu" in the context of the nineteenth century. It is a common lament that the "zoological garden," or *dōbutsuen*, was not called the *dōbutsugakuen*, an appellation that would emphasize the scientific nature of the institution via the appendix "gaku," commonly rendered as "to study" or as a marker of disciplinarity such as "dōbutsu*gaku*," or "zoology." The point here is that *dōbutsu* itself carried this specialized meaning in the mid-nineteenth cen-tury, but that it was quickly naturalized so that the term appeared as a simple marker of "animals" by the end the century.

34. Tony Bennett, "The Exhibitionary Complex," in *Culture/Power/History: A Reader in Contemporary Social Theory*, ed. Nicholas B. Dirks, Geoff Eley, and Sherry B. Ortner (Princeton, N.J.: Princeton University Press, 1994), 137. See also Bennett, *The Birth of the Museum*, and Timothy Mitchell, *Colonizing Egypt*, especially xii.

35. Japan's first modern penitentiary opened at Kajibashi in Tokyo in 1874 on land that is now occupied by Tokyo Station. See Daniel V. Botsman, *Punishment and Power in the Making of Modern Japan* (Princeton, N.J.: Princeton University Press, 2005), 162. Foucault's classic work: Michel Foucault, *Discipline and Punish: The Birth of the Prison*, trans. Alan Sheridan, 2d ed. (New York: Vintage Books, 1995).

36. Watanabe Morio, "Media to shite no dōbutsuen," in *Dōbutsuen to iu media*, ed. Watanae Morio (Tokyo: Seikyūsha Raiburarī, 2000), 89–115.

37. Foucault, *Discipline and Punish*, 203. The Shogunate kept no permanent collection of animals. For a discussion of early-modern Japanese animal exhibition, see my "Didactic Nature," in *JAPANimals: History and Culture in Japan's Animal Life*, ed. Gregory M. Pflugfelder and Brett L. Walker (Ann Arbor: University of Michigan Center for Japanese Studies, 2005).

38. On biopower in Japan and its empire, see Takashi Fujitani, *Race for Empire: Koreans as Japanese and Japanese as Americans during World War II* (Berkeley: University of California Press, 2011), especially 35–40. See also Mark Driscoll, *Absolute Erotic, Absolute Grotesque: The Living, Dead, and Undead in Japan's Imperialism, 1895–1945* (Durham, N.C.: Duke University Press, 2010).

39. Michel Foucault, *The History of Sexuality, Vol. 1: An Introduction* (New York: Vintage, 1980), 142–143.

40. Bennett, "Exhibitionary Complex," 130. I am drawing here and elsewhere on Louis Althusser's "Ideology and Ideological State Apparatuses," in *Lenin and Philosophy and Other Essays* (New York: Monthly Review Press, 1971).

41. Koga Tadamichi, "Dōbutsuen no fukkō," *Bungei shunjū* 27, no. 3 (March 1, 1949).

42. Kume would go on to become a professor at Tokyo University and one of Japan's foremost historians. His notes on the mission's travels were not published until 1878. They went through several rewrites and edits before publication. Because of this, they are best read as policy documents rather than as a simple "diary." I am grateful to Claire Cooper for underlining this insight and for her work with these documents. *Rekishika kume kunitake ten* (Tokyo: Kumebijutsukan, 1991), 43.

43. Kume Kunitake, *Iwakura Embassy, 1871–1873: A True Account of the Ambassador Extraordinary and Plenipotentiary's Journey of Observation through the United States of America and Europe*, ed. Graham Healey and Chushichi Tsuzuki, 5 vols. (Princeton, N.J.: Princeton University Press, 2002), 2: 67. With very few exceptions, I have chosen to use the translations from the Healey and Tsuzuki editions. They are excellent and consistent. For the original, see Kume Kunitake, *Tokumei Zenken Taishi Bei-Ō kairan jikki* (Tōkyō: Dajōkan Kirokugakari, 1878), reprinted as Kume Kunitake, *Tokumei Zenken Taishi Bei-Ō kairan jikki* (Tokyo: Keiō Gijuku Daigaku Shuppankai, 2005), 2:

77–78. It is important to note that Kume does not use Fukuzawa's "dōbutsuen" when referring to what he calls the "jōrochi kāten," or "zoology garden." He is not consistent in his terminology, but in most cases he has chosen to use the term *kinjūen*, or "beast garden." On the effort to name the institution prior to Fukuzawa, see Sasaki, *Dōbutsuen no rekishi*, 7–36.

44. Sasaki, *Dōbutsuen no rekishi*, 2: 68.

45. Ibid.

46. Ibid. On the English valorization of "improvement" and the control of nature, see Richard Drayton, *Nature's Government: Science, Imperial Britain, and the "Improvement" of the World* (New Haven, Conn.: Yale University Press, 2000).

47. Kume, *Iwakura Embassy, 1871–1873*, 1: 69. See also Kume, *Tokumei Zenken Taishi Bei-Ō kairan jikki*, 1: 83–84.

48. Kume, *Iwakura Embassy, 1871–1873*, 1: 69.

49. Ibid., 3: 57–58. Kume, *Tokumei Zenken Taishi Bei-Ō kairan jikki*, 3: 262–263.

50. Kume, *Iwakura Embassy, 1871–1873*, 3: 57–58.

51. Sano Tsunetami, "Ōkoku hakurankai hōkokusho," May 1875; reprinted in Onshi Ueno Dōbutsuen, *Shiryōhen*, 9–10. On exhibition and its uses in modern Japan please see Angus Lockyer, "Japan at the Exhibition, 1867–1970," Ph.D. dissertation, Stanford University, 2000, especially pp. 79–123.

52. Hijikata Hisamoto, "Toshoryō hakubutsukan kara teikoku hakubutsukan e," in "Reikoku Meiji 22" ledger, Tokyo Zoological Park Society Archives, May 16, 1889.

53. By way of comparison, the average cost of ten kilos of white rice in Tokyo at the time was eighty-two *sen*. A bowl of *soba* noodles cost just under one *sen*. For the Ishiki kaii jōrei, see Ogi Shinzō, Kumakura Isao, and Ueno Chizuko, eds., *Fūzoku sei*, Nihon kindai shisō shiryō 23 (Tokyo: Iwanami Shoten, 1990), 3.

54. Onshi Ueno Dōbutsuen, *Shiryō hen*, 73–79.

55. Kuki Ryūichi, "Teian," March 1889. Reprinted in Onshi Ueno Dōbutsuen, *Shiryōhen*, 19.

56. Onshi Ueno Dōbutsuen, *Shiryōhen*, 93–100.

57. Gordon, *Labor and Imperial Democracy in Prewar Japan*, especially pp. 26–63.

58. For Ishikawa's biography, see, "Rōkagakusha no shuki," in *Ishikawa Chiyomatsu zenshū*, vol. 4, ed. Ishikawa Chiyomatsu zenshū kankōkai (Tokyo: Kōbunsha, 1935), especially 71–160. Itō was also director of the Koishikawa Botanical Garden, a remnant of the Tokugawa interest in *materia medica* placed under the administration of the new university in 1877. The presence of this garden helps to explain the absence of a botanical garden in the Ueno Park complex. Sugimoto Isao, *Itō Keisuke* (Tokyo: Yoshikawa Kōbunkan, 1960). See also, Doi Yasuhiro, *Nihon hatsu no rigaku hakase: Itō Keisuke no kenkyū* (Tokyo: Koseisha, 2005).

59. Itō was the first Japanese to systematically apply Linnaean classifications, in his 1829 botanical guide, *Taisei honzō meiso*. Although Yōan's neologism "kingdom" (*kai*) remains in use today, the modern terms for phylum (*mon*), class (*kō*), order (*moku*), family (*ka*), genus (*zoku*), and species (*shu*) all have

Tokugawa-era precedents, and it was Itō who began the process of translation. Ueno Masuzō, *Nihon dōbutsgakushi* (Tokyo: Yazaka Shobō, 1987), 362–420.

60. For the full text, see Ishikawa Chiyomatsu, "Dōbutsu shinkaron," in *Ishikawa Chiyomatsu zenshū*, vol. 1; Edward Sylvester Morse, *Japan Day by Day 1877, 1878–79*, vol. 1 (Boston: Houghton Mifflin, 1912), 339–340.

61. *Ishikawa zenshū*, vol. 1, 7–8; Morse, *Japan Day by Day*, 339–334. On the development of zoology at Tokyo University, see Ueno Masuzō, *Nihon dōbutsugakushi*, 495–502.

62. *Ishikawa zenshū*, vol. 1, 17.

63. Ibid., 75. Morse's lecture was just the first in a series focused on the application of social evolution. Ernest Fenollosa followed with a series on social evolution and religion. It is worth noting that Ishikawa was a prolific participant in social Darwinian debate across his career. For an especially trenchant piece, see his *Ningen no shinka* reprinted in *Ishikawa zenshū*, vol. 8, originally published in 1917. The piece, where Ishikawa outlines a theory of nationalist self-sacrifice in biological terms, is among the most important entries from a professional scientist in the development of fascism in Japan. The fact that it is rarely cited in postwar scholarship—in Japanese or English—helps us to see exactly how neglected scientific discourse has been in historical writing on Japanese intellectual history and political culture.

64. Ibid. For an excellent analysis of the development of biology and evolutionary theory in Japan, see Clinton Godart, "Darwin in Japan: Evolutionary Theory and Japan's Modernity (1820–1970)," Ph.D. dissertation, University of Chicago, 2009, especially 55–65.

65. Samuel George Morton and George Combe, *Crania Americana; or, a comparative View of the Skulls of Various Aboriginal Nations of North and South America. To Which Is Prefixed an Essay on the Varieties of the Human Species* (Philadelphia: J. Dobson and Marshall Simpkin, 1839). For the discussion of phrenology, see *Ishikawa zenshū*, vol. 1, 74.

66. For Lamarck's entry into these debates, see Jean-Baptiste Lamarck, *Système des animaux sans vertèbres* (Paris: Chez Deterville, 1801). See also, Richard W. Burkhardt, *The Spirit of System: Lamarck and Evolutionary Biology* (Cambridge, Mass.: Harvard University Press, 1995).

67. *Ishikawa zenshū*, vol. 1, 75. Unlike Darwin, who argued that advantageous traits were passed down solely through the reproduction of inborn traits, Lamarck argued that characteristics acquired during an organism's lifetime may be inherited by offspring. On the history of Darwinian thought in Europe, see Robert J. Richards, *The Romantic Conception of Life: Science and Philosophy in the Age of Goethe* (Chicago: University of Chicago Press, 2002), and Robert J. Richards, *Darwin and the Emergence of Evolutionary Theories of Mind and Behavior* (Chicago: University of Chicago Press, 1987).

68. On George Bigot, see *Bigō Nihon sōbyoshū*, ed. Isao Shimizu (Tokyo: Iwanami Shoten, 1986), 226, and *Zoku Bigō Nihon sōbyoshū*, ed. Isao Shimizu (Tokyo: Iwanami Shoten, 1992), 229.

69. Isao Shimizu, *Bigō Nihon sōbyoshū*, 229.

70. It is important to note that the characters used for "evolution," or *shinka*, imply a sense of forward progress; see Yokoyama Toshiaki, *Nihon shinka shisōshi: Meiji jidai no shinka shisō* (Tokyo: Shinsui, 2005).

71. Thus, in part, the importance of art, where aesthetics and reason combined in the nineteenth century. I am drawing here on W.J.T. Mitchell, "Illusion: Looking at Animals Looking," in *Picture Theory: Essays on Verbal and Visual Representation* (Chicago: University of Chicago Press, 1994).

72. Emiko Ohnuki-Tierney, *The Monkey as Mirror: Symbolic Transformations in Japanese History and Ritual* (Princeton, N.J.: Princeton University Press, 1987).

73. Cited in Migita Hiroki, *Tennōsei to shinkaron* (Tokyo: Seikyusha, 2009), 27–30.

74. On Oka, see Yokoyama Toshiaki, *Nihon shinka shisōshi: Meiji jidai no shinka shisō* (Tokyo: Shinsui, 2005), 61–129; see also Godart, "Darwin in Japan."

75. On Katō, see Tanaka, "The Essentialization of Nature," 89–92; Julia Adeney Thomas, "Katō Hiroyuki: Turning Nature into Time," in *Reconfiguring Modernity*, 84–110; Yokoyama Toshiaki, *Nihon shinka shisōshi*, 130–182.

76. Tanaka, "The Essentialization of Nature," 89–92. Ishikawa Chiyomatsu, "Shōrai no ningen, ketsuron," in *Ningen no shinka*, 374–380; on progress and "enlightenment," see especially 354–357.

77. Ishikawa Chiyomatsu, *Seibutsu no rekishi* (Tokyo: Arusu, 1929), 244–246.

78. I am drawing here on Harriet Ritvo's work on Victorian Britain, where the class system picked up and amplified notions of natural selection and superiority. See Ritvo, *The Animal Estate: The English and Other Creatures in the Victorian Age* (Cambridge, Mass.: Harvard University Press, 1987), 29. Something similar happened in Japan, where former samurai such as Ishikawa, Katō, and Tanaka tended to assume leadership positions in the new Meiji order.

CHAPTER 2

1. Komori Atsushi, the main author of the Ueno Zoo's official centennial history and a prolific amateur historian, has argued that Japanese zoos entered a period of "stagnation" early in the twentieth century. While much of Komori's work has informed my own—no other scholar knew more about the institution than he—this characterization does not hold. Rather, we would do better to think about the early twentieth century as a time of normalization, wherein attendance continued to grow steadily along with the institution's improved status in metropolitan life. It is only against the backdrop of the Ueno Zoo's otherwise spectacular growth over the course of a full century that these years can be seen as "stagnant." Komori Atsushi, "Ueno dōbutsuen no ayumi," *Dōbutsu to dōbutsuen* 32, no. 5 (1980): 18. Likewise, Sasaki Tokio laments the absence of an explicit scientific research agenda in the gardens following the resignation of Ishikawa Chiyomatsu. It is clear that Japan saw a growing separation between professional scientists—now located primarily in universities

and research laboratories—and the work of civic institutions such as the zoological garden during this era. The pursuit of professional distinction pursued by Udagawa, Itō, and Tanaka in the nineteenth century was a normal part of the social landscape by the early twentieth century. See, Sasaki Tokio, *Dōbutsuen no rekishi: Nihon ni okeru dōbutsuen no seiritsu* (Tokyo: Nishida Shoten, 1975).

2. I am drawing here on Harriet Ritvo's path-breaking work on the connections between zoological gardens and empire; see Harriet Ritvo, *The Animal Estate: The English and Other Creatures in the Victorian Age* (Cambridge, Mass.: Harvard University Press, 1987). See especially "Exotic Captives," pp. 205–242. See also, Randy Malamud, *Reading Zoos: Representations of Animals and Captivity* (New York: New York University Press, 1998). On the relationship between representation and empire—the "dreamwork of imperialism"— see W.J.T. Mitchell, "Imperial Landscape," in *Landscape and Power* (Chicago: University of Chicago Press, 1994), 5–34.

3. I have found William Leach's work on the emergence of a new American consumer culture useful here. See William Leach, *Land of Desire: Merchants, Power, and the Rise of a New American Culture* (New York: Vintage, 1994). On childhood in modern Japan, see Mark Jones, *Children as Treasures: Childhood and the Middle Class in Early Twentieth Century Japan* (Cambridge, Mass.: Harvard University Asia Center, 2010). I am grateful to Hue-Tam Ho Tai for her thoughts on the importance of the relationship between the physical and the imagined empire.

4. Ritvo makes precisely this point in reference to the London Zoo, a model for Ueno. See Ritvo, *The Animal Estate*. See also Kay Anderson, "Animals, Science, and Spectacle in the City," in *Animal Geographies: Place, Politics, and Identity in the Nature-Culture Borderlands,* ed. Jennifer Wolch and Jody Emel (New York: Verso, 1998), 27–50.

5. Prasenjit Duara also suggests the importance of "nature" and the "natural" to the discourse and practices of empire. See, for example, Prasenjit Duara, "The Authenticity of Spaces," in *Soverignty and Authenticity: Manchukuo and the East Asian Modern* (New York: Rowman & Littlefield, 2003), 171–177. As Duara makes clear, Japanese imperialism and the empire itself were central to changing conceptions of nature in East Asia and to the environmental history of Northeast Asia overall. Work on Hokkaido prior to its formal incorporation into the Japanese nation-state by David Howell and Brett Walker suggests the significance of related frontier dynamics to national formation in Japan prior to the modern era. Brett L. Walker, *The Conquest of Ainu Lands: Ecology and Culture in Japanese Expansion, 1590–1800* (Berkeley: University of California Press, 2006), and David L. Howell, *Capitalism from Within: Economy, Society, and the State in a Japanese Fishery* (Berkeley: University of California Press, 1995). See also Kären Wigen, *The Making of a Japanese Periphery, 1750–1920* (Berkeley: University of California Press, 1995).

6. There has been a good deal of recent research on the contested nature of Japanese imperialism. For a representative works, see Jun Uchida, *Brokers of Empire: Japanese Settler Colonialism in Korea, 1876–1945* (Cambridge, Mass.: Harvard University Asia Center, 2011) and Daqing Yang, *Technology of Em-*

pire: Telecommunications and Japanese Expansion in Asia, 1883–1945 (Cambridge, Mass.: Harvard University Asia Center, 2011). Uchida and Yang remind us that imperialism was a cultural phenomenon in the early decades of the twentieth century, and that expansionism could not work without mass mobilization at home. Empire generated mass consent on the home front in part through the work of exhibition and spectacle. For the seminal work along these lines, see Jennifer Robertson, *Takarazuka: Sexual Politics and Popular Culture in Modern Japan* (Berkeley: University of California Press, 1998). See also, Louise Young, *Japan's Total Empire: Manchuria and the Culture of Wartime Imperialism* (Berkeley: University of California Press, 1998).

7. On animals and the commodity fetish, see Nicole Shukin, *Animal Capital: Rendering Life in Biopolitical Times* (Minneapolis: University of Minnesota Press, 2009).

8. The literature on "social problems" in Japanese history is especially rich. For two classic examples, see Sheldon Garon, *Molding Japanese Minds: The State in Everyday Life* (Princeton, N.J.: Princeton University Press, 1998) and Carol Gluck, "Social Foundations," in *Japan's Modern Myths: Ideology in the Late Meiji Period* (Princeton, N.J.: Princeton University Press, 1987), 157–212. For a new look at "urban problems" in Japanese public discourse, see Shindō Muneyuki and Matsumoto Yosho, eds., *Zasshi 'toshi mondai' ni miru toshi mondai, 1925–1945* (Tokyo: Iwanami Shoten, 2010).

9. Karl Popper, "Criticism of the Pro-Naturalistic Doctrines," especially "Is There a Law of Evolution? Laws and Trends," in *The Poverty of Historicism*, 2nd ed. (New York: Routledge, 2002), 96–149. On the social sciences in Japan, see Andrew E. Barshay, *The Social Sciences in Modern Japan: The Marxian and Modernist Traditions* (Berkeley: University of California Press, 2007).

10. W.J.T. Mitchell makes much the same point about the appeal of landscape painting. Mitchell, "Imperial Landscape," especially 13–16.

11. Gitarō Kurokawa, *Dōbutsuen keiei hōshin* (Tokyo: Ueno Dōbutsuen, 1926). On the naturalization of ideology, see especially Louis Althusser, "Ideology and Ideological Apparatus (Notes towards an Investigation)," in *Lenin and Philosophy and Other Essays* (New York: Monthly Review Press, 2001), 85–126.

12. On Koga's career and biography, see Sasaki Toshio, *Dōbutsuen no rekishi: Nihon ni okeru dōbutsuen no seiritsu* (Tokyo: Nishida Shoten, 1975), 269–287.

13. This account is indebted to Harry D. Harootunian, *Overcome by Modernity: History, Culture, and Community in Interwar Japan* (Princeton, N.J.: Princeton University Press, 2000). Also, E. Sydney Crawcour, "Industrialization and Technological Change," in *Cambridge History of Japan*, vol. 6, ed. Peter Duus (New York: Cambridge University Press, 1986), 385–450; Koji Taira, "Economic Development, Labor Markets and Industrial Relations, 1905–1955," in *Cambridge History of Japan*, 606–653.

14. Yanagita Kunio, "Fūkō suii," in *Yangita Kunio zenshū*, vol. 26 (Tokyo: Chikuma Shobō, 1990), 122–152.

15. Hasegawa Nyozekan, "Ryokuchi bunka no Nihonteki tokuchō," in *Kōen ryokuchi* 3, no. 10 (October 1939): 2–3. Koga Tadamichi, "Dōbutsu shiiku kōza (1–10)," *Kōen ryokuchi* 3–4 (1939).

16. Koga Tadamichi, "Dōbutsu no shiiku kōza," *Kōen ryokuchi* 3, no. 1 (January 1939): 47. It is in the writings of Koga and others like him that we find the closest Japanese analog to the American "wilderness ideal." It was a vision that absorbed many Japanese intellectuals and writers in the mid-twentieth century. For the idea's clearest constituency, see the magazine *Parks and Green-swards* (*Kōen ryokuchi*), published by the Parks and Open Space Association of Japan. The Society was founded in 1936, and though many of its members did not advocate along the same lines as Koga and Inoshita, its journal contains numerous articles outlining something like the American idealization of wilderness. Certainly many of its authors worked within the framework that I describe as "ecological modernity." Thomas R.H. Havens has also touched on many of these issues. See, Thomas R.H. Havens, *Parkscapes: Green Spaces in Modern Japan* (Honolulu: University of Hawaii Press, 2011).

17. Ibid. For a related analysis, see Mitchell, "Imperial Landscape," 15. For a similar argument, see Tsutsui Akio, "Waga kuni dōbutsuen no kaizen," in *Dōbutsu oyobi shokubutsu* 9, no. 3 (September 1935): 91–97.

18. Koga's careful use of the terms *ningen* and *jinrui* is telling. The former implied a cultured, rational existence, while the latter, which literally means "human type," was freighted with biological meaning. There were "types" of shellfish (*kairui*), mammals (*honyūrui*), and so on. "Rui" is used to mark "genus" in the Linnaean nomenclature created in the nineteenth century, and it was often associated with notions of biological race. "Ningen," in contrast, has a history reaching back to Confucian notions of moral being that were central to philosophies during the early-modern Tokugawa era and earlier. "Jinrui" implied a modern, scientific understanding of the human being. These terms could, at times, define the limits of moral consideration. To be labeled "jinrui" rather than "ningen" was to be framed biologically rather than in the language of personhood. The resonance here with the notion of "bare life" described by Georgio Agamben is striking. Koga, "Dōbutsu no shiiku kōza," 48–49. Giorgio Agamben, *The Open: Man and Animal* (Stanford, Calif.: Stanford University Press, 2003), and Giorgio Agamben, *Homo Sacer: Sovereign Power and Bare Life* (Stanford, Calif.: Stanford University Press, 1998).

19. Koga, "Dōbutsu no shiiku kōza," 47.

20. Ibid., 48. For an inversion of the same argument as a critique of both the zoological garden and imperialism itself, see Komori Atsushi, "Dōbutsuen nit-suite no gimon," *Dōbutsu bungaku* 47 (1938): 16–19. Komori is eloquent in his criticism, arguing that the "zoological garden teaches young children an imperious attitude towards nature [*tenzen*]," and that it further inverts the process of animalization, "animalizing people through brutality and de-animalizing animals through removal from the wild." Such criticism was rare in print before the war.

21. Koga, "Dōbutsu no shiiku kōza," 47–48.

22. Koga's language is revealing of the crucial separation between the zoo and a "real" nature assumed to reside elsewhere. People must be able to feel *as if* they are in nature. Ibid., 46.

23. On biophilia, see Edward O. Wilson, *Biophilia* (Cambridge, Mass.: Harvard University Press, 1984). For a related approach to Japan, see Stephen R.

Kellert, "The Biological Basis for Human Values of Nature," in *The Biophilia Hypothesis*, ed. Stephen R. Kellert and Edward O. Wilson (New York: Island Press, 1993), 42–72. On "reality effects," see Roland Barthes, *The Rustle of Language*, trans. R. Howard (Berkeley: University of California Press, 1989). Indeed, zoo displays worked much like the literary texts considered by Barthes, who argued that the referent of such effects was not reality itself but *realism*, the notion of a reality external to the text that was itself an effect of that text. Much the same thing could be said of zoo exhibits that gestured to a separate nature that was never there in the first place. Zoo animals bred in captivity become icons of a natural world that is imagined to be elsewhere. On the notion of "improvement" in the colonization of the natural world, see Richard Drayton, *Nature's Government: Science, Imperial Britain, and the "Improvement" of the World* (New Haven, Conn.: Yale University Press, 2000).

24. On parks and green space, see Thomas R.H. Havens, *Parkscapes*. See also Maruyama Atsushi, *Kindai Nihon kōenshi no kenkyū* (Kyoto: Shibunkaku, 1994).

25. On park budgets, see Tokyo-to, *Ueno dōbutsuen hyakunenshi, shiryōhen* (Tokyo: Dai-Ichi Hoki, 1982), 259–268.

26. I am drawing here on William Leach's analysis of similar dynamics in U.S. department stores; see Leach, *Land of Desire*.

27. Ishikawa Chiyomatsu, *Dōbutsu chikuyōjin oyobi entei kokoroe* (Tokyo: Teishitsu Hakubutsukan, 1887).

28. Tokyo-to, *Ueno dōbutsuen hyakunenshi, shiryōhen*, 843.

29. Leach, *Land of Desire*, 63.

30. John Berger, "Why Look at Animals?" in *About Looking* (New York: Pantheon Books, 1980).

31. Susan G. Davis, *Spectacular Nature: Corporate Culture and the Sea World Experience* (Berkeley: University of California Press, 1997), 77–116.

32. Erving Goffman, *The Presentation of Self in Everyday Life* (Woodstock, N.Y.: Overlook Press, 1973).

33. For a discussion of similar dynamics in the construction of the "Sea World Experience," see Davis, *Spectacular Nature*, 109–110.

34. On Hagenbeck, see Nigel Rothfels, *Savages and Beasts: The Birth of the Modern Zoo* (Baltimore, Md.: Johns Hopkins University Press). See also Eric Ames, *Carl Hagenbeck's Empire of Entertainments* (Seattle: University of Washington Press, 2009).

35. For a detailed treatment of this dynamic, see Rothfels, *Savages and Beasts*, 141–188.

36. Amemiya Ikusaku, "Shiiku no hongi," in *Saishū to shiiku* 1, no. 5 (1939): 223. Jean Baudrillard makes a similar argument about the coincidence between animals and humans in "The Animals: Territory and Metamorphosis," in *Simulacra and Simulation* (Ann Arbor: University of Michigan Press, 1994), 129–142. On anomie, see Emile Durkheim, *On Suicide* (New York: Penguin, 2006).

37. Tokyo-to, *Ueno dōbutsuen hyakunenshi, tsūshihen*, 106–107.

38. Sasaki, *Dōbutsuen no rekishi*, 242.

39. Ibid., 242–244.

40. Tokyo-to, *Ueno dōbutsuen hyakunenshi, tsūshihen*, 53.

41. Ibid., 65.

42. "Ueno Dōbutsuen," *Shōnen sekai* 8, no. 4 (1902): 116–117.

43. I am drawing here on William Leach's insightful reading of American consumer culture; see Leach, *Land of Desire*.

44. Tokyo-to, *Ueno dōbutsuen hyakunenshi, shiryōhen*, 567.

45. For a summary of the zoo's wartime acquisitions, see ibid., 142–157. Total votes were somewhere in the hundreds. As such, the list of possible names was quite lengthy.

46. Masahisa Narioka, *Hyō to heitai—yasei ni katta aijō no kiseki* (Tokyo: Jippi Shuppan, 1967).

47. Monbusho Shakai Kyōikukyoku, *Kyoikuteki kanran shisetsu ichiran* (Tokyo: Monbusho, 1938). Total attendance at occupied Taiwan's ten officially recognized cultural institutions was approximately 1,949,000 in 1938.

48. Ibid. See also "Kōkai jitsubutsu kyōiku kikan ichiran," *Hakubutsukan kenkyū* 3, no. 8 (August 1930): 1–4. For a special issue on cultural institutions in colonial Korea, see *Hakubutsukan kenkyū* 8, no. 4 (April 1935).

49. For detailed descriptions and plans for the Shinkyō exhibition grounds in general, see Mitaka Ken'ichi, "Kokuritsu hakubutsukan kensetsu no undo nitsuite," *Hakubutsukan kenkyū* 13, no. 1 (February 1940): 10.

50. Koga Tadamichi, "Sensō to dōbutsuen" *Bungei shunjū* 17, no. 21 (November 1939): 21–26. Nakamata Atsushi, "Kokuto ni kizuku dai dōshokubutsuen," *Shin Manshū* 4, no. 9 (September 1940): 68–69.

51. Atsushi, "Kokuto ni kizuku dai dōshokubutsuen," 68–69.

52. Koga Tadamichi, "Sensō to dōbutsuen," *Bungei shunjū* 17, no. 21 (November, 1939): 23.

53. Nakamata, "Kokuto ni kizuku dai dōshokubutsuen"; Kenneth Whyte, *The Uncrowned King: The Sensational Rise of William Randolph Hearst* (Berkeley, Calif.: Counterpoint, 2009). Koga, "Sensō to dōbutsuen."

54. Fujisawa Takeo, *Nanpō kagaku kikō—Nanpō kensetsu to kagaku gijutsu* (Tokyo: Kagakushugi Kōgyōsha, 1943). For another telling example, see *Daitōa no dōbutsu* (Osaka: Seikanbō, 1943). See also, Miyoshi Hōjū, *Nan'yō dōbutsushi* (Tokyo: Modan Nihonsha, 1943).

55. Ibid.

56. Tōman mōjūgari iinchō, "Tōman mōjūgari annai." Dated 1939.

57. The journal *Saishu to shiiku*, which began publication in 1939 was regularly filled with advertisements for and articles about such events. The magazine was, in many ways, Japan's version of *National Geographic*. For the first issue, see Saishū to Shiiku no Kai and Nihon Kagaku Kyōkai, "Saishū to shiiku," *Saishu to shiiku* 1, no. 1 (1939).

CHAPTER 3

1. For a summary of the period leading to the outbreak of war, see Michael A. Barnhart, *Japan Prepares for Total War: The Search for Economic Security, 1919–1941* (Ithaca, N.Y.: Cornell University Press, 1987), 290. See also Peter

Duus, Ramon H. Myers, and Mark R. Peattie, *The Japanese Wartime Empire, 1931–1945* (Princeton, N.J.: Princeton University Press, 1996).

2. See William Tsutsui, "Landscapes in the Dark Valley: Toward an Environmental History of Wartime Japan," *Environmental History* 8, no. 2 (April 2003): 294–311. See also, Kurasawa Aiko, *Shigen no sensō: 'Dai tōa kyōei ken' no jinryū-monoryū* (Tokyo: Iwanami, 2012). On war and the natural world see, Edmund Russell, *War and Nature: Fighting Humans and Insects with Chemicals from World War I to Silent Spring* (New York: Cambridge University Press, 2001).

3. Nōrinsho Baseikyoku, "Zensen to jūgo no uma—aiba no hi ni saishite," in *Shūhō* no. 337 (March 31, 1943): 21.

4. This listing considers only those animals put to use in considerable numbers at the front. If we step back and consider the use of animals in military research, industrial production, and other sectors of the war effort, the range of species expands considerably.

5. I am drawing here on Georgio Agamben's response to Carl Schmitt's theorization of the "state of exception" in which sovereignty is defined as the capacity to *choose* to suspend the rule of law in a "state of emergency." Schmitt was a main theorist of the Nazi legal system. Agamben argues that the "state of exception"—defined by Schmitt as akin to the more commonly referenced "state of emergency"—became normalized in the course of the twentieth century. Though often disavowed or dismissed as provisional, it in fact remains latent in most modern legal systems, ready for invocation. The "state of exception" thus must be understood as constitutive of the normal political order. This dynamic was certainly present in wartime Japan. See Agamben, *State of Exception* (Chicago: University of Chicago Press, 2005).

6. Julia Adeney Thomas, *Reconfiguring Modernity: Concepts of Nature in Japanese Political Ideology* (Berkeley: University of California Press, 2001), 179–208. See also, Aaron Skabelund, "Dogs of War: Mobilizing All Creatures Great and Small," in *Empire of Dogs: Canines, Japan, and the Making of the Modern Imperial World* (Ithaca, N.Y.: Cornell University Press, 2011).

7. For an analysis of the role of "science," as rhetoric and practice, in the Japanese empire, Hiromi Mizuno, *Science for the Empire: Scientific Nationalism in Modern Japan* (Stanford, Calif.: Stanford University Press, 2010).

8. Nihon dōbutsuen suizokukan kyōkai, "Dōbutsuen suizokukan shisetsu no senjika ni okeru yūkōnaru keiei hōshin," Tokyo, Tokyo City Government, 1943.

9. *Ueno Dōbutsuen moyoshimono*, 1937–1943, vols. 15–22, misc. pages.

10. Lee Kennedy Pennington, "Wartorn Japan: Disabled Veterans and Society, 1931–1952," Ph.D. dissertation, Columbia University, 2005, pp. 62–68.

11. Nihon dōbutsuen suizokukan kyōkai, "Dōbutsuen suizokukan shisetsu no senjika ni okeru yūkōnaru keiei hōshin."

12. Tokyo-to, *Ueno Dōbutsuen hyakunenshi tsūshihen* (Tokyo: Dai-Ichi Hoki, 1982), 184.

13. For the two lengthy meditations on the uses of "nature" as an ideological tool in wartime Japan, see Emiko Ohnuki-Tierney, *Kamikaze, Cherry Blossoms,*

and Nationalisms: The Militarization of Aesthetics in Japanese History (Chicago: University of Chicago Press, 2002) and Julia Adeney Thomas, *Reconfiguring Modernity*.

14. Ohnuki-Tierney, *Kamikaze, Cherry Blossoms, and Nationalisms*. (I would like to thank Kenji Tierney for pointing me to this reference.) On breeding and the cult of purity, see Imagawa Isao, *Inu no gendaishi* (Tokyo: Gendai Shokan, 1996). Aaron Skabelund builds on this foundation in his *Empire of Dogs*. See also, Elmer Veldkamp, "Eiyū to natta inutachi: gunken irei to dōbutsu kuyō no henyō," in *Hito to dōbutsu no Nihonshi: dōbutsu to gendai shakai*, ed. Suga Yutaka (Tokyo: Yoshikawa Kōbunkan, 2009), 44–68.

15. A *kadomatsu* is a ritual object commonly displayed in Japanese homes at New Year's.

16. Monokami Satoshi, "Nihon ni okeru 'tora,'" *Dōbutsubungaku* 416 (October 1938): 2–15.

17. Harriet Ritvo, *The Animal Estate: The English and Other Creatures in the Victorian Age* (Cambridge, Mass.: Harvard University Press, 1989), 28.

18. William Swainson, *Animals in Menageries* (London: Longman, Orme, Brown, Green, and Longmans, 1830), 104. Quoted in ibid.

19. The most dramatic ideological delivery of this sort took a somewhat more columbaceous form. At several points during the war children were encouraged to write letters to soldiers at the front, which were then said to be delivered by masses of military messenger pigeons (*gunyō bato*) released at the close of zoo festivals. In reality the letters were most likely collected and forwarded by normal military post. Tokyo-to, *Ueno Dōbutsuen hyakunenshi, shiryōhen* (Tokyo: Dai-Ichi Hoki, 1982), 666.

20. For an in-depth treatment of the question of suasion in modern Japanese state-society relations, see Sheldon M. Garon, *Molding Japanese Minds: The State in Everyday Life* (Princeton, N.J.: Princeton University Press, 1997).

21. Such stamps provide patrons with a souvenir. Thus the stamp works not only as a keepsake but also as a memento intended to spur recollections inflected by the ideology of the given event. These simple markers also work to spark desire, fueling the nostalgic urge to return to a given place. This pamphlet, published by the Office of Equine Management (Basei kyoku) within the Ministry of Agriculture and Forestry, may be found in volume 16 of the Moyoshimono series held by the Tokyo Zoological Park Society archives. These volumes are roughly arranged by year. They hold thousands of documents, many of them without explicit publication information, that have been simply bound together, apparently in the order in which they were originally filed. Materials range from handwritten memoranda to blueprints to pamphlets of the sort cited here. Basei kyoku, *Gunba no Issho* (Tokyo: Baseikyoku, 1938).

22. Ibid.

23. "Haru same kemuru dōbutsuen de monoshizuka na ireisai," *Tokyo shōgakusei shinbun*, March 10, 1940.

24. On the power of such cherry blossom images, see Ohnuki-Tierney, *Kamikaze, Cherry Blossoms, and Nationalisms*. The use of flora as a mask for military ideology, which is perhaps surprising to those unfamiliar with Japan's cherry blossom obsession, was hardly unique to Japan. As George Mosse points

out, England has its "flowers of Dover" and the Nazi fascination with the deep, enclosed spaces of the forest is well known. Mosse, *Fallen Soldiers: Reshaping the Memory of the World Wars* (New York: Oxford University Press, 1990). See also, Simon Schama, *Landscape and Memory* (New York: Vintage, 1996).

25. Such ritualized performances of grief were not limited to the zoological gardens. Services were held throughout the home islands and in the empire as well. See "Shina jihen to dōbutsu," *Dōbutsubungaku* 41 (1938): 50–53.

26. Ginjirō Takeichi, *Fukoku kyōba—uma kara mita kindai Nihon* (Tokyo: Kodansha Sensho Mechie, 1999), 196–198. Shirayuki was put out to stud in 1942.

27. Hirohito was understood to share a deep and genuine affinity with the natural world in general. Kokuritsu Kagaku Hakubutsukan, *Tennō heika no seibutsugaku gokenkyū* (Tokyo: Kokuritsu Kagaku Hakubutsukan, 1988). See also Junzō Fujikashi, *Kōshitsu shashi taikan* (Tokyo: Tōkō Kyōkai, 1950), and Noboru Ono, *Tennō no sugao* (Tokyo: Kindai Shobō, 1949).

28. Most horses were used for transport by troops. Even officers rarely rode horseback in the combat zone.

29. Takeichi, *Fukoku kyōba*, 211–212. For examples of other songs, see "Gunba" and "Uma," both of which set poems by the Meiji emperor on the nobility of war horses to music. Music in both cases was by Motoi Nagayo. Like many others, these tunes were approved by the Ministry of Education for use in school instruction and music class.

30. The song was ubiquitous throughout the war. This rendering is translated from the text as reproduced inside the front cover of "Aiba shingun ka," *Gunjin engo* 4, no. 1 (January, 1942): 1.

31. Imagawa Isao, *Inu no gendai shi* (Tokyo: Gendai Shokan, 1996), 7–78. See also Aaron Herald Skabelund, "Loyalty and Civilization: A Canine History of Japan, 1850–2000," Ph.D. dissertation, Columbia University. See also, Showakan, *Senchū sengo o tomonishita dōbutsutachi* (Tokyo: Showakan, 2008).

32. Shirasaki Iwahide, "Tōyō heiwa no tame naraba," *Jōdo* 4, no. 3 (March 1938): 8–9.

33. Ibid., 9.

34. Yoshimura, "Tomo ni shinu ki no aiba datta," in *Shina jihen jūgunki shūroku*, vol. 3 (Tokyo: Kōa Kyōkai, 1943).

35. Bukkyō Rengō, *Rengō kokudachi* (Tokyo: Bukkyō Rengō, 1939).

36. Ibid.

37. Ibid.

38. Takeichi, *Fukoku kyōba*, 209–211. Mayumi Itoh deals briefly with related issues in her *Japanese Wartime Zoo Policy: The Silent Victims of World War II* (New York: Palgrave Macmillan, 2010), 28–30.

39. Ibid.

40. Ibid. See also Teikoku Bahitsu Kyōkai, *'Aiba no hi' shisetsu* (Tokyo: Teikoku Bahitsu Kyōkai, 1939). A statue commemorating the nation's military animals remains on the grounds of the Yasukuni shrine to this day.

41. Takeichi, *Fukoku kyōba*, 209–211.

42. Nōrinshō Baseikyoku, "Zen sen to jūgo no uma," *Shūhō*, no. 337 (March 31, 1943): 23.

43. Koga graduated with a degree in veterinary medicine from Tokyo Imperial University in 1928. After graduation he entered the Imperial Army, where he joined First Cavalry as a second lieutenant. Most graduates in veterinary medicine followed this path into military service in the prewar years. Koga left military service after only 9 months in order to work at the Ueno Zoo. He returned to formal military duties in July of 1941.

44. For an in-depth discussion of such rites, see Barbara Ambros, *Bones of Contention: Animals and Religion in Contemporary Japan* (Honolulu: University of Hawaii Press, 2012). For Daimaru's survey, see Daimaru Hideshi, "Dōbutsu irei ya dōbutsu aigo no monyumento nitsuite no ankēto chōsa," Hiroshima, 2002. See also, Kojima Yoshiyuki, "Shinbutsu to dōbutsu," in *Hito to dōbutsu no Nihonshi*, ed. Namamura Ikuo and Miura Sukeyuki (Tokyo: Yoshikawa kōbunkan, 2009), 74–101 and Fujii Hiroaki, "Dōbutsu shoku to dōbutsu kuyō," in *Hito to dōbutsu no Nihonshi*, 223–240.

45. Barbara Ambros, "Masking Commodification and Sacrilising Consumption: The Emergence of Animal Memorial Rites," in *Bones of Contention*, 51–89. Nakamaki Hirochika, "Memorials of Interrupted Lives in Modern Japan: From Ex Post Facto Treatment to Intensification Devices," in *Perspectives on Social Memory in Japan*, ed. Tsu Yun Hui, Jan van Bremen, and Eyal Ben-Ari, 55–56.

CHAPTER 4

1. This literature is varied and rich. I have benefited here from the following: Louise Young, "War Fever," in *Japan's Total Empire: Manchuria and the Culture of Wartime Imperialism* (Berkeley: University of California Press, 1998), 55–114; Ben-Ami Shillony, *Politics and Culture in Wartime Japan* (Oxford: Clarendon Press, 1981); Alan Tansman, *The Aesthetic of Japanese Fascism* (Berkeley: University of California Press, 2009); James Dorsey, "Literary Trops, Rhetorical Looping, and the Nine Gods of War: 'Fascist Proclivities' Made Real," in *The Culture of Japanese Fascism*, ed. Alan Tansman (Berkeley: University of California Press, 2009), 409–430; Ellen Scattschneider, "The Work of Sacrifice in the Age of Mechanical Reproduction: Bride Dolls and Ritual Appropriation at Yasukuni Shrine," in *The Culture of Japanese Fascism*, 296–320. For a theorization of sacrifice in the modern political economy that resonates with the events in 1943 Japan, see Georges Bataille, *The Accursed Share, Volume 1: Consumption*, trans. Robert Hurley (New York: Zone Books, 1991). I follow Andrew Gordon's logic in the identification of "fascism" in wartime Japan. Although often helpful in other ways, I am unconvinced by arguments surrounding the particularity or uniqueness of the Japanese situation, often framed by such terms as "ultranationalism" or "corporatism." Andrew Gordon, "Imperial Fascism, 1935–40" and "Conclusion," in *Labor and Imperial Democracy in Prewar Japan* (Berkeley: University of California Press, 1991), 302–342. See also, Gregory Kasza, *The State and Mass Media in Japan, 1918–1945* (Berkeley: University of California Press, 1988); Peter Duus and Daniel Okamoto, "Fascism and the History of Pre-War Japan: The Failure of a Concept," *Journal of Asian Studies* 39 (November 1979): 65–76.

2. The elephant called Wanri was also sometimes called Wang Li, Wangli, or Hanako. I have chosen to use "Wanri" because it is a direct transliteration of the name most often used by zookeepers themselves. Likewise, I have chosen to render "Tonky" and "John" as they appear in primary documents from the time of the killings rather than as they do in the numerous memorials, memoirs, diaries, and accounts written after the fact. Koga Tadamichi regularly used the Roman alphabet to write these animal's names in correspondence and so on. See, for example, *Dōbutsu shiiku roku*, Showa 18 (1943), Tokyo Zoological Park Society archives.

3. Shibuya Shinkichi, *Zō no namida* (Tokyo: Nichigei Shuppan, 1972).

4. Robert Darnton, *The Great Cat Massacre and Other Episodes in French Cultural History* (New York: Vintage Books, 1985). Fukuda Saburō, *Jitsuroku— Ueno Dōbutsuen* (Tokyo: Mainichi Shinbunsha, 1968).

5. Koga Tadamichi, "Sensō to dōbutsuen," *Bungei shunjū* 17, no. 21 (November 1939): 21–26. Both Fukuda and Koga noted after the war that they were aware of bombings in London and Berlin, and Koga addressed similar issues in the 1939 *Bungei shunjū* article cited above. Likewise, these questions were addressed at the 1943 meeting of the Japan Association of Zoos and Aquariums. After the war, Fukuda suggested that the rumors had been worse than the reality. Rumor had it that an elephant had been killed in an English raid on Berlin, and that other animals had to be shot as they escaped. Fukuda Saburō, *Jitsuroku*, 81–83. Snakes and spiders at London's Regent's Park Zoo were, in fact, killed soon after the commencement of hostilities, but many other large animals remained on display until well into the conflict. The Monkey Hill took a direct hit while polar bears and large cats were kept in carefully secured cages at night. The Belgrade Zoological Garden was also bombed in 1941 (and again in 1944), and reports circulated in Japan that animals had run amok in the city as it burned. "The Animals in the Zoo Don't Mind the Raids," *The War Illustrated* 3, no. 63 (November 15, 1940): 526–527.

6. On efforts to respond to such issues through policy, see Nihon Dōbutsuen Suizokukan Kyōkai, "Dōbutsuen suizokukan shisetsu no senjika ni okeru yū-kōnaru keiei hōshin," Tokyo, Tokyo City Government, 1943. This report and many of the specific papers from the 1943 conference of the Japanese Association of Zoos and Aquariums (JAZA) illustrate the depth of Japanese knowledge about events overseas. I am grateful to JAZA staff for opening their collection of wartime materials to me. Although the association does not keep a formal archive, numerous materials survived. For Ōdachi's basic biography, see Hamada-shi, *Hamadashi shi* (Hamada: Hamada-shi Shi Hensan Iinkai, 1973), 442–448.

7. For a treatment of Ōdachi's decision, see "Hito to kenbutsu no sokai" and "dōbutsuen no mōjū o shobun," in *Ōdachi Shigeo*, ed. Ōdachi Shigeo Denki Kankō Kai (Tokyo: Ōdachi Shigeo Denki Kankō Kai, 1956), 231–240. For Fukuda's response to the orders in real time memos and notes, see Fukuda Saburō, *Senjū-sengo roku 2—mōjū shobun*. Unpublished manuscript dated 1943.

8. Darnton, *The Great Cat Massacre*, 5.

9. For a public discussion by Ōdachi of the war's impact on everyday life and his thinking on the need for total mobilization, see Ōdachi, *Kessen no*

Tomin Seikatsu (Tokyo: Kessen Seikatsu Jissen Kyokakai, 1944). See also, Ōda-chi, *Ōdachi Shigeo*.

10. On the history of Asakusa's Sensōji temple, see Nam-Lin Hur, *Prayer and Play in Late Tokugawa Japan: Asakusa Sensōji and Edo Society* (Cambridge, Mass.: Harvard University Press, 2000). For a clear treatment of the events of 1943, see Tokyo-to, *Ueno Dōbutsuen hyakunenshi, tsūshihen* (Tokyo: Dai-ichi Hoki, 1982), 165–196.

11. See, for example, Nobusuke Takatsukasa, *Chōrui* (Tokyo: Iwanami Sho-ten, 1930).

12. Tokyo-to, *Ueno Dōbutsuen hyakunenshi, tsūshihen* (Tokyo: Dai-Ichi Hoki, 1982), 177.

13. "'Jikyoku sutemi' no mōjū: seidai ni karen na tama o nagusamu," *Yomi-uri shinbun*, September 5, 1943, 3.

14. As Akiyama points out, the term used for "martyr" or "self-abnegation" (*sutemi*), which I have glossed here as "giving oneself," implies a conscious choice on the part of the victim. A different reading of the same characters—*shashin*—is used to indicate the renunciation of the flesh that comes with enter-ing the priesthood. It can also mean to "risk one's life in for others," a reading that was used in descriptions of wartime heroes. It was an idea that resonated with the fascist demand that all concerns—bodily, ideological, and spiritual—be subordinated to the preservation of the nation. This notion of voluntary death is, as Mauss and Hubert point out, significant in that it removes the burden from the sacrificer, smoothing over the murderous aspects of the sacrificial act. Akiyama Masami, *Dōbutsuen no Shōwa shi* (Tokyo: Dēta Hausu, 1995); Henri Hubert and Marcel Mauss, *Sacrifice: Its Nature and Function* (London: Cohen and West, 1964), 35.

15. Inoshita Kiyoshi, *Ueno Onshi Kōen Dōbutsuen mōjū hijō shochi hō-koku* (Tokyo: Ueno Onshi Kō en Dōbutsuen, 1943). Reprinted in Tokyo-to, *Ueno Dōbutsuen hyakunenshi, shiryōhen*, 738–739. See also, "Mōjū shobun no hi," in *Senjū-sengo roku 2*.

16. Ōdachi, *Ōdachi Shigeo*, 235–238. Ōdachi, *Kessen no Tomin Seikatsu*, 2, 26–28. Koga Tadamichi, "Dōbutsu to watakusi," *Ueno* 23, no. 3 (1962).

17. Kiyosawa Kiyoshi, *Ankoku nikki* (Tokyo: Tōyō Keizai Shinpōsha, 1954). John W. Dower, "Sensational Rumors, Seditious Graffiti, and the Nightmares of the Thought Police," in *Japan in War and Peace: Selected Essays* (New York: The New Press, 1993), 101–154.

18. As one might expect, Ōdachi was a ubiquitous media presence in 1943. The zoological garden was by no means the only lever that he used to try to shift public policy and perception, but it was among the earliest and most public. Thomas R.H. Havens has shown how broader changes in home front policy were put in place in the final two years of the war. Thomas R.H. Havens, *Valley of Darkness: The Japanese People and World War Two* (New York: Norton, 1978).

19. Ōdachi, *Ōdachi Shigeo*, 236.

20. Ibid., 237.

21. As Lee Pennington points out, historical memory and public memory have tended to locate the maturation of this orthodoxy at much earlier points in time. This trick of historical vision, in which understandings of Japanese fascism

are refracted through the blood-covered lens of 1945, has occluded the more incremental emergence of what historical anthropologist Emiko Ohnuki-Tierney has described as "pro rege et patria mori" ideology. See Emiko Ohnuki-Tierney, *Kamikaze, Cherry Blossoms, and Nationalisms: The Militarization of Aesthetics in Japanese History* (Chicago: University of Chicago Press, 2002).

22. Ōdachi certainly understood the war in starkly Manichean terms. At the close of his essay on "life in wartime," a tour de force of rational moblization and fascist rhetoric, he writes, "If we cannot accomplish these goals [of total mobilization] it is not that we will lose, but that if we lose Japan will cease to exist, and so we have no choice to but to endure." He also made similar remarks in numerous newpaper articles. Ōdachi, *Kessen no Tomin Seikatsu*, 29. As I suggest in the following chapter, the emperor's position at once within and beyond the scope of ecological modernity, as human and something more than human, resonates in important ways with Georgio Agamben's meditations on sovereign power and bare life. See Georgio Agamben, *Homo Sacer: Sovereign Power and Bare Life* (Stanford, Calif.: Stanford University Press, 1998).

23. Ōdachi, *Ōdachi Shigeo*, 237; Ōdachi, *Kessen no tomin seikatsu*, 1–6, 29.

24. Tokyo-to, *Ueno Dōbutsuen hyakunenshi, tsūshihen*, 170–171. See also Koga Tadamichi, "Omoide no ki," *Dōbutsu to Dōbutsuen* (October 1962): 6–9; Koga Tadamichi, "Dōbutsu to watakushi," *Ueno* 23, no. 3 (1962).

25. Robert Thomas Tierney, *Tropics of Savagery: The Culture of Japanese Empire in Comparative Frame* (Berkeley: University of California Press, 2010).

26. Hubert and Mauss, *Sacrifice*, 9–12, 28–29.

27. On the arrival of various animals, see Tokyo-to, *Ueno Dōbutsuen hyakunenshi, shiryōhen* (Tokyo: Dai-ichi hoki, 1982), 613–631.

28. *Mainichi Shinbun*, September 3, 1943, 3. Also pasted in Fukuda's handwritten diary, under September 1. Other papers editorialized on the announcement. The Yomiuri, for example, cast the event in the saddest possible terms from September 3, publishing the announcement under the title: "The skin of beloved 'heros' remains: memorial service for animals sacrificed for the emergency [*jikyoku*]." "Onajimi no 'yūshi' hifu ni nokoshite: jikyoku sutemi no junjita mōjū no ireisai," *Yomiuri shibun*, September 3, 1943, 3.

29. Hubert and Mauss, *Sacrifice*, 27.

30. René Girard, *Violence and the Sacred* (Baltimore: Johns Hopkins University Press, 1977).

31. Hubert and Mauss, *Sacrifice*, 24.

32. "Zen mōjū kairanu tabi e," *Mainichi shinbun*, September 4, 1942.

33. American Pet Products Manufacturers Association, APPMA's 2005–2006 National Pet Owners Survey (NPOS) (Greenwich: American Pet Products Association, Inc., 2006).

34. On pet keeping, see Ambros, *Bones of Contention*, and Skabelund, *Empire of Dogs*.

35. "Zen mōjū kairanu tabi e."

36. Ibid.

37. Quoted in Fukuda Saburō, *Jitsuroku*, 183. Appended in Fukuda Saburō, *Personal Diary* (Tokyo: Zoological Society, 1943). It is worth questioning the

authorship of this letter, which reads as if it may have been written with the help of a parent or perhaps even by an adult posing as a youngster. In either event, the emotional performance of the letter remains unchanged, illustrating a conversion of grief and sadness into rage. The letter does bear the marks of having been mailed, but no envelope has survived.

38. Ohnuki-Tierney, *Kamikaze, Cherry Blossoms, and Nationalisms*.

39. Fukuda, *Jitsuroku*, 183.

40. Alan Tansman offers an argument along just these lines in his excellent intellectual and literary history of Japanese fascism; see *The Aesthetics of Japanese Fascism* (Durham, N.C.: Duke University Press, 2009).

41. Fukuda, *Jitsuroku*, 182.

42. Hubert and Mauss, *Sacrifice*, 32.

43. Agamben, *Homo Sacer*.

44. For a discussion of taxonomy and its social uses in Japan, see Brett L. Walker, *The Lost Wolves of Japan* (Seattle: University of Washington Press, 2005), especially pp. 24–56.

45. Ueno Dōbutsuen, *Omonaru kiken dōbutsu yakubutsu chishi ryō* (Ueno Zoological Gardens, no date). Partially reproduced in Tokyo-to, *Ueno Dōbutsuen hyakunenshi, shiryōhen*, 731–732.

46. "Beppyō (1): dōbutsu bungyō ichiranhyō," in *Senjū-sengo roku* 2. Partially reprinted in Tokyo-to, *Ueno Dōbutsuen hyakunenshi, shiryōhen*, 730–732.

47. For the institution's reorganization of personnel in preparation for air raids, see *Tōkyō-shi shiminkyoku kōenka tokusetsu bōgodan Ueno onshi kōen dōbutsuen bundan kisoku* (Tokyo: Tokyo-shi Shiminkyoku Kōenka, 1941). Reproduced in Tokyo-to, *Ueno Dōbutsuen hyakunenshi, shiryōhen*, 732–734.

48. Tokyo-to, *Omonaru kiken dōbutsu yakubutsu chishi ryō*. It is worth noting that these dosages were estimates and that they did not take a specific animal's weight or other physical characteristics into account. For efforts to prepare for bombings more generally, with notes on response to orders from Ōdachi via Inoshita's office, see "Dōbutsuen hijōsochi yōan," unpublished collection of memoranda, 1943.

49. As noted in the introduction to this book, the question of animal agency and action is hugely complex. I understand these issues on a spectrum that runs within and across species boundaries. For two key discussions of related issues, see Peter Singer, *Animal Liberation: The Definitve Class of the Animal Movement* (New York: Harper Perennial Modern Classics, 2009); Cary Wolfe, *What Is Posthumanism?* (Minneapolis: University of Minnesota Press, 2009).

50. Though rarity played a part as far back as the early twentieth century, an animal's economic value (as both an attraction and in raw monetary terms) was the most important factor in selecting whether or not it would be killed, kept, or traded by the zoo. Obviously, despite ubiquitous conservationist rhetoric, financial concerns remain paramount at many zoological gardens to this day. Mark Cioc, *The Game of Conservation: International Treaties to Protect the World's Migratory Animals* (Athens: Ohio University Press, 2009); Mark V. Barrow, *Nature's Ghosts: Confronting Extinction from the Age of Jefferson to the Age of Ecology* (Chicago: The University of Chicago Press, 2009).

51. Fukuda, *Jitsuroku*, 36–44.

52. Ibid., 84–90.

53. For a discussion of similar choices made in European and North American contexts, see Randy Malamud, *Reading Zoos: Representations of Animals and Captivity* (New York: New York University Press, 1998), 179–224. On the killing of Chunhee, the elephant star of London's Exeter Exchange, once the animal was redefined as a threat to public safety, see Harriet Ritvo, *The Animal Estate: the English and Other Creatures in the Victorian Age* (Cambridge, Mass.: Harvard University Press, 1987), 226.

54. Fukuda, *Personal Diary*. See also Tokyo-to, *Ueno Dōbutsuen hyakunenshi, tsūshihen*, 170.

55. Fukuda, *Personal Diary*, 181.

56. Fukuda, *Jitsuroku*, 174.

57. Watanabe Waichirō, "Dōbutsu aigo undō o kataru," *Dōbutsubungaku* 87 (September 1942): 57.

58. Tokyo-to, *Ueno Dōbutsuen hyakunenshi, shiryōhen*, 731.

59. Fukuda, *Jitsuroku*, 175.

60. Ibid., 176.

61. Ibid., 176–177.

62. Tokyo-to, *Ueno Dōbutsuen hyakunenshi, tsūshihen*, 174. See also Fukuda, *Jitsuroku*, 175–176.

63. See Nakashima Mitsuo, *Rikugun jūi gakkō* (Tokyo: Rikugun Jūi Gakkō Kai, 1996), 157; Tokyo-to, *Ueno Dōbutsuen hyakunenshi, shiryōhen*, 740–741.

64. Inoshita, *Ueno Onshi Kōen Dōbutsuen mōjū hijō shochi hōkoku*.

65. Personal communication, Ezawa Sōji to Fukuda Saburō. Also reprinted in Tokyo-to, *Ueno Dōbutsuen hyakunenshi, shiryōhen*, 738.

66. Tokyo-to, *Ueno Dōbutsuen hyakunenshi, tsūshihen*, 172.

67. "Dōbutsu sōkai," in *Senjū-sengo roku* 2

68. Ōdachi, *Ōdachi Shigeo*, 236.

69. Fukuda, *Personal Diary*.

70. Inoshita, *Ueno Onshi Kōen Dōbutsuen mōjū hijō shochi hōkoku*.

71. Ibid.

72. "Kūshū ni sonaete shochi," *Asahi shinbun*, September 3, 1943, 3. The scientific aspects of the slaughter would be reported publicly later in the war. See, for example, "Akasareta 'zō no himitsu,'" *Asahi shinbun*, December 11, 1943, 3. For the record of the autopsy itself, see "Taiheiyō sensō senchū gisei ni natta Ueno Dōbutsuen shiiku dōbutsu no bōken nitsuite—*himitsu*," in *Senjū-sengo roku* 2.

73. Fukuda, *Jitsuroku*, 174.

74. Ibid., 180.

75. Ibid.

76. Fukuda Saburō, "Wanri shin nitsuite," in *Senjū-sengo roku* 2. Tokyo-to, *Ueno Dōbutsuen hyakunenshi, shiryōhen*, 735.

77. "Dōbutsu ireisai no dai 2 tai," *Asahi shinbun*, December 3, 1943, 2.

78. "Osaka de mo mōjū shobun," *Asahi shinbun*, September 4, 1943, 3. On the order to kill large animals held in circuses and other private institutions

and businesses, see "Dōbutsu ireisai no dai 2 tai," *Asahi shinbun*, December 3, 1943, 2.

79. Tsuchiya Yukio and Takebe Motoichirō, *Kawaisōna zō* (Tokyo: Kin no Hoshisha, 1970). Published in English as Yukio Tsuchiya and Ted Lewin, *Faithful Elephants: A True Story of Animals, People, and War* (Mooloolaba: Sandpiper, 1997).

80. Front jacket of *Kawaisōna zō* (2007 edition).

81. Hasegawa Ushio, "Zō mo kawaisō–mōjū gyakusatsu shinwa hihan," in *Hasegawa Ushio hihanshū: Sensō jidō bungaku wa jujitsu o tsutaetekita ka*, 8–30. Hasegawa's work merit's particular attention. Certain of the arguments laid out here are echoed in one way or another in Hasegawa's work, especially our shared focus on Ōdachi's motives. I am grateful for his insightful reading of postwar memory culture and children's literature. We seem to have arrived at similar points via different paths. Or perhaps he, too, was inspired to pursue this problem by Komori Atsushi's uncharacteristic use of the word "shock" (*shokku*) in the encyclopedic one-hundred-year history of the Ueno Zoo, as I was. The word, in quotations in the text, is itself an echo of Koga Tadamichi's language in the postwar years. Komori was the person most responsible for the care of the archive at the Ueno Zoo in the postwar years. I am grateful to his family and his friends at the Tokyo Zoological Park Society for sharing his records, writings, and commitment to open scholarly dialogue. Please see the bibliography for his collected works; please also note that he was the lead (but by no means only) author of the *Ueno Dōbutsuen hyakunenshi* that is cited so often here.

82. Yoshikuni Igarashi, "Re-Presenting Trauma in Late 1960s Japan," in *Bodies of Memory: Narratives of War in Postwar Japanese Culture, 1945–1970* (Princeton, N.J.: Princeton University Press, 2000), 164–198. See also Carol Gluck, "The Past in the Present," in *Postwar Japan as History*, ed. Andrew Gordon (Berkeley: University of California Press, 1993), 64–96.

83. Hasegawa, "Zō mo kawaisō," 8–30.

CHAPTER 5

1. Komori Atsushi, "Bambi: Fuarin to wakarete Ueno e," *Dōbutsu to Dōbutsuen*, July 1, 1951, 4–5. For a further example of the Disneyfication of the zoo, see Koga Tadamichi, *Dōbutsuen shinpan shōgakusei zenshū* (Tokyo: Chikuma Shobō, 1952).

2. *Uma*, directed by Yamamoto Kajirō et al. (Tokyo: Tōei Kabushiki Kaisha, 1941).

3. Matt Cartmill, "The Bambi Syndrome," in *A View to a Death in the Morning: Hunting and Nature Through History* (Cambridge, Mass.: Harvard University Press, 1996), 161–171.

4. Victoria De Grazia, *Irresistible Empire: America's Advance through Twentieth-century Europe* (Cambridge, Mass.: Belknap Press of Harvard University Press, 2005); Gordon Andrew, "Consumption, Leisure and the Middle Class in Transwar Japan," *Social Science Japan Journal* 10, no. 1 (April 2007): 1–21.

5. Anne Allison, "Enchanted Commodities," in *Millennial Monsters: Japanese Toys and the Global Imagination* (Berkeley: University of California Press, 1996), 1–34.

6. On Disney in Japan, see Eishi Katsura, *Tōkyō Dizunī Rando no shinwagaku* (Tokyo: Seikyūsha, 1999).

7. Thanks to Greg Wheeler for pointing me to this quotation, found in John W. Dower, *Embracing Defeat: Japan in the Wake of World War II* (New York: W.W. Norton & Co., 1999), 551, 556.

8. Gregg Mitman, *Reel Nature: America's Romance with Wildlife on Films* (Cambridge, Mass.: Harvard University Press, 1999), 111; Jennifer Price, *Flight Maps: Adventures with Nature in Modern America* (New York: Basic Books, 1999); Lisa McGirr, *Suburban Warriors: The Origins of the New American Right* (Princeton, N.J.: Princeton University Press, 2001); Elaine Tyler May, *Homeward Bound: American Families in the Cold War Era* (New York: Basic Books, 1988). On the American idealization of wilderness and its troubling ramifications, see William Cronon, "The Trouble with Wilderness; or, Getting Back to the Wrong Nature," in *Uncommon Ground: Toward Reinventing Nature*, ed. William Cronon (New York: W.W. Norton & Company, 1995), 69–90.

9. For an example of this phenomenon, see Yasugi Ryūichi, *Dōbutsu no kodomotachi* (Tokyo: Kōbunsha, 1951), especially "Kodomo no sekai," 13–15; Yasugi Ryūichi, "Ningen wa hoka no ikimono to doko ga chigauka?" in *Dōbutsu no kodomotachi* (Tokyo: Kōbunsha, 1951), 135–154.

10. For a citation of the zoo as an emblem of the future, see C.S. Babia, *Nihon no shōrai* (Tokyo: Nihon Kashikai, 1952).

11. Koga Tadamichi, "Dōbutsuen no kinkyō," *Tabi*, May 1949, 182. Reprinted in Koga Tadamichi, *Dōbutsu to dōbutsuen* (Tokyo: Kadokawa Shoten, 1951).

12. Koga Tadamichi, "Prospectus," official correspondence addressed to GHQ from Tokyo Dōbutsuen Kyōkai, October 1948.

13. As Stefan Tanaka has argued, there is a gap between "childhood" (as a category of representation generally associated with innocence) and the "child" (as an individual). Stefan Tanaka, "Childhood," in *New Times in Modern Japan* (Princeton N.J.: Princeton University Press, 2004), 179–181. On spectacle and escape, see Michael Sorkin, "See You in Disneyland," in *Variations on a Theme Park: The New American City and the End of Public Space* (New York: Hill and Wang, 1992).

14. We might call this process more exactly "de-imperialization," as I do above, but I have chosen instead to use the more familiar term "decolonization" here as a gloss on the complex dynamics of postimperial change in post-1945 Japan. I have selected the term for two specific reasons. First, "decolonization" allows us to maintain an international focus rather than collapsing back into the habits of nation-centered history. As I argue in the remainder of this section, Japan's "decolonization" under American command was part of a regional process. Further, this process was never completed. Postwar Japan and Japanese retained patterns and dynamics developed during the age of overseas expansion. Second, "decolonization" accommodates the fact that Japan remained *imperial* after the war in the sense that the emperor remained unimpeached due to U.S.

intervention on behalf of the imperial institution in general and Hirohito specifically. On the distinction and relationship between decolonization and deimperialization, see Kuan-Hsing Chen, *Asia as Method: Toward Deimperialization* (Durham, N.C.: Duke University Press, 2010), especially "Deimperialization: Club 51 and the Imperialist Assumption of Democracy," pp. 161–210.

15. Lori Watt, *When Empire Comes Home: Repatriation and Reintegration in Postwar Japan* (Cambridge, Mass.: Harvard University Asia Center, distributed by Harvard University Press, 2009).

16. Kristen Ross uncovers a related process at work in postwar France, arguing persuasively that modernization and decolonization, though separated in most accounts, were deeply interrelated in the French move away from the war; see Kristin Ross, *Fast Cars, Clean Bodies: Decolonization and the Reordering of French Culture* (Cambridge, Mass.: MIT Press, 1995).

17. Koga, "*Dōbutsuen no kinkyō,*"184.

18. Watt, *When Empire Comes Home,* 4.

19. SCAP authorities undertook an in-depth review of the nation's cultural resources in 1945 and 1946. See, for example, Allied Operational and Occupation Headquarters, World War II, Supreme Commander for the Allied Powers and Civil Information and Education Section Religion and Cultural Resources Division Arts and Monuments Branch, *Zoological Gardens, Botanical Gardens, and Aquaria in Japan* (Tokyo: National Archives Record Service, 1946).

20. Koga Tadamichi, *Sekai no dōbutsuen meguri* (Tokyo: Nihonjidōbunko-kankōkai, 1957). See also Nakagawa Shirō, *Dōbutsuen no Shōwashi*, vol. 1 (Tokyo: Taiyō Kikaku Shuppan, 1989), especially 16–17.

21. Dower, *Embracing Defeat.*

22. Koga Tadamichi, "Sengo no sesō to dōbutsuen," *Tabi,* June 1947. Reprinted in Koga, *Dōbutsu to dōbutsuen,* 206.

23. Koga Tadamichi, "Dōbutsuen no fukkō," *Bungei shunjū* 27, no. 3 (March 1, 1949): 7.

24. Mitman, *Reel Nature.* See also Walter Benjamin, "The Work of Art in the Age of Mechanical Reproduction," in *Illuminations,* ed. Walter Benjamin and Hannah Arendt (New York: Schocken, 1969), 217–253; Nigel Rothfels, *Representing Animals* (Bloomington: Indiana University Press, 2002).

25. Koga, "Dōbutsuen no fukkō," 7.

26. Koga, "Sengo no sesō to dōbutsuen," 206. For similar arguments, see also Koga Tadamichi, "Ōbei dōbutsuen shisatsuki 4" *Kōen ryokuchi* 15, no. 1 (1953).

27. Koga, "Sengo no sesō to dōbutsuen," 206.

28. *The Sons of Pig* 1, no. 1 (November 1948).

29. There were at least seven such sales and festivals in the period between 1946 and 1949. For details, see Tokyo-to, *Ueno Dōbutsuen hyakunenshi, shiryōhen* (Tokyo: Dai-Ichi Hoki, 1982), 678.

30. For an argument on a similar transformation in representations of the body across the same period, see Yoshikuni Igarashi, "The Age of the Body," in *Bodies of Memory: Narratives of War in Postwar Japanese Culture, 1945–1970* (Princeton, N.J.: Princeton University Press, 2000), 47–72.

31. On the history of the Monkey Train, or "Saru densha," see Horiuchi Naoya, *Osaru densha monogatari* (Tokyo: Kanransha, 1998).

32. Carol Gluck, "The Past in the Present," in *Postwar Japan as History*, ed. Andrew Gordon (Berkeley: University of California Press, 1993), 93; Yoshikuni Igarashi, *Bodies of Memory: Narratives of War in Postwar Japanese Culture, 1945–1970* (Princeton, N.J.: Princeton University Press, 2000), 14, 19–46.

33. Koga, *Sekai no dōbutsuen meguri*.

34. Ibid., 8–9.

35. Akira Mizuta Lippit, *Electric Animal: Toward a Rhetoric of Wildlife* (Minneapolis: University of Minnesota Press, 2000), 2.

36. Koga Tadamichi, "Dōbutsuen wa donna yakume o motteiruka," in *Sekai no dōbutsuen meguri*, 8.

37. Fairfield Osborn, *Our Plundered Planet* (Boston: Brown, 1948). For a treatment of the history of this idea as it impacted policymaking, see Matthew James Connelly, *Fatal Misconception: The Struggle to Control World Population* (Cambridge, Mass.: Belknap Press of Harvard University Press, 2008).

38. As the success of Disney's film in postwar Anglo-American markets illustrates, this discourse of vanishing nature was broadly resonant as the global postwar became entangled in the atomic politics of the Cold War.

39. Koga, *Sekai no dōbutsuen meguri*, 8, 53, 127, 178.

40. Osborn, *Our Plundered Planet*.

41. Koga, "Dōbutsuen no kinkyō," 182–183. On suffering and the body during this era, see Igarashi, "The Age of the Body," 47–72.

42. Koga, "Dōbutsuen no fukkō," 7. For the history of these regulations vis-à-vis cetaceans, see Watanabe Hiroyuki, *Hogei mondai no rekishi shakaigaku: kin-gendai Nihon ni okeru kujira to ningen* (Tokyo: Tōshindō, 2006), 222.

43. Koga, "Dōbutsuen no kinkyō," 182–183; *Taitō-kushi, shimohen* (Tokyo: Tōkyō Taitō-kuyakusho, 1955), 1893.

44. Henri Hubert and Marcel Mauss, *Sacrifice: Its Nature and Function* (London: Cohen and West, 1964). Mary Douglas, "No Free Gifts," in *The Gift: The Form and Reason for Exchange in Archaic Socities*, 2nd ed. (New York: Routledge, 2005), ix–xxiii.

45. I am grateful to Ken Kawata for discussions on this point. On the politics of institutional status, see Jesse Donahue and Erik Trump, *The Politics of Zoos: Exotic Animals and Their Protectors* (DeKalb: Northern Illinois University Press, 2006).

46. Koga Tadamichi, "Kodomo dōbutsuen," *PTA*, May 1948. Reprinted in Koga, *Dōbutsu to dōbutsuen*, 199.

47. Koga, "Sengo no sesō to dōbutsuen, 209.

48. Koga, "Kodomo dōbutsuen,"198–199.

49. Sonya O. Rose, "Cultural Analysis and Moral Discourses: Episodes, Continuities, and Transformations," in *Beyond the Cultural Turn: New Directions in the Study of Society and Culture*, ed. Victoria E. Bonnell, Lynn Avery Hunt, and Richard Biernacki (Berkeley: University of California Press, 1999), 217–238. Quoted in David Richard Ambaras, *Bad Youth: Juvenile Delinquency and the Politics of Everyday Life in Modern Japan* (Berkeley: University of California Press, 2005), 188.

50. Koga Tadamichi, "Kodomo dōbutsuen," 199.

51. Quoted in Koga Tadamichi, "Jinbutsu hōmon," *Saishū to shiiku* 24, no. 5 (May 1962): 27. Emphasis in original.

52. Koga, "Dōbutsuen no fukkō," 7. For a particularly detailed and conscious effort to rebuild the gardens as an emblem of revival, see Ueno Dōbutsuen, "Fukkō ni maishinchū no Ueno Dōbutsuen [Hand-Written Document]," 1946.

53. Koga, "Kodomo dōbutsuen," 198–199.

54. Koga, "Sengo no sesō to dōbutsuen," 203–206; Ambaras, *Bad Youth*.

55. Koga, "Kodomo dōbutsuen," 201. See also Nippashi Kazuaki, "Kodomo dōbutsuen o megutte," *Dōbutsuen Kenkyū* 4, no. 1 (2000): 200.

56. Koga, "Sengo no sesō to dōbutsuen," 200.

57. Ibid., 199.

58. Koga, "Kodomo dōbutsuen," 201.

59. "'Dōbutsu' tessaku o yaburu—nichiyō no dōbutsuen suto de jūmanen fui," *Yomiuri shimbun*, March 28, 1948, 5.

60. Kiyomizu Kengo, "Ikinobita zō: Senzen senchū no Higashiyama Dō-shokubutsuen," *Hakubutsukanshi kenkyū* 4 (1996): 1–11.

61. Richard W. Burkhardt, *Patterns of Behavior: Konrad Lorenz, Niko Tinbergen, and the Founding of Ethology* (Chicago: University of Chicago Press, 2005); Koga Tadamichi, *Dōbutsu no aijō*, ed. Kagaku Yomiuri Henshūbu, vol. 116 (Tokyo: Matsumoto Saburō, 1959).

62. Joyce Poole, *Coming of Age with Elephants: A Memoir* (New York: Hyperion, 1996); Gregg Mitman, "Pachyderm Personalities: The Media of Science, Politics, and Conversation," in *Thinking with Animals: New Perspectives on Anthropomorphism*, ed. Lorraine Daston and Gregg Mitman (New York: Columbia University Press, 2005), 175–195.

63. Poole, *Coming of Age with Elephants*. See also Mitman, *Reel Nature*; Eric L. Santner, *Stranded Objects: Mourning, Memory, and Film in Postwar Germany* (Ithaca, N.Y.: Cornell University Press, 1990).

64. Shibuya Shinkichi, *Zō no namida* (Tokyo: Nichigei Shuppan, 1972), 41.

65. *Tokyo mainichi shinbun*, February 27, 1949. See also Tokyo-to, *Ueno Dōbutsuen hyakunenshi, tsūshihen*, 241.

66. Materials taken from two sources: *Taitō-kushi, shimohen*, 1893–1902; *Taitō-kushi, shakai bunka hen* (Tokyo: Tōkyō-to Taitō-kuyakusho, 1966). And Tokyo-to, *Ueno Dōbutsuen hyakunenshi, tsūshihen*, 242.

67. Ibid.

68. Tokyo-to, *Ueno Dōbutsuen hyakunenshi tsūshihen*, 242.

69. James C. Scott, "Beyond the War of Words: Cautious Resistance and Calculated Conformity," in *Weapons of the Weak: Everyday Forms of Peasant Resistance* (New Haven, Conn.: Yale University Press, 1985), 241–303. Scott's ideas are in many ways the frame for my treatment of children and child actors under Allied occupation.

70. Koga, "Sengo no sesō to dōbutsuen," 202.

71. Komori Atsushi, "Indira to Yoshida shushō," in *Mōhitotsu no dōbutsuen shi* (Tokyo: Maruzen, 1997), 94–98

72. Asano Akihiko, *Shōwa o hashitta ressha monogatari: tetsudōshi o irodoru jūgo no meibamen* (Tokyo: JTB, 2001); Tetsudō shiryō kenkyūkai, *Zō wa kisha ni noreruka* (Tokyo: JTB, 2003).

73. "Nihon no yoikotachi e," *Kodomo shinbun*, September 10, 1949. For the use of "mascot," see "Nihon no kodomotachi e okuru kotoba," *Dōbutsuen shinbun*, October 15, 1949.

74. Tokyo-to, *Ueno Dōbutsuen hyakunenshi, tsūshihen*, 245; Jawaharlal Nehru, "Message for Japanese Children [Correspondence]," New Delhi, 1949. Indeed, shared Buddhist culture was a cornerstone of wartime connections between Japan and the Indian National Army.

75. Tokyo-to, *Ueno Dōbutsuen hyakunenshi, tsūshihen*, 245; Nehru, "Message for Japanese Children."

76. Ibid.

77. Shibuya, *Zō no namida*, 36.

78. For basic information, see Tokyo-to, *Ueno Dōbutsuen hyakunenshi, shiryōhen*, 678. For detailed recounting, see Ueno dōbutsuen, *Moyoshimono*, Showa 9.

79. Tokyo-to, *Ueno Dōbutsuen hyakunenshi, shiryōhen*, 773.

80. Ibid., 787.

81. Quotation may be found in Ueno Dōbutsuen, "Moyoshimono Folder, Shōwa 24 [Folder of hand-written documents gathered together by year]," 1949.

82. Tooth size, especially the highly visible maxillary canines of the upper jaw, are one of the key physical differences between humans and chimpanzees, and Suzie's nearly inch-long canines were normal for her species and age.

83. Tokyo-to, *Ueno Dōbutsuen hyakunenshi tsūshihen*, 361–362

84. On the symbolism of the postwar emperor, see Kenneth J. Ruoff, *The People's Emperor: Democracy and the Japanese Monarchy* (Cambridge, Mass.: Harvard University Asia Center, 2003); Dower on "Becoming Human" in *Embracing Defeat*, 308–318.

85. www.ndl.go.jp/constitution/e/. The emperor presaged the crux of the revised constitution with his so-called declaration of humanity on January 1, 1946. Though Hirohito never explicitly defined himself as "human" in the speech, he did attack the "false conception that the emperor is divine." Dower on "Becoming Human," in *Embracing Defeat*, 308–318.

86. Ono Noboru, *Tennō no sugao—Tenno "Hirohito" as It Really Is* (Tokyo: Kindai Shobō, 1946), 42. Morris Low offers a treatment of "The Emperor as Scientist" in his *Japan on Display: Photography and the Emperor* (New York: Routledge, 2006), 122–135.

87. Ono, *Tennō no sugao*, 40–42. *Tennō heika no seibutsugaku gokenkyū* (Tokyo: Kokuritsu Kagaku Hakubutsukan, 1989).

88. *Tonosama seibutsugaku no keifu* (Tokyo: Kagaku Asahi, 1991).

CHAPTER 6

1. Inoue Hisashi, "Panda shon takenawa," *Shūkan asashi* 10 (November, 1972). Quoted in Nakagawa Shirō, *Jaianto panda no shiiku: Ueno Dōbutsuen*

ni okeru 20-nen no kiroku (Tokyo: Tokyo dōbutsuen kyōkai, 1995), 197. Tigers and bamboo were commonly paired in Japanese painting in the early-modern Tokugawa period and before. Bamboo, emblematic of the cat's place in the natural world, was thought to augment the appearance of ferocity, and the combination gradually became a metaphor for complementariness.

2. In the interest of consistency and because our main concerns reside in Japan, I have chosen to use the Ueno Zoo's own Romanizations for the animals' names. In each case, the pandas were given names in Chinese characters (*kanji*) that may be read differently in Chinese and Japanese. "Ling Ling," for example, may be rendered as "Lin Lin." The exceptions, seen below, come with animals housed outside of Japan such as the pair of pandas given to the United States following President Richard M. Nixon's visit to the PRC in 1971. In that case, I have used the English transliterations in common usage at the time.

3. Among other things, these controversial "rent-a-panda" contracts, as the biologist George B. Schaller—World Wildlife Fund affiliate and director of science at the Wildlife Conservation Society in New York (associated with the Bronx Zoo)—has called them, stipulated that breeding should be encouraged and that all offspring must remain the property of the PRC. A prominent conservation biologist, Schaller played an important role in negotiations between the PRC and WWF surrounding panda conservation and lending practices. On the development and implications of panda leasing, see George B. Schaller, *The Last Panda* (Chicago: University of Chicago Press, 1993), 235–249.

4. Nakagawa, *Jaianto panda no shiiku*, 181.

5. Ibid., 180–181.

6. I am drawing here on Dipesh Chakrabarty, "The Climate of History: Four Theses," *Critical Inquiry* 35 (Winter 2009), especially pp. 201–207. The historian Brett L. Walker has explored these questions in his writing on Japanese wolves, highly social creatures with agendas that reach beyond the simple pursuit of food and reproduction. The ethologist Marc Bekoff has shown how animals—including human beings—become tied into one another's emotional lives. Walker, *The Lost Wolves of Japan* (Seattle: University of Washington Press, 2005); Marc Bekoff, *The Emotional Lives of Animals: A Leading Scientist Explores Animal Joy, Sorrow, and Empathy* (New York: New World Library, 2008). For an effort to parse the interrelationship between historical time and evolutionary or deep history, see Edmund Russell, *Evolutionary History: Uniting History and Biology to Understand Life on Earth* (New York: Cambridge University Press, 2011).

7. Collingwood is quoted in Chakrabarty, "The Climate of History: Four Theses," *Critical Inquiry* 35 (Winter 2009): 203. For the original, see R.G. Collingwood, *The Idea of History* (New York: Oxford University Press, 1946), 320. It is important to note that Nakagawa did not exempt himself from this process. Even as keepers and others at the zoo sought to impose their wills on the bears, he argued, they became subject to the influence of genetic predisposition. Nakagawa, *Jaianto panda no shiiku*, 189. For an innovative argument that moves beyond the traditional separation between natural history and human history in the study of Japan, see Brett L. Walker, *Toxic Archipelago: A History of Industrial Disease in Japan* (Seattle: University of Washington Press, 2010).

On animals in media, see Gregg Mitman, *Reel Nature: America's Romance with Wildlife on Film* (Seattle: University of Washington Press, 2009). For a related but quite different approach to the relationship between animals and technology, see Etienne Benson, *Wired Wilderness: Technologies of Track and the Making of Modern Wildlife* (Baltimore: Johns Hopkins University Press, 2010).

8. Nakagawa, *Jaianto panda no shiiku*, 180–181; Konrad Lorenz, *Über Tierisches und Menschliches Verhalten* [Studies in Animal and Human Behavior], trans. Robert Martin (Cambridge, Mass.: Harvard University Press, 1970); Ramona Morris and Desmond Morris, *Men and Pandas* (New York: McGraw-Hill, 1967).

9. Nakagawa, *Jaianto panda no shiiku*, 181.

10. Konrad Lorenz, "Part and Parcel in Animal and Human Societies," in *Über Tierisches und Menschliches Verhalten* [Studies in Animal and Human Behaviour], trans. Robert Martin, vol. 2 (Cambridge, Mass.: Harvard University Press, 1970), 156. For an in-depth treatment of Lorenz's role in the formation of ethology as a discipline, see Richard W. Burkhardt, *Patterns of Behavior: Konrad Lorenz, Niko Tinbergen, and the Founding of Ethology* (Chicago: University of Chicago Press, 2005), especially ch. 3, "Konrad Lorenz and the Conceptual Foundations of Ethology," 127–186. See also Stephen Jay Gould, "A Biological Homage to Mickey Mouse," in *The Panda's Thumb: More Reflections in Natural History* (New York: Norton, 1980), 102.

11. Lorenz, "Part and Parcel in Animal and Human Societies," 156.

12. Gould, "A Biological Homage to Mickey Mouse," 101–102.

13. Ibid., 101; Burkhardt, *Patterns of Behavior*.

14. Ramona Morris and Desmond Morris, "The Appeal of the Panda," in *Men and Pandas*, 220–232. See also Bob Mullan and Garry Marvin, *Zoo Culture: The Book about Watching People Watch Animals*, 2nd ed. (Champaign: University of Illinois Press, 1999), 24–25.

15. Nakagawa, *Jaianto panda no shiiku*, 181–182, 200.

16. Ibid.

17. Narushima Nobuo, "Jaianto panda no hanshoku sakusen," in *21-seiki no dōbutsuen to kishō dōbutsu no hanshoku* (Tokyo: Nihon Hanshoku Seibutsu Gakkai, 2001), 22.

18. Gould, "A Biological Homage to Mickey Mouse," 95–107; W.J.T. Mitchell, "The Totem Animal of Modernity," in *The Last Dinosaur Book: The Life and Times of a Cultural Icon* (Chicago: University of Chicago Press, 1998), 77–87; Manuel J. Salesa et al., "Evidence of a False Thumb in a Fossil Carnivore Clarifies the Evolution of Pandas," *PNAS* 103, no. 2 (January 2006): 379–382.

19. "'VIP' panda-chan," *Sankei shinbun*, October 5, 1972; "Panda wa yorokondeiru ka?" *Mainichi shinbun*, May 17, 1973.

20. Nakagawa, *Jaianto panda no shiiku*, 200.

21. Captive breeding may, of course, emerge as a reasonable alternative to habitat preservation with time and work. For PRC efforts on this score, see www.panda.org.cn/, accessed January 1, 2013.

22. Emiko Ohnuki-Tierney, *Kamikaze, Cherry Blossoms, and Nationalisms: The Militarization of Aesthetics in Japanese History* (Chicago: University of Chicago Press, 2002), especially 3–4. For the importance of meconnaissance to

the social mechanism of the gift, see Pierre Bourdieu, *Outline of a Theory of Practice*, trans. Richard Nice (New York: Cambridge University Press, 1977), especially 3–15.

23. Morris and Morris, *Men and Pandas*; Ramona Morris, Desmond Morris, and Jonathan Barzdo, *The Giant Panda* (New York: Penguin Books, 1982), 192.

24. On Nixon and Mao, see Joseph Fewsmith, "Reaction, Resurgence, and Succession: Chinese Politics since Tiananmen," in *The Politics of China: Sixty Years of the People's Republic of China*, ed. Roderick MacFarquhar (Cambridge: Cambridge University Press, 1994), 468–527. See also, Roderick MacFarquhar and Michael Schoenhals, *Mao's Last Revolution* (Cambridge, Mass.: Harvard University Press, 2006)

25. Schaller, *The Last Panda*.

26. On the campaign, see ch. 4 of Jesse Donahue and Erik Trump, *The Politics of Zoos: Exotic Animals and Their Protectors* (DeKalb: Northern Illinois University Press, 2006). On the echo of postcolonial themes in conservation in general: Ramachandra Guha, "Radical American Environmentalism and Wilderness Preservation: A Third World Critique," *Environmental Ethics* 11, no. 1 (Spring 1989): 71–83.

27. Nakagawa, *Jaianto panda no shiiku*, 201; "The IUCN Red List of Endangered Species," International Union for Conservation of Nature and Natural Resources, accessed July 10, 2010 at www.iucnredlist.org/.

28. Scott O'Bryan, *The Growth Idea: Purpose and Prosperity in Postwar Japan* (Honolulu: University of Hawaii Press, 2009).

29. "Tanjō!! Panda kisha," *Nihon keizai shinbun*, November 11, 1972.

30. Yamashita Kyōko, Nihon Hōsō Kyōkai and Purojekuto X Seisakuhan, *Komikku-ban Purojekuto X chōsenshatachi. Panda ga Nihon ni yattekita Kankan jūbyō, shirarezaru 11-nichikan* (Tokyo: Aozora Shuppan, 2004); Nihon Hōsō Kyōkai, *Tsubasa yo yomigaere* (Tokyo: Nihon Hōsō Shuppan Kyōkai, 2000). There is a surprising number of official histories and popular hagiographies of the zoo's staff, most recently a 2000 episode of NHK television's patriotic *Project X~Challengers* series, which have framed the arrival of Kang Kang and Lan Lan as a shock in and of itself, an echo of the Nixon shocks. The *Project X* episode heightens the drama surrounding Kang Kang and Lan Lan, emphasizing the zoo's role as a site for technical success: "They succeeded in keeping the exotic animals alive," the narrator gravely intones.

31. Tokyo-to, *Ueno Dōbutsuen hyakunenshi, shiryōhen* (Tokyo: Dai-Ichi Hoki, 1982), 407.

32. Ibid., 406.

33. "Kenbutsu yūsen ka, hogo yūsen ka," *Asahi shinbun*, October 11, 1972.

34. "Japan Society for the Prevention of Cruelty to Animals," accessed June 25, 2010, at www.jspca.or.jp/.

35. "Kenbutsu yūsen ka, hogo yūsen ka," 13.

36. "Panda sōdatsu 'kūchūsen,' " *Yomiuri shinbun*, October 13, 1972.

37. Quoted in Tokyo-to, *Ueno Dōbutsuen hyakunenshi tsūshihen* (Tokyo: Dai-Ichi Hoki, 1982), 410.

38. Quoted in ibid.

39. "Yume wa nani? Mochiron panda," *Yomiuri shinbun*, November 5, 1972.

40. Nakagawa, *Jaianto panda no shiiku*, 200.

41. Ibid., 202–204.

42. "Tanjō!! Panda kasha."

43. Ibid.

44. Ibid.

45. Ibid.

46. Nakagawa, *Jaianto panda no shiiku*, 184.

47. Ibid., 182.

48. "Panda!" *Shūkan Asahi* 10 (November 3, 1972): 12–18. Cited in Nakagawa, *Jaianto panda no shiiku*, 184. *Sankei shinbun*, October 22, 1977. Quoted in ibid.

49. "Tareme de kawaii," *Tokyo shinbun*, November 6, 1972.

50. "Yume wa nani? Mochiron panda," 14.

51. "Panda kyōsōkyoku," *Tokyo shinbun*, November 6, 1972.

52. "Sugatamienedo 'netsuretsu kangei,'" *Nippon keizai shinbun*, October 29, 1972, 1.

53. "Panda kyōsōkyoku," 3. Also, "Panda-chan mitayo demo . . ." *Yomiuri shinbun*, November 6, 1972.

54. Ibid.

55. "Panda-chan mitayo demo . . . ," 14.

56. "Tareme de kawaii," 3.

57. John Berger, "Why Look at Animals?" in *About Looking* (New York: Vintage, 1992), 23, 24.

58. Ibid., 22.

59. "Nihao minasan, yōkoso panda," *Nihon keizai shinbun*, October 29, 1972; "Panda daun," *Sankei shinbun*, November 8, 1972.

60. "Panda-chan 'honjitsu wa kyūgyō' desu," *Yomiuru shinbun*, November 8, 1972; "Ningen tsukare? Panda-chan," *Tokyo shinbun*, November 5, 1972.

61. "'Ueno VIP' daun, kyō wa 'kōkaishimasen,'" *Mainichi shinbun*, November 8, 1972.

62. "Panda wa shūkyū futsuka," *Sankei shinbun*, November 9, 1972; "Panda mo 'shūkyū futsukasei' kyō kara kōkai mo wazuka nijikan," *Tokyo shinbun*, November 9, 1972, 9; "Genki ni aikyō furimaku," *Yomiuru shinbun*, November 11, 1972.

63. "Genki ni aikyō furimaku."

64. On legislation related to animals and animal welfare in Japan, see Aoki Hitoshi, *Nihon no dōbutsu hō* (Tokyo: Tokyo Daigaku Shuppan, 2009). See also Aoki Hitoshi, *Hō to dōbutsu* (Tokyo: Meiseki Shoten, 2004).

65. "Panda gotten wa gōkaban," *Sankei shinbun*, December 16, 1972.

66. Tokyo-to, *Ueno Dōbutsuen hyakunenshi, shiryōhen*, 406.

67. "Panda wa yorokondeiru ka?"

68. "Pandasha ni naze taikin kakeru," *Sankei shinbun*, May 17, 1973.

69. "'Pandasha hihan' ni hitokoto," *Sankei shinbun*, May 17, 1973.

70. Nakagawa, *Jaianto panda no shiiku*, 185–192.

71. "Aoenpitsu," *Asahi shinbun*, June 2, 1983, p. 8.

72. In this case, the whole was worth more than the parts. The original doll—assembled as a "mother and child"—was sold for 4500 yen. Nakagawa, *Jaianto panda no shiiku,* 187.

73. Copyright number 1570222, filed February 25, 1983.

74. For images of the dolls in question, see Nakagawa, *Jaianto panda no shiiku,* 188.

75. Ibid., 189.

76. Iwataki Tsuneo, "Shizenbutsu o moshita shōhin no sōsakusei to wa," in *Nikkei dezain,* June 1989, pp. 8–18. Reprinted in Nikkei dezain ed., *Dezain no funsō to hanrei* (Tokyo: Nikkei BP sha, 1992), 22–30. On the implications of ownership and animals, see Harriet Ritvo, "Possessing Mother Nature: Genetic Capital in Eighteenth-Century Britain," in *Noble Cows and Hybrid Zebras: Essays on Animals and History* (Charlottesville: University of Virginia Press, 2010), 157–176.

77. See, for example, Karl Marx, "The Chapter on Capital," in *Grundrisse* (New York: Penguin Classics, 1993), 239–882, especially 489–490. See also, John Bellamy Foster, *Marx's Ecology: Materialism and Nature* (New York: Monthly Review Press, 2000).

78. The centrality of this discussion to the zoo itself was reflected in the subtitle of the institution's 90-year commemorative history, co-authored by numerous Ueno Zoo and TZPS employees and alumni: *The Present and Future of Ueno Zoo: Toward a Reconciliation of Humans and Nature,* Tokyo Dōbutsuen Suizokukan Kyōkai ed., *Ueno Dōbutsuen no genjō to shōrai: ningen to shizen no chōwa e* (Tokyo: Tokyo Dōbutsuen Suizokukan Kyōkai, 1972).

79. Nakagawa, *Jaianto panda no shiiku,* 192.

80. Ibid., 189, 197–201.

81. "Kenbutsu yūsen ka, hogo yūsen ka," 13.

82. Tokyo-to, *Ueno Dōbutsuen hyakunenshi tsūshihen,* 410.

83. Nakagawa, *Jaianto panda no shiiku,* 185.

84. Nihon Hōsō Kyōkai and Purojekuto X Seisakuhan, *Komikku-ban Purojekuto X chōsenshatachi*; Nihon Hōsō Kyōkai, *Tsubasa o yomigaere*; Nakagawa, *Jaianto panda no shiiku,* 3–5; Morris and Morris, *Men and Pandas*; D. Dwight Davis, *The Giant Panda: A Morphological Study of Evolutionary Mechanisms* (Chicago: Chicago Natural History Museum, 1964).

85. On the tense relationship between the WWF and the PRC, see Schaller, *The Last Panda.*

86. For a summary of the "whaling problem" in Japan and the development of a Japanese conservation ethic, see Watanabe Hiroyuki, *Hogei mondai no rekishi shakaigaku: kin-gendai Nihon ni okeru kujira to ningen* (Tokyo: Tōshindō, 2006), 222. I am grateful to Jakobina Arch for bringing this and other books on the topic to my attention.

87. "Yasei dōbutsu kaimasen," *Yomiuri shinbun,* November 28, 1972.

88. Donahue and Trump, *The Politics of Zoos*; David Hancocks, *A Different Nature: The Paradoxical World of Zoos and Their Uncertain Future* (Berkeley: University of California Press, 2001).

89. "Yasei dōbutsu kaimasen," 10.

90. Ibid.; Elizabeth Hanson, *Animal Attractions: Nature on Display in American Zoos* (Princeton, N.J.: Princeton University Press, 2002), 184–186.

91. D.J. Shepherdson, "Tracing the Path of Environmental Enrichment in Zoos," in *Second Nature—Environmental Enrichment for Captive Animals*, ed. D.J. Shepherdson, J.D. Mellen, and M. Hutchins (London: Smithsonian Institution Press, 1998), 1–12.

92. For the institution's arguments on this point as expressed to Tokyo city officials, see Ueno Dōbutsuen, *Ueno Dōbutsuen hakusho* (Tokyo: Ueno Dōbutsuen, 1975), 2.

93. *Ueno Dōbutsuen no ayumi—kaien 120-shūnen kinen, 1982–2002* (Tokyo: Tokyo-to Ueno Onshi Dōbutsuen), 44.

94. Sekai Shizen Hogo Kikin Nihon Iinkai, ed., *WWF nijūnenshi* (Tokyo: Sekai Shizen Hogo Kikin Nihon Iinkai, 1994).

95. See Ken Kawata, "Zoological Gardens of Japan," in *Zoo and Aquarium History: Ancient Animal Collections to Zoological Gardens*, ed. Vernon Kisling (New York: CRC Press, 2001), 295–330. In the 1950s Koga pioneered the use of artificial insemination in captive bird breeding.

96. Komiya Teruyuki and Fukuda Toyofumi, *Hontō no ookisa dōbutsuen* (Tokyo: Gakushū Kenkyūsha, 2008).

97. Nakagawa Shirō, "Chūgoku no panda to dōbutsuen (1)," *Dōbutsu to dōbutsuen*, July, 1973, pp. 4–8; Nakagawa, *Jaianto panda no shiiku*, 29.

98. I am grateful to Ellen Schattschattschneider for this attribution.

99. Nakagawa, *Jaianto panda no shiiku*, 29.

100. Ibid., 185.

101. Convention on International Trade in Endangered Species of Wild Fauna and Flora, *Appendices I, II, and III* (Geneva: International Environment House, 2010); Donahue and Trump, *The Politics of Zoos*, 108–139; Hancocks, *A Different Nature*.

102. Roger Courtney, *Strategic Management for Voluntary Nonprofit Organizations* (New York: Routledge, 2002), 235–241; Morris and Morris, *Men and Pandas*, 134–145, 220–225.

103. Schaller, *The Last Panda*, 244–245.

104. Nakagawa, *Jaianto panda no shiiku*, 29–30.

105. Ibid., 28–30, 186.

106. Narushima, *Jaianto panda no hanshoku sakusen*, 24.

107. Edmund Russell, "The Garden in the Machine: Toward an Evolutionary History of Technology," in *Industrializing Organisms: Introducing Evolutionary History*, ed. Philip Scranton and Susan R. Schrepfer (New York: Routledge, 2004), 1–18.

108. Narushima, *Jaianto panda no hanshoku sakusen*, 22.

109. Nakagawa, *Jaianto panda no shiiku*, 37.

110. Narushima, *Jaianto panda no hanshoku sakusen*, 22–26.

111. Ibid., 24–26.

112. Berger, "Why Look at Animals?" 19.

113. Nakagawa, *Jaianto panda no shiiku*, 180; Aoki, *Hō to dōbutsu*, 17–47.

EPILOGUE

1. The commonalities across national boundaries are palpable here. For a closely related analysis, see Michael Bess, *The Light-Green Society: Ecology and Technological Modernity in France, 1960–2000* (Chicago: University of Chicago Press, 2003).

2. Ishihara Shintarō and Morita Akio, *"Nō" to ieru Nihon: shin Nichi-Bei kankei no kādo* (Tokyo: Kōbunsha, 1989). "Ishihara chiji—hatsugen kara," *Asahi shinbun*, March 1, 2011.

3. "Ueno Zoo Fears Visitor Numbers Will Fall after Panda's Death," *Yomiuri shinbun*, May 3, 2008.

4. Tōkyō-to Onshi Ueno Dōbutsuen, *Ueno Dōbutsuen no nyuen shazō* (Tokyo: Tokyo dōbutsuen kyokai, 1984), 53.

5. "Panda ga yatte kita: Ōhashi Nozomisan, panda kangei taishi ninmei," *Asahi shinbun*, February 27, 2011.

6. "Ishihara chiji—hatsugen kara," *Asahi shinbun*, March 1, 2011.

7. "Ishihara chiji no '*sensen, kakukaku*' hatsugen ni Chūgoku hanpatsu," *Asahi shinbun*, June 30, 2012, 37.

8. "Inexperience to Blame for Baby Panda Death," *Xinhua*, July 18, 2012. This number is nonetheless a marked improvement over those from earlier decades. Strikingly absent from these reports were discussions of panda habitat more broadly. Both the Wolong and Chengdu preserves in Western China appear to be under considerable pressure from local communities. They have also transformed themselves into tourist destinations akin to zoological gardens. See http://www.chinawolong.com.

9. Ibid.

10. Nakagawa Shirō, *Jaianto panda no shiiku: Ueno Dōbutsuen ni okeru 20-nen no kiroku* (Tokyo: Tokyo dōbutsuen kyōkai, 1995), 181.

11. Timothy Mitchell, *Colonizing Egypt* (Berkeley: University of California Press, 1991), xiii. On the history of "resources" in modern Japan, see Satō Jin, *"Motazaru kuni" no shigenron* (Tokyo: Tokyo Daigaku Shuppan, 2011).

12. Mitchell, *Colonizing Egypt*, xiii, 6–7, 18. For work on the history of expositions in Japan, see Angus Lockyer, "Japan at the Exhibitions, 1867–1970," Ph.D. dissertation, Stanford University; Angus Lockyer, "Expo Fascism? Ideology, Representation, Economy," in *The Culture of Japanese Fascism*, ed. Alan Tansman (Durham, N.C.: Duke University Press, 2009).

13. Mitchell, *Colonizing Egypt*, xiv.

14. Ueno Dōbutsuen, *Shin Dōbutsu Kōen Chōsakokusho* (Tokyo: Ueno Dōbutsuen, 1975). See also Tokyo-to, *Ueno Dōbutsuen hyakunenshi, shiryōhen*, 411–436.

15. Nakagawa, *Jaianto panda no shiiku*, 180; Aoki, *Hō to dōbutsu*, 17–47.

16. Brett L. Walker, *Toxic Archipelago: A History of Industrial Disease in Japan* (Seattle: University of Washington Press, 2010).

17. P.J. Crutzen and E.F. Stoermer, "The 'Anthropocene,'" *Global Change Newsletter* 41 (2000): 17; Paul J. Crutzen, "Geology of Mankind," *Nature* 415 (January 3, 2002): 23.

Bibliography

PUBLISHED PRIMARY SOURCES IN ENGLISH AND JAPANESE

Abe, Yoshio. *Shina honyū dōbutsushi*. Tokyo: Meguro Shoten, 1944.

"Aiba shingun ka." *Gunjin engo*, vol. 4, no. 1 (January 1942): 1.

Allied Operational and Occupation Headquarters, World War II, Supreme Commander for the Allied Powers, and Civil Information and Education Section Religion and Cultural Resources Division Arts and Monuments Branch. *Zoological Gardens, Botanical Gardens, and Aquaria in Japan*. National Archives Record Service, 1946.

Amemiya, Ikusaku. "Shiiku no hongi." *Saishū to shiiku*, vol. 1 no. 5 (1939): 222–224.

Association of Zoos and Aquariums. "Zoo and Aquarium Statistics." Accessed July 4, 2010, www.aza.org/About/detail.aspx?id=2962&terms=annual+attendance.

Babia, C.S. *Nihon no shōrai*. Tokyo: Nihon Kashikai, 1952.

Basei kyoku. *Gunyō hogo ba futsū tanren no sankō*. Tokyo: Baseikyoku, 1940.

Bigot, Georges. *Tōbaé: Journal Satirique*. Yokahama: On S'abonne au Club Hotel, 1887–1889.

Bukkyō Rengō. *Rengō kokudachi*. Tokyo: Bukkyō Rengō, 1939.

Convention on International Trade in Endangered Species of Wild Fauna and Flora. *Appendices I, II, and III*. Geneva: International Environment House, 2010.

Department of Home Affairs. *Preservation of Natural Monuments in Japan*. Tokyo: Department of Home Affairs, 1926.

Food and Agriculture Organization of the United Nations. "Livestock's Long Shadow: Environmental Issues and Options." FAO Corporate Document Repository. Accessed June 15, 2010, www.fao.org.ezp-prod1.hul.harvard.edu/docrep/010/a0701e/a0701e00.htm.

Fujikashi, Junzō. *Kōshitsu shashi taikan.* Tokyo: Tōkō Kyōkai, 1950.

Fujisawa, Takeo. *Nanpō kagaku kikō—nanpō kensetsu to kagaku gijutsu.* Tokyo: Kagakushugi Kōgyōsha, 1943.

Fukuda, Saburō. *Dōbutsuen hijō shochi yōkō.* Tokyo: Tokyo-to Onshi Ueno Dōbutsuen, 1941.

———. *Jitsuroku—Ueno Dōbutsuen.* Tokyo: Mainichi Shinbunsha, 1968.

———. *Nanpō kagaku kikō.* Tokyo: Kagakushugi Kōgyōsha, 1943.

———. *Personal Diary.* Tokyo Zoological Society, 1942.

Fukuzawa, Yukichi. *Seiyō jijō.* Tokyo: Shokodo, 1870.

———. "Seiyō jijō." Accessed May 1, 2012, http://project.lib.keio.ac.jp/.

Gakusei—isshūnen kinen gō, vol. 2. Tokyo: Tokyo Toyamabō, 1911.

Hakubutsukyoku. "Dai ichi go reppinkan." *Kokuritsu Hakubutsukan hyakunen shi—shiryō hen,* edited by Tokyo Kokuritsu Hakubutsukan. Tokyo: Dai-Ichi Hōki Shuppan, 1973.

Hasegawa, Nyozekan. "Ryokuchi bunka no Nihon teki tokuchō." *Kōen ryokuchi,* vol. 3, no. 10 (October 1939): 2–3.

Hiraiwa, Yoneichi. "Ori no jū." *Dōbutsubungaku,* vol. 82 (1941): 24–27.

Hoshiai, Masaji. *Beikokunai kaku hakubutsukan no kyōiku jigyō nitsuite.* Tokyo: Tokyo Kagaku Hakubutsukan, 1932.

Inoshita, Kiyoshi. *Ueno Onshi Kōen Dōbutsuen mōjū hijō shochi hōkoku.* Tokyo: Ueno Onshi Kōen Dōbutsuen, 1943.

Ise, Masasuke. "Gunba monogatari—kijin mo nakashimuru gunba no isaoshi." *Shin seinen* (December 1937).

Ishikawa, Chiyomatsu. *Dōbutsu chikuyōjin oyobi entei kokoroe.* Tokyo: Teishitsu Hakubutsukan, 1887.

———. *Dōbutsuen annai.* Tokyo: Tokyo Teishitsu Hakubutsukan, 1902.

———. "Inu no hanashi." *Shōnen sekai,* vol. 16, no. 1 (1921): 20–25.

———. *Ishikawa Chiyomatsu zenshū,* edited by Ishikawa Chiyomatsu zenshū kankōkai, vol. 1–8. Tokyo: Kōbunsha, 1946.

———. *Ningen no shinka.* Tokyo: Dai Nihon Gakujutsu Kyokai, 1917.

———. *Seibutsu no rekishi.* Tokyo: Arusu, 1929

———. *Ueno Dōbutsuen annai.* Tokyo: Teishitsu Hakubutsukan, 1903.

"Ishiki kaii jorei." *Fuzoku/Sei: Nihon kindai shiso taikei,* vol. 23, edited by Shinzo Ogi, Isao Kumakura, Chizuko Ueno.Tokyo: Iwanami Shoten, 1990.

"Ishiki kaii jorei zukai." *Meiji bunka zenshu,* vol. 8. Tokyo: Nihon Hyōronsha, 1929.

Jikken tanuki no kaikata. Tokyo: Nishigahara Kankōkai, 1939.

Kagaku no shōri. Tokyo: Seibundō Shinkōsha, 1946.

Kagaku Yomiuri Henshūbu. *Dōbutsu no aijyō.* Tokyo: Jitsugyō no Nihonsha, 1961.

Kashioka, Tamio. "Dōbutsuen ron." *Tokyo kōtō jūi gakkō kai shi,* vol. 5 (Tokyo: Tokyo Kōtō Jui Gakkō Kai, 1935).

Kawamura, Tamiji. "Dōbutsuen to suizokukan," *Shizen kagaku,* vol. 1, no. 1 (1926): 103–145.

Kingston, William. "Sōretsu naru mōjūgari." *Gakusei,* vol. 1, no. 1 (May 5, 1910): 44–49.

Kitamura, Eiji. *Yōitachi no kenkyū.* Tokyo: Bunkeisha, 1930.

Koga, Tadamichi. "Dainikai Nichibei minkan kankyō kaigi ni shussekishite."
Kankyōhō kenkyū, vol. 16 (November 1983): 165–171.

———. "Dōbutsuen e no shōtai." *Shisei*, vol. 5, no. 5 (May 1965).

———. "Dōbutsuen no fukkō." *Bungei shunjū*, vol. 27, no. 3 (March 1, 1949).

———. "Dōbutsuen no keiei." *Meisō*, vol. 4, no. 1–2 (May 1935): 222–225.

———. "Dōbutsuen no kinkyō." *Tabi*, May 1949.

———. *Dōbutsuen shinpan shōgakusei zenshū.* Tokyo: Chikuma Shobō, 1952.

———. "Dōbutsuen to "hakubutukanhou" narabi ni "dōbutsu hogo oyobi kanri
ni kansuru hōritsu." *Museum Studies*, vol. 14, no. 5 (May 1979): 14–17.

———. *Dōbutsu no aijō*, edited by Kagaku Yomiuri Henshūbu. Tokyo: Matsumoto Saburō, 1959.

———. "Dōbutsu no shiiku kōza." *Kōen ryokuchi*, vol. 3, no. 1 (January 1939):
47–55.

———. "Dōbutsu shiiku kōza (1–10)." *Kōen ryokuchi*, vols. 3–4 (1939).

———. "Dōbutsu shiiku kōza (1–10)." *Kōen ryokuchi*, vols. 4–5 (May 1939).

———. *Dōbutsu to dōbutsuen.* Tokyo: Kadokawa shoten, 1951.

———. "Dōbutsu to watakushi." *Ueno*, vol. 23, no. 3 (1962).

———. "Gendai no kateikyōiku ni tsuite—Hitokoto." *Shakaikyōiku*, vol. 33,
no. 1 (January 1978): 21–22.

———. "Jinbutsu hōmon." *Saishū to shiiku*, vol. 24, no. 5 (May, 1962).

———. *Kansatsu ehon: Kindaa bukku, kodomo dōbutsuen.* Tokyo: Fureburukan, 1949.

———. "Kodomo dōbutsuen." *PTA*, May 1948.

———. "Kodomo dōbutsuen." *Tabi*, June 1947.

———. *Koga Tadamichi sono hito to bun*, edited by Koga Tadamichi-sensei
Kinen Jigyō Jikkō Iinkai. Tokyo: Koga Tadamichi Kinenjigyōkai, 1988.

———. *Ōbei dōbutsuen shisatsuki.* Tokyo: Dōbutsuen Kyōkai, 1953.

———. "Ōbei dōbutsuen shisatsuki -1-." *Kōen ryokuchi*, vol. 13, no. 3 (1951):
23–36.

———. "Ōbei dōbutsuen shisatsuki -2-." *Kōen ryokuchi*, vol. 14, no. 1 (April
1952): 11–24.

———. "Ōbei dōbutsuen shisatsuki -3-." *Kōen ryokuchi*, vol. 14, no. 2 (1952):
31–46.

———. "Ōbei dōbutsuen shisatsuki -4-." *Kōen ryokuchi*, vol. 15, no. 1 (1953):
31–44.

———. "Omoide no ki." *Dōbutsu to dōbutsuen*, October 1962, 6–9.

———. "Prospectus, Official Correspondence Addressed to GHQ from Tokyo.
Dōbutsuen Kyōkai," October 1948.

———. "Sekai no dōbutsuen." *Shōsetsu kōen*, vol. 2, no. 10 (October 1951):
76–77.

———. *Sekai no dōbutsuen meguri.* Tokyo: Nihon Jidō Bunko, 1957.

———. "Sengo no sesō to dōbutsuen." *Tabi*, June 1947.

———. "Sensō to dōbutsuen." *Bungei shunjū*, vol. 17, no. 21 (November 1939):
21–26.

———. "Subete wa seibutugakuteki hōsoku no moto ni—Watashi no kyōiku-
kan." *The Curriculum*, vol. 68 (August 1954): 22–23.

———. "Waga kuni no dōbutsuen no kinkyō." *Shakaikyōiku,* vol. 9, no. 8 (August 1954): 89–92.

———. "Watashi no dōbutsuen funsenki." *Gekkan shin jiyū kurabu,* vol. 3, no. 23 (March 1979): 130–137.

———. *Watashi no mita dōbutsu no seikatsu.* Tokyo: Sanseidō, 1940.

———. "Watashi to shakaikyōiku—Hakubutsukanhō no seitei ni atari." *Shakaikyōiku,* vol. 19, no. 10 (October 1964): 54–56.

Koga, Tadamichi and Kin'ichi Ishikawa. "Dōbutsushi—Ori no naka no dōbutsu wa hatashite fukō ka? (Taidan)." *Nichiyōbi,* vol. 1, no. 3 (November 1951): 72–81.

Koga, Tadamichi and Yōhei Kōno. "Otona ni nattemo asobu no wa ningen dake." *Gekkan shin jiyū kurabu,* vol. 65 (January 1983): 84–93.

Kokuritsu kagaku hakubutsukan. *Tennō heika no seibutsugaku gokenkyū.* Tokyo: Kokuritsu Kagaku Hakubutsukan, 1988.

Komori, Atsushi. "Dōbutsuen nitsuite no gimon," *Dōbutsu bungaku,* vol. 47 (1938): 16–19.

Kuki Ryūichi. *Teian.* Tokyo: Kokuritsu Hakubutsukan, 1889.

Kume, Kunitake. *Tokumei Zenken Taisha Bei-Ō kairan jikki.* Tokyo: Dajōkan Kirokugakari, 1878.

———. *Tokumei Zenken Taisha Bei-Ō kairan jikki,* vol. 1–3. Tokyo: Keiō Gijuku Daigaku Shuppankai, 2005.

Kume, Kunitake, Graham Healey, and Chūshichi Tsuzuki, eds. *The Iwakura Embassy, 1871–73: A True Account of the Ambassador Extraordinary & Plenipotentiary's Journeys of Observation through the United States and Europe.* Princeton, N.J.: Princeton University Press, 2002.

Kurokawa, Gitarō. *Dōbutsuen keiei hōshin.* Tokyo: Ueno Dōbutsuen, 1926.

———. "Ueno Dōbutsuen no jinjū." *Ni roku shinpō,* vol. 9, no. 1 (1903).

Kurokawa, Yoshitarō. *Tochō nikki.* Tokyo: Ueno Dōbutsuen, 1927.

Lorenz, Konrad. "Autobiography." Nobelprize.org. Accessed January 30, 2013, www.nobelprize.org/nobel_prizes/medicine/laureates/1973/lorenz-autobio. html.

———. "Part and Parcel in Animal and Human Societies." In *Studies in Animal and Human Behaviour,* vol. 2, translated by Robert Martin. Cambridge, Mass.: Harvard University Press, 1970.

———. *Studies in Animal and Human Behaviour,* translated by Robert Martin. Cambridge, Mass.: Harvard University Press, 1970.

Machida, Hisanari. "Hakubutsukyoku dai san nenpō." In *Tokyo Kokuritsu Hakubutsukan hyaku nen shi,* edited by Tokyo Kokuritsu Hakubutsukan. Tokyo: Dai-Ichi Hōki Shuppan, 1973.

Matsudaira, Michio. *Jidō dōbutsugaku.* Tokyo: Kinransha, 1927.

Ministry of Agriculture, Forestry, and Fisheries. *Visual: Japan's Fisheries.* Tokyo: Fisheries Agency, 2009.

Mishima, Yasushichi. *Nūtoriya no yōshoku.* Tokyo: Ikuseisha, 1942.

Monbusho Shakai Kyōiku Kyoku. *Kyoikuteki kanran shisetsu ichiran.* Tokyo: Monbusho, 1938.

Monokami, Satoshi. "Nihon ni okeru 'tora.'" *Dōbutsubungaku,* vol. 416, (October 1938): 2–15.

Morris, Ramona and Desmond Morris. *Men and Pandas*. New York: McGraw-Hill, 1967.

Morse, Edward Sylvester. *Japan Day by Day 1877, 1878–79*, vol. 1. Boston: Houghton Mifflin, 1912.

Morton, Samuel George and George Combe. *Crania Americana; or, a comparative View of the Skulls of Various Aboriginal Nations of North and South America. To Which Is Prefixed an Essay on the Varieties of the Human Species*. Philadelphia: J. Dobson, J. and Marshall Simpkin, 1839.

Murakami, Haruki. *The Elephant Vanishes: Stories*. New York: A.A. Knopf, 1993.

———. *The Wind-up Bird Chronicle*, translated by Jay Rubin. New York: A. A. Knopf, 1997.

Nakagawa, Shirō. "Chūgoku no panda to dōbutsuen (1)." *Dōbutsu to dōbutsuen* (July 1973): 4–8.

———. *Dōbutsuen no Shōwashi 1*. Tokyo: Taiyō Kikaku Shuppan, 1989.

———. *Jaianto panda no shiiku: Ueno Dōbutsuen ni okeru 20-nen no kiroku*. Tokyo: Tokyo Dōbutsuen Kyōkai, 1995.

Nakamata, Atsushi. "Kokuto ni kizuku dai dōshokubutsuen," *Shin Manshū*, vol. 4, no. 9 (September 1940): 68–69.

NHK. *Purojekuto X Chōsenshatachi. Panda ga Nihon ni yattekita kankan jūbyō, shirarezaru 11-nichikan*. Tokyo: NHK Studios, 2006.

Nihon Dōbutsuen Suizokukan Kyōkai. "Dōbutsuen suizokukan shisetsu no senjika ni okeru yūkōnaru keiei hōshin." Tokyo: Tokyo City Government, 1943.

Nihon Jōba Kyōkai. *Aiba no hi*. Tokyo: Nihon Jōba Kyōkai, 1939.

Nōrinshō Baseikyoku. *Gunyō hogoba futsū tanren no sankō*. Tokyo: Nōrinshō, 1940.

———. "Zen sen to jūgo no uma." *Shūhō*, no. 337 (March 31, 1943).

Ōdachi, Shigeo. *Kessen no tomin seikatsu*. Tokyo: Kessen Seikatsu Jissen Kyokakai, 1944.

Ōdachi Shigeo Denki Kankō Kai. *Ōdachi Shigeo*. Tokyo: Ōdachi Shigeo Denki Kankō Kai, 1956.

Oka, Asajirō. "Ningen no senzo wa saru to kyōdō." *Gakusei* 5, no. 6 (June 1889): 8–14.

Okamatsu, Takeshi. "Dōbutsuen no kagami." *Dōbutsu to dōbutsuen*, vol. 21 (October 1951): 8.

Omochabako shiriizu daisanwa: Ehon 1936-nen. Tokyo: J&O Studios, 1936.

Ono, Noboru. *Tennō no sugao—Tenno "Hirohito" as It Really Is*. Tokyo: Kindai Shobō, 1949.

Onshi Ueno Dōbutsuen. *Onshi Ueno Dōbutsuen sōritsu 70 shūnen kinen shōshi*. Tokyo: Tokyo-to, 1952.

Osborn, Fairfield. *Our Plundered Planet*. Boston: Brown, 1948.

Perry, Matthew. *The Japan Expedition, 1852–1854: The Personal Journal of Commodore Matthew C. Perry*. Washington, D.C.: Smithsonian, 1968.

Rikugun Jūi Dan. *Rekishi ni arawaretaru gunyō dōbutsu no eisei to senō to no kankei*, vol. 321. Tokyo: Rikugun Jūi Dan Hō, 1936.

Saishin gyūnyū no chishiki. Tokyo: Imperial Milk Association, 1937.

San-X Company. "San-X Netto: Tarepanda Sama." Accessed July 5, 2010, www
.san-x.co.jp/suama/suama.html.

Shibata, Keisai. "Shōni o seiō no gai o ronzu." *Dai Nihon shiritsu eiseikai zasshi*, vol. 11 (1884): 8–11.

Shibuya, Shinkichi. *Zō no namida*. Tokyo: Nichigei Shuppan, 1972.

Shima, Jirō. *Hakubutsu kyōjūhō*. Tokyo: Hokuō Saburō, 1877.

Shimizu. "Ikinobita zō." *Hakubutsukanshi kenkyū*, vol. 4 (1996).

Shirasaki, Iwahide. "Tōyō heiwa no tame naraba." *Jōdo*, vol. 4, no. 3 (March 1938).

Sugi, Yasusaburō. *Kagaku no furusato*. Tokyo: Sekai Bunka Kyōkai, 1946.

Takahashi, Onojirō. *Aiba dokuhon*. Tokyo: Takahashi Shoten, 1933.

Takashima, Haruo. *Dōbutsu tōrai monogatari*. Tokyo: Gakufū Shoinkan, 1955.

Takatsukasa, Nobusuke. *Chōrui*. Tokyo: Iwanami Shoten, 1930.

Tanaka, Atsushi. *Jūi kaibō hen*. Tokyo: Yūrindō, 1886.

Tanaka, Yoshio. *Dōbutsugaku*. Tokyo: Hakubutsukan, 1874.

———. *Kyōiku dōbutsuen*. Tokyo: Gakureikan, 1893.

Tanaka, Yoshio and Nakajima Gyōzan, eds. *Dōbutsu kinmō*. Tokyo: Hakubutsukan, 1875.

Teikoku Bahitsu Kyōkai. *'Aiba no hi' shisetsu*. Tokyo: Teikoku Bahitsu Kyōkai, 1939.

———. *Doitsu gunba shiyō hō*. Tokyo: Teikoku Bahitsu Kyōkai, 1938.

Tokyo-shi. *Nissen shinzen no zō*. Tokyo: Tokyo-shi, 1935.

Tokyo-shi Shiminkyoku kōenka. *Tokyo-shi shiminkyoku kōenka tokusetsu bōgodan Ueno onshi kōen dōbutsuen bundan kisoku*. Tokyo: Tokyo-shi Jimin Kyoku Kōenka, 1941.

Tsuchiya, Yukio and Ted Lewin. *Faithful Elephants: A True Story of Animals, People, and War*. Mooloolaba: Sandpiper, 1997.

Tsuchiya, Yukio and Motoichirō Takebe. *Kawaisōna zō*. Tokyo: Kin No Hoshisha, 1970.

———. *Kawaisōna zō*. Tokyo: Kin No Hoshisha, 2007.

Tsunetami, Sano. "Ōkoku hakurankai hōkokusho." Tokyo: Kokuritsu Hakubutsukan, May 1875.

Tsutsui, Akio. "Waga kuni dōbutsuen no kaizen." *Dōbutsu oyobi shokubutsu*, vol. 9, no. 3 (September 1935): 91–97.

Uchida, Shigeru. *Futsū dōbutsu zusetsu*. Tokyo: Shugakudo Shoten, 1915.

Udagawa Yōan. "Botanika kyō." Accessed June 28, 2012, http://archive.wul.waseda.ac.jp/kosho/bunko08/bunko08_a0208/bunko08_a0208.html.

Ueno Dōbutsuen. *Shin dōbutsu kōen chōsa koku sho*. Tokyo: Ueno Dōbutsuen, 1975.

———. *Ueno Dōbutsuen hakusho*. Tokyo: Ueno Dōbutsuen, 1975.

"Ueno Dōbutsuen." *Shōnen sekai*, vol. 8, no. 4 (1902).

Watanabe, Waichirō. "Dōbutsu aigo undō o kataru." *Dōbutsubungaku*, vol. 87 (September 1942).

World Association of Zoos and Aquariums. "WAZA: World Association of Zoos and Aquariums." Accessed June 15, 2006, www.waza.org/en/site/home.

Uma. Directed by Kajirō Yamamoto, Hideko Takamine, Chieko Takehisa and Kamatari Fujiwara. Tokyo: Tōei Kabushiki Kaisha, 1941 (VHS).

WWF nijūnenshi. Tokyo: Sekai Shizen Hogo Kikin Nihon Iinkai, 1994.

Yamashita, Kyōko, Nihon Hōsō Kyōkai, and Purojekuto X Seisakuhan. *Panda ga Nihon ni yattekita Kankan jūbyō, shirarezaru 11-nichikan*. Tokyo: Aozora Shuppan, 2004.

Yanagita, Kunio. "Fūkō suii." *Yangita Kunio zenshū*, vol. 26, 122–152. Tokyo: Chikuma Shobō, 1990.

Yasugi, Ryūichi. *Dōbutsu no kodomotachi*. Tokyo: Kōbunsha, 1951.

———. "Kodomo no sekai." In *Dōbutsu no kodomotachi*, 13–15. Tokyo: Kōbunsha, 1951.

———. "Ningen wa hoka no ikimono to doko ga chigauka?" In *Dōbutsu no kodomotachi*, 135–154. Tokyo: Kōbunsha, 1951.

Yoshimura, Ichrō. *Gunyō dōbutsugaku (gunken gunbato gaku)*. Tokyo: Rikugun Jūi Gakkō, 1939.

Yoshimura, Masuzō. "Tomo ni shinu ki no aiba datta." In *Shina jihen jūgunki shūroku*, vol. 3. Tokyo: Kōa Kyōkai, 1943.

UNPUBLISHED PRIMARY SOURCES

Dōbutsu mokuroku, 130 vols., 1882–2012.

Hakurankai Jimukyoku. "Mokuroku."

Hayashi, Kenzō. "Shirokuma no kiji." In *Dōbutsu roku Meiji 24*. Tokyo: Zoological Society Archives, 1891.

"Hayashi Kenzō et al. to Hijikata Hisamoto." In *"Dōbutsuroku Meiji 24" ledger*. Tokyo: Zoological Society Archives, 1891.

Higuma byōjō no ken. Tokyo: Teikoku Hakubutsukan, 1892.

Hijikata, Hisamoto. "Toshoryō hakubutsukan kara teikoku hakubutsukan e." In *"Reikoku Meiji 22" ledger*: Tokyo: Zoological Society Archives, 1889.

"Ishikawa Chiyomatsu to Kubota Kazuo." In *"Dōbutsuroku Meiji 25" ledger*. Tokyo: Zoological Society Archives, 1892.

"Janson to Ishikawa Chiyomatsu." In *"Dōbutsuroku Meiji 25" ledger*. Tokyo: Zoological Society Archives, 1892.

Kawamura, Tamiji. "Dōbutsuen no kaizensaku," *Hakubutsukan kenkyū*, vol. 12 (December 1939): 2–5.

Leonard Rothbard, Captain Commanding QMC. Wakkanai Area 6th District 441st Counter Intelligence Corps Detachment. General Headquarters. Far East Command. "Letter Addressed to Curator Ueno Park Zoo," 1950.

Omonaru kiken dōbutsu yakubutsu chishi ryō. Tokyo: Ueno Zoological Gardens, no date.

Nehru, Jawaharlal. "Message for Japanese Children [Correspondence]." New Delhi, 1949.

Personal communication, Ezawa Sōji to Fukuda Saburō, 1943.

Senjū-sengo roku. 1940–1952.

Senjū-sengo roku 2—mōjū shobun. 1943.

"The Sons of Pig." Hand-written pamphlets. 1948–1951.

Tokyo-to Taitō-kuyakusho. *Taitō-kushi, shakai bunka hen*. Tokyo: Tokyo-to Taitō-kuyakusho, 1966.

Tokyo-to Taitō-kuyakusho. *Taitō-kushi, shimohen.* Tokyo: Tokyo Taitō-kuyakusho, 1955.

Tōman mōjūgari iinchō. "Tōman mōjūgari annai." 1939.

Ueno Dōbutsuen moyoshimono, 35 vols., 1882–1992.

PERIODICALS AND NEWSPAPERS

Asahi Shinbun, 1879.

Asahi shōgakusei shinbun, 1900.

Dōbutsu bungaku, 1934.

Dōbutsuen shinbun, 1949.

Dōbutsugaku zasshi, 1889.

Dōbutsukan kenkyū, 1992.

Dōbutsu to dōbutsuen, 1949.

Hakubutsukan kenyū, 1928.

Kōen ryokuchi, 1937.

Mainichi Shinbun, 1872.

Mainichi shōgakusei shinnbun, 1936.

Saishū to shiiku, 1939.

Shōkokumin shinbun, 1934.

Shōnen sekai, 1895.

Shumi no seibutsu, 1932.

Tokyo shinbun, 1888.

Tokyo shōgakusei shinbun.

Yomiuri Shinbun, 1874.

PRIMARY SOURCE COLLECTIONS

Ishikawa Chiyomatsu zenshū, edited by Ishikawa Chiyomatsu Zenshū Kankō-Kai, vol. 1–8. Tokyo: Kōbunsha, 1946.

Kajima, Takao. *Shiryō Nihon dōbutsu shi.* Tokyo: Yasaka Shōbō, 1977.

Tokyo Kokuritsu Hakubutsukan, ed. *Tokyo Kokuritsu Hakubutsukan hyaku nen shi—shiryō hen.* Tokyo: Dai-Ichi Hōki Shuppan, 1973.

Tokyo-to. *Ueno Dōbutsuen hyakunenshi, shiryō hen.* Tokyo: Dai-Ichi Hoki Shuppan, 1982.

JAPANESE-LANGUAGE SECONDARY SOURCES

Akiyama, Masami. *Dōbutsuen no Shōwa shi.* Tokyo: Dēta Hausu, 1995.

Aoki, Hitoshi. *Hō to dōbutsu.* Tokyo: Meiseki Shoten, 2004.

———. *Nihon no dōbutsu hō.* Tokyo: Tokyo Daigaku Shuppan, 2009.

Asakura, Shigeharu. *Dōbutsuen to watashi.* Tokyo: Kaiyūsha, 1994.

Asano, Akihiko. *Shōwa o hashitta ressha monogatari: tetsudōshi o irodoru jūgo no meibamen.* Tokyo: JTP, 2001.

Bigot, Georges and Tōru Haga. *Bigō sobyō korekushon.* Tokyo: Iwanami Shoten, 1989.

Daimaru, Hideshi. "Dōbutsuen suizokukan ni okeru dōbutsu ireihi no secchi jōkyō." Daikyūkai Hito to Dōbutsu no Kankei Gakkai Gakujutsu Taikai, March 21, 2003.

Doi, Yasuhiro. *Itō Keisuke no kenkyū*. Tokyo: Koseisha, 2005.

Endō, Shōji. *Honzōgaku to yōgaku—Ono Razan gakutō no kenkyū*. Tokyo: Shibunkaku Shuppan, 2003.

Hamada-shi. *Hamadashi shi*. Hamada: Hamada-shi Shi Hensan Iinkai, 1973.

Hase, Toshio. *Nihon no kankyō hogo undō*. Tokyo: Tōshindō, 2002.

Hasegawa, Ushio. *Jidō sensō yomimono no kindai*. Tokyo Kyūzansha, 1999.

———. "Zō mo kawaisō -mōjū gyakusetsu shinwa hihan." In *Sensō jidō bungaku wa jujitsu o tsutaetekita ka Hasegawa Ushio hihanshū*, 8–30. Tokyo: Nashinokisha, 2000.

Horiuchi, Naoya. *Osaru densha monogatari*. Tokyo: Kanransha, 1998.

Iida-shi bijutsu hakubutsukan, *Tanaka Yoshio*. Iida: Iida-shi Bijutsu Hakubutsukan, 1999.

Imagawa, Isao. *Inu no gendai shi*. Tokyo: Gendai Shokan, 1996.

Imanishi, Sukeyuki. *Ireba o shita roba no hanashi*. Tokyo: Gin no Hoshi, 1971.

Inoue, Kentarō. *Nihon kankyōshi gaisetsu*. Okayama-shi: Daigaku Kyōiku Shuppan, 2006.

Ishida, Osamu. *Gendai Nihonjin no dōbutsukan: dōbutsu to no ayashigena kankei*. Tokyo: Biingu Netto Puresu, 2008.

———. *Ueno Dōbutsuen*. Tokyo Kōen Bunko. Tokyo: Tokyo-to Kōen Kyōkai, 1991.

———, et al. "Nihonjin no dōbutsukan: kono jūnenkan no suii." *Dōbutsukan kenkyū*, vol 8 (2004): 17–32.

Isono, Naohide. "Shinkaron no Nihon e no dōnyū." In *Mōsu to Nihon*, edited by Takeshi Moriya. Tokyo: Shōgakkan, 1988.

———. "Umi o koetekita chōjū tachi." In *Mono no imeji: Honzō to hakubutsugaku e no shōtai*, edited by Keiji Yamada. Tokyo: Asahi Shinbunsha, 1994.

Izono, Naohide, Ryūzō Kakizawa, Seiichi Kashiwabara, Masayasu Konishi, and Shirō Matsuyama. *Tono sama no seibutsu gaku keifu*. Tokyo: Kagaku Asahi, 1991.

Katō, Hidetoshi. *Toshi to goraku*. Tokyo: Kashima Shuppanka, 1969.

Katsura, Eishi. *Tokyo Dizunī Rando no shinwagaku*. Tokyo: Seikyūsha, 1999.

Kawai, Masao and Hanihara Kazurō, eds. *Dōbutsu to bunmei*. Tokyo: Asakura Shoten, 1995.

Kinoshita, Naoyuki. "Dōbutsuen e Ikō." In *Kankyō: bunka to seisaku*, edited by Sumio Matsunaga and Toshihiko Itō, 205–227. Tokyo: Tōshindō, 2008.

———. "Dōbutsutachi no Hōmudorama—dōbutsuen to Nihonjin no monogatari o tsumugu (2)." *Tosho*, vol. 727 (2009): 30–35.

———. "Osarudensha wa yuku yo—dōbutsuen to Nihonjin no monogatari o tsumugu (3)." *Tosho*, vol. 728 (2009): 26–32.

———. "Sakadachisuru zō—dōbutsuen to Nihonjin no monogatari o tsumugu (1)." *Tosho*, vol. 726 (2009): 24–30.

Kitazawa, Noriaki. *Me no shinden: "Bijuntsu" juyōshi nōto*. Tokyo: Bijutsu Shuppansha, 1989.

Kiyomizu, Kengo. "Ikinobita zō: Senzen senchū no Higashiyama Dōshokubutsuen." *Hakubutsukanshi kenkyū*, vol. 4 (1996): 1–11.

Koizumi, Makoto. *Dōbutsuen*. Tokyo: Iwanami Shoten, 1933.

Komiya, Teruyuki. *Monogatari—Ueno Dōbutsuen no reskishi: Enchō ga kataru dōbutsutachi no 140 nen*. Tokyo: Chūō Shunsho, 2010.

———. *Mukashi mukashi no Uenō Dōbutsuen, e hagaki monogatari*. Tokyo: Kyūryūdo, 2012.

———. "Shu no hozon to dōbutsuen." In *21-seiki no dōbutsuen to kishō dōbutsu no hanshoku*, vol. 22. Tokyo: Nihon Hanshoku Seibutsu Gakkai, 2001.

Komiya, Teruyuki and Toyofumi Fukuda. *Hontō no ookisa dōbutsuen*. Tokyo: Gakushū Kenkyūsha, 2008.

Komori, Atsushi. "Bambi: Fuarin to wakarete Ueno e." *Dōbutsu to dōbutsuen* (July 1, 1951): 4–5.

———. *Mō hitotsu no Ueno Dōbutsuen shi*. Tokyo: Maruzen Kabushiki Kaisha, 1997.

Kubo, Toshimichi. "Ōkubo Toshimichi bunsho." In *Nihon kagaku gijutsu shi taikei*, edited by Nihon Kagaku Kyōkai. Tokyo: Daiichi Hōki Shuppan, 1964.

Kume Bijutsuka. *Rekishika kume kunitake ten*. Tokyo: Kume Bijutsuka, 1991.

Kurasawa, Aiko. *Shigen no sensō: 'Dai tōa kyōei ken' no jinryū-monoryū*. Tokyo: Iwanami Shoten, 2012.

Maruyama, Atsushi. *Kindai Nihon kōen shi no kenkyū*. Tokyo: Shibunkaku, 1994.

Migita, Hiroki. *Tennōsei to shinkaron*. Tokyo: Seikyusha, 2009.

Mihashi, Osamu. *Meiji no seikatsushi—sabetsu no shinseishi*. Tokyo: Nihon Editaasukuru, 1999.

Nakamura, Ikuo. "'Dōbutsu kuyō' wa nan no tame ni—gendai Nihon no shizen ninshiki no arikata." *Tōhakugaku*, vol. 3 (October 1997): 268–279.

———. *Saishi to kugi: Nihonjin no shizenkan-dōbutsukan*. Kyoto: Hōzōkan, 2001.

Nakamura, Teiri. *Nihonjin no dōbutsukan—Henshintan no rekishi*. Tokyo: Kaimeisha, 1984.

Nakashima, Mitsuo. *Rikugun Jūi Gakkō*. Tokyo: Rikugun Jūi Gakkō Kai, 1996.

Narioka, Masahisa. *Hyō to heitai—yasei ni katta aijō no kiseki*. Tokyo: Jippi Shuppan, 1967.

Narushima, Nobuo. "Jaianto panda no hanshoku sakusen." In *21-seiki no dōbutsuen to kishō dōbutsu no hanshoku*, vol. 22. Tokyo: Nihon Hanshoku Seibutsu Gakkai, 2001.

Nippashi, Kazuaki. "Kodomo dōbutsuen o megutte." *Dōbutsuen kenkyu*, vol. 4, no. 1 (2000): 10–11.

———. "Nihon no dōbutsuen no rekishi." In *Dōbutsuen to iu media*, edited by Morio Watanabe. Tokyo: Seikyūsha, 2000.

Nishimoto, Toyohiro. "Dōbutsukan non hensen." In *Hito to dōbutsu no Nihonshi: I, dōbutsu no kōkogaku*, 61–85. Tokyo: Yoshikawa Kōbunkan, 2009.

———. *Hito to dōbutsu no Nihonshi: I, dōbutsu no kōkogaku*. Tokyo: Yoshikawa Kōbunkan, 2009.

Nishimura, Saburō. *Bunmei no naka no hakubutsugaku: Seiyō to Nihon*. Tokyo: Kinokuniya Shoten, 1999.

————. *Rinne to sono shitotachi: Tanken hakubutsugaku no yoake*. Tokyo: Asahi Shinbunsha, 1997.

Nomura, Keisuke. *Edo no shizenshi: 'bukō sanbutsu shi' wo yomu*. Tokyo: Dōbutsusha, 2002.

Obinata, Sumio. *Kindai Nihon no keisatsu to chiiki shakai*. Tokyo: Chikuma Shobō, 2000.

Osamu, Ōba. "Kyōhō ban 'zo' no subete." In *Mono no imeji: Honzō to hakubutsugaku e no shōtai*, edited by Keiji Yamada, 92–114. Tokyo: Asahi Shinbunsha, 1994.

Sasaki, Toshio. *Dōbutsuen no rekishi: Nihon ni okeru dōbutsuen no seiritsu*. Tokyo: Nishida Shoten, 1975.

Satō, Jin. *'Motazaru kuni' no shigenron: jizoku kanō na kokudo o meguru mō hitotsu no chi*. Tokyo: Tokyo Daigaku Shuppan Kai, 2011.

Shimizu, Isao, ed. *Bigō Nihon sōbyoshū*. Tokyo: Iwanami Shoten, 1986
————. *Zoku Bigō Nihon sōbyoshū*. Tokyo: Iwanami Shoten, 1992.

Shōji, Endo. *Honzōgaku to yōgaku—Ono Razan gakutō no kenkyū*. Tokyo: Shibunkaku Shuppan, 2003.

Suga, Yutaka, ed. *Hito to dōbutsu no Nihonshi: 3, dōbutsu to gendai shakai*. Tokyo: Yoshikawa Kōbunkan, 2009.

Sugimoto, Isao. *Itō Keisuke*. Tokyo: Yoshikawa Kōbunkan, 1960.

Takeichi, Ginjirō. *Fukoku kyōba—uma kara mita kindai Nihon*. Tokyo: Kodansha Sensho Mechie, 1999.

Taki, Koji. *Tennō no shōzō*. Tokyo: Iwanami Shoten, 1988.

Tanaka, Seidai. *Nihon no kōen*. Tokyo: Shikashima, 1974.

Tanaka, Shigeo. *Tanaka Shigeo den*. Tokyo: Tōshin, 1983.

Terao, Gorō. *"Shizen" gainen no keisei shi: Chūgoku, Nihon, Yoroppa*. Tokyo: Nobunkyo, 2002.

Tetsudō Shiryō Kenkyūkai. *Zō wa kisha ni noreruka*. Tokyo: JTB, 2003.

Tokyo Kokuritsu Hakubutsukan, ed. *Tokyo Kokuritsu Hakubutsukan hyaku nen shi*. Tokyo: Dai-Ichi Hōki Shuppan, 1973.

Tokyo-to. *Ueno Dōbutsuen hyakunenshi, shiryōhen*. Tokyo: Dai-Ichi Hoki Shuppan, 1982.
————. *Ueno Dōbutsuen hyakunenshi, tsūshihen*. Tokyo: Dai-Ichi Hoki Shuppan, 1982.

Tokyo Zoological Park Society. *Koga Tadamichi shi tsuitō tokushūgo*, vol. 38. Tokyo: Tokyo Zoological Park Society, 1986.

Tsukamoto, Manabu. *Edo jidai jin to dōbutsu*. Tokyo: Nihon Editaasukuru, 1995.

Ueno, Masuzō. *Hakubutsugaku no jidai*. Tokyo: Yasaka Shobō, 1990.
————. *Hakubutsugakusha retsuden*. Tokyo: Yasaka Shobō, 1991.
————. "Jobun: Edo hakubutsugaku no romanchishizumu." In *Edo hakubutsugaku shūsei*, edited by Shomonaka Hiroshi, 12–15. Tokyo: Heibonsha, 1994.
————. *Nihon dōbutsugakushi*. Tokyo: Yazaka Shobō, 1987.
————. *Seiyō hakubutsugakusa retsuden: Arisutoteresu kara Dauin made*. Tokyo: Yushokan, 2009.

Ueno, Masuzō and Yabe Ichirō, ed. *Shokugaku keigen/Shokubutsugaku*. Tokyo: Kōwa Shuppan, 1980.

Veldkamp, Elmer. "Eiyū to natta inutachi: gun'yōken irei to dōbutsu kuyō no henyō." In *Hito to dōbutsu no Nihonshi*, edited by Suga, 44–68. Tokyo: Yoshikawa Kōbuukau, 2009.

Wako, Kenji. "Nichibei ni okeru dōbutsuen no hatten katei ni kansuru kenkyū." Ph.D. dissertation, University of Tokyo, 1993.

Watanabe, Hiroyuki. *Hogei mondai no rekishi shakaigaku: kin-gendai Nihon ni okeru kujira to ningen*. Tokyo: Tōshindō, 2006.

Watanabe, Morio. *Dōbutsuen to iu media*. Tokyo: Seikyusha, 2000.

———. "Media toshite no dōbutsuen." In *Dōbutsuen to iu media*, edited by Morio Watanabe, 9–52. Tokyo: Seikyusha, 2000.

Yanabe, Akira. *Honyaku no shisō—"shizen" to NATURE*. Tokyo: Chikuma Shobō, 1995.

Yano, Satoji. *Dōbutsu ehon wo meguru tanken*. Tokyo: Keisō Shobō, 2002.

Yokoyama, Toshiaki. *Nihon shinka shisōshi: Meiji jidai no shinka shisō*. Tokyo: Shinsui, 2005.

Yoshimi, Shun'ya. *Banpaku gensō: Sengo seiji no jubaku*. Tokyo: Chikuma Shobō, 2005.

———. *Hakurankai no seijigaku: Manazashi no kindai*. Tokyo: Chūō Kōronsha, 1992.

———. *Toshi no doramaturugī: Tokyo sakariba no shakaishi*. Tokyo: Kōbundō, 1987.

ENGLISH-LANGUAGE SECONDARY SOURCES

Adams, Carol J. *Neither Man nor Beast: Feminism and the Defense of Animals*. New York: Continuum, 1994.

———. *The Sexual Politics of Meat: A Feminist-Vegetarian Critical Theory*, 10th anniversary ed. New York: Continuum, 2000.

Adams, Carol J. and Josephine Donovan. *Animals and Women: Feminist Theoretical Explorations*. Durham, N.C.: Duke University Press, 1995.

Adorno, Theodor W. "Free Time." *The Culture Industry: Selected Essays on Mass Culture*, edited by Theodor W. Adorno and J. M. Bernstein, 187–197. New York: Routledge, 2001.

———. *Minima Moralia: Reflections from Damaged Life*. New York: Schocken Books, 1978.

Agamben, Giorgio. *Homo Sacer: Sovereign Power and Bare Life*. Stanford, Calif.: Stanford University Press, 1998.

———. *The Open: Man and Animal*. Stanford, Calif.: Stanford University Press, 2004.

———. *State of Exception*. Translated by Kevin Attell. Chicago: University of Chicago Press, 2005.

Allison, Anne. "Enchanted Commodities." In *Millennial Monsters: Japanese Toys and the Global Imagination*, 1–34. Berkeley: University of California Press, 1996.

Althusser, Louis. "Ideology and Ideological State Apparatus (Notes towards an Investigation)." In *Lenin and Philosophy, and Other Essays*, translated by Ben Brewster, 85–126. New York: Monthly Review Press, 2001.

Ambaras, David. *Bad Youth: Juvenile Delinquency and the Politics of Everyday Life in Modern Japan*. Berkeley: University of California Press, 2005.

Ambros, Barbara. *Bones of Contention: Animals and Religion in Contemporary Japan*. Honolulu: University of Hawaii Press, 2012.

American Pet Products Manufacturers Association. *APPMA's 2005–2006 National Pet Owners Survey (NPOS)*. Greenwich: American Pet Products Association, Inc., 2006.

Ames, Eric. *Carl Hagenbeck's Empire of Entertainments*. Seattle: University of Washington Press, 2009.

Anderson, Kay. "Animals, Science, and Spectacle in the City." In *Animal Geographies: Place, Politics, and Identity in the Nature-Culture Borderlands*, edited by Jennifer Wolch and Jody Emel, 27–50. New York: Verso, 1998.

Asma, Stephen T. *Stuffed Animals & Pickled Heads: The Culture and Evolution of Natural History Museums*. New York: Oxford University Press, 2001.

Asquith, Pamela J. and Arne Kalland. *Japanese Images of Nature: Cultural Perspectives*. Richmond: Curzon Press, 1997.

Baker, Steve. *Picturing the Beast: Animals, Identity, and Representation*. Urbana: University of Illinois Press, 2001.

———. *The Postmodern Animal*. London: Reaktion, 2000.

Bakhtin, M.M. *Rabelais and His World*. Bloomington: Indiana University Press, 1984.

Baratay, Eric and Elisabeth Hardouin-Fugier. *Zoo: A History of Zoological Gardens in the West*. London: Reaktion, 2002.

Barlow, Tani E. *Formations of Colonial Modernity in East Asia*. Durham, N.C.: Duke University Press, 1997.

Barnhart, Michael A. *Japan Prepares for Total War: The Search for Economic Security, 1919–1941*. Ithaca, N.Y.: Cornell University Press, 1987.

Barret, Brendan F.D. *Ecological Modernization and Japan*. New York: Routledge, 2005.

Barringer, T.J. "The South Kensington Museum and the Colonial Project." In *Colonialism and the Object: Empire, Material Culture, and the Museum*, edited by T.J. Barringer and Tom Flynn, 11–28. New York: Routledge, 1998.

Barringer, T.J. and Tom Flynn. *Colonialism and the Object: Empire, Material Culture, and the Museum*. New York: Routledge, 1998.

Barrow, Mark V. *Nature's Ghosts: Confronting Extinction from the Age of Jefferson to the Age of Ecology*. Chicago: The University of Chicago Press, 2009.

———. *A Passion for Birds: American Ornithology after Audubon*. Princeton, N.J.: Princeton University Press, 2000.

Barthes, Roland. *The Rustle of Language*. Translated by R. Howard. Berkeley: University of California Press, 1989.

Bartholomew, James R. *The Formation of Science in Japan: Building a Research Tradition*. New Haven, Conn.: Yale University Press, 1989.

Bataille, Georges. *The Accursed Share: An Essay on General Economy*. New York: Zone Books, 1988.

———. "Sacrifice, the Festival and the Principles of the Sacmonred World." In *The Bataille Reader*, edited by Fred Botting and Scott Wilson, 210–220. Malden, Mass.: Blackwell, 1997.

Bataille, Georges, Fred Botting, and Scott Wilson. *The Bataille Reader*. Blackwell Readers. Malden, Mass.: Blackwell, 1997.

Baudrillard, Jean. "The Animals: Territory and Metamorphoses." In *Simulacra and Simulation*, translated by Sheila Glaser, 129–142. Ann Arbor: University of Michigan Press, 1994.

Bauman, Zygmunt. *Modernity and the Holocaust*. Ithaca, N.Y.: Cornell University Press, 1991.

Benjamin, Walter. "On Some Motifs in Baudelaire." In *Illuminations*, translated by Harry Zohn, edited by Walter Benjamin and Hannah Arendt, 155–200. New York: Schocken, 1969.

———. "The Work of Art in the Age of Mechanical Reproduction." In *Illuminations*, translated by Harry Zohn, edited by Walter Benjamin and Hannah Arendt, 217–253. New York: Schocken, 1969.

Benjamin, Walter and Hannah Arendt. *Illuminations*. New York: Schocken, 1969.

Benjamin, Walter and Rolf Tiedemann. *The Arcades Project*. Cambridge, Mass.: Belknap Press, 1999.

Bennett, Tony. *The Birth of the Museum: History, Theory, Politics*. New York: Routledge, 1995.

———. "The Exhibitionary Complex." In *Culture/Power/History: A Reader in Contemporary Social Theory*, edited by Nicholas B. Dirks, Geoff Eley, and Sherry B. Ortner. Princeton, N.J.: Princeton University Press, 1994.

Berger, John. "Why Look at Animals?" In *About Looking*. New York: Pantheon Books, 1980.

Bess, Michael. *The Light-Green Society: Ecology and Technological Modernity in France, 1960–2000*. Chicago: University of Chicago Press, 2003.

Bhabha, Homi K. *The Location of Culture*. London; New York: Routledge, 1994.

———. "The Other Question: Stereotype, Discrimination and the Discourse of Colonialism." In *The Location of Culture*, 66–84. New York: Routledge, 1994.

Blacker, Carmen. *The Japanese Enlightenment: A Study of the Writings of Fukuzawa Yukichi*. New York: Cambridge University Press, 1964.

Botsman, Daniel V. *Punishment and Power in the Making of Modern Japan*. Princeton, N.J.: Princeton University Press, 2005.

Bourdieu, Pierre. *Outline of a Theory of Practice*. Translated by Richard Nice. New York: Cambridge University Press, 1977.

———. "The Specificity of the Scientific Field and the Social Conditions of the Progress of Reason." In *The Science Studies Reader*, edited by Mario Biagioli, 12–30. New York: Routledge, 1999.

Bulliet, Richard. *Hunters, Herders, and Hamburgers: The Past and Future of Human-Animal Relationships*. New York: Columbia University Press, 2005.

Burkhardt, Richard W. *Patterns of Behavior: Konrad Lorenz, Niko Tinbergen, and the Founding of Ethology*. Chicago: University of Chicago Press, 2005.

———. *The Spirit of System: Lamarck and Evolutionary Biology*. Cambridge, Mass.: Harvard University Press, 1995.

Cartmill, Matt. "The Bambi Syndrome." In *A View to a Death in the Morning: Hunting and Nature through History*, 161–171. Cambridge, Mass.: Harvard University Press, 1996.

Certeau, Michel de. *The Writing of History*. New York: Columbia University Press, 1988.

Chakrabarty, Dipesh. "The Climate of History: Four Theses." *Critical Inquiry* 35 (Winter 2009): 197–222.

Chapman, James. *The British at War: Cinema, State, and Propaganda, 1939–1945*. New York: St. Martin's Press, 1998.

Chen, Kuan-Hsing. *Asia as Method: Toward Deimperialization*. Durham, N.C.: Duke University Press, 2010.

———. "Deimperialization: Club 51 and the Imperialist Assumption of Democracy." In *Asia as Method: Toward Deimperialization*, 161–210. Durham, N.C.: Duke University Press, 2010.

Cioc, Mark. *The Game of Conservation: International Treaties to Protect the World's Migratory Animals*. Athens: Ohio University Press, 2009.

Clifford, James. *The Predicament of Culture Twentieth-Century Ethnography, Literature, and Art*. Cambridge, Mass.: Harvard University Press, 1988.

Connelly, Matthew James. *Fatal Misconception: The Struggle to Control World Population*. Cambridge, Mass: Belknap Press of Harvard University Press, 2008.

Convention on International Trade in Endangered Species of Wild Fauna and Flora. *Appendices I, II, and III*. Geneva: International Environment House, 2010.

Cosby, Alfred W. *Children of the Sun: A History of Humanity's Unappeasable Appetite for Energy*. New York: W.W. Norton & Company, 2006.

Courtney, Roger. *Strategic Management for Voluntary Nonprofit Organizations*. New York: Routledge, 2002.

Craig, Albert M. *Civilization and Enlightenment: The Early Thought of Fukuzawa Yukichi*. Cambridge, Mass.: Harvard University Press, 2009.

Crawcour, E. Sydney. "Industrialization and Technological Change." In *Cambridge History of Japan*, edited by Peter Duus, vol. 6, 385–450. New York: Cambridge University Press, 1986.

Cronon, William. "The Trouble with Wilderness; or, Getting Back to the Wrong Nature." In *Uncommon Ground: Toward Reinventing Nature*, edited by William Cronon, 69–90. New York: W.W. Norton & Company, 1995.

Crutzen, Paul J. "Geology of Mankind." *Nature*, vol. 3 no. 415 (January 3, 2002): 23.

Crutzen, Paul J. and Euguene F. Stoermer. "The Anthropocene." *IGBP Newsletter*, vol. 41 (2000): 17.

Cummings, e.e. "The Secret of the Zoo Exposed." In *e.e. Cummings: A Miscellany Revised*, edited by George Firmage, 174–178. New York: October House, 1927.

Cyranoski, D. "Japanese Call for More Bite in Animal Rules." *Nature*, vol. 434, no. 7029 (2005): 6.

———. "Row over Fate of Endangered Monkeys." *Nature*, vol. 408, no. 6810 (2000): 280.

———. "Slipshod Approvals Taint Japanese Animal Studies." *Nature*, vol. 430, no. 7001 (2004): 714.

Darnton, Robert. *The Great Cat Massacre and Other Episodes in French Cultural History*. New York: Vintage Books, 1985.

Das, Veena. "Language and Body: Transactions in the Construction of Pain." In *Social Suffering*, edited by Arthur Kleinman, 67–92. Berkeley: University of California Press, 1997.

Daston, Lorraine and Fernando Vidal. *The Moral Authority of Nature*. Chicago: University of Chicago Press, 2004.

Davey, G. "An Analysis of Country, Socio-Economic and Time Factors on Worldwide Zoo Attendance during a 40-Year Period." *International Zoo Yearbook*, vol. 41, no. 1 (March 26, 2007): 217–225.

Davis, D. Dwight. *The Giant Panda: A Morphological Study of Evolutionary Mechanisms*. Chicago: Chicago Natural History Museum, 1964.

Davis, Susan G. *Spectacular Nature: Corporate Culture and the Sea World Experience*. Berkeley: University of California Press, 1997.

Debord, Guy. *Society of the Spectacle*. Translated by Fredy Perlman and Jon Supak. Kalamazoo: Black & Red, 1977.

———. *The Society of the Spectacle*. Translated by Donald Nicholson-Smith. Cambridge, Mass.: Zone Books, 1994.

de Ganon, Pieter S. "Down the Rabbit Hole," *Past & Present*, vol. 213 (2011): 237–266.

De Grazia, Victoria. *Irresistible Empire: America's Advance through Twentieth-Century Europe*. Cambridge, Mass.: Belknap Press of Harvard University Press, 2005.

Derrida, Jacques. *Of Spirit: Heidegger and the Question*. Chicago: University of Chicago Press, 1989.

Desmond, Jane. "Displaying Death, Animating Life: Changing Fictions of 'Liveness' from Taxidermy to Animatronics." In *Representing Animals*, edited by Nigel Rothfels, 159–178. Bloomington: Indiana University Press, 2002.

Dirks, Nicholas B., Geoff Eley, and Sherry B. Ortner. *Culture/Power/History: A Reader in Contemporary Social Theory*. Princeton Studies in Culture/Power/History. Princeton, N.J.: Princeton University Press, 1994.

Doak, Kevin Michael. *Dreams of Difference: The Japan Romantic School and the Crisis of Modernity*. Berkeley: University of California Press, 1994.

———. *A History of Nationalism in Modern Japan: Placing the People*. Boston: Brill, 2007.

Donahue, Jesse and Erik Trump. *The Politics of Zoos: Exotic Animals and Their Protectors*. DeKalb: Northern Illinois University Press, 2006.

Dorfman, Ariel and Armand Mattelart. *How to Read Donald Duck: Imperialist Ideology in the Disney Comic*, 2nd enlarged edition. New York: International General, 1984.

Douglas, Mary. "No Free Gifts," In *The Gift: The Form and Reason for Exchange in Archaic Socities*, 2nd edition, ix–xxiii. New York: Routledge, 2005.

Dower, John W. "The Demonic Other." In *War without Mercy: Race and Power in the Pacific War*, 234–261. New York: Pantheon Books, 1986.

———. *Embracing Defeat: Japan in the Wake of World War II*. New York: W.W. Norton & Company, 1999.

———. *War without Mercy: Race and Power in the Pacific War*. New York: Pantheon Books, 1986.

Drayton, Richard Harry. *Nature's Government: Science, Imperial Britain, and the "Improvement" of the World*. New Haven, Conn.: Yale University Press, 2000.

Driscoll, Mark. *Absolute Erotic, Absolute Grotesque: The Living, Dead, and Undead in Japan's Imperialism, 1895–1945*. Durham, N.C.: Duke University Press, 2010.

Durkheim, Émile. *The Elementary Forms of Religious Life*. Translated by E. Fields. New York: Free Press, 1995.

———. *On Suicide*. Translated by Robin Buss. New York: Penguin, 2006.

Durkheim, Émile, Marcel Mauss, and Rodney Needham. *Primitive Classification*. Chicago: University of Chicago Press, 1963.

Duus, Peter. *The Abacus and the Sword: The Japanese Penetration of Korea, 1895–1910*. Berkeley: University of California Press, 1995.

———, ed. *The Japanese Discovery of America: A Brief History with Documents*. The Bedford Series in History and Culture. Boston: Bedford Books, 1997.

Duus, Peter, Ramon Hawley Myers, and Mark R. Peattie. *The Japanese Informal Empire in China, 1895–1937*. Princeton, N.J.: Princeton University Press, 1989.

Duus, Peter, Ramon Hawley Myers, Mark R. Peattie, and Wanyao Zhou. *The Japanese Wartime Empire, 1931–1945*. Princeton, N.J.: Princeton University Press, 1996.

Figal, Gerald. *Civilization and Monsters: Spirits of Modernity in Meiji Japan*. Durham, N.C.: Duke University Press, 1999.

Fisher, James. *Zoos of the World*. London: Aldus, 1966.

Fisher, Philip. *Hard Facts: Setting and Form in the American Novel*. New York: Oxford University Press, 1987.

Foster, Michael Dylan. *Pandemonium and Parade: Japanese Monsters and the Culture of Yokai*. Berkeley: University of California Press, 2008.

Foucault, Michel. *Discipline and Punish: The Birth of the Prison*. Translated by Alan Sheridan. New York: Vintage Books, 1979.

———. *The Foucault Reader*. Edited by Paul Rabinow. New York: Pantheon Books, 1984.

———. *The History of Sexuality, Vol. 1: An Introduction*. New York: Vintage, 1980.

———. *The Order of Things: An Archaeology of the Human Sciences*. Translated by Alan Sheridan. New York: Vintage Books, 1973.

Freud, Sigmund. *Totem and Taboo; Some Points of Agreement between the Mental Lives of Savages and Neurotics*. New York: Norton, 1952.

Fritzsche, Peter. *Reading Berlin 1900*. Cambridge, Mass.: Harvard University Press, 1996.

Fudge, Erica. *Perceiving Animals: Humans and Beasts in Early Modern English Culture*. New York: St. Martin's Press, 2000.

————. *Renaissance Beasts: Of Animals, Humans, and Other Wonderful Creatures.* Urbana: University of Illinois Press, 2004.

Fudge, Erica, Ruth Gilbert, and S. J. Wiseman. *At the Borders of the Human: Beasts, Bodies, and Natural Philosophy in the Early Modern Period.* New York: St. Martin's Press, 1999.

Fujitani, Takashi. *Splendid Monarchy: Power and Pageantry in Modern Japan.* Berkeley: University of California Press, 1996.

————. *Race for Empire: Koreans as Japanese and Japanese as Americans during World War II.* Berkeley: University of California Press, 2011.

Garon, Sheldon M. *Molding Japanese Minds: The State in Everyday Life.* Princeton, N.J.: Princeton University Press, 1997.

————. *The State and Labor in Modern Japan.* Berkeley: University of California Press, 1990.

Giddens, Anthony. *The Consequences of Modernity.* Stanford, Calif.: Stanford University Press, 1990.

Girard, René. *The Scapegoat.* Translated by Yvonne Freccero. London: Athlone, 1986.

————. *Violence and the Sacred.* Translated by Patrick Gregory. Baltimore: Johns Hopkins University Press, 1977.

Girard, René, João Cezar de Castro Rocha, and Pierpaolo Antonello. *Evolution and Conversion: Dialogues on the Origins of Culture.* New York: T&T Clark, 2007.

Gluck, Carol. "The Invention of Edo." In *Mirror of Modernity: Invented Traditions of Modern Japan*, edited by Stephen Vlastos, 262–283. Berkeley: University of California Press, 1998.

————. *Japan's Modern Myths: Ideology in the Late Meiji Period.* Princeton, N.J.: Princeton University Press, 1985.

————"Meiji for Our Time." In *New Directions in the Study of Meiji Japan*, edited by Helen Hardacre and Adam L. Kern, 11–28. New York: Brill, 1997.

————. "Operations of Memory: "Comfort Women" and the World." In *Ruptured Histories: War, Memory, and the Post-Cold War in Asia,* edited by Sheila Miyoshi Jager and Rana Mitter, 47–77. Cambridge, Mass.: Harvard University Press, 2007.

————. "The Past in the Present." In *Postwar Japan as History*, edited by Andrew Gordon, 64–96. Berkeley: University of California Press, 1993.

Godart, Clinton. "Darwin in Japan: Evolutionary Theory and Japan's Modernity (1820–1970)." Ph.D. dissertation, University of Chicago, 2009.

Goffman, Erving. *The Presentation of Self in Everyday Life.* Woodstock, N.Y.: Overlook Press, 1973.

Gordon, Andrew. "Consumption, Leisure and the Middle Class in Transwar Japan." *Social Science Japan Journal*, vol. 10, no. 1 (2007): 1–21.

————. *Labor and Imperial Democracy in Prewar Japan.* Berkeley: University of California Press, 1991.

————. *A Modern History of Japan: From Tokugawa Times to the Present.* New York: Oxford University Press, 2003.

————. *Postwar Japan as History.* Berkeley: University of California Press, 1993.

Gould, Stephen Jay. "A Biological Homage to Mickey Mouse." In *The Panda's Thumb: More Reflections in Natural History*, 95–107. New York: Norton, 1980.

———. *The Panda's Thumb: More Reflections in Natural History*. New York: Norton, 1980.

Greene, Ann. "War Horses: Equine Technology in the American Civil War." In *Industrializing Organisms: Introducing Evolutionary History*, edited by Philip Scranton, 143–166. New York: Routledge, 2004.

Guha, Ramachandra. "Radical American Environmentalism and Wilderness Preservation: A Third World Critique." *Environmental Ethics*, vol. 11, no. 1 (Spring 1989): 71–83.

Hall, John W. "Changing Conceptions of the Modernization of Japan." In *Changing Japanese Attitudes toward Modernization*, edited by Marius B. Jansen. Princeton, N.J.: Princeton University Press, 1965.

Hancocks, David. *A Different Nature: The Paradoxical World of Zoos and Their Uncertain Future*. Berkeley: University of California Press, 2001.

Hanes, Jeffrey. "Media Culture in Taishō Osaka." In *Japan's Competing Modernities: Issues in Culture and Democracy*, edited by Sharon A. Minichiello, 267–288. Honolulu: University of Hawaii Press, 1998.

Hanes, Jeffrey E. and Hajime Seki. *The City as Subject: Seki Hajime and the Reinvention of Modern Osaka*. Berkeley: University of California Press, 2002.

Hanson, Elizabeth. *Animal Attractions: Nature on Display in American Zoos*. Princeton, N.J.: Princeton University Press, 2002.

Haraway, Donna. *A Cyborg Manifesto: Science, Technology, and Socialist-Feminism in the Late Twentieth Century*. New York: Routledge, 1992.

———. *Primate Visions: Gender, Race, and Nature in the World of Modern Science*. New York: Routledge, 1989.

———. *Simians, Cyborgs, and Women: The Reinvention of Nature*. New York: Routledge, 1991.

———. "Teddy Bear Patriarchy: Taxidermy in the Garden of Eden, New York City, 1908–1936." In *Culture/Power/History: A Reader in Contemporary Social Theory*, edited by Nicholas Dirks, Geoff Eley, and Sherry Ortner, 49–95. Princeton, N.J.: Princeton University Press, 1994.

Hardacre, Helen. *Shinto and the State, 1868–1988*. Princeton, N.J.: Princeton University Press, 1991.

Harootunian, Harry D. *History's Disquiet Modernity, Cultural Practice, and the Question of Everyday Life*. New York: Columbia University Press, 2000.

———. *Overcome by Modernity: History, Culture, and Community in Interwar Japan*. Princeton, N.J.: Princeton University Press, 2000.

Harris, Daniel. *Cute, Quaint, Hungry, and Romantic: The Aesthetics of Consumerism*. New York: Basic Books, 2000.

Havens, Thomas R.H. *Farm and Nation in Modern Japan: Agrarian Nationalism, 1870–1940*. Princeton, N.J.: Princeton University Press, 1974.

———. *Parkscapes: Green Spaces in Modern Japan*. Honolulu: University of Hawaii Press, 2012.

———. *Valley of Darkness: The Japanese People and World War Two*. New York: Norton, 1978.

Heidegger, Martin. *The Question Concerning Technology, and Other Essays.* New York: Harper & Row, 1977.

Herbert, T. Walter. *Sexual Violence and American Manhood.* Cambridge, Mass.: Harvard University Press, 2002.

Hoage, R. J., William A. Deiss, and National Zoological Park (U.S.). *New Worlds, New Animals: From Menagerie to Zoological Park in the Nineteenth Century.* Baltimore: Johns Hopkins University Press, 1996.

Howell, David Luke. *Capitalism from Within: Economy, Society, and the State in a Japanese Fishery.* Berkeley: University of California Press, 1995.

———. *Geographies of Identity in Nineteenth-Century Japan.* Berkeley: University of California Press, 2005.

Howland, Douglas. "Society Reified: Herbert Spencer and Political Theory in Early Meiji Japan." *Comparative Studies in Society and History*, vol. 42, no. 1 (January 2000): 67–86.

———. *Translating the West: Language and Political Reason in Nineteenth-Century Japan.* Honolulu: University of Hawaii Press, 2001.

Hubert, Henri, Marcel Mauss, and W. D. Halls. *Sacrifice: Its Nature and Function.* London: Cohen and West, 1964.

Hur, Nam-Lin. *Prayer and Play in Late Tokugawa Japan: Asakusa Sensōji and Edo Society.* Cambridge, Mass.: Harvard University Asia Center; Distributed by Harvard University Press, 2000.

Igarashi, Yoshikuni. "The Age of the Body." In *Bodies of Memory: Narratives of War in Postwar Japanese Culture, 1945–1970*, 47–72. Princeton, N.J.: Princeton University Press, 2000.

———. *Bodies of Memory: Narratives of War in Postwar Japanese Culture, 1945–1970.* Princeton, N.J.: Princeton University Press, 2000.

Ingold, Tim. *The Appropriation of Nature: Essays on Human Ecology and Social Relations.* Iowa City: University of Iowa Press, 1987.

———. *Hunters, Pastoralists, and Ranchers: Reindeer Economics and Their Transformations.* New York: Cambridge University Press, 1980.

———. *What Is an Animal?* Boston: Unwin Hyman, 1988.

Ito, Mayumi. *Japanese Wartime Zoo Policy: The Silent Victims of World War II.* New York: PalgraveMacMillan, 2010.

"IUCN—What Is Diversity in Crisis?" Accessed July 8, 2011, www.iucn.org /what/tpas/biodiversity/about/biodiversity_crisis/.

Jasanoff, Sheila. *The Fifth Branch: Science Advisers as Policymakers.* Cambridge, Mass.: Harvard University Press, 1998.

———. "The Idiom of Co-production." In *States of Knowledge: The Co-production of Science and Social Order*, edited by Sheila Jasanoff. New York: Routledge, 2004.

Jewett, Andrew. *Science, Democracy, and the American University.* Cambridge: Cambridge University Press, 2012.

Jones, Mark. *Children as Treasures: Childhood and the Middle Class in Early Twentieth Century Japan.* Cambridge, Mass.: Harvard University Asia Center, 2010.

Kalland, Arne. "Culture in Japanese Nature," *Asian Perceptions of Nature: A Critical Approach*, edited by O. Bruun and Arne Kalland. London: Curzon, 1995.

———. "Management by Totemization: Whale Symbolism and the Anti-Whaling Campaign." *Arctic*, vol. 46, no. 2 (1993).

———. *Unveiling the Whale: Discourses on Whales and Whaling*. New York: Berghan Books, 2003.

Kappeler, Susanne. "Speciesism, Racism, Nationalism . . . or the Power of Scientific Subjectivity." In *Animals and Women: Feminist Theoretical Explorations*, edited by Carol Adams and Josephine Donovan, 320–352. Durham, N.C.: Duke University Press, 1995.

Karatani, Kōjin. *Origins of Modern Japanese Literature*. Durham, N.C.: Duke University Press, 1993.

Karlin, Jason Gregory. "The Empire of Fashion: Taste, Gender, and Nation in Modern Japan." Ph.D. dissertation, University of Illinois at Urbana-Champaign, 2002.

Kawata, Ken. "Don't Hit an Elephant, It's Cruel!" *Alive*, June 1983, pp. 2–6.

———. "History of Traveling Menageries of Japan." *Bandwagon*, November-December 2005, pp. 44–51.

———. "Zoological Gardens of Japan." In *Zoo and Aquarium History: Ancient Animal Collections to Zoological Gardens*, edited by Vernon N. Kisling, Jr., 295–330. New York: CRC Press, 2001.

Kellert, S. "Attitudes, Knowledge and Behaviour toward Wildlife among the Industrial Superpowers: United States, Japan and Germany." *Journal of Social Issues*, vol. 49, no. 1 (1993): 53–69.

———. "The Biological Basis for Human Values of Nature." *The Biophilia Hypothesis*, edited by Stephen R. Kellert and Edward O. Wilson, 42–72. New York: Island Press, 1993.

Kete, Kathleen. *The Beast in the Boudoir: Petkeeping in Nineteenth-Century Paris*. Berkeley: University of California Press, 1994.

Kisling, Vernon N., ed. *Zoo and Aquarium History: Ancient Animal Collections to Zoological Gardens*. Boca Raton, Fla.: CRC Press, 2001.

Knight, C.H. "The Bear as Barometer: The Japanese Response to Human-Bear Conflict." Ph.D. dissertation, University of Canterberry, 2007.

Knight, John. "Feeding Mr. Monkey: Cross-Species Food 'Exchange' in Japanese Monkey Parks." In *Animals in Person: Cultural Perspectives on Human-Animal Intimacy*, edited by John Knight, 231–253. Oxford: Berg, 2005.

———. *Waiting for Wolves in Japan: An Anthropological Study of People-Wildlife Relations*. Oxford: Oxford University Press, 2003.

———, ed. *Wildlife in Asia: Cultural Perspectives*. London: RoutledgeCurzon, 2004.

Kornicki, Peter. "Public Display and Changing Values: Early Meiji Exhibitions and Their Precursors." *Monumenta Nipponica*, vol. 49 (1994): 167–196.

Koschmann, Victor J. "Modernization and Democratic Values: The 'Japanese Model' in the 1960s." In *Staging Growth: Modernization, Development, and the Global Cold War*, edited by David Engermann, Nils Gilman, Mark

Haefele, and Michael E. Latham. Amherst: University of Massachusetts Press, 2003.

Kushner, Barak. *The Thought War: Japanese Imperial Propaganda.* Honolulu: University of Hawaii Press, 2006.

LaFleur, William. *The Karma of Words: Buddhism and the Literary Arts in Medieval Japan.* Berkeley: University of California Press, 1983.

Lamarck, Jean-Baptiste. *Système des animaux sans vertèbres.* Paris: Chez Deterville, 1801.

Lansbury, Coral. *The Old Brown Dog: Women, Workers, and Vivisection in Edwardian England.* Madison: University of Wisconsin Press, 1985.

Laqueur, Thomas W. "Bodies, Details, and the Humanitarian Narrative." In *The New Cultural History,* edited by Lynn Hunt, 176–204. Berkeley: University of California Press, 1989.

Latour, Bruno. *We Have Never Been Modern.* Translated by Catherine Porter. Cambridge, Mass.: Harvard University Press, 1993.

Leach, William. *Land of Desire: Merchants, Power and the Rise of a New American Culture.* New York: Vintage Books, 1994.

Lévi-Strauss, Claude. *Totemism.* Translated by Rodney Needham. Harmondsworth: Penguin, 1969.

Lippit, Akira Mizuta. *Electric Animal: Toward a Rhetoric of Wildlife.* Minneapolis: University of Minnesota Press, 2000.

Litten, Frederick S. "Starving the Elephants: The Slaughter of Animals in Wartime Tokyo's Ueno Zoo." *Asia-Pacific Journal,* vol. 38, no. 3 (2009).

Liu, Jiangu, Marc Linderman, Zhiyun Ouyang, Li An, Jian Yang, and Hemin Zhang. "Ecological Degradation in Protected Areas: The Case of Wolong Nature Reserve for Giant Pandas." *Science,* vol. 292, no. 5514 (April 6, 2001): 98–101.

Liu, Jianguo, Zhiyun Ouyang, William W. Taylor, Richard S. Groop, Yingchung Tan, and Heming Zhang. "A Framework for Evaluating Human Factors on Wildlife Habitat: The Case of Giant Pandas." *Conservation Biology,* vol. 13, no. 6 (December 1999): 1360–1370.

Lockyer, Angus. "Expo Fascism? Ideology, Representation, Economy." In *The Culture of Japanese Fascism,* edited by Alan Tansman. Durham, N.C.: Duke University Press, 2009.

———. "Japan at the Exhibitions, 1867–1970." Ph.D. dissertation, Stanford University, 2000.

Low, Morris. *Japan on Display: Photography and the Emperor.* New York: Routledge, 2006.

Malamud, Randy. *Reading Zoos: Representations of Animals and Captivity.* New York: New York University Press, 1998.

Marcon, Federico. "Inventorying Nature: Tokugawa Yoshimune and the Sponsorhip of *Honzōgaku* in Eighteenth-Century Japan." In *Japan at Nature's Edge: The Environmental Context of a Global Power,* edited by Ian Miller, Julia Adeney Thomas, and Brett Walker. Honolulu: University of Hawaii Press, 2013.

———. *The Knowledge of Nature and the Nature of Knowledge in Early-Modern Japan.* Unpublished book manuscript, 2011.

Marris, Emma. *Rambunctious Garden: Saving Nature in a Post-Wild World.* New York: Bloomsbury, 2011.

Marvin, Bob and Garry Mullan. *Zoo Culture: The Book about Watching People Watch Animals,* 2nd ed. Champaign: University of Illinois Press, 1999.

Marzuluff, John M., Eric Shulenberger, Wilifried Endlicher, Marina Alberti, Gordon Bradley, Lare Ryan, Ute Simon, and Craig Zumbrennen, eds. *Urban Ecology: An International Perspective on Interaction between Humans and Nature.* New York: Springer, 2008.

Mauss, Marcel. *The Gift: The Form and Reason for Exchange in Archaic Societies.* Translated by W.D. Halls. New York: W.W. Norton & Company, 1990.

McClintock, Anne. *Imperial Leather: Race, Gender, and Sexuality in the Colonial Conquest.* New York: Routledge, 1995.

McGirr, Lisa. *Suburban Warriors: The Origins of the New American Right.* Princeton, N.J.: Princeton University Press, 2001.

McNeill, John Robert. *Something New under the Sun: An Environmental History of the Twentieth-Century World.* New York: W.W. Norton & Company, 2000.

Miller, Ian Jared. "Didactic Nature." In *JAPANimals: History and Culture in Japan's Animal Life,* edited by Gregory M. Pflugfelder and Brett L. Walker. Ann Arbor: University of Michigan Center for Japanese Studies, 2005.

Mitchell, Timothy. *Colonising Egypt.* Berkeley: University of California Press, 1988.

———. *Rule of Experts: Egypt, Techno-Politics, Modernity.* Berkeley: University of California Press, 2002.

Mitchell, W.J.T. "Illusion: Looking at Animals Looking." In *Picture Theory: Essays on Verbal and Visual Representation,* 329–344. Chicago: University of Chicago Press, 1994.

———. "Imperial Landscape." In *Landscape and Power,* 5–34. Chicago: University of Chicago Press, 1994.

———. *The Last Dinosaur Book: The Life and Times of a Cultural Icon.* Chicago: University of Chicago Press, 1998.

Mitman, Gregg. *Breathing Space: How Allergies Shape Our Lives and Landscapes.* New Haven, Conn.: Yale University Press, 2007.

———. "Pachyderm Personalities: The Media of Science, Politics, and Conversation." In *Thinking with Animals: New Perspectives on Anthropomorphism,* edited by Lorraine Daston and Gregg Mitman, 175–195. New York: Columbia University Press, 2005.

———. *Reel Nature: America's Romance with Wildlife on Films.* Cambridge, Mass.: Harvard University Press, 1999.

———. *The State of Nature: Ecology, Community, and American Social Thought, 1900–1950.* Chicago: University of Chicago Press, 1992.

———. "When Nature *Is* the Zoo: Vision and Power in the Art and Science of Natural History." *Osiris,* vol. 11 (1996): 117–143.

Mizruchi, Susan L. *The Science of Sacrifice: American Literature and Modern Social Theory.* Princeton, N.J.: Princeton University Press, 1998.

Mizuno, Hiromi. *Science for the Empire: Scientific Nationalism in Modern Japan.* Stanford, Calif.: Stanford University Press, 2010.

Mol, Arthur P. J. *The Ecological Modernization of the Global Economy.* Cambridge, Mass.: MIT Press, 2001.

Mol, Arthur P. J., David A. Sonnenfeld, and Gert Spaargaren, eds. *The Ecological Modernization Reader.* New York: Routledge, 2009.

Morris, Ramona, Desmond Morris, and Jonathan Barzdo. *The Giant Panda.* New York: Penguin Books, 1982.

Morris-Suzuki, Tessa. "Concepts of Nature and Technology in Pre-Industrial Japan." *East Asian History*, vol. 1 (1991): 81–96.

———. *Re-Inventing Japan: Time, Space, Nation.* Armonk, N.Y.: M.E. Sharpe, 1998.

———. *The Technological Transformation of Japan: From the Seventeenth to the Twenty-First Century.* Cambridge: Cambridge University Press, 1994.

Morton, Oliver. *Eating the Sun: How Plants Power the Planet.* New York: HarperCollins, 2009.

Mosse, George L. *Fallen Soldiers: Reshaping the Memory of the World Wars.* New York: Oxford University Press, 1990.

Mullin, Molly H. "Mirrors and Windows: Sociocultural Studies of Human-Animal Relationships." *Annual Review of Anthropology*, vol. 28 (1999): 201–224.

Namaura, Takafusa. "Depression, Recovery, and War." In *Cambridge History of Japan*, vol. 6, edited by Peter Duus, 451–467. New York: Cambridge University Press, 1986.

O'Bryan, Scott. *The Growth Idea: Purpose and Prosperity in Postwar Japan.* Honolulu: University of Hawaii Press, 2009.

Ohnuki-Tierney, Emiko. *Kamikaze, Cherry Blossoms, and Nationalisms: The Militarization of Aesthetics in Japanese History.* Chicago: University of Chicago Press, 2002.

———. *The Monkey as Mirror: Symbolic Transformations in Japanese History and Ritual.* Princeton, N.J.: Princeton University Press, 1987.

Peattie, Mark. *Nan'yō: The Rise and Fall of the Japanese in Micronesia, 1885–1945.* Honolulu: University of Hawaii Press, 1988.

Pflugfelder, Gregory M. *Cartographies of Desire: Male-Male Sexuality in Japanese Discourse, 1600–1950.* Berkeley: University of California Press, 1999.

Pflugfelder, Gregory M. and Brett L. Walker, eds. *JAPANimals: History and Culture in Japan's Animal Life.* Ann Arbor: University of Michigan, 2005.

Poole, Joyce. *Coming of Age with Elephants: A Memoir.* New York: Hyperion, 1996.

Popper, Karl. *The Poverty of Historicism*, 2nd ed. New York: Routledge, 2002.

Prakash, Gyan. *Another Reason: Science and the Imagination of Modern India.* Princeton, N.J.: Princeton University Press, 1999.

———. "Staging Science." In *Another Reason: Science and the Imagination of Modern India*, 17–48. Princeton, N.J.: Princeton University Press, 1999.

Pratt, Mary Louise. *Imperial Eyes: Travel Writing and Transculturation.* New York: Routledge, 1992.

Price, Jennifer. *Flight Maps: Adventures with Nature in Modern America.* New York: Basic Books, 1999.

Pyne, Lydia V. and Stephen J. Pyle. *The Last Lost World: Ice Ages, Human Origins, and the Invention of the Pleistocene*. New York: Viking, 2012.

Regan, Tom. *The Case for Animal Rights*. Berkeley: University of California Press, 1983.

———. *Empty Cages: Facing the Challenge of Animal Rights*. Lanham, Md.: Rowman & Littlefield, 2004.

Richards, Robert J. *Darwin and the Emergence of Evolutionary Theories of Mind and Behavior*. Chicago: University of Chicago Press, 1987.

———. *The Romantic Conception of Life: Science and Philosophy in the Age of Goethe*. Chicago: University of Chicago Press, 2002.

Richards, Thomas. *The Imperial Archive: Knowledge and the Fantasy of Empire*. New York: Verso, 1993.

Ritvo, Harriet. *The Animal Estate: The English and Other Creatures in the Victorian Age*. Cambridge, Mass.: Harvard University Press, 1987.

———. *Noble Cows and Hybrid Zebras: Essays on Animals and History*. Charlottesville: University of Virginia Press, 2012.

———. *The Platypus and the Mermaid, and Other Figments of the Classifying Imagination*. Cambridge, Mass.: Harvard University Press, 1997.

———. "Possessing Mother Nature: Genetic Capital in Eighteenth-Century Britain." In *Noble Cows and Hybrid Zebras: Essays on Animals and History*, 157–176. Charlottesville: University of Virginia Press, 2010.

Robertson, Jennifer. "Empire of Nostalgia: Rethinking 'Internationalization' in Japan Today." *Theory, Culture and Society*, vol. 14, no. 4 (1997): 97–122.

———. "Japan's First Cyborg? Miss Nippon, Eugenics, and Wartime Technologies of Beauty, Body, and Blood." *Body & Society*, vol. 7, no. 1 (2001): 1.

———. "Robo Sapiens Japanicus: Humanoid Robots and the Posthuman Family." *Critical Asian Studies*, vol. 39, no. 3 (2007): 369–398.

———. *Takarazuka: Sexual Politics and Popular Culture in Modern Japan*. Berkeley: University of California Press, 1998.

Rose, Sonya O. "Cultural Analysis and Moral Discourses: Episodes, Continuities, and Transformations." In *Beyond the Cultural Turn: New Directions in the Study of Society and Culture*, edited by Victoria E. Bonnell, Lynn Avery Hunt, and Richard Biernacki, 217–238. Berkeley: University of California Press, 1999.

Rosenzweig, Roy and Elizabeth Blackmar. *The Park and the People: A History of Central Park*. Ithaca, N.Y.: Cornell University Press, 1992.

Ross, Kristin. *Fast Cars, Clean Bodies: Decolonization and the Reordering of French Culture*. Cambridge, Mass.: MIT Press, 1995.

Rothfels, Nigel. *Representing Animals*. Bloomington: Indiana University Press, 2002.

———. *Savages and Beasts: The Birth of the Modern Zoo*. Baltimore: Johns Hopkins University Press, 2002.

Ruddiman, William F. *Plows, Plagues, and Petroleum: How Humans Took Control of Climate*. Princeton, N.J.: Princeton University Press, 2010.

Russell, Edmund. *Evolutionary History: Uniting History and Biology to Understand Life on Earth*. New York: Cambridge University Press, 2011.

————. *War and Nature: Fighting Humans and Insects with Chemicals from World War I to Silent Spring*. New York: Cambridge University Press, 2001.

Sachs, Aaron. *Arcadian America: The Death and Life of an Environmental Tradition*. New Haven, Conn.: Yale University Press, 2013.

Salesa, Manuel J., Mauricio Anton, Stephane Peigne, and George Morales. "Evidence of a False Thumb in a Fossil Carnivore Clarifies the Evolution of Pandas." *PNAS*, vol. 103, no. 2 (January 2006): 379–382.

Sand, Jordan. *House and Home in Modern Japan: Architecture, Domestic Space, and Bourgeois Culture, 1880–1930*. Cambridge, Mass.: Harvard University Press, 2005.

————"Was Meiji Taste in Interiors 'Orientalist'?" *positions*, vol. 8, no. 3 (Winter 2000): 637.

Santner, Eric L. *Stranded Objects: Mourning, Memory, and Film in Postwar Germany*. Ithaca, N.Y.: Cornell University Press, 1990.

Sax, Boria. *Animals in the Third Reich: Pets, Scapegoats, and the Holocaust*. New York: Continuum, 2000.

Schaller, George B. "Bamboo Shortage Not Only Cause of Panda Decline." *Nature*, vol. 327 (1987): 562.

————. *The Giant Pandas of Wolong*. Chicago: University of Chicago Press, 1985.

————. *The Last Panda*. Chicago: University of Chicago Press, 1993.

Schattschneider, Ellen. "The Bloodstained Doll: Violence and the Gift in Wartime Japan." *The Journal of Japanese Studies*, vol. 31, no. 2 (2005): 329–356.

————"The Work of Sacrifice in the Age of Mechanical Reproduction: Bride Dolls and the Enigma of Fascist Aesthetics at Yasukuni Shrine." In *The Culture of Japanese Fascism*, edited by Alan Tansman, 296–320. Durham, N.C.: Duke University Press, 2009.

Schiebinger, Londa L. *Plants and Empire: Colonial Bioprospecting in the Atlantic World*. Cambridge, Mass.: Harvard University Press, 2004.

Scholtmeijer, Marian. *Animal Victims in Modern Fiction: From Sanctity to Sacrifice*. Toronto: University of Toronto Press, 1993.

Scott, James C. "Beyond the War of Words: Cautious Resistance and Calculated Conformity." In *Weapons of the Weak: Everyday Forms of Peasant Resistance*, 241–303. New Haven, Conn.: Yale University Press, 1985.

Scranton, Philip and Susan R. Schrepfer. *Industrializing Organisms: Introducing Evolutionary History*. New York: Routledge, 2004.

Screech, Timon. *The Western Scientific Gaze and Popular Imagery in Later Edo Japan: The Lens within the Heart*. New York: Cambridge University Press, 1996.

Selin, Helaine and Arne Kalland. *Nature across Cultures: Views of Nature and the Environment in Non-western Cultures*. Boston: Kluwer Academic Publishers, 2003.

Seraphim, Franziska. *War Memory and Social Politics in Japan, 1945–2005*. Cambridge, Mass.: Harvard University Press, 2006.

Shepard, Paul. *The Others: How Animals Made Us Human*. Washington, D.C.: Island Press, 1996.

Shepherdson, D.J. "Tracing the Path of Environmental Enrichment in Zoos." In *Second Nature—Environmental Enrichment for Captive Animals*, edited by D.J. Shepherdson, J.D. Mellen, and M. Hutchins, 1–12. London: Smithsonian Institution Press, 1998.

Shirane, Haruo. *Japan and the Culture of the Four Seasons: Nature, Literature, and the Arts*. New York: Columbia University Press, 2013.

Shukin, Nicole. *Animal Capital: Rendering Life in Biopolitical Times*. Minneapolis: University of Minneapolis Press, 2009.

Silverberg, Miriam. "Constructing the Japanese Ethnography of Modernity." *Journal of Asian Studies*, vol. 51, no. 1 (February 1992): 30–54.

Singer, Peter. *Animal Liberation*, 2nd ed. New York: Random House, 1990.

———. *Animal Liberation: A New Ethics for Our Treatment of Animals*. New York: Random House, 1975.

Skabelund, Aaron Herald. *Empire of Dogs: Canines, Japan, and the Making of the Modern Imperial World*. Ithaca, N.Y.: Cornell University Press, 2011.

———. "Fascism's Furry Friends: Dogs, National Identity, and Purity of Blood in 1930s Japan." In *The Culture of Japanese Fascism*, edited by Alan Tansman. Durham, N.C.: Duke University Press, 2009.

Sorkin, Michael. "See You in Disneyland." In *Variations on a Theme Park: The New American City and the End of Public Space*. New York: Hill and Wang, 1992.

Soulé, Michael E. and Gary Lease, eds. *Reinventing Nature? Responses to Postmodern Deconstruction*. Washington, D.C.: Island Press, 1995.

Spang, Rebecca L. "'And They Ate the Zoo': Relating Gastronomic Exoticism in the Siege of Paris." *MLN*, vol. 107, no. 4 (September 1992): 752–773.

Sterckx, Roel. *The Animal and the Daemon in Early China*. Albany: State University of New York Press, 2002.

Taira, Koji. "Economic Development, Labor Markets and Industrial Relations, 1905–1955." In *Cambridge History of Japan*, vol. 6, edited by Peter Duus, 606–653. New York: Cambridge University Press, 1986.

Tanaka, Stefan. *Japan's Orient: Rendering Pasts into History*. Berkeley: University of California Press, 1993.

———. *New Times in Modern Japan*. Princeton, N.J.: Princeton University Press, 2004.

Tansman, Alan, ed. *The Culture of Japanese Fascism*. Durham, N.C.: Duke University Press, 2009.

Tapper, Richard L. "Animality, Humanity, Morality, Society." In *What Is an Animal?* edited by Tim Ingold, 47–62. New York: Routledge, 1988.

Thal, Sarah E. *Rearranging the Landscape of the Gods: The Politics of a Pilgrimage Site in Japan, 1573–1912*. Chicago: University of Chicago Press, 2005.

———. "What Is Meiji?" In *New Directions in the Study of Meiji Japan*, edited by Helen Hardacre and Adam L. Kern, 29–32. New York: Brill, 1997.

Thomas, Julia Adeney. "The Exquisite Corpses of Nature and History: The Case of the Korean DMZ." *The Asia-Pacific Journal*, vol. 43 (October 6, 2009).

———. "From Modernity with Freedom to Sustainability with Decency: Politicizing Passivity." In *The Future of Environmental History: Needs and Op-

portunities, edited by Kimberly Coulter and Christof Mauch. Munich: University of Munich, March 2011.

———. "Not Yet Far Enough." *American Historical Review*, vol. 117, no. 3 (June 2012).

———. *Reconfiguring Modernity: Concepts of Nature in Japanese Political Ideology.* Berkeley: University of California Press, 2001.

———. "'To Become as One Dead': Nature and the Political Subject in Modern Japan." In *The Moral Authority of Nature*, edited by Lorraine Daston and Fernando Vidal, 308–330. Chicago: University of Chicago Press, 2004.

Thomas, Keith. *Man and the Natural World: Changing Attitudes in England, 1500–1800.* New York: Oxford University Press, 1996.

Tierney, Robert Thomas. *Tropics of Savagery: The Culture of Japanese Empire in Comparative Frame.* Berkeley: University of California Press, 2010.

Toby, Ronald P. "Carnival of the Aliens: Korean Embassies in Edo-period Art and Popular Culture." *Monumenta Nipponica*, vol. 41, no. 4 (Winter 1986): 415–456.

Tseng, Alice Yu-Ting. *The Imperial Museums of Meiji Japan: Architecture and the Art of the Nation.* Seattle: University of Washington Press, 2008.

Tsutsui, William. *Godzilla On My Mind: Fifty Years of the King of Monsters.* New York: Palgrave Macmillan, 2004.

———. "Landscapes in the Dark Valley: Toward an Environmental History of Wartime Japan." *Environmental History*, vol. 8, no. 2 (April 2003): 294–311.

Tuan, Yi-fu. *Dominance and Affection: The Making of Pets.* New Haven, Conn.: Yale University Press, 1984.

Walker, Brett L. "Commercial Growth and Environmental Change in Early Modern Japan: Hachinohe's Wild Boar Famine or 1749." *Journal of Asian Studies*, vol. 60, no. 2 (May 2001): 329–351.

———. *The Conquest of Ainu Lands: Ecology and Culture in Japanese Expansion, 1590–1800.* Berkeley: University of California Press, 2001.

———. "Foreign Contagions: Ainu Medical Culture and Conquest." In *Ainu: Spirit of a Northern People*, edited by William Fitzhugh Dubreuil and Chisato, 102–107. Washington, D.C.: University of Washington Press, 1999.

———. *The Lost Wolves of Japan.* Seattle: University of Washington Press, 2005.

———. *Toxic Archipelago: A History of Industrial Disease in Japan.* Seattle: University of Washington Press, 2010.

Watt, Lori. *When Empire Comes Home: Repatriation and Reintegration in Postwar Japan.* Cambridge, Mass.: Harvard University Press, 2009.

Whyte, Kenneth. *The Uncrowned King: The Sensational Rise of William Randolph Hearst.* Berkeley: Counterpoint, 2009.

Wigen, Kären. "Mapping Early Modernity: Geographical Meditations on a Comparative Concept." *Early Modern Japan Newsletter*, vol. 5, no. 2 (1995): 1–13.

Willis, R.G. *Man and Beast.* London: Hart-Davis, MacGibbon, 1974.

Wilson, Edward O. *Biophilia.* Cambridge, Mass.: Harvard University Press, 1984.

Wolch, Jennifer R. and Jody Emel. *Animal Geographies: Place, Politics, and Identity in the Nature-Culture Borderlands.* New York: Verso, 1998.

Yanni, Carla. *Nature's Museums: Victorian Science and the Architecture of Display.* Baltimore: Johns Hopkins University Press, 1999.

Young, Louise. *Japan's Total Empire: Manchuria and the Culture of Wartime Imperialism.* Berkeley: University of California Press, 1998.

Young, Robert. *Colonial Desire: Hybridity in Theory, Culture, and Race.* New York: Routledge, 1995.

Index

acquired characteristics, inheritance of, 53, 57, 256n67

acquisition(s): colonial, 83–86; of elephants, 186–88; of pandas, 206–11; postwar, 171–72, 175–76; through breeding, 221–22

Agamben, Georgio, 140, 263n6

agency, 11, 14, 196

Aikawa Motomu, 79

Akao Naoto, 217–18

Akiyama Chieko, 161

Ali (lion), 152

alienation, 20, 67–69, 118, 170, 236–37

Allied occupation: animal acquisitions during, 173–76; Animal Kinder Garten and, 176–80; arrival of elephants during, 186–88; *Bambi* and, 165–66; decolonization and, 167–73; elephant mania during, 180–85; Hirohito and, 188–92; Ueno Zoo during, 167–68

All Nippon Airways (ANA), 209

Ambros, Barbara, 28, 119, 249n1

An An (panda), 202–3

Ānanda, 26, 250n4

Animal Evolution (Ishikawa), 50–53

"Animal Festival Commemorative Zoo Map," 60fig.

Animal Hall, 35–36

Animal Kinder Garten, 176–80

Animal Memorial, 98, 117, 118–19

animal(s): in Anthropocene, 8–12; as communication, 66; as compelling subjects, 13–14; encounter between humans and, 70–71; as exhibition, 17; as fabricated category, 6; giving and exchanging, 83–84, 175–76, 186–88, 203–5, 221–22; human beings as, 168; imperialism and, 65, 67; as living machines, 35; in modern political economy, 6; in modern warfare, 96–97; moral treatment of, 149–50, 179–80; separation of art and, 37; separation of humans and, 27–28, 29, 68–69; touching, 74. See also *dōbutsu*; military animals

animal veterans. *See* military animals

Anthropocene, 8–12, 195, 231, 238, 245n21

Aoyama Hiroko, 127

Arashiro Masaichi, 111

artifice, authenticity and, 19

artificial insemination, 226–29

Asano Mitsuyoshi, 207, 208, 221

attendance, at Ueno Zoo, 48, 133, 171

Attu, 100

authenticity, 19, 236–37

backstage, 75–76

Bactrian camels, 82–83

Bambi, 165–66

Bambi (deer), 165

bamboo, 278n1

STUDIES OF THE WEATHERHEAD EAST ASIAN INSTITUTE

Columbia University

Selected Titles

(Complete list at: www.columbia.edu/cu/weai/weatherhead-studies.html)

Beyond the Metropolis: Second Cities and Modern Life in Interwar Japan by Louise Young. University of California Press, 2013.

Redacted: The Archives of Censorship in Postwar Japan, by Jonathan E. Abel. University of California Press, 2012.

Occupying Power: Sex Workers and Servicemen in Postwar Japan, by Sarah Kovner. Stanford University Press, 2012.

Empire of Dogs: Canines, Japan, and the Making of the Modern Imperial World, by Aaron Herald Skabelund. Cornell University Press, 2011.

Russo-Japanese Relations, 1905–17: From enemies to allies, by Peter Berton. Routledge, 2011.

Realms of Literacy: Early Japan and the History of Writing, by David Lurie. Harvard University Asia Series, 2011.

Planning for Empire: Reform Bureaucrats and the Japanese Wartime State, by Janis Mimura. Cornell University Press, 2011

Passage to Manhood: Youth Migration, Heroin, and AIDS in Southwest China, by Shao-hua Liu. Stanford University Press, 2010

Imperial Japan at its Zenith: The Wartime Celebration of the Empire's 2,600th Anniversary, by Kenneth J. Ruoff. Cornell University Press, 2010

Behind the Gate: Inventing Students in Beijing, by Fabio Lanza. Columbia University Press, 2010

Postwar History Education in Japan and the Germanys: Guilty Lessons, by Julian Dierkes. Routledge, 2010

The Aesthetics of Japanese Fascism, by Alan Tansman. University of California Press, 2009

The Growth Idea: Purpose and Prosperity in Postwar Japan, by Scott O'Bryan. University of Hawai'i Press, 2009

National History and the World of Nations: Capital, State, and the Rhetoric of History in Japan, France, and the United States, by Christopher Hill. Duke University Press, 2008

Leprosy in China: A History, by Angela Ki Che Leung. Columbia University Press, 2008

Kingdom of Beauty: Mingei and the Politics of Folk Art in Imperial Japan, by Kim Brandt. Duke University Press, 2007.

Mediasphere Shanghai: The Aesthetics of Cultural Production, by Alexander Des Forges. University of Hawai'i Press, 2007.

Modern Passings: Death Rites, Politics, and Social Change in Imperial Japan, by Andrew Bernstein. University of Hawai'i Press, 2006.

The Making of the "Rape of Nanjing": The History and Memory of the Nanjing Massacre in Japan, China, and the United States, by Takashi Yoshida. Oxford University Press, 2006.